The Utility of Splendor

The Utility of Splendor

Ceremony, Social Life, and Architecture
at the Court of Bavaria, 1600–1800

Samuel John Klingensmith

Edited for publication by
Christian F. Otto and Mark Ashton

The University of Chicago Press / Chicago and London

Samuel John Klingensmith (1949–1986) was assistant professor of art history at Tulane University. Christian F. Otto is professor of the history of architecture at Cornell University. Mark Ashton is an independent scholar.

The University of Chicago Press, Chicago 60637
The University of Chicago Press, Ltd., London
© 1993 by The University of Chicago
All rights reserved. Published 1993
Printed in the United States of America
02 01 00 99 98 97 96 95 94 93   5 4 3 2 1

ISBN (cloth): 0-226-44330-2

Publication of this book has been aided by a grant from the Millard Meiss Publication Fund of the College Art Association

Library of Congress Cataloging-in-Publication Data

Klingensmith, Samuel John.
    The utility of splendor: ceremony, social life, and architecture at the court of Bavaria, 1600–1800 / Samuel John Klingensmith; edited for publication by Christian F. Otto and Mark Ashton.
        p.   cm.
    Includes bibliographical references and index.
    ISBN 0-226-44330-2
    1. Palaces—Germany—Bavaria.   2. Architecture, Modern—17th–18th centuries—Germany—Bavaria.   3. Bavaria (Germany)—Kings and rulers—Dwellings.
    4. Bavaria (Germany)—Courts and courtiers.   5. Bavaria (Germany)—Social life and customs.   I. Otto, Christian F.   II. Ashton, Mark.   III. Title.
    NA7740.K55   1993
    725'.17'09433—dc20   93-17138
                                                                                               CIP

Contents

Illustrations

Plans (following index)

Editors' Preface

This book brings to general view the scholarship of a historian of architecture who was denied by an early death the joy of guiding his work to print. *The Utility of Splendor* is a study of the enormous palaces of seventeenth- and eighteenth-century southern Germany as working buildings, structures whose seemingly endless tracts of elaborately decorated rooms are here understood in new ways through the reconstruction of the private, social, and civic life that fostered them and filled them. The research entailed in this task matched the scale of the buildings themselves.

Samuel John Klingensmith was a doctoral candidate at Cornell University when he undertook the research and writing of the dissertation that bears the main title of this book. He completed his work and was awarded the Ph.D. in August of 1986, just before beginning his duties as Assistant Professor of Architecture at Tulane University. In October of the same year he was shot and killed while walking on a New Orleans street, victim of one of the numberless random acts of violence that plague us. His loss robbed family and friends of his company and love, as it deprived those with a historical interest in architecture of the scholarship that his considerable talents would have continued to direct and shape.

Like every scholar, Sam had hoped to see his dissertation reach print in some form. Scholars who knew Sam's work recognized both its quality and its contribution to the field of architectural history, and decided to try to fulfill that hope after his death. With the interest and support of Sam's parents, Clarence and Margaret Klingensmith of Alfred, New York, the editors found a publisher in the University of Chicago Press.

As editors, we have striven to increase the concision of Sam's discussion and its accessibility to non-experts, which required cutting, rearranging, and clarifying some of the text. Although a few books and articles pertinent to his argument have been published since Sam finished writing, we chose not to augment the scholarship, even through bibliographic entries. To start such an effort would have been to embark on an uncharted course destined to end in a new work that was neither Sam's nor ours. As it stands, we feel confident that Sam would recognize the book as his own and object to little that we did, even though he would inevitably have done it differently.

We and the Klingensmith family thank Tulane University's School of Architecture and the Millard Meiss Fund of the College Art Association for underwriting the costs of color printing. Professor Emerita Esther Gordon Dotson of Cornell University cheerfully contributed her translations of passages from French and Italian sources. The professionalism of the University of Chicago Press made working with it a pleasure.

Acknowledgment

The family of Samuel John Klingensmith expresses its gratitude to the editors, Dr. Christian Otto and Dr. Mark Ashton, for preparing this work for publication. We feel that their care and attention have added much to the work that Sam was undertaking before his untimely death.

Preface

In the two centuries from 1600 to 1800 the electors of Bavaria, like their fellow princes of the Holy Roman Empire, built on a prodigious scale. In the process they succeeded in substantially remaking the physical milieu of the Bavarian court. When they couldn't build, they dreamed of building. "What I need are country houses," wrote Elector Max Emanuel to his mistress, Gräfin Arco, "country houses, gardens, and forests." This was written from Brussels in 1705, toward the beginning of what would turn out to be ten long years of penurious exile for the unfortunate ruler. Max Emanuel deeply regretted having to leave behind his half-finished palaces in the environs of Munich. These were, as he put it, "my 'créatures' and the only object of my love in Bavaria." "I couldn't live these days without making plans," he continued. "I fill the pages with my scribbles, but have no illusions about realizing these. Who knows, they might be useful someday. When I look at my drawings, the mere thought of future building projects is a source of excitement."[1]

Statements such as these have often been rightly seen as an expression of the intense personal interest that Baroque rulers took in building palaces. Max Emanuel himself is credited with the design of the Pagodenburg, one of the diminutive *maisons de plaisance* that went up in the park at Nymphenburg shortly after his return from exile. His active involvement in the affairs of his court building office is well documented. Building was part of the profession of ruler, on a par with statecraft, warfare, ceremonies, and hunting.

Historians have long realized that a passion for architecture was not the only factor that motivated the building of palaces, even though this often seems to be the only way to account for the incredible volume of building activity or for the fact that these sizable and magnificent structures sometimes bear little apparent relationship to political and economic realities. We can agree with the assertion by Richard Sedlmaier and Rudolf Pfister in their 1923 monograph on the Würzburg Residenz: "Here in Würzburg, too, it was not the need for certain rooms or the fulfillment of a well-defined program of functional requirements that provided the impetus for the project, but instead, quite simply, the will to erect a monument. And thus construction began long before the eventual use of the rooms had been clarified."[2] This led the authors to feel justified in focusing almost exclusively on the building as pure form. But we now recognize that there is no absolute polarity between aesthetics and functionality. However important the urge toward monumentality might have been in bringing Baroque palaces into being, these buildings did serve social and political purposes and did fulfill functional needs, whether well or poorly. The representational character of Baroque palaces, with their rigid axiality, open *cours d'honneur,* centrally placed staircases and ceremonial halls, and long, symmetrical flights of rooms, has blinded us to the purposes served by representation itself and to the fact that these buildings were as much *machines à habiter* as Le Corbusier's early residential projects or the *Minimalwohnungen* of the Weimar Republic.

This was an age that took external phenomena to be a representation of the underlying order of things. Christian Wolff wrote in his *Vernünftige Gedanken von dem gesellschaftlichen Leben der Menschen* (1721), "The average person, dependent on his senses and unable to reason, is incapable of comprehending the majesty of the king. But through the things that meet the eye and in turn activate the other senses, he receives a clear, if imprecise, idea of this majesty, or power and authority. We see, then, that an impressive court with its ceremonies is not something superfluous, much less reprehensible."[3] In an age that held such beliefs, we should expect architectural form and function to have had a very special rapport.

During the seventeenth and eighteenth centuries, court and state were not entirely distinct, and the physical settings of princely domestic life and territorial government were not entirely separated. Residences and offices were not only often in the same palace, for the prince they were often in the same rooms. A prince lived and worked at the top of a huge, pyramidal "household" composed of family members, officials, courtiers, and servants, and the palace formed the physical setting for all their activities.

For an understanding of the Baroque court as a social institution and an instrument of absolutist sovereignty, we are highly indebted to

Norbert Elias, whose pioneering 1969 study, *The Court Society,* has led to further work by such scholars as Jürgen Freiherr von Kruedener and Hubert Ehalt. An important component of Elias's work was an explication of the role played by ceremonial in binding prince and courtier to one another and in fixing rank among courtiers, while at the same time allowing the prince latitude to manipulate this connection for his own purposes. Ceremonial provided the context within which a society that found its ultimate justification in prestige rather than wealth pursued its objectives. The function of ceremonial in rendering social relationships visible was seen by Elias as analogous to the representational character of Baroque secular architecture. This seemed to offer a framework for understanding the cultural significance of the palace.

The particulars of ceremonial, as manifested in such activities as attendance at court, the prince's Lever and Coucher, dining in state, and the reception of princely guests and diplomats, have been less exhaustively studied. Thus the programmatic determinants of the palace plan remain largely uninvestigated. Hugh Murray Baillie's 1967 essay "Etiquette and the Planning of the State Apartments in Baroque Palaces" served an essential purpose in raising pertinent issues and suggesting a framework for further research. Valuable additional contributions have been made by Wilfried Hansmann in his 1972 study of the building history of Schloss Brühl and by Karin Plodeck in her detailed analysis (also of 1972) of ceremonial at the court of Brandenburg-Ansbach.[4] In neither of these works, however, is the relationship between court usage and the palace plan central to the author's subject.

This relationship forms the focus of the present study. In order to explore the theme in depth, the material studied was limited to a single court. The court of Bavaria suits the purpose well. Although it cannot without much qualification be taken as typical of German courts during the seventeenth and eighteenth centuries, it was one of the largest and most important of them. The Wittelsbach dynasty, which had ruled Bavaria since the early Middle Ages and achieved the electoral dignity in 1623, was a ranking dynasty within the empire, reigning over territories that figured as sizable and prosperous in German-speaking lands.

Two avenues of investigation are pursued here. First, the relative status of the wide spectrum of residences available to the Bavarian court is clarified. In the eighteenth century, these ranged in scale from the vast Residenzschloss in Munich, a veritable city-within-the-city; to large country houses such as Nymphenburg and Schleissheim, suitable for prolonged summer residence; to the Parkburgen at Nymphenburg, private retreats of only one apartment. General patterns of court usage and court dwelling are examined in the context of the building histories of these houses. This forms the subject of chapters 2 and 3. Chapters 4, 5, and 6 turn to the principal rooms—the apartments and halls—of the major residences, where the private life of the ruling family and the public life of the court were concentrated, and examine internal patterns of usage. The focus is on life at the top of the court hierarchy, among those persons for whom all this splendour was created. Life "below stairs," in the chancelleries, kitchens, and stables, is looked at less closely.

The present work draws primarily on archival material, both published and unpublished. Secondary studies on court life in Munich during the seventeenth and eighteenth centuries are virtually nonexistent. The notable exception is Eberhard Straub's *Repraesentatio maiestatis oder churbayerische Freudenfeste* of 1969, a compendious investigation of festivities at the Bavarian electoral court that charts developments in festival form and content. Several recent biographies of the Wittelsbach rulers—Roswitha von Bary's on Henriette Adelaide (1980), Ludwig Hüttl's on Max Emanuel (1976), and Peter Claus Hartmann's on Karl Albrecht (1985)—attempt to portray their subjects against the social background of the courts over which they presided and in the process provide useful information on court life.[5] Although many aspects of the architectural history of the palaces have received attention from scholars over the past century, definitive, up-to-date monographs on the buildings are lacking. Our knowledge of their physical evolution is thus uneven.[6]

Fortunately, the available primary documentation, although it cannot provide answers to all questions, is rich enough to allow general patterns of use to emerge. Most courts kept thorough, often voluminous, records regarding public life at court, and in this the Bavarian court was typical.[7] Court usage was described in published regulations that came in different guises. These are discussed in chapter 1.

Extensive material can be found on the ceremonies and festivities occasioned by state and dynastic events. Particularly momentous events were often memorialized in special vanity publications, a vehicle of self-representation highly characteristic of the absolutist court. Since rank and precedence were such fundamental preoccupations of the age, the ruler needed to be very exact in his dealings with foreign princes and their envoys, and there is probably more information to be had on the conduct of diplomatic audiences than on any other element of court life.[8]

Not surprisingly, the private aspects of court life receive considerably less recognition in the records. A researcher is largely dependent on the circumstantial evidence that can be gleaned from a wide variety of sometimes unlikely sources, often by reading between the lines. Daily life at the French court is well known today, partly because the king was such an accessible figure, but also because prolific and perceptive memoirists took it upon themselves to describe the vast panorama of Versailles in minute detail. An equivalent literary tradition was lacking in Munich. The few extant memoirs are better characterized as diaries, in that they record daily occurrences in a matter-of-fact manner and abjure discursive commentary on court affairs or political developments. They are nonetheless enormously useful, although often silent about details that their authors clearly took for granted. Two such works stand out: the diary kept during the period 1717–60 by Maximilian Graf von Preysing, holder of various high court offices and a trusted companion of Elector Karl Albrecht; and the journal of Princess Maria Anna Josepha, Karl Albrecht's third daughter, covering the period 1740–76.[9] Also useful in filling in details are accounts written by foreign visitors, particularly persons who had entrée at court and were in a position to attend social functions.[10]

Records pertaining to the buildings cannot be overlooked. Architectural plans are indispensable in forming a picture of the layout of the apartments, and there is adequate, though hardly abundant, plan material. Furniture inventories, which in the eighteenth century were prepared periodically for each palace, prove to be helpful in clarifying room designations and in determining the allocation of apartments among minor family members, not to speak of the insights to be gained from knowing what pieces of furniture stood in the rooms.[11]

The contemporary German literature on Hofwesen (the study of the usages and the structure of the princely court) provides a valuable framework for interpreting the specific material gathered on the Bavarian court. These treatises vary in scope and intent. Gottfried Stieve's *Europäisches Hof-Ceremoniel* (1715) is limited to describing the ceremonial governing the interaction of princes and their envoys. Julius Bernhard von Rohr's *Einleitung zur Ceremoniel-Wissenschaft der grossen Herren* (1729) takes on the subject of ceremonial more broadly, as it applied to the full spectrum of events and activities at court—from coronations and state visits to the Lever, Coucher, and other daily rituals. A tiny volume, it was intended as a vade mecum for foreigners who had business at particular courts. Friedrich Carl von Moser's *Teutsches Hof-Recht* (1754–55) and Franciscus Philippus Florinus's *Oeconomus prudens et legalis continuatis* (1719), both encyclopedic works, treat not only ceremonial but also the duties of the entire hierarchy of court officers and servants, the functioning of service offices, and the architectural requirements of the palace and its subsidiary buildings. All of these treatises purport to describe existing conditions and are generally free of idealization.[12]

Recreating daily life in past centuries is very much like solving a jigsaw puzzle. Disparate bits of information must be painstakingly pieced together, and one must be constantly alert to the potential significance of unprepossessing scraps of documents. Clues, laboriously pursued, often lead nowhere. But the challenge Baillie set himself in his essay—"out of anecdotes to write history"—is a fascinating one and has been a constant inspiration in the present endeavor.

The Utility of Splendor

1

Introduction

The rulers of the Middle Ages had been nomads, moving among dwellings scattered throughout their realms with greater or lesser frequency over the course of the year. The rulers of the early modern period were likewise nomads. Unlike their medieval predecessors, however, they moved always in reference to a fixed Residenzort, or location of official residence, where government offices were settled and where for governmental purposes the ruler was considered to reside even when he was staying elsewhere. The Bavarian electors of the seventeenth and eighteenth centuries seldom strayed too far from Munich, their Residenzort. Their itineraries took them mostly to country houses in its immediate vicinity and less frequently to more distant ones. The latter structures, inherited from past centuries, experienced for the most part only minor renovation and redecoration during these years. The major architectural efforts of the seventeenth and eighteenth centuries were concentrated in the capital and its environs.

The change over the centuries in the pattern of princely dwelling is reflected in differences in the functional complexion of the body of houses available to the ruler and his court. Whereas the houses between which medieval rulers moved were roughly equivalent in status, the houses of the seventeenth and eighteenth centuries were differentiated in purpose and use. In Bavaria, only the Residenz in Munich (fig. 1) possessed full Residenz character. Nymphenburg and Schleissheim, the two country houses most extensively occupied by the court in the eighteenth century, played less all-encompassing roles, despite the fact that they were often referred to as Residenzschloss or (official palace) or Residenz- und Lustschloss (official and country palace). The smaller country houses erected during the eighteenth century addressed very specific recreational

Fig. 1. Munich, Residenz, aerial view by Michael Wening, looking east, with Schwabingergasse (Residenzstrasse) in foreground, engraving, ca. 1700. (Bayerische Verwaltung der staatlichen Schlösser, Gärten und Seen, Munich)

needs. The one at Fürstenried was built as a lodge from which to hunt deer in the surrounding forest. The *maisons de plaisance* in the Nymphenburg park were private retreats, miniature palaces where only a limited retinue could be accommodated: the Badenburg was a bathing pavilion, the Pagodenburg a place to rest and dine after playing on the adjacent pall-mall, and the Amalienburg a lodge from which to shoot pheasants.

Contemporary theoretical literature on Hofwesen (conduct of the court) included extensive discussion of the function and character of Residenzschlösser. Friedrich Carl von Moser's *Teutsches Hof-Recht* of 1754–55 provides a succinct definition: "The Residenz is the regular, permanent dwelling of the ruler in the place where the court and the councils

have their seat. Here the ruler is at home and the prescriptions of ceremonial are to be seen in practice."[1] The definition in Johann Heinrich
Zedler's *Universal-Lexikon* (1742) is similar: "The Residenz is that city in
which a potentate or prince holds court and in which the higher councils,
such as State, Court of Chamber, Privy, and others that administer the
routine business of state, remain."[2]

The Residenz—or at least the Residenzstadt—thus united the dual
functions of court and government in one place, although neither definition is entirely clear about the extent to which the two were accommodated under the single roof of the Residenzschloss. "Residenz" could
refer both to the ruler's palace and to the city or town in which it was
located. Government functions were often housed not in the palace, but
in the city. In Munich, only those organs of government closest to the
ruler had space in the Residenz. Nor was it ever possible to lodge all
persons attached to the court in the palace. Only a small percentage of
the Bavarian household lived in the Residenz.

The second part of Moser's definition provides the clue to understanding the significance of the Residenzschloss. As the place where the ruler
was "at home," the palace was preeminently the seat of ceremonies. It
was to be distinguished from the ruler's Lustschlösser in this regard. In
the Residenz the ruler appeared as "head of his people and in the full
radiance of his hereditary or acquired dignities." In the country he was
instead "the ranking private individual" and allowed himself welcome
respite from the burden of public duties and the straitjacket of ceremonial. "It is taken for granted that the Residenz is the seat of ceremony. If
ceremonial may be diminished in the country, the dignity of the prince
and the strictures of court regulations do not permit this in the Residenz."[3] In the Residenz the ruler lived surrounded by retainers who enjoyed certain traditional rights of entrée, granting them admission to the
palace and the apartment of the elector up to a designated room or point;
but such rights did not automatically extend to palaces of non-Residenz
status. Only in the Residenz was the ruler obliged to receive foreign
princes and their envoys, and it was there—not in the country houses—
that he made his public appearances. The government remained behind
when the prince journeyed to his Lustschlösser, from which he returned
to Munich for public and state ceremonies even during the extended
summer sojourn out of town. According to Moser, it was common practice that while the prince was staying in the country, state correspondence
was issued using the name of the Residenzstadt as its place of origin.[4]

The program of a Residenzschloss was vast. A "complete Residenz-
haus" required, according to Franciscus Philippus Florinus, not only

living quarters for the ruler and his family, but also spacious and magnificent Säle (halls), galleries, a chapel, lodgings for foreign princes and their retinues, rooms for chancellery and councils, for kitchen, cellar, and stables.[5] Obviously, concluded Florinus, these functions could not be accommodated in a "simple building," although elsewhere he implied that it was desirable to unite them all in the Residenzschloss itself. Where this was not possible, then "it is customary to house certain functions, those not immediately necessary to the service of the prince (especially government offices and stables), in separate buildings, but not too far away."[6]

Most Residenzschlösser, as Moser wrote, featured three stories, in addition to cellars and attics. The ground floor, at least in urban palaces, was normally given over to services and government offices. In the country the prince and his family usually preferred to live on the ground floor; in the city both state and private apartments, as well as guest suites, were found on the second floor. Ladies and gentlemen who lodged at court were put up on the third floor, where there might also be apartments for family and guests, if space was tight on the second. Servants lived "under the roof."[7]

Although large, neither Nymphenburg nor Schleissheim could function as a complete Residenz. Neither palace was equipped to accommodate government functions, other than the innermost functions of the cabinet, nor did either contain spacious guest suites such as those that had been erected specifically for the purpose in the Residenz. Indeed, visitors lodged at Nymphenburg sometimes displaced members of the family. Only the apartments in the Residenz itself had the full complement of anterooms required by the ceremonial usage discussed in chapters 4, 5, and 6. In the country houses, by contrast, public ceremonies did not as a rule take place, and it was not necessary to maintain the prescribed sequence of anterooms. More space could therefore be devoted specifically to private and social purposes. For example, the large Säle in the Residenz were guard chambers that served as places of waiting for the court and as settings for public ceremonies; they were thus an integral component of the apartments. In the Lustschlösser, such halls were placed in the center of the plan, not integrated into the apartments, and they were intended preeminently as Festsäle in the strictest sense of the word—halls for banquets, balls, and other festivities. The time spent in the country was given over to pleasurable pursuits. Entrée to the country houses was not as liberal as that to the Residenz, and a relaxed ceremonial prevailed.

In order to understand the functional composition of the palace plan, a concerted look at ceremonial usage and at basic patterns of everyday existence is necessary. Life at court may be seen to have operated in three spheres: the public, the private, and the social, each of which received recognition in the physical organization of the palace. Correspondingly, the prince may be seen to have embodied three roles: head of state, private individual, and leader, or at least host, of court society. The relative importance of these roles varied from court to court. At some courts, the public and private spheres were kept distinctly separate; at others, they overlapped. At some courts, the social sphere was hardly present.

Along with the outside personages whose interactions with the ruler occasioned some of the activity in the public and social realms, the participants in these mixed fields of operation were the ruler and the immense body of attendants called his household—government officers, courtiers, servants, and of course members of his family. Officials, who at the highest levels were also courtiers, dispatched the affairs of an increasingly intricate government structure extending its authority to aspects of life previously unregulated. Courtiers, attached to the prince's service and dependent upon his bounty, engaged in a relentless round of rituals and amusements, lending prestige to their benefactor through their collective splendor. Life at the top of this social organism was governed by elaborate codes of ceremonial that affected even the minutiae of everyday existence. Mastering the complexities of ceremonial became the métier of the courtier and a means of distinguishing himself from other elements of society. Armies of servants ministered to their superiors, performing tasks that we now would consider demeaning or superfluous.

During the seventeenth and eighteenth centuries, the conduct of the public sphere of court life was increasingly directed by written instructions. Routine matters were formulated into Ordnungen (regulations or orders) of various sorts that were issued periodically—at the beginning of a reign, or when the prince felt that certain rules were falling into disregard and needed reinforcement, or when he wished to alter past practice. General Hofordnungen (court regulations) consisted principally of guidelines for the deportment of persons attached to the court; they were addressed to the entire household. Other regulations set forth procedures to be followed by the staffs of particular court offices or departments—such as the Kammerordnungen (orders for the chamber), which governed the elector's personal household and are thus of particular importance in understanding how his apartment functioned. Among the regulations covering specific activities were the Aufwartungs-Ordnungen (orders of waiting), which spelled out in sometimes pedantic detail the hierarchy of entrée to the sequence of rooms preceding the bedchamber of a ruler's apartment; by the early eighteenth century these were issued in most courts. In addition, individual officers and servants received their own Dienst-Instruktionen (service instructions; in effect, job descriptions). Special events like births, marriages, accessions, and visits of foreign princes called for complex ceremonies and commemorative festivities. Agendas and plans for them were outlined in protocols and memoranda, many of which were saved as models for future occasions or as references for disputes of precedence or ceremony involving state receptions and diplomatic audiences.[8]

During the eighteenth century nearly all German courts published annual Hofkalender (court calendars) listing scheduled holidays and ceremonies and complete directories of the personal households of each member of the elector's family. An expression of princely status as well as of bureaucratic management, the calendars served to notify, coordinate, and inform participants and observers. They would have been especially useful to foreign diplomats, gentlemen, and adventurers curious about the relative ranks of courtiers to be encountered, and they suggest that courts had become too large to be understood without their help.

The first Bavarian Hofkalender appeared in 1727; the first with a directory in 1738. They present a court of well over a thousand persons who revolved around the elector and his family. The court of Elector Karl Albrecht, under whom the Hofkalender was first issued, included the immediate family—his wife and children—and a "second family"—his brother Ferdinand with his wife and children. Both families took part in court ceremonies and festivities, and it was customary for foreign envoys to request and receive public audiences with each. Households changed with births, deaths, marriages, and the movements of members from place to place, and participation in public ceremonies depended partly on the personality of the individual. Karl Albrecht's mother, for example, took little part in court ceremony.

Around the family were grouped the high court officers. In the seventeenth and eighteenth centuries the Bavarian court was divided into four offices, following the imperial model: those of the Obristhofmeister (chief steward), Obristkämmerer (chief chamberlain), Obristhofmarschall (chief marshal), and Obriststallmeister (chief master of the stables). These offices were virtually monopolized by a handful of noble families. Their incumbents often held additional posts on the inner state councils and were the confidants of the electors in the direction of foreign policy.

Under the four high offices were others, also as a rule reserved to the nobility: the Obristküchenmeister (chief master of the kitchen), Obristsilberkämmerer (chief chamberlain of the silver), and Intendants of the Hofoper (court opera) and Hofmusik (court musicians). The Obristjägermeister (chief master of the hunt) and the Obristfalkenmeister (chief master of the falcons) oversaw offices that were independent of the four high offices. All these officers exercised general supervisory control over the personnel under their jurisdiction, but by the eighteenth century their functions had become primarily ceremonial; indeed, their presence was mandatory at public and state ceremonies, where they might have prescribed duties. The day-to-day administrative work of running the office was in the hands of a Stabscommissarius (staff commissioner), assisted by secretaries and bookkeepers.

The ranking court officer was the Obristhofmeister, who had supervision over the entire household. To his office belonged the personnel of the court chapel, the elector's confessor, the court doctors and druggists, the singers and other personnel of the Hofkapellenmusik (court chapel musicians) and the Hofoper, the two regiments of guardsmen (Hartschier, halberdiers, and Trabanten, or gentlemen-at-arms), the persons responsible for the custody and security of the palace and its furnishing, the Hofbauamt (court building office), and the court artists and artisans.

The Obristkämmerer headed the elector's personal household. The most important of his ceremonial duties was arranging audiences with foreign envoys and receiving them when they arrived at the Residenz. Under his jurisdiction stood the electoral Kämmerer or Kammerherren (chamberlains), nobles who waited on the elector closely during the course of the day and performed ceremonial services at his Lever and Coucher and when he dined in private. The title was granted to many individuals as an honorary distinction. The ranks of the Kämmerer were very large in the eighteenth century; only a handful had actual service. Also under the jurisdiction of the Obristkämmerer were the servants responsible for the elector's personal needs and for maintaining order in his apartment: the Kammerfourier (quartermaster), who arranged the personal accommodations of the elector when he traveled and who performed much of the administrative work involved in regulating ceremonial; the Kammerdiener (valets), many of whom, like the Kämmerer, were titular (Kammerdiener was the honorary title granted to persons of middle-class origin); the Kammerportiers and Kabinetts-Portiers (doormen), charged with controlling access to the rooms of the apartment; and the Guardarobadiener (wardrobe attendants).

The Obristhofmarschall was responsible for arranging the accommodation of the court on trips and for arranging that of princely guests and envoys and their suites (through a Hoffourier). He presided at state or public dinners, orchestrating the ceremonial services of the other court officers—including the electoral Truchsesse (stewards), a body of noble officers who stood under his jurisdiction. Like the Kämmerer, the Truchsesse served purely ceremonial functions, mostly involving table service. They were of lesser rank than the Kämmerer and were never as numerous. Most of the personnel in the Obristhofmarschall's jurisdiction belonged to the kitchen, cellar, and silver offices, under the immediate control of the Obristküchenmeister and Obristsilberkämmerer. These two officers employed a multitude of servants, ranging from a provision master, pantlers, sommeliers, a variety of cooks, servants responsible for the care of the table silver and table linen, and Tafeldecker (table setters), down to the menial servants involved in preparing and storing food and in washing dishes.

The Obriststallmeister had charge not only of the stables, but also of the electoral Edelknaben (pages). As in the Middle Ages, pages were raised at court under the supervision of a Hofmeister and a small corps of instructors, and they performed a variety of minor ceremonial duties. For the son of a noble house, service as a page was an introduction to a later appointment as a Truchsess or Kämmerer. The Obriststallmeister also had jurisdiction over the instrumentalists of the Hofmusik, the court trumpeters and drummers, the Hoflakaien (court lackeys), the court dwarfs, and the Sesselträger (sedan-chair bearers).

The households of other family members were personal households and normally included a confessor, a small body of Kammerdiener, a secretary, an accountant, and other miscellaneous servants. All of these stood under an Obristhofmeister, equivalent to the elector's Obristkämmerer. Male members of the family also had their own Kämmerer and, if they were under age, tutors. The electress and the princesses had their ladies-in-waiting (Kammerdamen and Hofdamen), who were supervised by an Obristhofmeisterin and her second-in-command, a Fräulein-Hofmeisterin. Although the ladies-in-waiting had once formed a sort of noble court "academy" very much like the pages, by the seventeenth and eighteenth centuries their duties were mostly ceremonial, and they were the constant companions of their mistresses.

The palaces large enough to accommodate such households and hosts of officers were organized around the suites of rooms, or apartments, in which the public and private spheres of court life met. An often-noted characteristic of the principal apartments of German Residenzschlösser in the eighteenth century is the large number of rooms preceding the bedchamber, in marked contrast to French royal palaces, where there were far fewer anterooms. Even a ruler as politically insignificant as the Prince-Bishop of Würzburg had more anterooms than the King of France. In Germany, Louis XIV's apartments in the Louvre and Versailles would have been sufficient only for a prince of very minor standing.

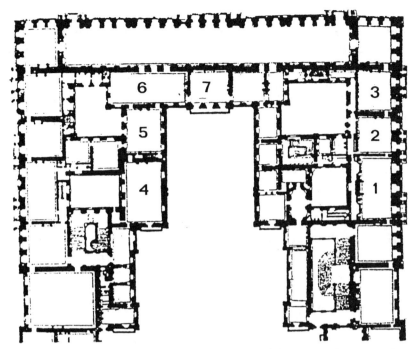

Fig. 2. Versailles, Château, partial plan of piano nobile showing locations of first and second (after 1701) apartments of Louis XIV. First apartment: 1, *salle des gardes;* 2, antechamber; 3, chamber. Second apartment: 4, *salle des gardes;* 5, first antechamber; 6, second antechamber; 7, chamber.

This variance in the plans of German and French apartments resulted from differing conceptions of the boundaries between the public and private lives of the sovereign and from differing ways of acknowledging distinctions in rank among courtiers. The French king was unique among European rulers in the lack of privacy surrounding his daily life. He was almost always accessible to his courtiers, which often aroused shocked comment from foreign visitors. The public and private realms were barely distinguishable. Mundane events that for us are affairs of our private lives assumed the solemn character of acts of state. Acts of state, such as diplomatic audiences, seemed like private, domestic events, because they were conducted in exactly the same surroundings. Louis XIV's Lever and Coucher were witnessed by multitudes of officers and gentlemen. Even when the king dined in private in his bedchamber, a group of ranking courtiers stood in attendance in respectful silence, while the door to the room remained open.

The public nature of the French royal regimen is reflected in two features of the apartment plan (fig. 2). First of all, the bedchamber possessed an importance for the representational life of the king and court that it utterly lacked in Germany. It functioned as a room of audience, where the king received ambassadors, minor sovereigns, and cadet members of regnant families, as well as being the site of the Lever and Coucher. The living rooms of the king were located behind the bedchamber. Directly behind was the grand cabinet, where council meetings, private audiences, and court presentations were held and where the king heard ministerial reports. Secondly, the antechamber preceded the bedchamber directly, with no intervening room. In France, where all distinctions in rank were considered to disappear in the presence of the sovereign, all persons of quality had entrée to the antechamber to wait on the king. Not more than two places of waiting were necessary in French royal apartments— the antechamber for courtiers and the guard chamber for liveried servants.

The Munich court patterned its ceremonial after the Burgundian-Spanish model that had been introduced in Austria by Emperor Charles V and had gradually come to pervade imperial court life under his sixteenth-century successors. Beginning around 1550, the elements of this ceremonial were adopted by many of the emperor's German vassals, particularly by the Catholic princes, who maintained close political and cultural bonds with Vienna. The earliest evidence for the existence of Spanish ceremonial at the Munich court is found in the earliest surviving Bavarian court regulations from the 1580s and 1590s.

Spanish-imperial ceremonial contrasted with the traditions of the French court in that a sharp distinction was maintained between the public and private realms. The public appearances of the prince were limited to certain occasions, leaving him free to conduct his daily life largely in private. Daily events such as the Lever, Coucher, dinner, and supper were domestic rituals involving primarily only the officers and servants of the immediate personal household. The prince dined in public in his anterooms on certain days—notably Sundays and holidays—but otherwise he dined privately in his bedchamber or cabinet, without observers on hand.

The bedchamber was therefore a private room. Public functions took place in the anterooms, which served to shield the bedchamber from the outside. Because audiences (even public audiences) were essentially private transactions between the prince and the envoy, the apartment needed a separate audience chamber, in addition to the guard chamber or Saal and the antechamber. The Grosses Cabinet, in which the prince lived and worked, was typically located in front of the bedchamber—rather than behind it, as in the French king's apartment. Princes of any consequence had more than one antechamber. The number of anterooms could be an expression of status, and a prince could be as pretentious as he wished in this regard. Entrée at the German courts was not as liberal as at the French court and was characterized by a greater insistence on preserving the visibility of distinctions in rank. Hierarchies of rank were made to correspond to the hierarchy of anterooms, with entrée to the individual rooms becoming increasingly restrictive the closer one approached the bedchamber.

The multiplicity of anterooms in German palaces reached a peak in the eighteenth century, and the phenomenon was seen by many contemporary writers on Hofwesen as a sign of the times. In the Munich Residenz, the proliferation of anterooms in the elector's apartment came about gradually over the course of the seventeenth and eighteenth centuries, as successive reconstructions of the apartment resulted in the insertion of additional rooms. The sequence of anterooms reached its greatest extent under Elector Karl Albrecht, who in the 1730s transformed the apartment into the suite of rooms known today as the Reiche Zimmer (opulent rooms; plan D, 3–11). In the apartment's previous incarnation called the Alexanderzimmer, dating from the early 1680s, the anterooms had consisted of guard chamber (the so-called Herkules-Saal), Ritterstube (knights' social room, an outer antechamber), antechamber, audience chamber, and Grosses Cabinet (inner audience chamber), followed by the bedchamber (plan C, 1–11). The Reiche Zimmer included an additional audience chamber, the Grosses Audienzzimmer, between the first audience chamber and the Grosses Cabinet.

This increase in the length of the public zone of the apartment must be seen against two concurrent phenomena: the demographic growth of the court, and the increasing elaboration of the ceremonial governing public or state ceremonies and patterns of court attendance. A numerous and magnificent court, with its ceremonial and its pageantry, was both an expression and an instrument of absolutist authority. It served above all as a means of domesticating the nobility, who were no longer free to participate in political processes as they had been within the frame work of the medieval Ständestaat, or corporate state. Rendered powerless through their economic dependence on the prince, the nobles were reduced to vying among themselves for the advantages that the prince could confer— government posts and benefices, as well as purely honorary (but also potent) marks of prestige. The privilege of noble rank came to be measured more and more in terms of one's proximity to the person of the prince. In the seventeenth and eighteenth centuries, the highest Bavarian court offices were held by the most august representatives of the Estates.[9]

The growth of the Bavarian court can be seen in the records. A description of the Bavarian household prepared in 1615 lists over 770 persons, about 520 of them clearly distinguishable as court personnel, the remainder primarily as personnel of the councils and chancelleries.[10] The household seems to have been reduced somewhat during the height of the Thirty Years' War, but thereafter it increased again steadily, reaching a peak in the second half of the eighteenth century.[11] A description of the household from 1705 lists some 1,030 persons, of whom about 720 were court personnel.[12] By 1738, court personnel had almost doubled in number; the court directory in the Hofkalender for that year lists some 1,340 posts. The Hofkalender for 1781 lists 2,140.[13]

This increase was most striking at the very top of the court hierarchy, among purely honorary officers, who served only to augment the elector's prestige.[14] Growth is registered, however, at all levels of the household, down to the menial servants of the kitchens and stables, and is also significant in the ranks of such conspicuously visible servants as mounted guardsmen and liveried lackeys.[15]

Impetus for the development of complex ceremonial at the German courts came partly from increased contact during the late sixteenth and seventeenth centuries with the highly evolved ceremonies of Romance cultures. The lengthy negotiations that ended in the Peace of Westphalia in 1648 brought many German princes face to face for the first time with foreign ambassadors well versed in a ceremonial emphasizing elaborate formal displays of courtesy and respect.[16] In the case of Bavaria, this evolution was also motivated by the political ambitions of Dukes Max Emanuel and Karl Albrecht. Not satisfied with the status of elector, which had been obtained by Maximilian I in 1623, these two rulers concentrated their politics on yet further dynastic elevation. This political program, which was out of all proportion to the resources of a small state such as Bavaria and which brought with it political disaster and financial ruin, was finally realized in Karl Albrecht's brief, ill-fated reign as Emperor Charles VII from 1742 to 1745.

In 1739, shortly after the completion of the Reiche Zimmer, Karl Albrecht published a new Aufwartungs-Ordnung designed to coordinate the rules with the new physical circumstances of the apartment. The increase in the number of anterooms meant that further distinctions in rank could be drawn and certain courtiers could be assigned to rooms more elevated than those they had previously been privileged to enter. The insertion of an additional audience chamber also made it possible to distinguish among foreign envoys by granting those of higher status audience in the Grosses Audienzzimmer.

Diplomatic receptions were the most common of the state ceremonies that took place at court. Since sovereigns met in person infrequently, political intercourse unfolded largely through diplomatic channels. The German princes conducted much of their diplomatic business through special envoys, rather than permanent or resident ones, and they received in person representatives from a wide spectrum of political entities. Public audiences were thus a frequent event at court.

The period 1600–1800 witnessed a tremendous increase in the elaboration of the diplomatic reception and its capacity to differentiate nuances in political meaning. Maximilian I greeted ambassadors from the emperor and other crowned heads of state in person, in either the Ritterstube or the antechamber. Envoys from lesser princes were not greeted in the anterooms; instead, the elector waited for them in the audience chamber. Maximilian's successors stopped greeting envoys themselves, except on extraordinary occasions, and began delegating this task to their high court officers. This implied a general increase in ceremoniousness; the elector, in not greeting envoys in person, was behaving with greater consciousness of his own dignity. At the same time, sending officers to greet envoys meant that many envoys who under Maximilian would not have been specially greeted in the anterooms could now be granted this honor. During the mid-eighteenth century, particularly after the completion of the Reiche Zimmer, the reception reached its most complex stage. It became standard procedure to greet envoys of any importance with three officers, each stationed at a different meeting point. At its most circumstantial, the reception was spread out over the entire path of approach from the staircase to the antechamber.

The French court diverged from the courts that followed the Spanish-imperial model not only in the nature of the public-private relationship, but also in the character of its social life. Under Louis XIV, with large numbers of courtiers present at Versailles on a more or less permanent basis, the court became a focus for aristocratic social life. The king entertained his court. The centerpiece of the social schedule was the Appartement, an evening reception held two or three times a week, at which there were cards, music, dancing, and refreshment. Appartements alternated with theatrical performances. Balls and banquets were staged on special occasions. During the late years of Louis XIV's reign, leadership in fashion and manners passed to the emerging salon culture of aristocratic Paris. Under Louis XIV's successors, the court was never able to recapture its role as arbiter of polite society, but its social institutions nonetheless remained vital fixtures of court life.

The emperor, on the other hand, did not entertain or play host to his court on a regular, continuous basis. The festivities produced at the imperial court, which were renowned for their artistic brilliance, were limited in number, and there was no year-round weekly schedule of receptions and theatrical performances. The exclusivity of private life extended to the social sphere as well and contributed to the imperial court's reputation for ceremonious austerity.

This was also true of the Munich court in the early seventeenth century, during the reign of Maximilian I, whose elevated sense of purpose as a sovereign found expression in the remote dignity of Spanish ceremonial. Under the later electors, however, things began to change. Maximilian's successor, Ferdinand Maria, was wed to a Savoyard princess, Henriette Adelaide, who had grown up at a court where a Gallic style of life prevailed. Henriette Adelaide brought with her a taste for festivities and entertainment and a familiarity with the easier tone of French court society. A forceful personality, whose cultural influence in her adopted land was profound, she succeeded in instilling these values and predilections in her children.

By the eighteenth century, social institutions had developed that established the court as an active social center. In the mid-1680s Max Emanuel, Ferdinand Maria's successor, began the custom of holding Appartements on the model of those held at Versailles. Another type of reception, the Accademie, appears with regularity as early as the 1720s. In the eighteenth century we also find that the electoral family dined regularly in company with their courtiers. The increasing freedom with which the electors consorted with their suites induced Max III Joseph in 1774 to simplify the ceremonial in effect on social occasions. This had no bearing on the ceremonial governing public functions, which remained as elaborate as ever, nor did it diminish the exclusivity of private life. Max III Joseph, in fact, on his accession in 1745, decided to retain the apartment adjacent to the Reiche Zimmer that he had occupied as electoral prince. This became his private apartment, where he lived and worked, and the Reiche Zimmer were left as a state apartment serving public and social functions.

It was in the service of the social sphere that new room types appeared in the apartments of the Residenz. Max Emanuel's Alexanderzimmer included a suite of four rooms, the so-called Sommerzimmer (summer rooms; plan C, 10), that are distinct in plan but also represent an extension of the private zone of the apartment. The evidence is fairly conclusive that these rooms served as the setting for the Appartements. As these were relatively exclusive receptions, attended by a limited circle of courtiers, they could not be held in the Säle or the outer anterooms, to which a wider body of persons had entrée under the published Ordnungen.

When the Sommerzimmer were demolished to make way for the Reiche Zimmer in the 1730s, the picture gallery connected to the new apartment, the so-called Grüne Galerie (green gallery; plan D, 10), assumed the function of the destroyed rooms, becoming a reception suite. The gallery was in turn connected by means of a new staircase to various new rooms on the ground floor ranged along the garden, thus increasing the number of rooms that could be, and sometimes were, opened during the Appartements. The need or desire to accommodate exclusive social functions also seems to account for the creation of a gallery along the garden front of the central pavilion of Schleissheim, an unusual plan feature hitherto unexplained.

The increasing number of rooms designated and used specifically as dining rooms also signaled an expanding social sphere, for in them the prince ate in the company of courtiers—not in private, as he did in his chambers, nor in public, as he did in the anterooms (usually the Ritterstube), following traditional ceremony. Dining rooms are first found—as early as 1720—in the country houses, where life was more casual than in the Residenz. In the country, the electoral family had probably dined in company with their courtiers from a fairly early date. The first instance of a dining room in the Residenz occurs in the Grüne Galerie (plan D, 10), one of whose end salons was called Speise-Saal (dining hall) in contemporary records. It was followed by a dining room erected next to the gallery on the site of a demolished staircase under Max III Joseph in 1764 (plan D, 11). By this time, dining in company had become the most common mode of dining at court, in the Residenz as well as in the country houses. Public dinners, at which the traditional ceremonial still prevailed and which were held as before in the anterooms, notably the Ritterstube, became less and less frequent.

In their studies of the Baroque court, both Baillie and Straub—one writing on the apartment plan, the other on court festivities—seek, as a secondary goal, a clarification of the nature and extent of French cultural influence on Germany in the seventeenth and eighteenth centuries. Both reach the same conclusion: French influence was strong in the fields of fashion and manners, not to speak of architectural style, but left ceremonial and the basic patterns of court life untouched. Baillie wrote:

> Old-fashioned as it was, it was the Imperial Court that set the standard for the German princes. They might import French mistresses, French cooks and dancing-masters, perhaps eventually French craftsmen and architects, but if they felt any urge to assert their independence of their suzerain, they did so not

by following the customs of the French court but by imitating those of the Imperial Court even more closely than before. What France exported was fashion, not ceremonial.[17]

He failed to recognize, however, that there was more to it. Evolution in fashion and manners required a forum in which fashion could be displayed and manners exercised, and French influence thus extended to the development of new social institutions as well. These institutions in turn found their expression and setting in the palace plan. It was this situation that led contemporary commentators such as Karl Ludwig Freiherr von Pöllnitz and Gian Lodovico Bianconi to portray the Bavarian court as a place where the ceremoniousness of the imperial court in Vienna and the *galanterie* of French society met in perfect harmony.

2

The Residenz in Munich

On November 8, 1918, King Ludwig III of Bavaria and his immediate family stepped into a motorcar and drove out of the Munich Residenz under cover of night, not stopping until they had crossed the Austrian frontier. Bavaria was left to seek its destiny in a republican century, and the Residenz, as the king's cousin Adalbert wrote, "ceased to be a Residenz."[1]

This venerable structure had served as the principal seat of the Wittelsbach dynasty for four centuries. In that time it had grown from a small, fortified stronghold into an expansive complex of multiple wings grouped around a succession of courtyards. In 1701, Michael Wening, who left us one of the most thorough descriptions of the Residenz, counted 2,060 windows, 4 large courtyards, 20 Festsäle, 16 long galleries, 4 chapels, 16 kitchens, and 12 cellars.[2] The building was extraordinary among German Residenzschlösser for its size—as commentators, both partial and impartial, noted time and time again.

Although each ruler left his mark, the Residenz was principally the work of Maximilian I (reigned 1597–1651). Maximilian transformed the haphazard accumulation of individual buildings he had inherited from his predecessors into a fittingly magnificent seat for the dynasty and gave the Residenz the general form that it retained through the eighteenth century. Later rulers frequently renovated and redecorated within the palace, but there were no major additions until the erection of architect Leo von Klenze's Festsaalbau (festival hall block) and Königsbau (king's block) under King Ludwig I (1825–48).

Maximilian's building campaigns increased the area of the Residenz significantly and made it possible to fulfill with ease virtually all the programmatic demands posed by the court in the seventeenth and eighteenth centuries. The continuous growth of the Bavarian household during that time would have severely strained the capacities of a lesser building, but basic internal patterns of usage established under Maximilian endured until the end of the period. In radically remodeled building tracts between the Antiquarium and the Schwabingergasse, Maximilian located a new court chapel and apartments for himself and his consort (plans A, B).[3] This part of the palace became and remained the focus for the public life of the court and the private lives of the electors. In Maximilian's Kaiserhofbau (emperor's block; plan A, block around 18), spacious Festsäle and state apartments provided a sumptuous setting for visits of the emperor and other exalted guests. The ground floor of the Kaiserhofbau, with its orderly sequences of large, vaulted chambers, greatly augmented the palace's capacity to accommodate under one roof the subsidiary functions of court and government.

In their treatises on Hofwesen, neither Moser nor Florinus gives conclusive prescriptions for the plan of a Residenzschloss; indeed, they seem to have been somewhat nonplussed by the great variety in the palace architecture of Europe. Both take for granted, however, that the demands of representation will be met, and both emphasize the importance of forecourts, which by distancing the Residenz from surrounding structures allow it to assert itself as an architectural monument. "It is almost universally assumed," wrote Florinus, "that a Residenz will have two wing buildings forming an attractive Hof-Platz in front, which can be closed with an ornamental iron grille. In this way the palace presents itself, revealing to the world its major elements." Florinus was particularly taken with the plan of Versailles, whose succession of courtyards opening into one another he likened to the wings of a theater stage. But he wrote equally approvingly of the alternative scheme of principal courtyards completely enclosed by the building, citing Salzdahlum, with its well-ordered sequence of three interior courtyards, as exemplary.[4]

The major failing of Maximilian's Residenz was the lack of a monumental exterior, for however impressive the new facade along the Schwabingergasse was, it could not be appreciated from a distance. This was the most often heard criticism of the building, especially after Versailles had come to be widely emulated in Germany. Although reconstruction projects of the late eighteenth century attempted to rectify the situation, it was left to von Klenze in the nineteenth to provide the Residenz with facades of a character befitting the building's noble purpose.

The Residenz before Maximilian I

The Residenz that Maximilian inherited on his accession in 1597 was the result of slightly over two centuries of building activity. The oldest part of the complex originated in the 1380s as a fortified Wasserburg (stronghold protected by water), in which the dukes sought refuge from an often hostile citizenry. It became a residence in the early sixteenth century, after which the old ducal residence acquired the name Alter Hof (old court). The Alter Hof was built into the northeast corner of the earliest ring of city walls in the later thirteenth century, probably after 1255, when Bavaria was divided into the separate Wittelsbach duchies of Upper and Lower Bavaria and Munich was established as the principal seat of the former. By the early fourteenth century, municipal expansion had prompted the erection of a new ring of fortifications, more than tripling the enclosed area of the city and stranding the Alter Hof unstrategically in the city's midst (fig. 3). Tense relations between the dukes and the citizens of Munich reached a climax in 1385, when the dukes ended an open revolt with a show of force that brought the city to submission. In addition to paying a large indemnity, the citizenry consented to the erection of a fortified Burg called the Neuveste (new fortress), with its own gate toward the outside so that the dukes could enter and leave without hindrance.[5]

The Neuveste (fig. 4) was erected at the northeast extremity of the new walls in an angle of the moat.[6] It began as a relatively modest fortress incorporating two of the existing towers of the city wall as part of its defenses; the complex included a keep (the Silberturm, or silver tower) in the southwest corner, a gable-roofed Pallas, and a gatehouse guarding the access bridge from the north, grouped around an inner courtyard. Short sections of the city wall were demolished to allow excavation of a moat along the south and west sides. Over the course of the fifteenth century, the dukes strengthened the defenses of the Neuveste through the construction of new walls and towers, partly as a response to advances in artillery technology; but they added very little in the way of living quarters, and the seat of the ducal household remained the Alter Hof. An agreement of 1466 with the city established that the dukes could not set up housekeeping in the Neuveste, and they were prohibited from entering the fortress with more than a handful of retainers.[7]

Not until the reign of Wilhelm IV (1508–50) was there a conclusive transfer of residence from the Alter Hof to the Neuveste. Wilhelm laid out (from 1518) a magnificent Lustgarten (pleasure garden; visible in fig. 5 on the right) east of the Neuveste on the far side of the moat; he later decided to enlarge and modernize the Neuveste.[8] The old Pallas and the smaller structures that had grown up around it were entirely inadequate to accommodate the ducal household. Since advances in firearms had rendered a fortress such as the Neuveste obsolete, living quarters could be erected on the site of the earlier fortifications, reducing the

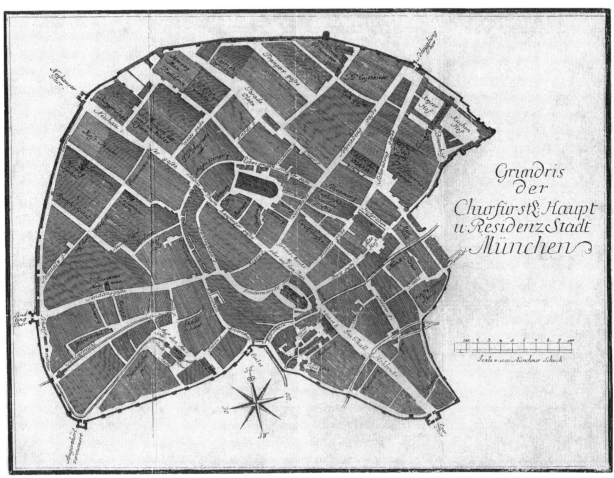

Fig. 3. Munich, plan by Lorenz Westenrieder, 1782. Residenz in northeast (upper right) corner of wall; Alter Hof below it. (Klingensmith)

Fig. 4. Munich, Residenz, reconstruction drawing of the Neuveste around 1570 by Otto Meitinger, 1970. Polygonal structure in right center is the Rundstubenbau; low gable at upper end of roof terrace is the Georgskapelle. (Meitinger)

problems of expanding. The most significant addition undertaken by Wilhelm was the Rundstubenbau (block with curved rooms), an oddly shaped structure located at the southeast corner of the Neuveste that culminated in a semicircular projection built over the foundations of a former bastion (plan A, 1; fig. 4). Also of significance was the rebuilding of the court Chapel of St. George, the Georgskapelle (plan A, 3; fig. 4), north of the Rundstubenbau and separated from it by an open section of the Zwinger (outermost courtyard). The new chapel was dedicated in 1540.

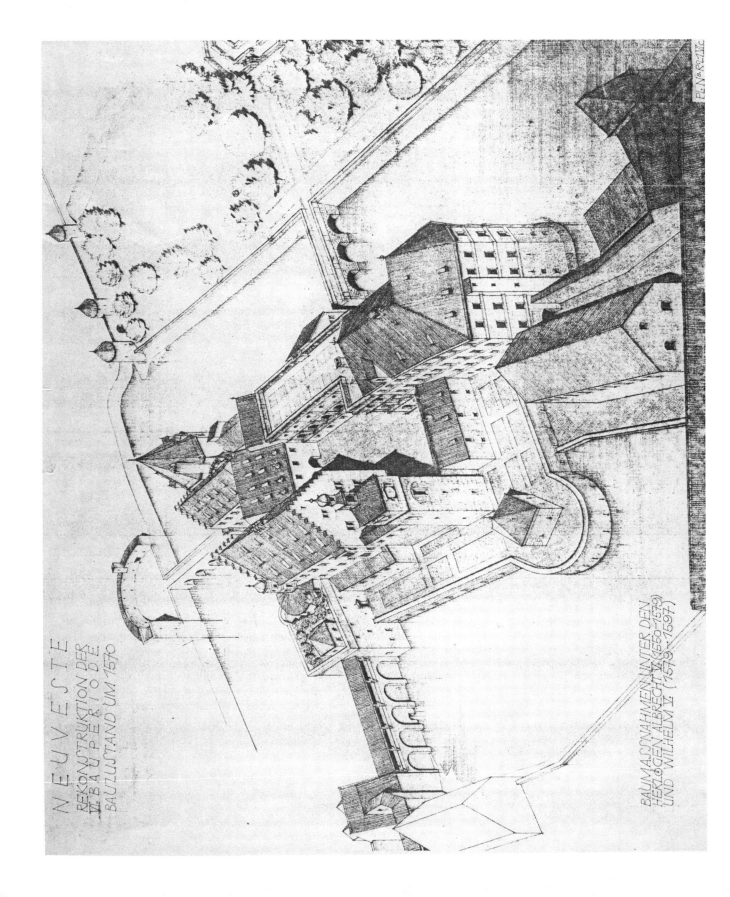

NEUVESTE
REKONSTRUKTION DER
IV. BAUPERIODE
BAUZUSTAND UM 1570

BAUMASSNAHMEN UNTER DEN
HERZÖGEN ALBRECHT V. (1550-1579)
UND WILHELM V. (1579-1597)

PL.1 No R24K

Fig. 5. Munich, view by Wenzel Hollar, detail showing the Residenz as it existed in 1605–11, engraving, 1623. (Bayerische Verwaltung der staatlichen Schlösser, Gärten und Seen, Munich)

The Neuveste reached its greatest extent under Wilhelm's two successors. Albrecht V (1550–79) raised the Rundstubenbau two stories, making a total of four stories crowned with an imposing hipped roof.[9] Between the Rundstubenbau and the Georgskapelle, the Georgs-Saal (George's Hall; plan A, 2) the Neuveste's most resplendent feature, was erected from 1558 to 1562 by court architect Wilhelm Egkl. This, the first of the Residenz's Festsäle, had richly painted walls and eight arched windows along each of the long sides to provide a fitting setting for court festivities, including the 1568 wedding ceremonies of Wilhelm V and Renata of Lorraine.[10]

Under Albrecht V, the Neuveste also began to relinquish its role as nucleus of the Residenz complex. As a setting for the activities of a Renaissance court and as a repository for Albrecht's growing collections of art and antiquities, it proved to be too circumscribed a structure; and the first of the buildings beyond the moat to the south and west, which became the new core of the Residenz, were begun. The land on which they were built was acquired piecemeal from various private owners. It was bounded on the north and east by the city walls; on the west by the Schwabingergasse, lined solidly with private houses; and on the south by two conventual institutions, the Franziskanerkloster and the Riedlkloster. (Fig. 5, although later in date, gives an indication of the situation.)

Albrecht V, whose zeal as a collector was intense enough to arouse concern over state finances among his councillors, was the first German ruler to erect special buildings for the display of his collections.[11] In 1563–67, a building went up directly north of the Alter Hof to serve the dual purpose of housing stables on the ground floor and a Kunstkammer (art gallery), containing paintings and all manner of objets d'art, on the upper floors.[12]

In 1568, Albrecht decided to erect another, more ambitious museum building, the Antiquarium, in which to house his collection of antique statuary and his library.[13] Originally freestanding, it was a narrow rectangle sited more or less parallel to the south arm of the moat (plan A, 20; fig. 5, the long tract below 21). The ground floor is occupied by a barrel-vaulted hall, seventeen bays in length (originally somewhat longer), the vault penetrated by lunettes placed very high in the wall. The statuary was arranged on pedestals and in niches along the walls. How the second floor, where the library was housed, was originally reached, and how it was laid out, cannot be determined with certainty, as the very meager documentation from this earliest period of the Antiquarium's history is contradictory on these points.[14] Construction proceeded from 1568 to 1571 under the direction of Wilhelm Egkl; the ground-floor hall received its final decoration in the 1580s, when the vaults were painted with allegorical figures and views of Bavarian cities and castles.

Wilhelm V (1579–97) was the first ruler to take up residence outside the Neuveste. In the first years of his reign the library was removed, probably to a building next to the stables, and the duke's living quarters were installed above the Antiquarium.[15] At the same time, or shortly thereafter, a new building tract was erected at the east end of the Antiquarium. It contained a spacious Saal on the upper floor, the so-called Schwarzer Saal (black, or dark, hall; plan A, 8). which was probably intended to serve as an approach to the new ducal apartment.[16]

The apartment above the Antiquarium seems to have been only a temporary expedient, however, for in 1581 a new residential tract was begun immediately west of the Antiquarium under the direction of architect Friedrich Sustris. This structure had three wings grouped around a small landscaped courtyard now called the Grottenhof (grotto court; plan A, 12). Behind the main wing on the south, a new garden (the Residenzgarten; plan A, 13) was laid out. Little is known about the interior of this structure, often referred to as the Gartenbau (garden block), before it was radically changed by Maximilian after 1600. Presumably, the ground floor contained a long garden hall facing the Residenzgarten and a flight of rooms facing the Grottenhof. The east wing featured a loggia opening onto the Grottenhof, reflected by a loggia in the opposite wing that was destroyed in the eighteenth century to make way for a suite of rooms.[17]

Simultaneously with the erection of the Gartenbau (finished in 1586), Wilhelm's mother, Duchess Anna of Austria, built a Witwensitz (widow's residence) for herself at the west end of the Residenzgarten, on property purchased by Albrecht V for this purpose in 1578.[18] After Anna died in 1590, the Witwenbau (widow's block; plan A, 14) was adapted to serve as a dependency of residential tracts erected to the north along the Schwabingergasse; around 1610, the ground floor was turned into a Gartenhalle (garden hall) forming the western terminus of the Residenzgarten.[19]

In 1591–94, Wilhelm erected a residence for Hereditary Prince Maximilian, who returned to Munich in 1591 from his studies at the university in Ingolstadt in order to begin an apprenticeship in the affairs of government.[20] The so-called Erbprinzenbau (hereditary prince's block; plan A, 17) was built over the Jägergassl at its intersection with the Schwabingergasse.[21] Three-bay sections on either side of the street were linked by a center section straddling an arched gateway. The house was connected to Wilhelm's Gartenbau by a rear wing containing a chapel (on the site of the later Hofkapelle). How far the enclosure of the Jägergassl on its north side had progressed under Wilhelm V is uncertain. In any case, the Herkules-Saal (plan B, 3) already existed on its present site, having been erected in all likelihood under Albrecht V.[22] It is probable that the Hofdamenstock (ladies-in-waiting tract; plan A, 19), which would have joined the Herkules-Saal with the north section of the Erbprinzenbau, was also erected under Wilhelm.[23]

Two further structures outside the walls of the Neuveste went up during Wilhelm's reign. A Ballhaus, (plan A, 6) featuring a large hall suitable for playing the various ball games then popular in court circles, was erected immediately south of the Rundstubenbau, on land reclaimed from the moat.[24] Along the north side of what would become the Brunnenhof (fountain court; plan A, 9), an open arcaded passageway was constructed to join the new residential tracts at the west with the south entrance of the Neuveste.[25]

The Residenz under Maximilian I (1597–1651)

The sixteenth century witnessed Bavaria's entrance into the world of pan-European politics, as the consolidation of ducal authority under Albrecht IV, who had permanently reunited Upper and Lower Bavaria, increased opportunities for exercising political initiative both at home and abroad. The counterreformatory zeal of the sixteenth-century dukes, particularly Albrecht V, earned them international reputations as defenders of the faith in central Europe and brought them into close contact with the papacy and with Spain, both of whom sought Bavaria's assistance in checking the spread of Protestantism within the empire. The military activity entailed in expanding political involvement, as well as the expenses incurred through a rapidly growing court, ambitious building programs, and lavish patronage of the arts, resulted in a mounting state deficit. Wilhelm V felt himself unable to deal with impending bankruptcy, and in 1594 he took on Maximilian as co-regent. In 1597, Wilhelm abdicated in favor of his highly capable heir.[26]

Maximilian I figures as the second great state-builder of the dynasty, after Albrecht IV. An extraordinarily energetic ruler, Maximilian had a well-developed concept of raison d'état and a sobering sense of the gravity of his responsibilities toward God, the Church, his people, and his dynasty. His first task as Wilhelm's successor was to reform state finances. Sound financial administration assumed a fundamental place in his political theories (which he expounded in his famous *monita paterna*) and led to reforms in other aspects of government. The *Codex maximilianus,* published in 1616, established a uniform code of law for the entire realm. The treasury that Maximilian accumulated enabled him to create a standing army and a provincial militia, while the Hapsburgs continued to rely on mercenary troops. However selfless Maximilian might have been in his dedication to the profession of government, however frugal and pious, he was also conscious of the need to represent authority. Although by no means extravagant, his court was every bit as magnificent as those of his father and grandfather; and with the resources he gathered, he undertook building programs far more ambitious than theirs.

Very shortly after his accession, Maximilian embarked on a twenty-year campaign of renovation and extension that left virtually no part of the Residenz untouched and that almost doubled the area of the complex. His work may be divided into two phases. In the first decade of the seventeenth century, his efforts, limited by financial constraints, were concentrated on filling out the existing Residenz and tying together its disparate elements. This was coupled with extensive interior renovation and redecoration. The second decade of the century saw the addition of the Kaiserhofbau (plan A, block around 18), which expanded the Residenz north to the city wall and gave it a long and impressive facade (Schaufassade) facing the Schwabingergasse.

The results of the first phase are well documented in Philipp Hainhofer's account of his visit to the Bavarian court in 1611, written at a point when the first phase was essentially complete and work on the Kaiserhofbau was about to begin. Hainhofer, an Augsburg patrician and connoisseur of art, was on familiar terms with Wilhelm and Maximilian. Maximilian valued his artistic expertise and honored him with long private audiences during his visit, which had as its purpose negotiating the sale of various objets d'art. Hainhofer made further trips to Munich in 1612, 1613, and 1636. Although all his travel accounts offer invaluable information on court life, only in the first does he treat the reader to a thorough description of the Residenz, as well as of the treasures contained in the Antiquarium, Kunstkammer, and library. Visual evidence for the work of the first phase is provided by the Hollar Plan (fig. 5), the earliest extant plan depiction of the Residenz; published in 1623, it shows the building as it existed sometime between 1605 and 1611.[27]

Maximilian installed apartments for himself and his first consort, Elisabeth of Lorraine, in the tracts around the Grottenhof and along the Schwabingergasse. Hainhofer notes the location of their apartments as follows: "The duke's rooms look out on both sides onto the gardens; the duchess's rooms are along the street and look into Graf von Rechberg's house."[28] In order to accommodate the duchess's apartment (plan B, 11–15), Maximilian had the Erbprinzenbau, erected hardly a decade previously, demolished and rebuilt, at the same time extending it to the south by several bays. This new wing did not reach all the way to the Witwenbau, but remained separated from it by a one-story building, a former private house that had been in Maximilian's possession since 1599.[29] On the level of the piano nobile, this property was not to be incorporated into the plan of the Residenz until the construction of the Goldener Saal (golden hall; plan D, 15) in the 1660s. Meanwhile, it remained open; a corridor connected the back rooms of the electress's apartment with the gallery on the upper floor of the Witwenbau that is listed in a 1638 furniture inventory as belonging to her suite. The electress's apartment was approached from the Herkules-Saal (plan B, 3) via a corridor in the Hofdamenstock. It could also be approached more directly by means of a staircase (plan B, between 16 and 12) adjacent to the first room of her apartment, Tafelstube (social room with a dining table, later called the Lederner Saal [leather hall] or Hartschiersaal; plan B, 11). Various private cabinets seem to have been located behind the chapel and/or facing the Residenzgarten.[30]

In 1601–3, a new and larger court chapel (Plan B, 16) was erected in place of the Erbprinzenkapelle. This Hofkapelle did not attain its present form, however, until 1630, when the nave was enlarged by one bay and the choir was added.[31] On the upper floor of the west wing of the Grottenhofbau, an intricately decorated Kammerkapelle (chamber chapel, known as the Schöne or Reiche Kapelle; plan B, 17), intended to house the most valuable pieces of the dynasty's collection of holy relics, was installed and consecrated in 1607.[32]

The Herkules-Saal was radically renovated during the first several years of the seventeenth century. It was raised in height, so that it towered over all other elements of the Residenz; this is evident in Hollar's view (fig. 5, above 3). The walls were painted with depictions of the accomplishments of Maximilian's Wittelsbach ancestors in the frieze zone in the intervals between high clerestory windows. These decorations were juxtaposed with newly woven tapestries representing the deeds of Hercules, a large statue of whom also stood on the mantel.[33] The Herkules-Saal became the means of access to the elector's apartment (plan B, 4–10). Hainhofer notes: "One passes through two Säle in order to reach ID the Duke. In the first of these, 100 Trabanten stand on two sides. . . . In the second (in which there are various painted *bayrische historia* round about at the top) stand 100 Corbiner."[34] The first Saal, in later descriptions often called the Vorsaal (forehall; plan B, 2), is the room at the top of the Breite Treppe (broad stairs; plan B, 1)—the new Residenz's principal staircase, which Maximilian built at the west end of the Brunnenhof. The second is the Herkules-Saal.

From the Herkules-Saal one passed directly into the elector's Ritterstube, or Tafelstube, which straddles the Kapellenhof (chapel courtyard; plan A, 11) at its point of juncture with the Brunnenhof. The remaining anterooms were ranged along the east side of the Grottenhof, the private rooms along the south side, between the two gardens. How and to what extent Maximilian might have rearranged the interior of these wings remains uncertain. We do know, however, that shortly before 1607 he constructed a Kammergalerie (chamber gallery; plan B, 8) facing the Residenzgarten, next to his bedroom; in 1607 and again in 1623, he had this gallery furnished with favorite paintings and objects from the Kunstkammer.[35] Described as "our newly erected Galeria, or Gang [passageway], which is directly adjacent to our Leibzimmer [bedroom] and which we use as our private Bibliothec [library]," it was paralleled by an altana, or roof terrace (plan B, 10), looking out over the Grottenhof.[36] This gallery survived until 1680–85, when Max Emanuel replaced it with a suite of rooms and built another altana on the next level.[37]

Between the two gardens on the ground floor there were various halls. Hainhofer notes: "Underneath the duke's Wohnzimmer [living rooms, or quarters] are nine vaulted *stantias,* painted with various figures by Peter Candid, furnished partly with beautiful stoves, partly with mantels on which stand antique busts and images, as also on the cornice (from which the tapestries hang). . . . These are thus the duke's Sommer Zimmer, in which he has cross-ventilation."[38] Hainhofer also describes a "long, open loggia, or Gang, paved with marble"; this faced the Residenzgarten.[39] At the west end of the garden, on the ground floor of the Witwenbau, there was an open Saal—also paved with marble and furnished with a fountain—from which "one can look through the entire garden."[40]

The enclosure of the open space in front of the Antiquarium was completed during this period, resulting in the oblong Brunnenhof (plan D).[41] On the long side opposite the Antiquarium, the existing arcade was enclosed, and a second-story corridor, later (after 1611) divided into a suite of rooms, was added above it.[42] This apartment (known today as the Charlottenzimmer after one of its nineteenth-century residents) became living quarters for the electoral children.[43] A double apartment, like that above the Antiquarium, it could be approached from both ends and could accommodate more than one occupant.

In the western short side of the Brunnenhof, a portal led to the Breite Treppe; from the eastern short side one reached (via a monumental dog-leg staircase of around 1600; plan A, next to 8) the Schwarzer Saal and the apartment over the Antiquarium. This apartment was used in the first half of the century as quarters for princely guests. An existing plan from the seventeenth century (plan A) seems to show a pair of apartments in this location. Hainhofer notes that "each room has a little room in which to keep *bagagi.* The rooms communicate with one another and each has an exit into a long corridor. The doors between the rooms are all double-bolted, so that when *mehr herrschaften* are lodged here, the rooms can be locked." He also describes a "grosse tafel stuben," where Maximilian had recently entertained envoys from the Protestant princes; this was the large room next to the octagon.[44] Henriette Adelaide occupied this apartment from 1652 until she was able to move into the new rooms she created in the electress's wing in the 1660s. It then became the apartment traditionally occupied by the electoral prince.[45]

When Hainhofer returned to Munich in 1612, a new, considerably more ambitious project was under way: "ID the Duke is now carrying out *einen starken Bau* and is demolishing many of the houses toward the city wall. This will certainly be a magnificent thing when it is finished."[46] This "solid building," the Kaiserhofbau (plan A, around court 18; plan B), begun no earlier than 1611 and finished probably around 1619, was a complex of four wings around a square courtyard, far vaster in scale than anything undertaken previously.[47] It is not possible to identify the architect or architects responsible for its design. While most nineteenth-century scholars attributed all design work, including architecture, decoration, and painting, to Peter Candid, the block has more recently been seen as the collective achievement of the court building office.[48]

The Hofdamenstock was taken as the point of departure. At right angles to it rose east and west wings, each featuring an apartment facing onto the Kaiserhof. These apartments were intended for the accommodation of the emperor and other exalted guests, a function they retained through the eighteenth century. The apartment in the west wing, today called the Steinzimmer (stone rooms) because of the lavish use of marble and scagliola for door surrounds and fireplaces, was known in the seventeenth and eighteenth centuries as the Kaiserappartement or Kaiserzimmer (emperor's rooms; plan B, 22–28).[49] The apartment opposite—now known as the Trierzimmer (plan B, 29–35) after Clemens Wenzeslaus of Saxony, Elector of Trier, who occupied a portion of this apartment in the late eighteenth century during lengthy visits with his Bavarian relatives—was originally called the Königliche Zimmer (royal rooms). Like the apartments around the Brunnenhof, this was a double apartment. Wening gives each half a separate designation; the north half he calls "Königlich-Zimmer," the south half "herzogliche oder Fürsten-Zimmer" (ducal or princes' rooms).[50] A French travel diary of 1661 describes the Steinzimmer as "the apartment reserved for the emperor when he comes to Munich" and the Trierzimmer as "the apartment reserved for foreign princes who happen to be passing by" (i.e., for those who were not on state visits but en route elsewhere).[51] The Habsburgs, who were related by marriage to the Wittelsbachs in almost every generation, were not infrequent guests in Munich on their trips to and from Frankfurt and Augsburg, where imperial coronations took place. The earliest recorded lodging of an imperial guest in the Kaiserhofbau is the 1636 visit of Emperor Ferdinand III (then King of Hungary and Bohemia), who is reported to have stayed in the "kaiserliche Neuen Zimmer."[52] During the visit of the imperial family in 1653, the emperor (Ferdinand III) stayed in the Kaiserzimmer, the empress in the south half of the Trierzimmer, and the newly crowned King of the Romans (later Ferdinand IV) in the north half.[53]

The ceremonial approach to these apartments was by way of the north wing of the Kaiserhofbau, where a triple-aisled vestibule (called the Halle zu den vier Schäften, after the four columns carrying its vaults) gave access to the monumental dog-leg Kaisertreppe (emperor's staircase; plan B, 19), which in turn opened into the enormous, double-story Kaisersaal (emperor's hall) centered on the garden facade (plan B, 20). The three paintings set into the ceiling of the Kaisersaal were allegories on sovereignty and princely virtue; on the walls were scenes from the Old Testament on one side and from classical history and mythology on the other.[54] The room thus owes its name not to its iconographical program, but to its function as a representational setting for imperial visits. It is to be distinguished from the roughly contemporary Kaisersaal in the Residenzschloss at Aschaffenburg (1605–14), whose program—23 relief panels representing scenes from the lives of the emperors from Julius Caesar to the reigning Emperor Matthias—was an explicit affirmation of the sanctity of the imperial ideal.[55]

Adjacent to the Kaisersaal on the west, a smaller Festsaal—called in the eighteenth century the Vierschimmelsaal (hall of the four white horses; plan B, 22), after the late-seventeenth-century ceiling fresco depicting Apollo in his quadriga—led directly into the Kaiserzimmer.[56] Both the Kaisersaal and the Vierschimmelsaal were sacrificed in 1799 to make way for living quarters for Karoline Friederike, wife of Max IV Joseph. A third Saal, on the opposite side of the staircase, provided access to the Trierzimmer. This Saal was redecorated in 1805, also as part of the renovations undertaken in this part of the palace for the family of Max IV Joseph; because of its white scagliola wall paneling, the room acquired the name Weisser Saal (white hall; plan B, 21).[57]

Easy communication through and around the Kaiserhofbau was afforded by the corridors backing the apartments along the outside. In the west wing, the exterior facade followed the line of the street, at an angle to the courtyard, and space was left between the Kaiserzimmer and the corridor for a flight of service rooms that were intended, Wening tells us, for the servants "whom an imperial or royal personage would need to have close at hand."[58]

As Brigitte Knüttel has pointed out, the Herkules-Saal played a determining role in the vertical dimensioning of the Kaiserhofbau.[59] The extreme height of this Saal necessitated the insertion of a mezzanine above the piano nobile. Here lodgings for court personnel were installed. Between ground floor and piano nobile was space for another mezzanine.[60]

Along the Schwabingergasse, the old and new wings were unified with, like the facades of the Kaiserhof, a painted order of giant pilasters standing on rusticated piers (fig. 6). The increased heights of the Kaiserhofbau required raising the roofline of the electress's wing, and the upper mezzanine was extended into this wing as well. The center bay of the facade was occupied by a bronze statue of the Madonna (the Patrona Bavariae) set in a niche within an aedicular frame. Two marble portals provided the only other architectural accents. The right portal led into the Kapellenhof, the principal ordinary entrance into the Residenz; the left portal, leading into the Kaiserhof, was normally kept closed and was opened only on ceremonial occasions.

North of the Kaiserhofbau, beyond the moat, Maximilian laid out a new Hofgarten (1613–17), which was included within the ring of earthenwork fortifications constructed around the city in 1619–38 (fig. 7). The western section of the garden was planted in four flower parterres focused on an octagonal tempietto. The eastern section, where the ground sloped off to a pond, lay on the site of an earlier garden laid out under Albrecht V, who had built here a garden house complete with a Festsaal and a small apartment. This house was later renovated to become one of the three pavilions terminating the Hofgarten on the east.[61]

Long, narrow wings with corridors on the ground floor and piano nobile were erected to connect the Kaiserhofbau with the Neuveste (plan A, flanking 10). The Pallas and the Silberturm were demolished, the remaining moat filled, and a new courtyard created—the Küchenhof (kitchen court), now the Apothekenhof, or apothecary's court (plan A, 10). In place of the Pallas, a smaller but likewise gable-roofed structure arose (the Hoher Stock, or tall tract; plan A, 4). Adjoining this on the west, a chapel (the Katherinenkapelle; plan A, 5) was installed along the corridor on the piano nobile. The Georgs-Saal and the Rundstubenbau remained; the former was given a new facade, with twin corner turrets and a painted order of giant pilasters, to serve as a fittingly monumental termination for the Küchenhof. Both the Hoher Stock and the Rundstubenbau contained apartments where princely guests and ranking ambassadors (mostly from the emperor), as well as members of the ruling family, were lodged.[62]

In size, scale, and magnificence, Maximilian's Residenz was without precedent in Germany. It was the first German Residenzschloss to be divested utterly of the character of a medieval stronghold—setting it apart from, for example, the otherwise modern palace at Aschaffenburg,

The Residenz in Munich

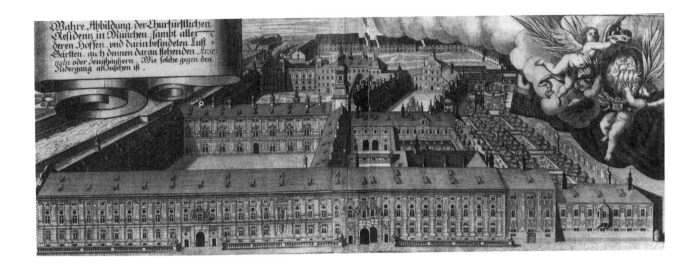

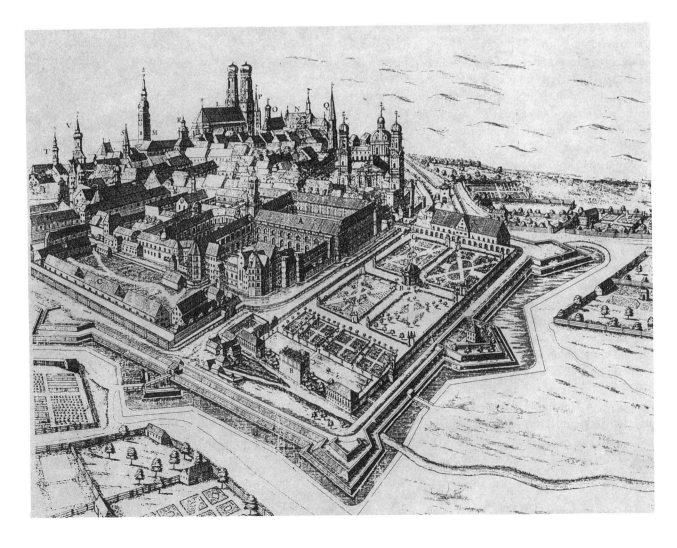

whose four massive corner towers lent it the aspect of a fortress. Above all, the architectural regularity of the Kaiserhofbau and the great length of the facade along the Schwabingergasse impressed contemporaries, even eighteenth-century writers who found the architecture outmoded. The Residenz is said to have served as the inspiration for Emperor Leopold I when he decided to enlarge the Hofburg after visiting Munich in 1658 on the way back from his coronation in Frankfurt.[63] But it was also the building's expansiveness, the almost baffling succession of courtyards and interior gardens produced by joining disparate elements, that made it unusual. This quality also did not escape contemporaries. Baldassare Pistorini was not merely flattering his employer or trotting out a literary cliché when he compared the Residenz—which he called a "sumptuous palace, an imperial rather than a ducal residence"—to a city: "In a corner of the electoral city of Munich there is situated another more delightful and more beautiful. If others have called the city a large palace, I will call this palace (it being the largest, richest, and noblest that can be seen, found, or imagined) a little city, because of the amplitude of its site, its majesty and grandeur, and no less because of its marvelous *struttura*."[64]

Maximilian's emergence early in his reign as the champion of the Catholic cause within the empire, a cause identified with the ideal of imperial unity, made the erection of a Residenz containing imperial guest suites and magnificent Festsäle of particular moment. In 1609, Maximilian played an instrumental role in the foundation of the Catholic League in reaction to the Union of Protestant Princes, founded the year before. The July meeting at which terms for the league were set convened in Munich; Maximilian was named director. The imperial family was conspicuously absent during the league's early planning stages, and it was only in 1610 that Archduke Ferdinand of Styria (later Emperor Ferdinand II) became a member. In October 1610, the negotiations between Catholics and Protestants that resulted in a temporary settlement of the Julich-Cleve succession took place in Munich, and the final settlement in 1613 was engineered by Maximilian. The extent of his reputation can be judged from the facts that France and Spain were prepared to back his candidacy as

---

Fig. 6. Munich, Residenz, view by Michael Wening, looking east toward Schwabingergasse facade, engraving, ca. 1700. (Österreichische National-bibliothek, Vienna)

Fig. 7. Munich, aerial view looking southwest by Michael Wening, detail showing Residenz and Hofgarten, engraving, ca. 1700. (Bayerische Verwaltung der staatlichen Schlösser, Gärten und Seen, Munich)

emperor on Rudolf II's death in 1612 and that several electors also expressed willingness to lend him their support. Realizing that his candidacy would run into serious opposition elsewhere and that a weakened House of Habsburg would not serve to further the Catholic cause, Maximilian rebuffed their overtures.

These political developments formed the background to the outbreak of the Thirty Years' War in 1618. Maximilian's initial military successes in Bohemia, where the Bavarian army was largely responsible for the spectacular imperial victory at White Mountain in 1620, and along the Rhine, where Bavaria and Spain together conquered the Palatinate, soon gave way to reversals. A Swedish invasion of Bavaria in 1632, during which Munich was occupied, was followed by repeated devastations by French and imperial troops, as southern Germany became one of the principal battlegrounds in a war that quickly accelerated into a continental struggle for hegemony between Habsburg and Bourbon. Bavaria derived certain political advantages from the war. Emperor Ferdinand II rewarded Maximilian in 1623 with elevation to the rank of Kurfürst (elector) of the Holy Roman Empire and in 1628 with possession of the Upper Palatinate, both confirmed by the Peace of Westphalia in 1648. These advantages were small, however, compared with the widespread economic devastation. Maximilian barely outlived the war, but he dedicated his last years to the task of reconstruction.[65]

The Residenz under Ferdinand Maria (1651–1679)

Maximilian's new Residenz was completed before the war made major building efforts unthinkable and limited construction to relatively insignificant renovation projects during the last thirty years of his reign. Maximilian's successor, Ferdinand Maria, introduces a long line of electors who left the structure of the Residenz intact while engaging in sometimes sweeping renovations of the interior to reflect changes in architectural taste, in living habits, or in the composition of the ruling family. This is not to say that Ferdinand Maria was inactive as a builder. His reign saw the erection of a court opera house on the Salvatorplatz (1654–55), generally recognized as the first detached theater building in Germany; a Turnierhaus (tournament house, or stadium, 1661; fig. 7) along the west side of the Hofgarten—an enormous structure with three tiers of galleries and capable, we are told, of holding ten thousand spectators; and the Theatinerkirche (Church of the Theatines, 1663ff.), which was built as a votive offering on the birth of Electoral Prince Max Emanuel in 1662 and which stood under the direct patronage of the elector and electress.[66]

Under Ferdinand Maria, Bavaria became a political pawn in the age-old struggle between France and Austria. Each of the two great powers sought to estrange Bavaria from the other and win it as a friendly buffer state.[67] Ferdinand Maria was only fifteen years old when he succeeded his father; and until he attained majority in 1654, the regency was held by Dowager Electress Maria Anna, a sister of Emperor Ferdinand III. Maria Anna's authority remained strong until her death in 1665, and she succeeded in keeping Bavaria on a pro-Habsburg, though outwardly neutral, course. Her influence on politics was all the more pronounced in that Ferdinand Maria, although certainly not the nonentity that some historians have made him out to be, was a reserved personality, lacking initiative and decisiveness, who regarded rulership as a painful obligation.[68]

Before his death, Maximilian had arranged a marriage for his son with Henriette Adelaide, daughter of the Duke of Savoy and, through her mother, a granddaughter of Henri IV of France. This arrangement came to fruition in 1652. The marriage, which was a departure from a long tradition of marital alliance with the Habsburgs, had first been suggested by Mazarin, who hoped thereby to bring Bavaria into the French camp. Maximilian saw instead the potential advantages to be had from alliance with another medium-sized state south of the Alps that had a similar interest in keeping both Habsburg and Bourbon at arm's length. With Henriette Adelaide's presence in Munich, however, the rivalry between these two houses became a domestic matter for the electoral family. Highly conscious of the exalted status her royal ancestry conferred on her, Henriette Adelaide could not forget that she had once been advanced as a potential bride for her cousin, Louis XIV. She was inclined to feel that she had married beneath her. Between her and her mother-in-law, an equally proud representative of the House of Habsburg, instant animosity arose. Maria Anna was offended by Henriette Adelaide's pretensions and her disdain for Germanic culture, and attempted to restrain her love for courtly pageantry and to limit the influence of the large Italian entourage Henriette Adelaide had brought with her.[69]

When Ferdinand III died in 1657, Louis XIV offered to back Ferdinand Maria's candidacy as emperor—a project enthusiastically endorsed by the young electress, who saw it as an opportunity for dynastic aggrandizement at Habsburg expense. Ferdinand Maria realistically declined to become involved and cast his vote for Leopold I. Leopold's repeated disregard for Bavaria's interests in the ensuing years, however, brought about a basic realignment of Bavaria. This development gained momentum after 1662, when Henriette Adelaide finally produced an heir, thereby augmenting her influence at court considerably. As pro-Austrian ministers died out, ministers who leaned toward the opposite side were appointed to replace them. In 1670, Bavaria entered into a treaty with France; in return for substantial subsidies, Bavaria guaranteed Louis XIV assistance in obtaining the Spanish inheritance by refusing to allow Austrian troops to cross Bavarian territory. Although Bavaria was hard-pressed to maintain its neutrality after Louis XIV began his offensive war against the Dutch in 1672, Ferdinand Maria's reign ended in 1679 without Bavaria having taken up arms. His reign had been one of unbroken peace and relative prosperity. The consequences of the precarious position in which Bavaria found itself through its alliance with a great power outside the empire would be realized only later—under his successor, Max Emanuel.

The work undertaken in the Residenz during Ferdinand Maria's reign involved preeminently the renovation of rooms for Henriette Adelaide. On her arrival in Munich in 1652, Henriette Adelaide was lodged for several days as a guest of honor in the Kaiserzimmer.[70] Since Electress Mother Maria Anna continued to occupy the electress's apartment, Henriette Adelaide moved into permanent quarters above the Antiquarium. In the early years of Ferdinand Maria's reign, Maria Anna retained effective control over court expenditures and permitted her daughter-in-law little freedom to engage in architectural projects. In 1658, however, Henriette Adelaide was able to erect a small gallery in which to display the numerous portraits in her possession.[71] This gallery looked out over the Residenzgarten from the east and was reached through the octagonal vestibule next to the Schwarzer Saal (plan A, 8).[72]

In 1664, shortly after the birth of Max Emanuel, Henriette Adelaide began to plan a radical transformation of the electress's apartment. Agostino Barelli, architect of the Theatinerkirche, was entrusted with the design of the new rooms. For their decoration, Henriette Adelaide sent to her brother, Karl Emanuel, Duke of Savoy, for sketches of ceilings and friezes.[73] After Maria Anna's death in 1665, the entire apartment could be included in the project, and it was decided to unite the disconnected tracts along the Schwabingergasse and along the garden and make of them a single ensemble.[74] This was achieved through the construction of a new room at their point of juncture. The finished apartment consisted of a flight of anterooms along the street, culminating in the Goldener Saal, or audience chamber (plan D, 12–15); a flight of private rooms along the garden (plan D, 16–18); and a gallery with two small cabinets in the former Witwenbau (plan D, 19–21). The rooms along the garden consisted of the Grottenzimmer, a private audience chamber; the Alkovenzimmer, or bedroom; and the Herzkabinett.[75] Scagliola wall paneling in the Herzkabinett and Grottenzimmer—as well as the wall fountain of the latter room, with its incrustation of shells and other marine exotica—belonged to the rooms created here in 1638–40 for Maria Anna. Ceilings and friezes were newly decorated by Henriette Adelaide. The Alkoven-zimmer was the most unusual room of the apartment and the one most specifically dependent on architectural precedent from Turin. The bed, which faced the entrance door, was set in a deep alcove and could be seen from the rest of the room through a sort of proscenium arch. For this, Henriette Adelaide had requested drawings of the Camera dell'Alcova in the Palazzo Reale in Turin, executed by Carlo Morello in 1663.[76] In the Witwenbau, the already existing gallery and its two end cabinets were redecorated. The gallery was furnished with paintings of the achievements and virtues of Maximilian I; the cabinets were decorated as a Liebeskabinett (cabinet of love) and a Rosen- und Lilienzimmer (rose and lily room). Along the south side of the Residenzgarten, a long, astoundingly narrow gallery was erected for the electress's library (plan D, 22).

Henriette Adelaide's apartment excited much admiration. S. Chapuzeau wrote in 1673, "Of all the sections of this vast palace, in which I often got lost, that of the electress is the richest and the most embellished as to ceilings, paneling, giltwork, chandeliers, large mirrors, precious furniture, and excellent paintings by the best masters of Flanders and of Italy."[77]

The electoral couple commissioned a description of the Residenz from Marchese Ranuccio Sforza Pallavicino, a gifted man of letters sent to the Bavarian court in 1666 by Henriette Adelaide's brother-in-law, the Duke of Parma. Pallavicino's work was published in 1667 under the title *I trionfi dell' architettura nella sontuosa Residenza di Monaco* (The triumphs of architecture in the sumptuous Residence in Munich) and appeared in updated German editions in 1685 (by Joanne Schmid) and 1719 (by Christoph Kalmbach).[78] Pallavicino devoted more attention to the electress's apartment than to any other part of the Residenz. He concentrated on the ceiling frescoes, for whose iconographical programs he offers exhaustive explanations. Unfortunately, he has virtually nothing to say about the furnishings of the rooms.

In April 1674, the first of three disastrous fires that ravaged the Residenz in the seventeenth and eighteenth centuries broke out in the quarters of the ladies-in-waiting, above the electress's anterooms, when a lady-in-waiting fell asleep over her evening devotions without having extinguished her candle. Before the fire could be brought under control, it caused widespread devastation to the recently furnished rooms in this part of the palace.[79] It spread east into the Hofdamenstock and north into the wing of the Kaiserzimmer, and was finally repelled by the fire walls separating the Herkules-Saal and the Kaisersaal from the rooms adjoining them. To the south, it was halted before the Goldener Saal by the gutting of the second antechamber. Restoration work on the Kaiserzimmer progressed very slowly, reaching completion only in the 1690s. The ceilings of the electress's anterooms were not restored.[80]

The Residenz under Max Emanuel (1679–1726)

Max Emanuel (reigned 1679–1726) figures as the second great palace builder of the dynasty. Unlike his illustrious grandfather and namesake, however, he focused his activities not on the improvement or enlargement of the Residenz, but on the erection of country palaces—and this on a scale previously unknown.

In the person of Max Emanuel there were concentrated to a high degree all the qualities that we associate with a Baroque prince—pursuit of dynastic prestige and military glory, desire for self-representation through a luxurious court housed in magnificent palaces, and an enormous appetite for "princely" diversions. He was raised by a Francophile mother who hired French tutors for him; and although an appreciation of the empire's oligarchic political traditions and of his grandfather's accomplishments formed part of his education, it was Louis XIV who was held up to him as a model to emulate.

The expansionist tendencies evident in Bavarian politics since the time of Albrecht V came to a climax in Max Emanuel's reign.[81] Dynastic interests had played an important role in the politics of his predecessors, but these interests had been balanced by attention to financial and judicial administration and had been tempered with realistic appraisals of Bavaria's political options. With Max Emanuel, the goal of dynastic aggrandizement became an obsession; he did not take much active interest in other objectives of statecraft, nor did he feel a sense of responsibility toward his lands.

Personally courageous and enterprising, Max Emanuel was incapable of sustained energy and lacking in self-discipline. "Although not without amiable qualities," wrote Fenelon, "the elector is infirm in his manner of life and depraved in his morals. He consoles himself with mistresses, passes his days in hunting, pipes on the flute, buys pictures, and runs up debts. He ruins his own land and does little good in the one to which he has been transferred [the Spanish Netherlands]."[82]

In the first two decades of his reign, Max Emanuel aligned himself with the emperor. Incensed at Louis XIV's capture of Strasbourg in 1681, he was persuaded to sign a treaty with Austria in 1683 for mutual protection against France and the Turks. In the Turkish campaigns of the 1680s in Hungary, Max Emanuel won fame as a courageous military leader, playing a decisive role at the relief of Vienna in 1683, as well as at the sieges of Buda in 1686 and Belgrade in 1688. In 1689, he fought for the emperor against the French in the Palatinate. The 1680s were the high point of Max Emanuel's career; it is worth noting that thirty years later, the only subject that could be found for the painting cycles in the Festsäle at Schleissheim was his victories in Hungary. Bavarian-Austrian friendship was sealed in 1685 with Max Emanuel's marriage to Archduchess Maria Antonia, Emperor Leopold's eldest daughter.

Maria Antonia's descent from Philip IV of Spain awakened the prospect of capturing all or a part of the Spanish inheritance for the Wittelsbachs on the death of Charles II. In 1691, Charles named Max Emanuel to the governorship of the Spanish Netherlands, for which he had negotiated relentlessly. The court was absent from Munich until 1701; Bavarian revenues, already severely strained by the costly Turkish campaigns, were diverted largely to Brussels, where Max Emanuel maintained an extravagant household. The birth of an heir, Joseph Ferdinand, in 1692 brought the Spanish inheritance considerably closer. Outraged at the discovery that France and the maritime powers had made secret plans for the division of Spain and its possessions, the Spanish Cortes persuaded Charles II in 1698 to name Joseph Ferdinand his universal heir; but the boy died prematurely in 1699, and Charles II revised his will in favor of Louis XIV's grandson, Philip of Anjou.

In the War of the Spanish Succession, Max Emanuel, against the better judgment of his ministers, allied himself with France, whose promises of subsidies and territorial gain or exchange were more tempting than those of Austria. Defeated by the Austrians and English at the Battle of Blenheim in 1704, Max Emanuel and his brother, Joseph Clemens, Elector of Cologne—France's only other ally—were forced to flee the empire. For their treasonous behavior, which amounted to an affront against the Imperial Peace (Reichsfrieden), Emperor Joseph I declared them imperial outlaws in 1706. Max Emanuel eventually was compelled to seek asylum in France, where he remained—penniless, inactive, and frustrated—until his lands were restored to him through the Peace of Rastatt in 1714.

When the electoral family reunited and reentered Munich in 1715, the Residenz must have seemed impossibly antiquated to a ruler who lived so much in the shadow of Louis XIV and whose politics centered so closely on the goal of dynastic aggrandizement. The location of the Residenz within the constricted setting of a walled capital still thoroughly medieval in character meant that the building could neither assert itself as an architectural monument nor be approached in a stately manner. To many commentators of the late seventeenth and eighteenth centuries, its courtyards and interior gardens made it seem more like a monastery than a palace. Most agreed that its principal claim to celebrity lay in its size and the magnificence of its interiors. Pöllnitz, for example, wrote in 1735:

> The palace of the elector is one of the vastest buildings in Europe, but it is much less beautiful than Misson and several other authors say; its size is its principal magnificence. The main facade, facing a rather narrow street, looks like a beautiful convent, an effect to which the image of the Virgin over the great portal very much contributes. What is most esteemed is the large apartment called the Emperor's Apartment.[83]

As early as Max Emanuel's accession, even the interior—however magnificent—was decidedly old-fashioned. The apartments of both elector and electress were squeezed irregularly into building tracts that lay at right angles to one another; moreover, the only truly representational suite of rooms, the Kaiserzimmer, had been decorated almost a century previously and was still in a state of partial ruin after the 1674 fire. With the exception of the electress's anterooms, which faced onto the narrow Schwabingergasse, and the Kaisersaal, the principal rooms of the palace were oriented inward, giving onto interior courtyards. None enjoyed the broad vista that had become virtually de rigueur by this time.[84]

Max Emanuel's contributions to the Residenz, which have not survived, were limited to the renovation of the elector's apartment. At the very beginning of his reign, he replaced the rooms of his father and grandfather with a new apartment known as the Alexanderzimmer (plan C, 1–11), after the ceiling frescoes that illustrated the deeds of Alexander the Great—an appropriate subject for a young ruler then achieving resounding success in battle.[85]

The Alexanderzimmer, begun in 1680 and finished in 1685, were designed and executed under the direction of court architect Enrico Zuccalli.[86] Zuccalli's design of the new apartment is recorded on a plan of the Residenz from 1616 to 1630, with proposed revisions on a flap that overlays the area of the Antiquarium and the southeast corner of the Grottenhofbau. It adds a new wing containing the elector's private rooms that extends eastward to the Antiquarium, thus reducing the size of the triangular courtyard behind it.[87] The anterooms along the east side of the Grottenhof remained as they were (plan C, 3, 4), but the changes south of them were radical (compare plan B, 7, 8, 10 with plan C, 5–11).

For descriptions of these rooms we are dependent on Schmid, Kalm-

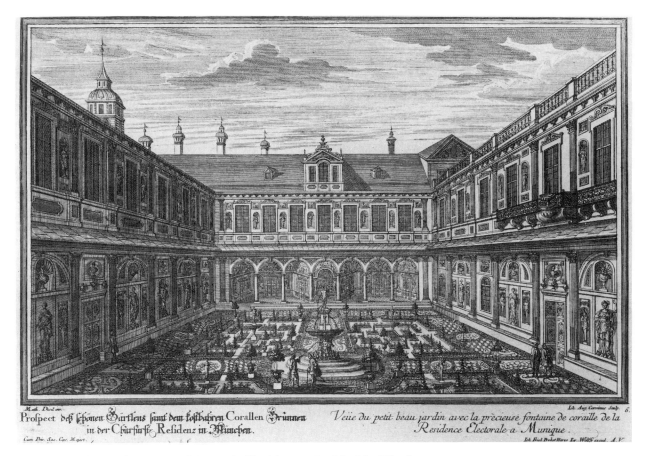

Prospect deß schönen Gärttens samt dem kostbahren Corallen Brunnen   Veüe du petit beau jardin avec la precieuse fontaine de coraille de la
        in der Churfürstl. Residenz in München.   Residence Electorale a Munique.

Fig. 8. Munich, Residenz, view of Grottenhof looking east by Matthias Diesel,
engraving, ca. 1720. (Staats- und Stadtbibliothek, Augsburg)

bach, and Wening.[88] The second audience chamber (plan C, 5) was followed by a bedroom with an alcove (plan C, 6), probably not unlike
Henriette Adelaide's bedroom. A Geheimes (privy) Cabinet (plan C, 7),
which looked out over the small rear courtyard, was reached from the
alcove. A dressing room (Ankleidezimmer; plan C, 8) adjoined the bedroom in the enfilade.[89] The most novel of the new rooms was found at
the very end of the new wing. Oval in shape, with openings into all adjacent spaces and onto a small balcony, this was in all probability the Holländisches (Dutch) or Spiegel (mirror) Cabinet described in the sources
(plan C, 9). It was furnished only in 1693–94 and was redecorated as a chapel (the Cäcilienkapelle) during the construction of the Reiche Zimmer.[90]
The walls of the Holländisches Cabinet were clad partly with mirrors and

partly with "Indian-style" woodwork; its floor, according to Kalmbach, was of majolica tiles, and there seem to have been quantities of porcelain on display. The ceiling, with its "perspective dome," was also at least partially mirrored. It seems to have been an early example—perhaps the earliest German example—of the fashion for exotic cabinets decorated with porcelain, lacquer, and mirrors that was to spread throughout Europe in the eighteenth century.

The south wing of the Grottenhofbau was also included in this renovation of the elector's apartment. Here a suite of four rooms known as the Sommerzimmer (plan C, 10) was created by enclosing the altana looking out over the Grottenhof.[91] The largest and most spectacular room of the suite was a picture gallery, where both Wening and Schmid noted paintings by Titian, Rubens, Dürer, Raphael, Veronese, and others. A door in its exterior wall gave access to a small balcony, where there was a little fountain (visible in fig. 8). Through the opposite wall one entered Maximilian's Kammergalerie (plan C, 11).[92] From the last of the Sommerzimmer, as Schmid and Wening tell us, one passed into the electress's apartment.

The Residenz under Karl Albrecht (1726–1745)

The last years of Max Emanuel's reign brought reconciliation with the emperor (not Joseph I, who died in 1711, but his brother, Charles VI). In 1717, Max Emanuel sent his heir, Karl Albrecht, to fight alongside Prince Eugene of Savoy at the reconquest of Belgrade. Karl Albrecht was wed to Joseph's daughter, Archduchess Maria Amalie, in 1722. Although Max Emanuel formally recognized the Pragmatic Sanction as part of the marriage agreement, the likely prospect of Charles VI dying without male issue activated hopes of asserting Bavaria's ancient claims to Austrian territories and of placing a second Wittelsbach on the imperial throne (the first having been Emperor Ludwig der Bayer in the fourteenth century). In a letter written shortly before his death in 1726, Max Emanuel exhorted Karl Albrecht to consider both these goals as his highest purpose in the years to come.[93]

Although Karl Albrecht's politics were not as narrowly focused on dynastic aggrandizement as Max Emanuel's had been, he did take his father's wishes to heart, and the goal of succeeding to Habsburg lands and dignities figured prominently in his diplomatic dealings with other states. He was able to win promises of support from France, as well as from many of his fellow princes of the empire, who could easily be induced to perceive Habsburg strength as a potential threat to their "liberties." When Charles VI died in 1740, Karl Albrecht moved quickly. A Bavarian-French army, with the elector in command, moved into Upper Austria and then on into Bohemia. In November 1741, Karl Albrecht was crowned King of Bohemia in Prague. While these events were taking place, the College of Electors was deliberating in Frankfurt; after heated debate, it voted in his favor. On February 12, 1742, he received the imperial crown from the hands of his brother, Clemens August, Elector of Cologne. Meanwhile, Austria mobilized its forces, marched into Bavaria, and took Munich. Over the next several years, the country was subjected intermittently to Austrian occupation as the fortunes of war shifted. Karl Albrecht evinced great energy as emperor, drafting proposals for the reform of the cumbersome imperial judicial system and the structure of imperial feudal law. Given the state of war, however, he was powerless to put any of these measures into execution. For Bavaria, the end to the War of the Austrian Succession came with Karl Albrecht's death in 1745. Happily, he was in possession of his capital at the time.

Under Karl Albrecht. the elector's apartment underwent one further reconstruction. The result was the rooms known at the time as the Schöne Zimmer (beautiful rooms) and today, because of the extraordinary lushness of their decor, as the Reiche Zimmer (plan D, 3–11).[94] They are the work of two architects, Joseph Effner and François de Cuvilliés the Elder.

The project was first commissioned by Max Emanuel from Effner on January 25, 1725. Its purpose was to provide the elector comfortable winter quarters in which to spend his declining years: "ICD has most graciously resolved to undertake highly necessary changes in the Residenz, in order that he might have a comfortable apartment for His Person in the wintertime, as he is at present chronically ill and has been subjected to all sorts of inconveniences that have prevented the desired recovery."[95] Originally the project seems to have been limited to the tract on the south side of the Grottenhof (possibly also including the rooms on the east side). After Max Emanuel's death on February 26, 1726, Karl Albrecht had the work continued and expanded the scope of the project to include not only the entire apartment upstairs, but also rooms on the ground floor.[96]

The new apartment was virtually complete when a fire broke out on December 14, 1729, destroying everything but the three anterooms (Ritterstube, antechamber, and first audience chamber; plan D, 2–4) and leaving the Grosses Audienzzimmer (the inner audience chamber of the Alexanderzimmer; plan D, 5) only partially undamaged. The gallery on the ground floor was also spared destruction.[97] Immediately the order was given to begin again, this time to new designs prepared by Cuvilliés. The work was finished in 1737.

The earlier Effner rooms spared by the fire were retained with only minor modifications. The private rooms of the apartment were the work of Cuvilliés: the Grosses Cabinet (or Konferenzzimmer), bedchamber, Spiegel Cabinet, and Cabinet der Miniatur-Gemälden (cabinet of miniature paintings; plan D, 6–9). These looked out over the Residenzgarten and were backed with service dégagements.[98] In a new wing built across the Residenzgarten, a picture gallery was installed, the Grüne Galerie (plan D, 10).[99] The gallery was tripartite, composed of a central section connecting two "salons." The north salon was demolished in 1826 to make way for the Königsbau. Direct access to the gallery could be had from the garden by means of an imperial-style staircase (plan D, 11). A vaulted vestibule and two further salons occupied the ground floor of the gallery wing. In 1764, under Max III Joseph, the staircase was removed and a dining room installed in its place; next to it, a new tract containing kitchens and pantries, as well as a smaller staircase leading down to the garden, was erected.[100]

Underneath the private rooms of the apartment, there was a portrait gallery (Ahnengalerie) on the site of the former garden hall, and at its far end was the Schatzkammer. The gallery was politically motivated. The over one hundred portraits of Wittelsbach ancestors—featuring three larger, almost full-length portraits of emperors Charlemagne, Theodo I, and Ludwig der Bayer in the center of the long wall—were a demonstration that Karl Albrecht's lineage was august enough to justify his claims to the imperial throne.[101] The same motives may be detected upstairs in the anterooms, where the overdoor panels are set with twelve portraits of Roman emperors, and in the Grüne Galerie, where there are busts of emperors in the woodwork.

Karl Albrecht also had a private apartment for himself, the Gelbes (yellow) Appartement, installed on the ground floor along the south side of the Grottenhof (fig. 9; beneath plan C, 10). It consisted of four rooms—two anterooms, a bedchamber, and a cabinet—and was entered from the room that served as the point of communication between the loggia of the Grottenhof, the Ahnengalerie, and the north garden salon.[102] The date of the erection of the Gelbes Appartement cannot be determined without

Fig. 9. Munich, Residenz, plan of ground floor by François de Cuvilliés, drawing formerly in the Bayerische Schlösser-Verwaltung, Museums-Abteilung, early 1760s. Schwabingergasse (west) facade at top. (Bayerische Verwaltung der staatlichen Schlösser, Gärten und Seen, Munich)

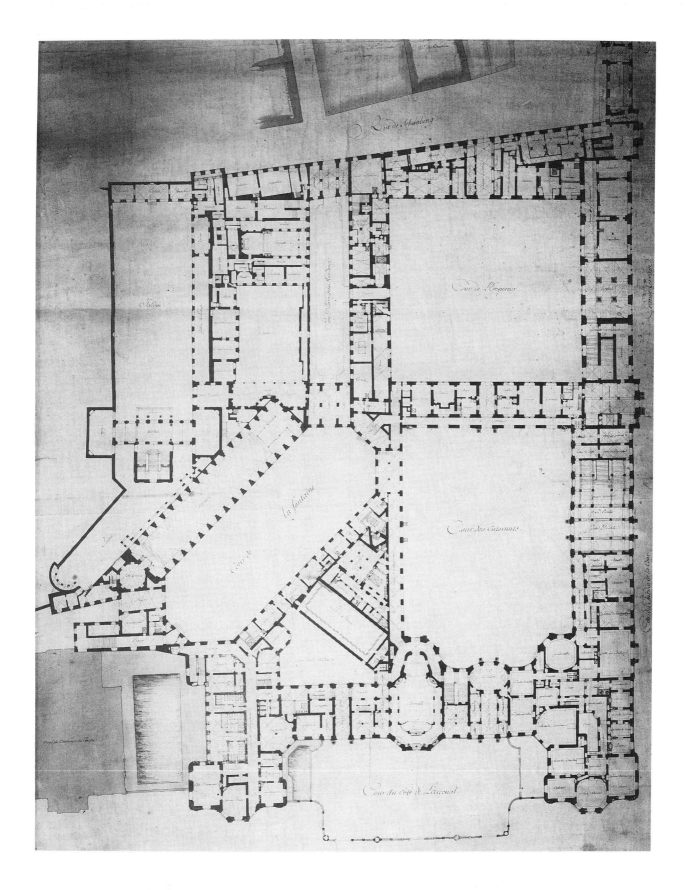

Rue de Schwabing

Cour de l'Empereur

Jardin

Cour de la fontaine

Cour des Cuisines

Cour du côté de L'arcenal

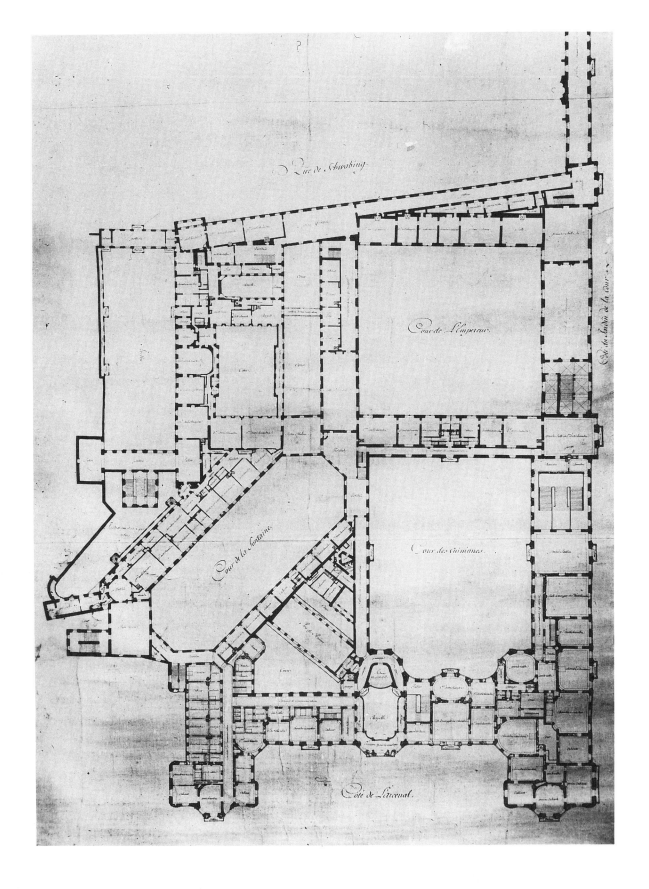

further research. In any case, it was in place by 1739; Graf von Preysing mentions in his diary that the elector spent some time there that year.[103]

The Residenz under Max III Joseph (1745–1777)

Karl Albrecht's successor, Max III Joseph, made his peace with Austria by renouncing all claims to Austrian territory and to the imperial title.[104] Under this elector, who sought to define a more realistic role for his state within the framework of the empire, Bavaria experienced an era of retrenchment and pursued a policy of determined neutrality. Military involvement in the Seven Years' War (1756–63) was kept to a minimum. Max III Joseph's reign, characterized by purposeful administrative and legal reform and noteworthy for advances in the field of education, served as Bavaria's introduction to the age of the Enlightenment.

On his accession in 1745, Max III Joseph decided to retain the apartment above the Antiquarium that he had occupied while electoral prince as "neue churfürstlichen Wohnzimmer" (new electoral living rooms). In 1746–48, these rooms were rather modestly renovated by court architect Johann Gunezrhainer into a pair of apartments for the elector and electress (plan D, 23–28, 30–35); beginning around 1762, the apartments were redecorated at greater expense by Cuvilliés.[105] Why Max III Joseph remained in this apartment is not known for certain. He may simply have felt more comfortable in these rooms, which were smaller and more intimate than the Reiche Zimmer; he may also have wished to disassociate himself in this way from his father's dynastic pretensions and the resultant political disaster.

To what extent Gunezrhainer might have altered the existing layout is not known.[106] Cuvilliés made one significant change in the plan of the electress's apartment. In 1760–61, her bedchamber, which until then had overlooked the old Residenzgarten (plan D, 17), was moved into the enfilade facing the Brunnenhof (plan D, 33).[107] This gave each apartment an identical sequence of anterooms—Ritterstube (the elector's Ritterstube, which was adjacent to the large Ritterstube of the Reiche Zimmer [plan D, 2], was called "kleine Ritterstube" in the 1769 furniture inventory), antechamber, and audience chamber.[108] The two cabinets in the enfilade belonged to the electress's apartment; the second of these, adjacent to the

Fig. 10. Munich, Residenz, plan of piano nobile by François de Cuvilliés, drawing formerly in the Bayerische Schlösser-Verwaltung, Museums-Abteilung, early 1760s. Schwabingergasse (west) facade at top. (Bayerische Verwaltung der staatlichen Schlösser, Gärten und Seen, Munich)

elector's bedchamber, housed her library (plan D, 35). Additional cabinets and service rooms were found in the rear enfilade. The apartments, particularly that of the electress, were well provided with service rooms—much better so, in fact, than any previous apartment in the Residenz.[109]

On the night of March 4, 1750, the third and last of the great fires in the Residenz broke out in the Neuveste. Apparently having started in the theater that had been installed in 1740 in the Georgs-Saal (plan A, 2), the fire spread along the north wing of the Küchenhof as far as the Trierzimmer and along the eastern side of the Residenz almost to the Brunnenhof before it could be contained. The Neuveste was left as little more than a burned-out ruin.[110] The Georgs-Saal was completely destroyed. Valuable living quarters for court personnel were lost. In the Hoher Stock and its adjoining structures (plan A, 4), the electoral Pagerie (pages' quarters) and the rooms of the court pharmacy (Hofapotheke) perished, as well as the two chapels. In the Rundstubenbau (plan A, 1), most of the rooms on the upper floors had been occupied by court ladies, several of whom lost their lives in trying to escape the flames. The Neuveste was rebuilt provisionally in a much reduced state, probably very shortly after the fire.[111] The walls were stabilized and repaired up to a height such that the buildings could be roofed above the first or second story. The ground floor continued to be used as the court pharmacy. In this form the Neuveste survived until it was demolished in 1830 to make way for von Klenze's Festsaalbau.

The one positive outcome of the fire was the Residenztheater (today the Altes Residenztheater), which was erected in 1751–55 to designs by Cuvilliés. The catastrophe had called attention to the fact that the danger of fire in theaters was abnormally great. It was thus thought desirable to keep the new building as isolated as possible. The site chosen was a segment of the Zwinger southeast of the Brunnenhof, a location that was also convenient to the principal apartments (figs. 11, 12, upper right).[112]

The Residenztheater, which in the eighteenth century was known as the Opera Haus, was the first theater building proper within the confines of the Residenz. Italian opera had been introduced in Munich by Maximilian I with a production in the Georgs-Saal in 1651; in that year, to celebrate the impending marriage of Ferdinand Maria and Henriette Adelaide, Maximilian ordered the erection of an opera house on the Salvatorplatz, which opened in 1655. The "Neues Opera Haus" in the Residenz was reserved exclusively for Italian opera seria. Other forms of court opera and court theater—Italian opera buffa and French comedy, introduced by Henriette Adelaide in 1671 and enormously popular under Max Emanuel and Karl Albrecht—were performed elsewhere: in the Theater am Salvatorplatz, in one of the Säle in the Residenz (notably the Schwarzer Saal or the Georgs-Saal), or in the Redoutensaal (hall for balls) erected in the Prannerstrasse in 1718.[113] Of the two carnival operas that Mozart composed for the Munich court, *La Finta Giardiniera* (1775), an opera buffa, was performed in the Redoutenhaus; *Idomeneo* (1771), an opera seria, played in the Opera Haus.

In the second half of the eighteenth century, the Theater am Salvatorplatz came to be accessible to a wider public, as a German-language drama directed at the middle classes experienced a tremendous surge. By the 1790s, however, the building had become so dilapidated that Karl Theodor, yielding to popular pressure, put the Opera Haus at the disposal of the public for plays of this nature as well as for the opera. It was then visited not only by those who were *hoffähig* (eligible to be presented at court), but by all who could pay the price of a seat. This measure was regarded as temporary, until plans for a new and large "national theater" could be realized. In 1819, Karl von Fischer's Hof- und Nationaltheater was opened, on a site adjoining that of the Opera Haus; and the latter reverted, although only briefly, to its role as a court theater.

In the early 1760s, Cuvilliés developed a project for "completing" the Residenz; the project exists in plan and elevation drawings (figs. 9, 10), as well as a large wooden model.[114] This was the first comprehensive plan for the extension of the Residenz since Maximilian's Kaiserhofbau. The project featured a new corps-de-logis on the site of the Neuveste (fig. 9, top). With end pavilions that projected far enough to create a shallow forecourt facing east, this would have given the Residenz the outward orientation and the magnificent approach it had previously lacked. A new, extraordinarily long facade was created on the north by repeating the facade of the new Küchenhof wing on the opposite side of the Kaisersaalbau.[115] The new corps-de-logis would have accommodated many of the functions that had been displaced with the loss of the Neuveste. The center pavilion was occupied by an enormous oblong chapel. Rooms for the Pagerie and the court pharmacy were found on the ground floor of the south wing. Upstairs there were three small apartments for Herrschaften (members of a ruling family), comparable in size to those in the Neuveste, as well as what look like lodgings for officials—probably intended for the court ladies who had formerly lived in the Rundstubenbau. The north wing, however, contained several apartments that can only have been meant as new apartments for the elector and electress, judging from the number and size of their rooms. The most elaborate of

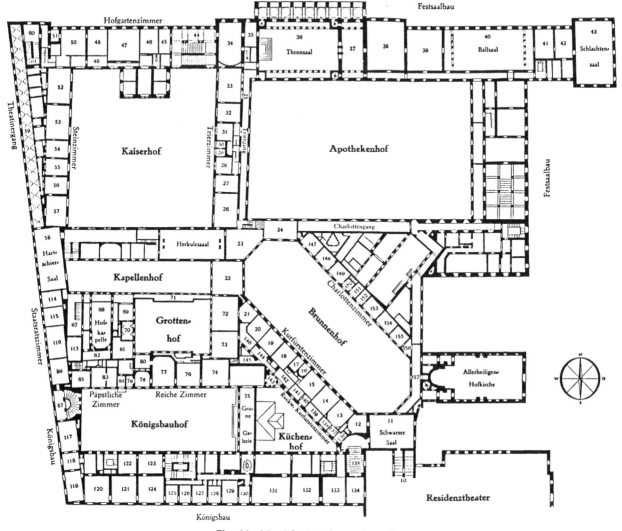

Fig. 11. Munich, Residenz, plan of piano nobile in 1937. (Thoma and Kreisel)

Fig. 12. Munich, Residenz, plan of ground floor by Maximilian von Verschaffelt, drawing, 1799. Schwabingergasse (west) facade at bottom. (Handschrift 64b, Plan 1, Geheimes Hausarchiv, Munich)

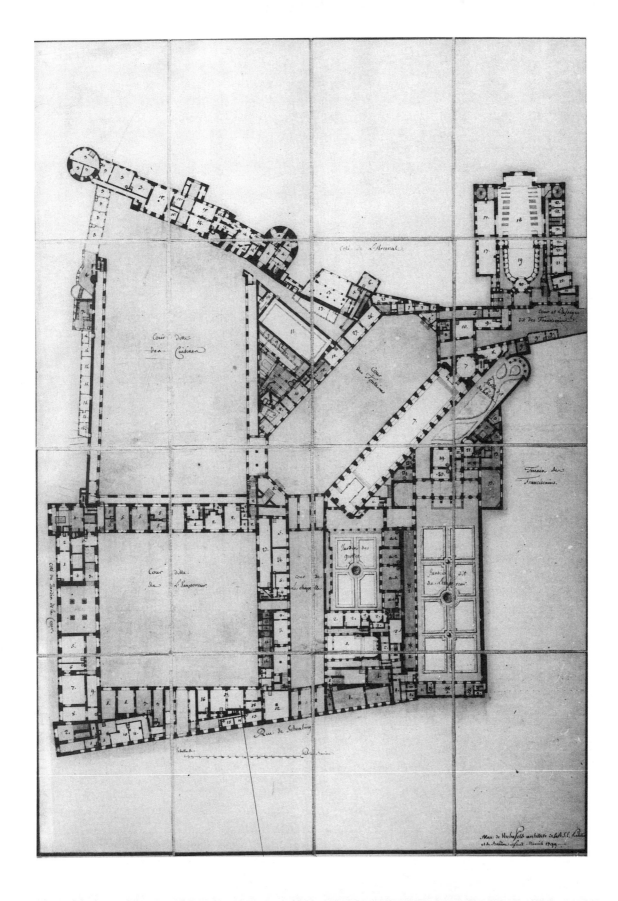

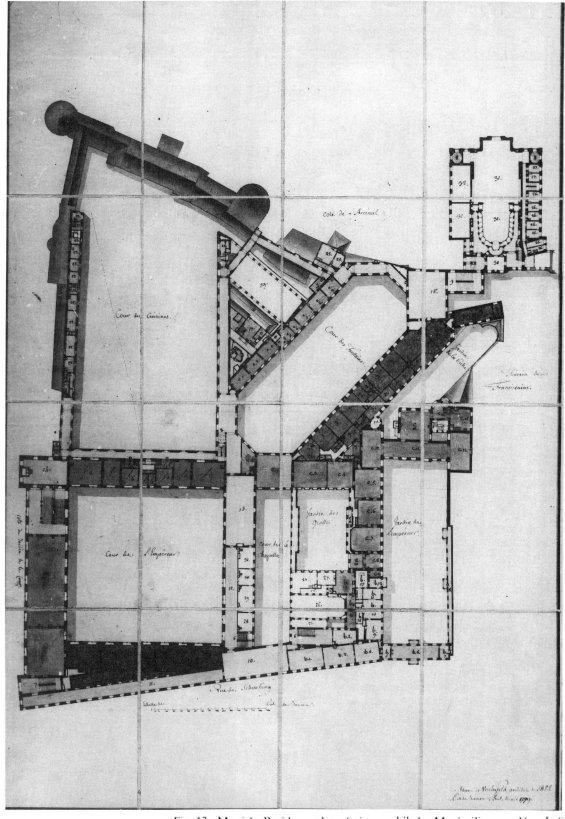

Fig. 13. Munich, Residenz, plan of piano nobile by Maximilian von Verschaffelt, drawing, 1799. Schwabingergasse (west) facade at bottom. (Handschrift 64b, Plan 3, Geheimes Hausarchiv, Munich)

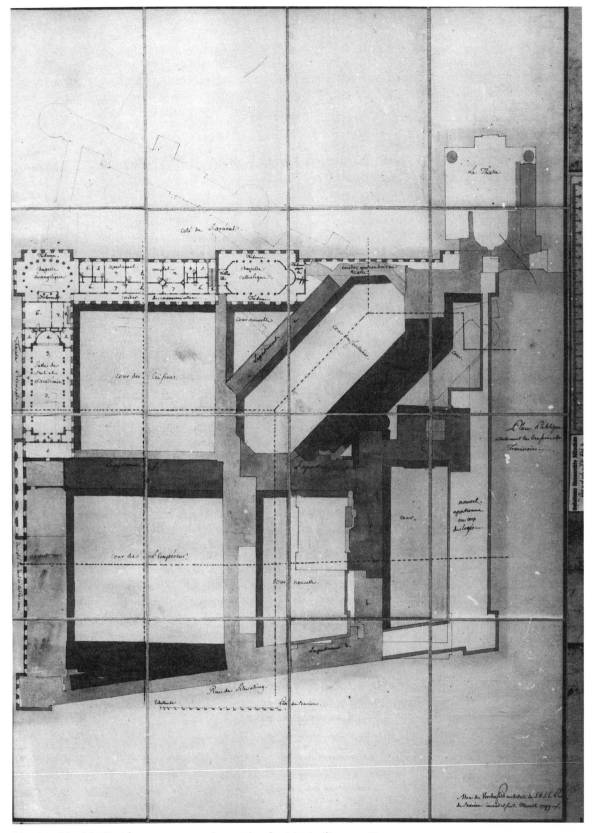

Fig. 14. Munich, Residenz, reconstruction project by Maximilian von Verschaffelt, plan of piano nobile, drawing, 1799. Schwabingergasse (west) facade
at bottom. (Handschrift 64b, Plan 6, Geheimes Hausarchiv, Munich)

these was ranged along the garden facade of the north wing and was reached by means of a hypostyle vestibule and an immense imperial-style staircase (figs. 9, 10, upper left side).

The Residenz under Karl Theodor (1777–1799) and Max IV Joseph (1799–1825)

Max III Joseph died childless and was succeeded by his distant cousin, Karl Theodor, Elector Palatine, head of the Palatine branch of the family. The succession should have been relatively painless, as it had been carefully arranged beforehand in a series of family agreements. Karl Theodor was not happy, however, with the stipulation establishing Munich as the capital of the new state of Kurpfalzbayern (Palatinate-Bavaria) that resulted from the union. He was reluctant to leave Mannheim, his old capital, which had become—largely through his own initiative and his enlightened policies—a cultural and intellectual center of some renown throughout Europe. He perceived Munich as backward and provincial by comparison. Karl Theodor entered into negotiations with Emperor Joseph II whereby Bavaria would be annexed to Austria in exchange for parts of the Austrian Netherlands, with the intention of forming a latter-day "Kingdom of Burgundy." The plan came very close to realization when Austrian troops marched into Bavarian territory in 1778; but the project was prevented through the intervention of Frederick the Great, who had no desire to see Austria enlarged at the expense of a medium-sized state so vital to maintaining the balance of power within the Empire. Bavaria's continued integrity as a state was guaranteed in the Treaty of Teschen, which ended this short War of the Bavarian Succession.[116]

When Karl Theodor himself died childless in 1799, Kurpfalzbayern passed undiminished to Max IV Joseph, head of the cadet line of Pfalz-Zweibrücken. Napoleon anointed him King of Bavaria in 1806, as Max I Joseph; through adroit diplomatic maneuvering, he was confirmed in this title at the Congress of Vienna. The abdication of his great-grandson Ludwig III in 1918 ended slightly over seven centuries of Wittelsbach rule in Bavaria.

Karl Theodor made no physical changes to the Residenz, where he lived alone for all but his last few years. His reign was notable not for court building projects, but for works that benefited the larger community, and it ushered in the tremendous expansion of the public realm that Munich experienced in the nineteenth century. In 1780–81, a picture gallery was erected above the arcade on the north side of the Hofgarten. A selection of paintings from the electoral collections was assembled here and became Munich's first public art gallery. For the first time, the public was admitted freely to the Hofgarten, to the park at Nymphenburg, and, as already noted, to the Residenztheater. The English Garden owes its beginnings to Karl Theodor, as does the demolition of the municipal fortifications, making possible a sequence of open spaces along the perimeter of the old city.

The first steps toward the radical reorganization of internal patterns of usage in the Residenz, a process that would be completed under Ludwig I, were taken by Max IV Joseph. On his accession in 1799, he decided to establish the Kaisersaalbau (which had the advantage of a view over the Hofgarten) as a center for the private life of his family (plan B, 19–22). A new apartment for Electress Karoline Friederike was installed in the Kaisersaal and Vierschimmelsaal (plan B, 20, 22; fig. 11). This apartment, known as the Hofgartenzimmer, was executed in 1799–1803 to designs by Charles-Pierre Puille. It was approached from the Kaisertreppe (plan B, 19) and consisted of seven rooms decorated in a Louis Seize style.[117] Although Max IV Joseph seems originally to have planned to occupy the Kaiserzimmer (plan B, 22–28), he eventually contented himself with very modest rooms on the third floor of the northwest pavilion. Ludwig I wrote that space was at such a premium in his father's quarters that when dinner was taken there on occasion, it was necessary to assemble in the bedroom. The Weisser Saal (plan B, 21) was redecorated in 1805 to become a dining room for the family.[118]

In 1799, Max IV Joseph commissioned designs for a new Festsaal (a "salle d'académie de musique, et de bal") and a Protestant chapel (Karoline Friederike was a Lutheran) from court architect Maximilian von Verschaffelt.[119] Verschaffelt took the opportunity to incorporate these spaces within a comprehensive plan for rebuilding the Residenz (figs. 13, 14) that was in certain respects a less ambitious version of the Cuvilliés design. The purpose of his proposal, as stated in the text accompanying the drawings, was to give the Residenz "a general form much more regular than the present one, and likewise an exterior appearance more closely related to and more suitable to its purpose."[120]

Nothing came of Verschaffelt's plan, nor of Karl von Fischer's several projects (1808–9) for a new wing along the north side of the vast open space (later the Max-Joseph-Platz) created in 1802–3 by the demolition of the Franziskanerkloster.[121] The financial strain of wartime precluded large-scale building enterprises, and Bavaria's elevation to the status of a monarchy in 1806 was not memorialized architecturally in the Residenz.[122] Furthermore, Max I Joseph was reluctant to complicate his old age with the aggravation of major renovations; he left it to Ludwig, who as crown prince demonstrated great enthusiasm for the fine arts, to transform the Residenz into a seat worthy of a king.[123]

Construction of the Königsbau (fig. 11,), designed by von Klenze, began very shortly after Ludwig's accession in 1825. The facade, modeled on that of the Palazzo Pitti, was monumental enough to give form to the Max-Joseph-Platz and to serve as a Schaufassade toward the city. The interior contained lavish apartments for the king and queen, as well as a suite of Festsäle for smaller court festivities. The Königsbau, finished in 1835, was followed in 1832–42 by von Klenze's Festsaalbau (fig. 11,), finally giving the Residenz a unified facade on the north.

The Accommodation of Subsidiary Functions

There are reasons that the foregoing building history of the Residenz has been told primarily from the point of view of the apartments and Festsäle. A palace such as the Residenz existed first and foremost to provide both living quarters for the sovereign and his family and a setting for court ceremonies and festivities. It was the fulfillment of these requirements that impelled major architectural efforts. Until the nineteenth century, subsidiary functions of court and state were rarely made the object of large-scale, monumental projects and were rarely given a significant role in determining the design of a palace. At best they were housed in seemingly orderly fashion in lateral building tracts or nearby structures— as at Versailles, for example, or the many other palaces erected during this period on fairly open sites. To what extent aesthetic considerations influenced the external form of such secondary buildings and prejudiced the internal functioning of court and state offices is difficult to determine.

The haphazard way in which subsidiary functions were accommodated in the Residenz can be analyzed in plans drawn by Verschaffelt in 1799 (figs. 12,13,). It resulted largely from the building's incremental history and the limited space for physical expansion. Rooms for the ladies-in-waiting are seen to be scattered throughout the palace, the administrative offices of the kitchens are nowhere near the kitchens themselves, and the rooms of the Geheimer Rat (privy council) are divided between two locations. The situation was made much worse when the partial destruction of the Neuveste in 1750 reduced the space available for a constantly growing court. Rooms for lodging personnel in the new opera house can hardly have been much of a substitute.[124]

Whether the inefficiencies resulting from such a plan mattered very much is another question. Large numbers of personnel were on hand to perform daily tasks. Court and state functions were distributed among many small and relatively self-sufficient jurisdictions. Each of the government councils had its own chancellery. Each of the offices involved with the preparation and service of food had its own administrators and secretaries. Meals were prepared not in one kitchen, but in several. If one had wanted to centralize the kitchens, one would have been hard-pressed to do so without major renovations.

The only semblance of orderliness is seen in the Kaiserhofbau. It contained not only magnificent apartments and Festsäle, but also spacious vaulted rooms on the ground floor for offices, mezzanines for lodging the household, and an enormous cellar in the Kaisersaal wing.

As the Alter Hof was abandoned as a residence in the fifteenth century, it was given over to subsidiary functions, chiefly to the chancelleries and council rooms of the various governmental bodies. The presence of state offices in the Alter Hof is recorded as early as 1470. In 1611, Hainhofer noted several there and in the library building next door.[125] In the seventeenth and eighteenth centuries, the higher organs of government—those most closely associated with the elector—had offices in the Residenz, while those involved with routine administrative business were housed either in the Alter Hof or elsewhere in the city.[126]

The ground floor of the Kaiserhofbau was clearly, perhaps chiefly, intended to house government offices. Wening describes "four vaulted rooms" in the Kaiserhofbau, with entrance from the Kapellenhof, dedicated to the Geheime Kanzlei (privy chancellery) and its Ratsstube (council room), as well as six additional rooms "for the extraordinary meetings of the councillors" (not the privy councillors, but presumably those of the Hofrat, or court council).[127] On Verschaffelt's plan, almost half the area on the ground floor of the Kaiserhofbau is occupied by state offices. Underneath the Kaiserzimmer there are six rooms (fig. 12, lower left; beneath plan B, 22–28) belonging to the *conseil intime* (inner council, or Geheimer Rat, which has four additional rooms below the dining room next to the Grüne Galerie). The rooms of the *revisoir* (Revisionsrat; the highest council of appeal in civil judicial matters) and those of the archives—the electoral archives, as well as the archives of the Order of the Knights of St. George—are found in the north wing, to either side of the hall with four columns (fig. 12, lower left side; beneath plan B, 19–20).[128] The *registrature d'état* (state registry office) is located in two rooms underneath the Herkules-Saal. The *départment des affaires étrangeres* (department of foreign affairs) is in the small apartment on the piano nobile of the Hofdamenstock, which formerly was used to lodge the very young electoral children and foreign envoys and later (under Max III Joseph) was divided among an office for the elector's cabinet secretary, a billiard room, and a studio where the elector worked on his lathe (plan B, between 11 and 3).[129] The *caisse de la chatouille electorale* (the Kabinettskasse, or privy purse) is found not in the Kaiserhofbau, but in three ground-floor rooms along the east end of the Brunnenhof (fig. 12, short upper arm of courtyard; plan A, 9).[130]

The kitchens and the related offices of the pantry, cellar, Silberkammer (silver chamber), and Leinwandkammer (table-linen chamber) took up more space on the ground floor of the palace than any other subsidiary function. The Silberkammer was located underneath the electress's anterooms, the Leinwandkammer under the Kaiserzimmer.[131] The various pantries and cellars were for the most part ranged along the west and north sides of the Küchenhof (plan A, 10), from which there was access to the extensive cellars under the Neuveste (plan A, 1–5), Ballhaus (plan A, 6), and the Kaisersaal wing.

The kitchen office was divided between the Hofküche (court kitchen), which prepared food for the court, and various other kitchens—chief among them the Mundküche (ruler's kitchen), which served the elector and the other Herrschaften. The largest kitchen was located in the triangular area between the Küchenhof, Brunnenhof, and Ballhaus (plan A). Here, according to Wening, were both the Hofküche and Mundküche, side by side. Cuvilliés's plan of the early 1760s (fig. 9) reveals that the court *pâtisserie* was also located here. The ladies and female servants had their own kitchen or kitchens in their living quarters, where they dined in their own Tafelzimmer (dining room). Wening also identifies a separate "Mundküche für die jungen Herrschaften" (eating kitchen for the young Herrschaften) on the ground floor of the Hofdamenstock, underneath the apartment. The kitchen erected in 1764 next to the Tafelzimmerbau (dining-room addition; plan D, 11) of the Reiche Zimmer was the first kitchen connected directly with a dining room.[132] We might expect the Mundküche to have been located here. While this may have been the case immediately after its erection, it was, according to Verschaffelt, the *confiserie* that occupied these rooms in 1799, when the Mundküche was on the ground floor of the Hofdamenstock (with additional space on the second floor of the Hofküche). Certain officials who had apartments in the Residenz, like the Leinwandmeisterin (mistress of the linens), had their own private kitchens. In the statistical summary at the end of his description, Wening gives a total of sixteen kitchens in the Residenz, many of which must have been such private kitchens.[133]

The male members of the household who were privileged to dine at court ate in one of the several Dirnitzen, large halls devoted to this purpose. From at least the late seventeenth century, the officers and gentlemen had their own dining room in the Neuveste. Wening notes a total of eight Dirnitzen, "darinn die Hof-Bediente gespeist werden" (in which those in court service are fed), but identifies only three of them—two on the ground floor of the Kaisersaal wing and one, the "schöne und grosse Dirnitz" (the prettiest and largest Dirnitz), underneath the Herkules-Saal (plan B, 3). Later documents, as well as the plans of Cuvilliés and Verschaffelt, note only this last one, which in 1600 was called the "neue Türniz" and seems to have been the principal dining room for servants.[134]

In the late eighteenth century, only a small percentage of the household lived in the Residenz. A description of persons having lodging in the Residenz from 1745 lists a total of 285, out of a household numbering 1,429 posts according to the 1747 Hofkalender. A similar description from 1771 totals 235; in 1769 the household numbered 1,525 persons.[135] In 1802 the Leinwandmeisterin, Frau Conjola, who like her predecessors had the right to live in the Residenz (in a small apartment adjacent to the Leinwandkammer [linens chamber]), submitted a petition requesting permission to use part of the Leinwandkammer as a lodging for her son-in-law, the Hofkellermeister (master of the court cellars). The request was denied on principle: "No Hofkellermeister has ever had free lodging in the Residenz. If his duties require his constant presence, then he should look around in the city for a nearby apartment. Otherwise, the Hofköche and other court servants could, for the same reasons, demand that they too be provided with apartments in the Residenz."[136]

The vast majority of those lodged in the Residenz fall into three groups: the ladies and female servants of the electress and the other female Herrschaften; the pages and their supervisors; and the staffs of the kitchen and pantry offices and the offices responsible for the custody and security of the palace.

A relatively high percentage of the female household lived in the Residenz. Of the twenty-one female members of the electress's household listed in the 1769 Hofkalender, from the Obristhofmeisterin and the Kammerdamen down to the maids and laundresses, fourteen had lodgings in the Residenz, according to the 1771 description. Eight ladies of the widowed Margravine of Baden–Baden lived in the palace. Ladies kept their own maids and servants; the electress's ladies had twenty-eight of these and the margravine's had fifteen. In addition, retired ladies and servants were often granted the privilege of continuing to occupy their old rooms; the 1771 description lists eight retired servants of the electress and two of the margravine. The rooms of the ladies were found throughout the palace, but were concentrated in the two mezzanines of the Hofdamenstock (plan D, between 1 and 12) and the upper mezzanine along the Schwabingergasse (plan D, 12–15). In this Frauenzimmer-Bereich (domain of ladies' rooms) there were also extensive wardrobes, as well as the ladies' dining rooms and kitchens.

The pages lived in dormitory rooms under the supervision of a Hofmeister and a *sous-gouverneur*. The Pagerie was located in the Neuveste (in the wing north of the Georgs-Saal; plan A, between 2 and 4) until this burned in 1750. It was then moved out of the Residenz until 1818.[137] The pages had various instructors (e.g,. a Mathematique- und Fortifications-Instructor, dancing and fencing masters) and were waited on by their own servants; several of these lived with their charges.[138]

The 1759 Hofkalender lists ninety-three persons belonging to the kitchen and pantry offices, from the Hofküchenamts-Commissarius (commissioner of the court kitchen office) down to the dishwashers and table setters. Of these, only twenty lived in the Residenz, according to the 1771 description. All, with the exception of a Hofzehrgaden-Officiant (pantry officer), were of the lowest ranks (apprentices, dishwashers, etc.). A handful of officials in charge of the palace, who were of bourgeois origins, were provided with lodgings. These included the Burgpfleger (concierge), the Hauspfleger (his second-in-command), and the Residenzgärtner. They had multiple-room apartments, where they lived with their families. In 1799, according to Verschaffelt's plan, the Burgpfleger had an apartment of seven rooms formerly assigned to Herrschaften on the ground floor of the Triertrakt (plan B, 29–35). The night watchmen, gatekeepers (Torsperrer), and persons responsible for lighting stoves and fireplaces were also housed in the Residenz.

Regarding the lodging of high court officers, Julius Bernhard von Rohr tells us in his *Einleitung zur Ceremoniel-Wissenschaft der grossen Herren* (1729) that although practices varied somewhat among the German courts, it was customary to house in the palace at most only officers closest to the prince and his family: "In some places, the princely residences are so laid out that the greatest and most necessary officers, who must be near the Herrschaften, are lodged there, either directly in the palace or in an attached subsidiary structure. At other courts, the important ministers and all the gentlemen reside in the city and, besides the ladies and the pages, only servants of the lowliest sort live in the palace."[139]

In the eighteenth century, none of the Bavarian court officers had apartments in the Residenz. They were, however, often granted rooms for their personal use during the day. An Instruktion of 1686 for the electress's Obristhofmeister states that he is to be provided with "a room at court . . . in which he can stay during the day," in order that he can wait on his mistress in the proper manner.[140] In the 1745 description, such rooms are noted for the Obristhofmarschall and the elector's cabinet secretary. The pair of Kämmerer who at any given time had service with the elector slept at court. The 1769 furniture inventory lists a room, not connected with the elector's apartment, "where the electoral gentlemen tend to congregate."

A small number of Kammerdiener and Portiers slept directly in the apartment. The 1745 description lists the following persons of the elector's household who sleep "wexlweis" (in rotation) at court: one Kämmerer, one Kammerdiener, one Portier "on the elector's side" (in the private apartment), one Portier "on the emperor's side" (in the Reiche Zimmer), and two persons in the Büchsenkammer (a back room). Certain of the Kammerdiener and/or Portiers slept in the antechambers. The furniture inventories (those for Nymphenburg and Schleissheim, as well as the 1769 Residenz inventory) list beds in many of the antechambers. These were trundle beds or cots that could be removed during the day.[141]

When the court was in residence at Nymphenburg in the summer, the high court officers were lodged in the palace. It was only essential members of the household, however, who were so provided for. This situation stands in marked contrast to that at Versailles, where large numbers of courtiers received apartments in the palace as a favor from the king. Although under Max Emanuel and his successors the Munich court was a very sociable place, it had none of the character of a perpetual weekend house party that we associate with the French court in the seventeenth and eighteenth centuries.

3

The Country Houses

There was hardly a prince in Germany, wrote Moser in his *Teutsches Hof-Recht* (1754–55), who did not have his "Nebenresidenzen" (subsidiary residences), by which he meant Lust- or Landschlösser (country palaces).[1] Although he stressed that a prince was free to choose his Residenzort as he saw fit, the implication was clear that this would be within the context of a city, as it had to be for economic reasons. Curiously, nowhere in his vast treatise did Moser mention the practice, so widespread in Germany in the seventeenth and eighteenth centuries, of founding new Residenzstädte away from the traditional capital—a practice that often yielded a discrepancy between the Hauptstadt (principal city) and the Residenzstadt (government seat). Although several of Max Emanuel's more grandiose preliminary projects for Schleissheim leave the suspicion that he might have had a new Residenz in mind, a relocation did not occur; and Bavaria demonstrated very clearly the sharp distinction that Moser drew between the unique, urban Residenz and its satellite Landschlösser.

"The temporary residence of the ruler in his country houses is useful and good," wrote Moser. Like any private gentleman, the prince deserved a change of scene, and it was only right that he should have this opportunity to escape the pressures of state affairs, the strictures of court ceremonial, and the importunity of those who had entrée at court. Here he was at greater liberty to do as he pleased and to determine the company he wished to keep.[2] Just as he should pursue his pleasures with moderation, however, so the prince should not stay too long in his Lustschlösser, nor withdraw too far from the public eye. A Lustschloss should be fairly close to the Residenz, so that affairs of state would not be prejudiced and there would be no inducement to establish a second household. Nor should it eclipse the Residenz in the magnificence of its architecture.[3]

Max Emanuel was the great builder of country houses of the Wittelsbach dynasty. Despite the nearly disastrous financial policies of his unstable reign, he built on a scale previously unknown and never attempted again. And unlike his predecessors, he was involved simultaneously on many projects, from substantial new residences at Nymphenburg and Schleissheim to diminutive garden pavilions such as the Pagodenburg and the Badenburg. His activity as a builder has all the appearance of a comprehensive program—largely successful—to extend and diversify the physical setting of the Bavarian court.

Country Residences before Max Emanuel

The Wittelsbach dukes and electors owned property throughout Bavaria, approximately 10 percent of all land being in their personal possession in 1760.[4] Only those estates and houses within convenient riding distance of the Residenzstadt played important roles in the life of the court after territorial authority was concentrated in Munich (see fig. 15). Some of these estates functioned as the residences of minor members of the family—for example, Schloss Blutenburg in Obermenzing and Schloss Neudeck on the east bank of the Isar. Other houses farther afield, such as Wasserburg am Inn, Haag, Schwaben, Lichtenberg am Lech, Starnberg, and Berg, were visited by the electors and the court infrequently but fairly regularly in the seventeenth and eighteenth centuries, when they provided overnight accommodations on trips and hunting expeditions. The latter two houses offered the pleasures of boating and fishing on the Starnbergersee, as well.

The country houses around Munich also served an important function as vantage points from which to meet exalted guests arriving on state visits. Traveling out from the Residenzstadt to greet princely visitors was a courtesy dictated by ceremonial; the distance traveled (as well as the size and magnificence of the entourage) was calculated to reflect the status of the visitor. In 1652, for example, on the occasion of Henriette Adelaide's arrival in Munich, the court went to Wasserburg am Inn to meet her. The initial encounter took place in a field one hour beyond Wasserburg, and the combined parties returned there to spend the first night. The procession back to Munich lasted two days, with stopovers at Haag and Schwaben.[5] For guests arriving from the west, Dachau was a convenient meeting point. In 1653, at the state visit of the imperial family, Ferdinand Maria traveled to Dachau two days beforehand to personally oversee preparations for their reception. When news of their approach arrived, he rode out to meet them and escorted them back to Dachau,

Fig. 15. Locations of Wittelsbach residences discussed in text, except Lichtenberg am Lech, about thirty miles west. (C.F. Otto)

where a state dinner was held in the evening. The formal entry into Munich took place the following day.[6]

Dachau

In the seventeenth century, the country houses that figured most prominently in the life of the court were Dachau and Schleissheim. Schloss Dachau is spectacularly situated. From the hilltop site that it shares with the town of the same name, rising abruptly from the surrounding marshlands, it commands a panoramic view over the Bavarian plateau to the southeast.

The Schloss (fig. 16) was largely the work of Albrecht V, under whom the existing house was transformed (from 1555 to 1573) into a substantial residence of four wings around a rectangular courtyard. Wening wrote that it boasted 400 windows, 108 habitable rooms, pleasant gardens and fountains all around, and a summer house standing on columns. The exterior was plain—"in the old style," according to Wening. On the interior, however, the principal rooms were furnished with extraordinary

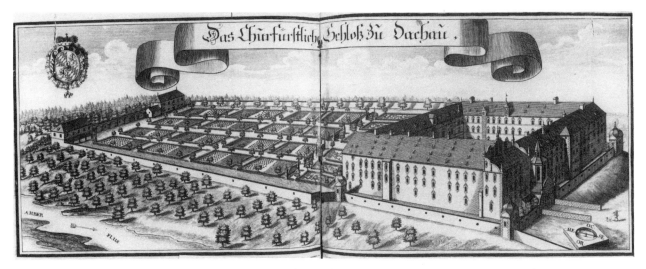

Fig. 16. Dachau, Schloss, view by Michael Wening, engraving, ca. 1700. On the compass, SE is north. (Österreichische Nationalbibliothek, Vienna)

magnificence. The Festsaal in the main wing overlooking the garden rivaled the roughly contemporary Georgs-Saal in the Neuveste in size and splendor; Max Emanuel deemed its ornately coffered wooden ceiling worthy of preservation during the redecoration in 1715–17. Although Schleissheim overtook Dachau in importance as a residence in the seventeenth century, both Maximilian and Ferdinand Maria spent considerable time at Dachau.[7]

Alt-Schleissheim

Shortly after accepting Maximilian as co-regent in 1594, Wilhelm V began to acquire land for a country retreat that was solitary and isolated, but easily reached from Munich and Dachau. Here at Schleissheim, Wilhelm began construction of a house and farm in 1597, the year of his final abdication. Essentially finished by 1600, the structure took the form of a long, narrow rectangle, with the house itself at the east end and wings containing barns, stables, other farm buildings, and quarters for household and estate personnel grouped around three courtyards to the west. Hainhofer visited the estate in 1611 and described in detail the farm buildings of this highly productive agricultural operation, organized on the most modern principles.[8] In the seventeenth and eighteenth centuries, Schleissheim also functioned as the electoral stud, and it remained an active farm until recently.

Fig. 17. Schleissheim, Alt-Schleissheim, view from southwest by Anton Wilhelm Ertel, engraving, 1687. From *Kurbayerisches Atlas.* (Bayerische Verwaltung der staatlichen Schlösser, Gärten und Seen, Munich)

Financial difficulties compelled Wilhelm to cede Schleissheim to Maximilian in 1616 in exchange for an annual pension.[9] Maximilian demolished his father's house, although not the other wings, and from 1616 to 1628 built a larger and more magnificent residence, the present-day Altes Schloss (fig. 17, east wing, at far right). The new building was dominated by the central Saalbau, which reached through the entire width of the structure and formed gabled pavilions on both the court and garden facades. Exterior staircases led directly into a barrel-vaulted Saal, which was flanked on each side by identical pairs of three-room apartments. The architecture of the exterior was rustic in character. At the south end of the building was the double-story Wilhelmskapelle, which Maximilian renovated. The renovation work also encompassed the subsidiary wings around the first courtyard, which were given an exterior treatment in keeping with the corps-de-logis. On completion of the work, more

The Country Houses

than two hundred rooms were available for the Herrschaften and court, increased from forty under Wilhelm.[10]

The Country Houses under Maximilian I

Under Maximilian, Schleissheim seems to have become the country residence preferred by the elector and his family. There is almost no information on annual itineraries of the court previous to the eighteenth century, when this was well documented in the indispensable diaries of Graf Maximilian von Preysing. In the Geheimes Hausarchiv in Munich, however, there is a diary kept by Obristhofmeister Graf Max Kurz during 1651, in which he exhaustively records the day-to-day activities of the Herrschaften.[11] It reveals that of the 104 nights the court spent outside Munich in that year, 63 were spent at Schleissheim, in short visits of not longer than two weeks. By comparison, the court spent five nights at Dachau, two at Schwaben, ten at Ingolstadt (where Maximilian died on September 27), and twenty-four elsewhere. This indicates the favored status Schleissheim enjoyed during at least the late years of Maximilian's reign.

Life in the country houses was simpler under Maximilian than it was during succeeding reigns. The goal of a visit to Schleissheim or Starnberg was relaxation in bucolic surroundings, not amusement in the lively company of courtiers. In 1655 Johann Mändl, president of the Hofkammer (court administrative office), prepared a memorandum criticizing mounting court expenditures. Among other things, he noted that whereas Maximilian had used to travel to Schleissheim with an entourage of not more than 60–70 persons, Ferdinand Maria couldn't do with fewer than 250–300.[12] When Hainhofer arrived in Munich in June 1636 on a diplomatic mission from the Duke of Braunschweig, he was informed that the elector and electress were on a ten-day retreat at Starnberg. Anxious to dispense with his business, Hainhofer decided to travel on to Starnberg, where he was told by an official that Maximilian was "in villa" and not receiving envoys. Even while at Schleissheim, the official went on to explain, the elector granted no audiences, as he kept no councillors or secretaries on hand and was thus not prepared to conduct business. Hainhofer insisted that his mission was purely ceremonial and could be quickly settled, but still Maximilian turned him down, directing him to report to the Hofmarschall in Munich.[13] On her arrival in Munich in 1652, Henriette Adelaide was shocked to find, as she wrote her mother in Turin, that Maria Anna made a practice of inspecting the kitchens and cow barns at Schleissheim. When it was suggested to her that she might do the same, she replied that she would obey if the electress mother ordered it, but she hardly considered it a fitting activity for a princess.[14]

The Country Houses under Ferdinand Maria

Ferdinand Maria's court was dominated by the electress mother, who maintained the ceremonious and somewhat rigid regimen that had prevailed under Maximilian. After her death in 1665, the wishes of Henriette Adelaide, who had grown up at the pleasure-seeking court of Savoy, determined the character of court life. The court was no less ceremonious than it had been, but it acquired a new emphasis on entertainment and amusement. The numerous festivals that Henriette Adelaide staged in the Residenz during the carnival season—the earliest in 1654—are well known. Carnival was now celebrated for weeks on end and without regard for the time of day. While Maria Anna was still alive, only rarely did social occasions last beyond midnight; now the court often danced into the morning hours.[15]

This change affected the use of the country residences; although they were probably no more extensively occupied than before, they were now exploited for a wider variety of recreational purposes. Ferdinand Maria and Henriette Adelaide shared a devotion to country life. The elector's preference for the out-of-doors probably had much to do with his poor vision, which made desk work a painful obligation. Only a strong sense of duty bound him to the Residenz, to councils, audiences, and ceremonies; he sought relief in the sports of hunting, riding, and boating, and he traveled frequently through Bavaria on tours of inspection.[16]

At Schleissheim, the improvements undertaken during his reign affected mostly the garden. North of the house, a new garden with covered arbors and an archery course was laid out. Elsewhere on the estate, there were now a manège and a redoubt in the middle of a pond, where one could practice shooting at painted targets. In 1656 a Ballhaus was erected.[17] In the house, the apartments of the elector and electress were lavishly redecorated. Schleissheim, wrote Chapuzeau in 1673, "is a perfectly beautiful house one league from Munich, where Their Electoral Highnesses ordinarily spend part of the summer."[18]

The Starnbergersee became a major attraction for the court with the construction of a flotilla of luxurious pleasure boats (fig. 18). As early

Fig. 18. Starnberg, Schloss, view with the Bucintoro by Michael Wening, engraving, ca. 1700. (Österreichische Nationalbibliothek, Vienna)

as the sixteenth century, the dukes of Bavaria had maintained boats on the lake; these were destroyed by the Swedes during the Thirty Years' War. In the early years of Ferdinand Maria's reign, the court made do with quite modest boats; but in 1662, after the birth of Max Emanuel, Ferdinand Maria decided to build a replica of the Bucintoro, the state barge of the Doge of Venice. He commissioned Francesco Santurini, a Venetian engineer and theater architect, with its design and construction. Of approximately the same size as its model, the Bavarian Bucintoro differed in its inner disposition. Instead of the one large salon of the doge's barge, it contained a suite of rooms for the electoral couple, including anterooms, a private room, and a Speise-Saal. In the following years, additional ships were built and the older ships were overhauled and used as escort vessels. Two smaller barges (one of them called the Kammerherrenschiff) and a swarm of gondolas and service ships— including "pantry ships" and a "kitchen ship" complete with stove— made up the fleet, which always sailed out in formation, the service ships at a respectful distance from the barges. Two thousand persons in all could be accommodated.[19]

A cruise in the Bucintoro became an inevitable part of the festivities during state visits of foreign princes. On board, one could dine in state, play cards, fish, swim, and hunt, all to the accompaniment of music and cannon salutes, and relish the lush scenery of the Alpine foothills. The best-documented festivity on the Starnbergersee was staged in 1672 for the Archbishop of Salzburg; the guests were treated to pearl fishing, fireworks, and a deer hunt, for which the animals were driven into the water to be shot from on board.[20]

Nymphenburg

On July 1, 1663, in gratitude for the birth of an heir the year before, Ferdinand Maria presented to his wife the properties of Menzing and Kemnat. Located northwest of Munich, both were productive agricultural estates favorably situated for summer residence and hunting excursions. Henriette Adelaide conceived the idea of building a villa here and wrote to her mother on July 5, requesting designs as well as suggestions for a new name for the property. On August 10, she sent a site plan and gave her mother an indication of the program she desired; the house should have four "appartements nobles," each with three antechambers, a bedchamber, two cabinets, and a garderobe. In the vicinity of Turin, her brother Karl Emanuel was building (from 1658) a magnificent *castello di caccia,* Venaria Reale, to designs by court architect Amedeo di Castellamonte; Henriette Adelaide clearly hoped to profit from ideas generated by this project. Toward the end of the year, two designs by Castellamonte arrived in Munich. The first, described as a "carré," was apparently a cubic structure; the other was presumably more strongly articulated on the exterior. Ferdinand Maria, as Henriette Adelaide wrote her mother, tended to prefer the carré; but neither design corresponded completely with their wishes, and she had taken the liberty of sending Castellamonte a memorandum detailing their needs and requesting improvements on the carré.[21] Nothing apparently came of this; finally, in the spring of 1664, the project was entrusted to Agostino Barelli, who was at that time occupied with the construction of the Theatinerkirche.

The resulting building (fig. 19) nonetheless owes much to precedent from Turin. The idea of the cubic block was retained from Castellamonte's initial design and is highly reminiscent of traditional Piedmontese villa architecture, which even in the seventeenth century adhered closely to the type of the Roman *villa suburbana.*[22] The plan of the piano nobile, with linear apartments grouped along both sides of a central *salle à l'italienne,* bears comparison with Castellamonte's original plan for the corps-de-logis of Venaria Reale. Construction was begun in September 1664, by which time a name had also been found. The name Nymphenburg was inspired by the so-called Green Bastion in the palace garden at Turin, where a sort of nymphaeum containing rooms lavishly frescoed with nymphs, nereids, and other deities of nature was set in

Fig. 19. Nymphenburg, Schloss, view by Michael Wening, engraving, ca. 1700. (Österreichische Nationalbibliothek, Vienna)

a bosquet garden. When she learned of its renovation in 1663–64, Henriette Adelaide decided to adopt similar motifs for the decoration of her house and chose a name that reflected the iconographical program very directly.[23]

Construction progressed slowly; funds had to be shared with the Theatinerkirche and the electress's apartment in the Residenz, and preference was given to the latter projects. In 1674, Barelli left Munich and supervision passed to Zuccalli, who also took over at the Theatinerkirche. By the end of 1675, according to building accounts, the house had been roofed and the interior plasterwork started. After Henriette Adelaide's death in 1676, work on the interior continued, at the wish of Ferdinand Maria, although it is doubtful that by his death in 1679 all the ceiling and wall paintings in the principal rooms were in place.[24]

The appearance of Henriette Adelaide's villa is recorded in Wening's engraving of about 1700 (fig. 19), which shows a cubic block of five stories diminishing in height toward the top, crowned with a high hipped roof. The exterior is simple in the extreme and totally without an order. In front of the house, a monumental double staircase gives direct access into the Saal, while under the stairs a triple-arched loggia leads to a groundfloor hall. Behind the house is an enclosed garden featuring a quincunx of fountains set within wedge-shaped *parterres en broderie*. An allée has been cleared through the woods, permitting a view of the parish church of Dorf Pipping in the distance. In the right foreground is the chapel of St. Magdalena and, on the opposite side, a building for court personnel, as well as farm buildings.

The Country Houses under Max Emanuel, 1679–1704

Max Emanuel made even greater demands on the country houses than his parents had. He was a notoriously restless and impetuous individual, accustomed to making decisions on the spur of the moment, and relentless travel from one residence to another characterized his entire reign. The itinerary was, it would seem, largely improvised and dictated by the pursuit of variety in his amusements. At least in the early years of his reign, he only reluctantly allowed duty to interfere with this self-indulgent life. Hardly was he back from one trip than he set off on another, with either a large or a small entourage, visiting Schleissheim and Nymphenburg most regularly but also going to the more distant Jagdschlösser (hunting palaces) with greater frequency than his predecessors had. As Conte Lantery, a Savoyard at the Munich court, reported in 1681, "he doesn't very much like staying in the city." [25]

The schedule of Max Emanuel's travels and activities in 1680—well documented in imperial and Savoyard diplomatic reports like most of his early reign—may be taken to illustrate the life of the young elector and his court. [26] December 1679 was spent mostly in Munich, although snowy days were taken up with sleigh excursions to Nymphenburg or Schleissheim, where the company dined and danced until late. Baroness Simeoni reported to Turin that on December 8 Max Emanuel drove out to Nymphenburg, spent the entire night dancing, and barely made it to early mass at the Theatinerkirche the next morning. After mass, he slept until 4 P.M., then returned to Nymphenburg. The elector and many of the gentlemen of his set were also training for the tournament planned as part of the procura wedding festivities of Max Emanuel's elder sister, Maria Anna Christina, with the grand dauphin in late January. On February 5, the princess began her journey to Paris, progressing in slow stages. On the seventh she arrived in Augsburg and was given a surprise reception by Max Emanuel, who had traveled there incognito. On the tenth he received her in the same manner in Ulm, where two days later brother and sister took final leave of each other.

The peripatetic life of the young elector and his circle continued. Much of May was spent at Nymphenburg, where Max Emanuel devoted himself to falconry. On May 29, after a long absence, he returned to Munich to attend a requiem mass for his father, only to leave the next day for Schleissheim. There he remained until July 7, when he returned to Munich to prepare for the celebration of his attainment of majority on July 11–14. On the seventeenth the court made a pilgrimage to Altötting and then spent some time at the Starnbergersee. On August 1 Max Emanuel was back in Munich to receive the traditional oath of fealty (Erbhuldigung) of the Estates. He passed most of August hunting in various parts of Bavaria and ended the month with a brief visit to Nürnberg to inspect the monuments and artistic treasures of the city. During the autumn he lived almost exclusively at Dachau and Schleissheim, finally returning to Munich on November 20 with the good intention of spending the whole winter in town.

The scale of Max Emanuel's activities as a builder of country houses, however, far exceeded the needs of recreation. The two major building projects of his reign—the new palace at Schleissheim and the expansion of Henriette Adelaide's villa at Nymphenburg—produced substantial edifices suited for accommodating a more numerous household than the Herrschaften with a limited retinue. Both were clearly planned to be major residences, although no evidence exists to suggest that Max Emanuel intended to remove the court permanently to the country or promote the development of Residenzstädte around the palaces capable of supporting the court.[27]

The planning of Schleissheim must be seen against the background of Max Emanuel's burgeoning political ambitions during the period from 1685, when his marriage with Maria Antonia first offered the possibility of capturing the Spanish inheritance, to 1699, when these hopes faded with the death of their son Joseph Ferdinand. In these years, numerous preliminary projects for Schleissheim were developed, several of them immoderately grandiose and hardly possible to realize without the resources of a major state to finance their construction. The conclusion that these projects grew in magnitude as the goal of dynastic aggrandizement became seemingly more concrete is inescapable.

Max Emanuel did not abandon his belief in the destiny of his house and person with the death of his son; if anything, his pursuit of greater glory intensified. Nor did he abandon Schleissheim. Construction of the new palace began only days after his return from the Spanish Netherlands in April 1701. The final project was somewhat reduced in scale, but still substantial enough to figure as a major residence. Although Max Eman-

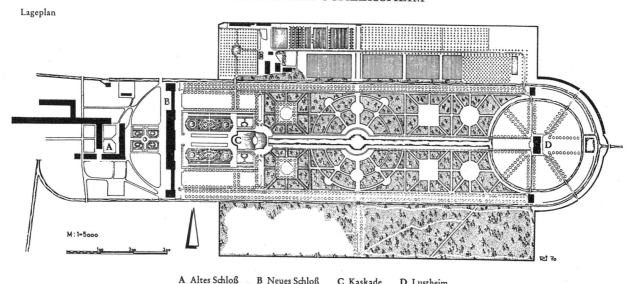

SCHLOSSPARK SCHLEISSHEIM

Lageplan

M : 1=5000

A Altes Schloß   B Neues Schloß   C Kaskade   D Lustheim

Fig. 20. Schleissheim, site plan in 1970. (Hager and Hojer, *Schleissheim Führer,* Bayerische Verwaltung der staatlichen Schlösser, Gärten und Seen, Munich, 1970)

uel was able to build only a fraction of it, he never gave up hope of finishing it as originally planned.

Neu-Schleissheim

Development at the Schleissheim site (fig. 20) began with the erection of Lustheim, a small *maison de plaisance* located east of the Altes Schloss and on axis with it (plate 2, fig. 21). The pretext for Lustheim was Max Emanuel's marriage with Maria Antonia in 1685, memorialized in the ceiling frescoes of the principal rooms. Construction began in May 1684 under Zuccalli's direction and seems to have proceeded rapidly, for by October of that year court painter Francesco Rosa had already been given a commission for ceiling frescoes. The Schloss seems to have been complete by 1689. On February 9, 1690, Max Emanuel entertained his imperial in-laws at Lustheim, where they dined in the Saal at midday and afterwards toured the estate buildings of the Altes Schloss.[28]

The earliest-known depiction of Lustheim appears on an aerial view of a garden design dating probably from the early 1690s. It shows Lustheim as the terminus of a vast formal garden extending eastward from either the Altes Schloss or a new palace placed just east of the old building.[29]

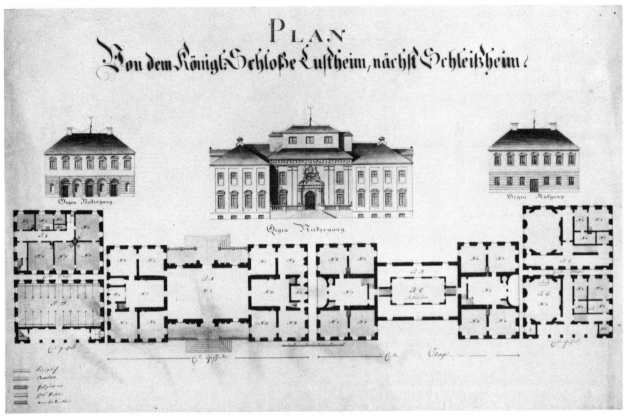

Fig. 21. Schleissheim, Lustheim, plans and west elevations by J. C. Altmannshofner, drawing, 1812. (Bayerische Verwaltung der staatlichen Schlösser, Gärten und Seen, Munich)

Lustheim is framed on either side by freestanding cubical pavilions. The pavilion on the south housed the Renatuskapelle (chapel of St. Renatus) and stood on the site of Wilhelm's earlier chapel of the same name. The north pavilion held stables for the ruler's personal horses (Leibpferde), with living quarters for personnel upstairs. The Schloss itself, perfectly symmetrical in plan, contained a central *salle à l'italienne* and identical four-room apartments to the sides, each grouped around a subsidiary Saal (fig. 21). The south apartment belonged to the elector, the north apartment to the electress. According to eighteenth-century furniture inventories, the floor above, similar in plan, contained eight Cavaliers-Zimmer.[30] In the basement there were, among other things, the kitchen and a vaulted Dirnitz underneath the Festsaal. The belvedere on the roof,

Chapter Three

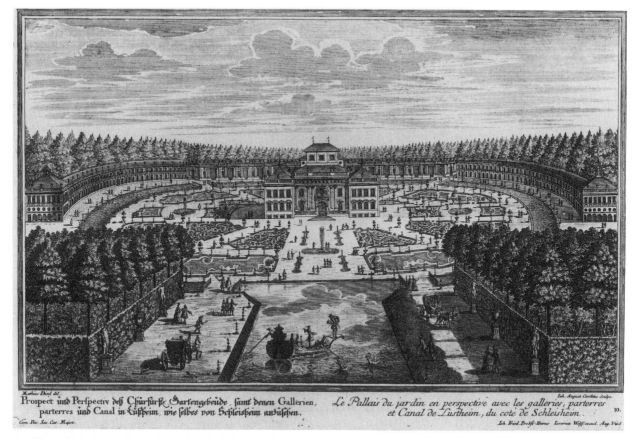

Fig. 22. Schleissheim, Lustheim, view looking east by Matthias Diesel, engraving, ca. 1720. (Staats- und Stadtbibliothek, Augsburg)

like the later open belvedere on the Amalienburg, was used as a vantage point for shooting fowl.

The same aerial view shows a semicircular allée connecting the two lateral pavilions. Eventually, a semicircular gallery or orangery arose in this position. It was first mentioned in 1694 but was not completed, if it ever was, until after 1716. As early as 1727, deterioration was recorded; toward mid-century the structure, having fallen into a state of serious disrepair, was removed.[31]

The gallery is seen in Diesel's view of around 1720 (fig. 22) and in two views of 1718, which show four segments.[32] The architecture of the two-story outer segments matches that of the lateral pavilions; the inner segments were, according to Diesel, one colossal story of alternating open and closed bays. The second floor of the outer segments probably contained the lodgings for gentlemen and domestics noted in the *Ausführliche Relation* of 1723; a plan of the gallery segment attached to the stable pavilion shows small, three-room apartments for courtiers on the upper floor and long, narrow halls on the ground floor that could belong to the orangery.[33]

The garden extending between Lustheim and the Altes Schloss, probably a continuation of plans formulated but never carried out under Ferdinand Maria, was apparently projected as early as the initial planning of Lustheim. Work on it proceeded through the late 1680s and 1690s, although the absence of the elector and the diversion of funds to Brussels meant that it was not pursued with great determination.[34] Canals, bordering the garden on the north and south and meeting in semicircular formation behind Lustheim, were excavated from 1687 to 1690 (fig. 20). They brought water from the Isar and the Würm, not only for irrigation, but also for the transport of building materials.[35] The delivery of trees to the Schleissheim site is recorded as early as 1688; in 1700, Zuccalli could report to the elector that the bosquets and allées had matured nicely.[36]

When Max Emanuel returned from Brussels in April 1701, the bosquet zone of the garden was essentially complete; the parterres in front of the as-yet-unbuilt new palace were unexecuted. The finished bosquet garden, visible in an aerial view of the site from around 1700, has retained its form to the present (fig. 20).[37] It consists of a large zone of concentric circular paths flanked by smaller units with alternating square and round *salles vertes* (originally including another pair of round units at the west, removed when the parterre was built). The garden was completed only after Max Emanuel's return from exile in 1715. Dominique Girard, a garden engineer whom the elector brought with him from Paris, prepared the final design. Executed beginning in 1717, the almost square area was divided into lateral strips of broderies and bosquets fronting the gallery wings of the palace and an inner zone featuring an allée of fountains and rectangular parterre units with four basins. An enormous cascade terminated the central axis on the east.[38]

Exactly when plans were first formulated for a new palace at Schleissheim cannot be determined with certainty. The earliest documentary evidence for active work on a new project dates from 1693. On April 15, Graf von der Wahl, head of the electoral Baudirektorium (construction directorate), wrote to Max Emanuel in Brussels warning him "that in these hard times it is advisable to curtail building projects somewhat, especially the very beautiful but also very costly plans that Zuccalli is bringing with him [from Munich]."[39]

Numerous preliminary designs produced by Zuccalli between 1693 and 1701 testify to the intensity of Max Emanuel's interest in the Schleissheim project during his long absence from Bavaria.[40] The diversity of the designs suggests a certain indecision about the form that the palace was to take, as well as a willingness to draw on ideas from a wide spectrum of models. None of the existing drawings is dated, and only by assuming that the building program escalated during the planning process can we order them into a plausible sequence. Initially, nothing more than a thorough modernization of the Altes Schloss was contemplated. The subsequent plans for a new palace east of the old building can be seen to grow from what looks like a sizable summer house to a major residence. Certain of the larger designs envisioned retaining the Altes Schloss as the fourth wing around a square *cour d'honneur.* Others eliminated the Altes Schloss or replaced it with a colonnade, in order to open up the *cour d'honneur* to a vast forecourt on the west.[41]

On January 8, 1700, Max Emanuel wrote Zuccalli ordering him to pursue design work on the new building at Schleissheim with all possible speed.[42] On April 3, Zuccalli sent three plan drawings to Brussels—a site plan, which he termed the "gran dissegno"; a plan of the ground floor; and a plan of the piano nobile. Of these drawings, only the ground-floor plan (fig. 23) exists; but we also have an aerial view of the Schleissheim site that corresponds in all respects with Zuccalli's description of the gran dissegno, a plan of the third mezzanine floor ("terzo piano de mezanini;" fig. 24), and an elevation of the court facade of the corps-de-logis (which Zuccalli sent to the elector slightly later; fig. 25). Attached to the letter in which Zuccalli announced the dispatch of the drawings is a legend identifying the numerical room designations.[43]

In this project, the principal structure is preceded by a forecourt less vast than that in several earlier projects, but still quite ample. Subsidiary functions (kennels, carriage houses, poultry yard, and covered manège) are housed in minor tracts forming small courtyards along the north side of the forecourt. Here Zuccalli also placed the "theatro per l'oppere et Comedie"; this was an unfavorable location for a theater, as Max Emanuel later complained, because of the distance from the corps-de-logis as well as the proximity of the kennels.[44] In subsequent designs, the theater was moved nearer the principal structure; the problem of its location, however, was never conclusively solved. Two *basses cours* flank the building on north and south; they are separated from the garden by the galleries connecting the corps-de-logis with the pavilions alongside the canals. The north courtyard is an open manège (adjacent to the covered manège); the south courtyard is labeled simply "piazza or garden."

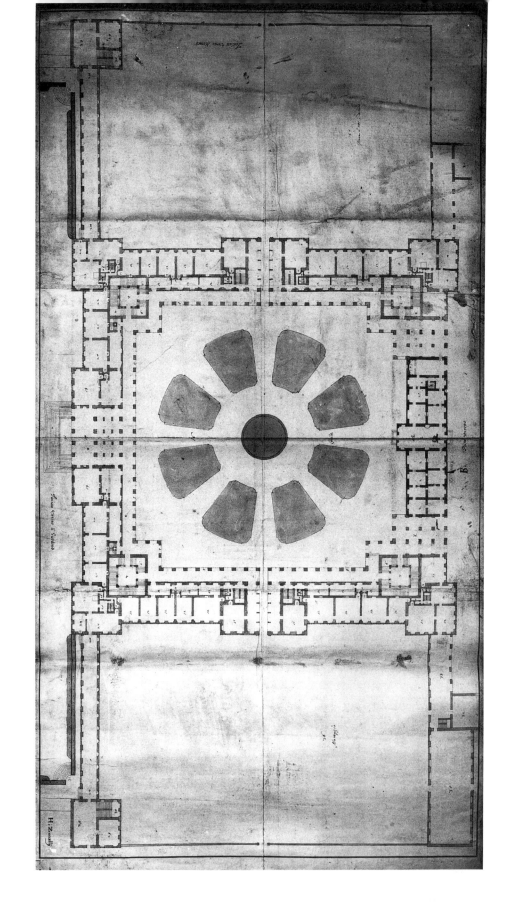

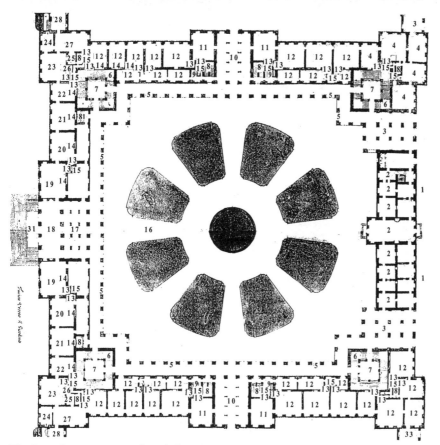

Fig. 23. Schleissheim, Neu-Schleissheim, project by Enrico Zuccalli, plan
of ground floor, drawing, 1700. Garden
(east) facade is at top. (Plansammlung
8269, Bayerisches Hauptstaatsarchiv,
Munich)

The legends to room numbers below are found in GHA, Korr Akt 753/42a (R220), where they were attached to Zuccalli's
letter to Max Emanuel of April 3, 1700, that accompanied the plans when they were sent from Munich to Brussels.

Primo dissegno in Grand de Piano Terreno, Lettera B:
 1. Vancorte
 2. Fabricha vecchia con Sala et Appartamenti latterali
    con la Capella
 3. Ingressi con Vestibboli nel secondo Cortile
 4. Abittatione per il Fattore
 5. Portici attorno il Cortile
 6. Scale principali
 7. Cortili delle Scale
 8. Scale particolari et secrette per la Communicatione
    de mezanini et parti superiori
 9. Lochi communi
10. Ingresso con suoi vestibboli della parti latterali
11. Stanze per Guardie et Ufficiali
12. Stanze per officy servitu et Ufficiali
13. Fornelli
14. Camini
15. Lochi per metter fuocho ne fornelli
16. Cortile con fontana nel mezo compartito a salicato
    et verdure
17. Vestibbolo
18. Loggia di Communicatione

19. Prima Anticamera del Piano Nobbile terreno sopra il
    Giardino
20. Seconda Anticamera
21. Camera d'Udienza
22. Gran Gabinetto
23. Camera da dormire
24. Gabinetto
25. Capella
26. Rittirata
27. Stanza di Passaggio
28. Galleria sopra il Giardino
29. Grotte et Communicatione dell appartamento sopra
    il Canale
30. Scale per ascender al Piano de sopra
31. Gradinate per descender nel giardino profondo
32. Cascate d'aqua
33. Portici che communicano alle Scuderie et Cavalleriza
34. Scuderie
35. Cavallerizza
36. Maneggio
37. Piaza ô ver Giardino

Fig. 24. Schleissheim, Neu-Schleiss-heim, project by Enrico Zuccalli, plan of mezzanine, drawing, 1700. Garden (east) facade at top. Legend to lost plan of the piano nobile is published here with the plan of the mezzanine (whose rooms are unnumbered). (Plansammlung 8283, Bayerisches Hauptstaatsarchiv, Munich)

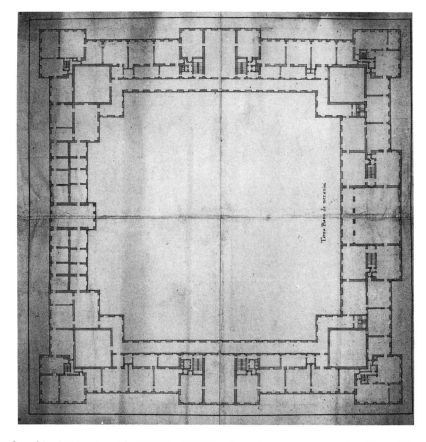

The legends to room numbers below are found in GHA, Korr Akt 753/42a (R220), where they were attached to Zuccalli's letter to Max Emanuel of April 3, 1700, that accompanied the plans when they were sent from Munich to Brussels.

Piano Nobbile, Lettera C:

 1. Sala grande
 2. Prima Anticamera
 3. Seconda anticamera
 4. Camera d'Udienza
 5. Gran Gabinetto
 6. Camera da Dormire
 7. Gabinetto
 8. Capella
 9. Rittirata
10. Camera di Passeggio
11. Scala secretta
12. Fornelli
13. Camini
14. Lochi da metter fuocho
15. Scala principale
16. Corridori che communicano alli appartimenti
17. Prima Stanza per la Bassa servitu
18. Stanza per Ufficiali
19. Stanza per l'aggiutanti di Camera
20. Sala per Appartimento de Prencipi
21. Anticamera
22. Camera d'Udienza
23. Camera da Dormire

24.
25. } Due Camera Communi
26. Anticamera
27. (omitted on original)
28. Camera d'Udienza
29. Camera da Dormire
30. Gabinetto
31. Stanze per la servitu et Passaggi
32. Scale
33. Lochi Communi
34. Salotto
35. Orattorio
36. Anticamera
37. Camera d'Udienza
38. Gabinetto
39. Camera da Dormire
40. Gabinetto
41. Galleria che communica alle scale et alli terrazzi
42. Riserve d'Aque per mandar alle fontane
43. Salotto
44. Scale
45. Terrazzo

Fig. 25. Schleissheim, Neu-Schleissheim, project by Enrico Zuccalli, elevation of court facade looking east, drawing, 1700. (Plansammlung 8262, Bayerisches Hauptstaatsarchiv, Munich)

Terminating the entire layout at the west and located the same distance from the palace as Lustheim to the east, there is a curious oval-shaped menagerie, or "Serragli per le fiere," set within a pentagonal redoubt.

On the piano nobile of the palace, the two principal apartments of the elector and electress face the garden and are approached from a central Saal, which occupies the entire breadth of the building from courtyard to garden. Other Säle in the centers of the side wings give access to "apartments for princes."[45] On the ground floor there are two summer apartments along the garden, identical in plan to those upstairs. There is no mention of guest apartments anywhere in the palace. On the ground floor of the side wings, there are rooms for offices and household officials ("Stanze per officy servitu et Ufficiali"); these are not specified in greater detail (except that the southwest corner pavilion contains an apartment for the concierge), nor are rooms for the chancellery and councils noted. Like the Residenz, the palace has two mezzanines. The first, between ground floor and piano nobile, contains service rooms for the apartments above and below it ("mezzanines to serve as wardrobes and to accommodate chamberlains and servants"); the second contains lodgings for ladies, gentlemen, and ministers. What purpose the Altes Schloss was to serve is barely addressed in the legend, which labels it simply "old building with a hall and lateral apartments, with the chapel." As no chapel is shown or described elsewhere in the palace, the Wilhelmskapelle was apparently to continue as the principal court chapel. In a letter Max Emanuel wrote after the decision had been made not to erect the side wings, or at any rate to postpone their erection, the elector noted that the Altes Schloss would contain lodgings for the concierge and for gentlemen.[46]

The palace in this project is similar in size to the Residenz, although it clearly would not be quite as large. It also repeats several features familiar from the Residenz that one associates with urban palaces in general: the quadrangular plan, the complete enclosure of the *cour d'honneur,* the placement of the piano nobile above a full ground floor and a mezzanine, and the location of offices on the ground floor. (Its references to Bernini's projects for the Louvre, the city residence of the kings of France, are also telling in this regard.) The project shows a full complement of apartments and Säle. We cannot be sure that these were meant to include guest apartments, although there was ample space for them; nor can we be sure that the extensive accommodations for offices include provision for government functions. The context of the palace, as portrayed in the aerial view, is distinctly rural. On all sides the building is surrounded by gardens, forests, and fields, and nowhere is there evidence of the town that would have been necessary to support the court on a permanent basis.

Max Emanuel solicited reactions to Zuccalli's project from his brother Joseph Clemens, Elector of Cologne, who replied in a detailed letter of July 4, 1700, complete with annotated plans. Joseph Clemens introduced his critique with the remark that the project was overly grandiose. "I must in conscience warn Your Electoral Highness that an able architect has said that even if Your Highness gave him 300,000 florins a year, he would not undertake to complete the task in ten years of work."[47] Despite these reservations, Joseph Clemens recommended removing the Altes Schloss, although he was aware of Max Emanuel's desire to keep it. The *cour d'honneur* could be better closed toward the forecourt with an iron grille, "as is the present practice in France in all the royal houses."[48]

Max Emanuel also had doubts about the practicality of such a vast project. In a memorandum entitled "Points on which a better explanation is desired from Zuccalli," the elector requested the architect to modify the corps-de-logis so that it could be erected as an autonomous structure and to explore ways of connecting it economically to the "fabrica vecchia (existing fabric)." Given the financial situation, erection of the side wings would probably have to be postponed.[49] The idea arose of connecting the two buildings with arcaded galleries supporting terraces on the level of the piano nobile.[50]

In his letter, Joseph Clemens identified major failings in the plan of the corps-de-logis. The centrally placed Hauptsaal (main hall) extending through the entire depth of the wing would impede communication between the apartments of the elector and electress. The treatment of the staircases was entirely unsatisfactory. Their location in the corners of the courtyard was a mistake, as "the stairway in fine buildings should always be the first thing one sees." Furthermore, they were inconveniently far from the Hauptsaal and the apartments. Joseph Clemens recommended that the two staircases in the corps-de-logis be moved in toward the center, so that they could be reached directly from the vestibule. In his memorandum Max Emanuel noted a discrepancy in the plan of the piano nobile; Zuccalli had designated the two rooms that formed the only logical means of communication between each staircase and the Hauptsaal as "rooms for the under servants" and "rooms for [household] officials." Max Emanuel requested that the architect either relocate the staircases adjacent to the Saal or transform the disrupting rooms into galleries by removing the partition walls.

Three plan drawings exist to document Zuccalli's attempts to satisfy the elector's demands. Two plans of the piano nobile, drawn on the same sheet (fig. 26), reduce the size of the Hauptsaal and add a centrally placed gallery along the garden facade in apparent response to the problem of communication between the apartments.[51] Any attempt to create an independent building out of the corps-de-logis of the earlier plan would run into difficulties because the staircases would protrude into the court. One of the drawings therefore shows the staircases with their open wells pulled into the mass of the building; the other moves the staircases into the central pavilion. Max Emanuel, as he wrote in a letter of July 30, 1700, preferred the staircases adjacent to the Saal.[52] In the third drawing, of the ground floor, imperial-type staircases have been substituted for the open-well staircases, probably because the former fit better into the available spaces next to the Saal.[53] This drawing also shows the corps-de-logis drawn for the first time as an autonomous structure.

Construction on the corps-de-logis began in April 1701. On April 14, only days after Max Emanuel's return to Munich, the cornerstone was laid.[54] The work progressed rapidly—too rapidly, apparently, for on July 7, 1702, the four piers in the center of the garden facade collapsed, bringing parts of the gallery above with them. Not satisfied with Zuccalli's attempts to explain the accident, Max Emanuel called together a commission of professionals, who submitted a report on July 29. This report reveals that by the date of the accident, the building was in large part complete and that a good beginning had been made with the roof-

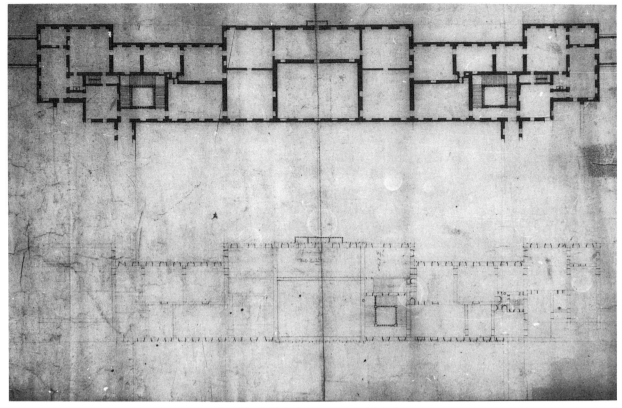

Fig. 26. Schleissheim, Neu-Schleissheim, two project plans of piano nobile, drawing, 1700–1701. East at top. (Plansammlung 8278, Bayerisches Hauptstaatsarchiv, Munich)

ing.[55] The commission's recommendations included rebuilding the faulty masonry in stone instead of brick and employing experienced personnel at the building site.

It was further suggested that the problem of the staircases (of which the one on the south had already been at least partially constructed) had not yet been adequately addressed, as the available space was too limited. The solution Zuccalli finally arrived at was to change the orientation of the stairs from east-west to north-south. This resulted in a more straightforward and strongly stated sequence of approach—from the courtyard, through vestibule and staircase, to the Saal above (plate 3, fig. 27).[56] Plans to erect a second, identical staircase north of the vestibule were eventually abandoned, and the space was used for a large room on each floor (plan F, 3, both floors). A plan drawing of the ground floor dating

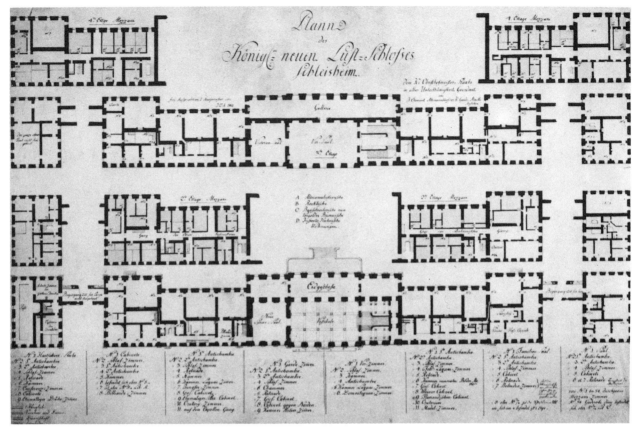

Fig. 27. Schleissheim, Neu-Schleissheim, plans by J. C. Altmannshofner, drawing, 1812. East facade at top. (Bayerische Verwaltung der staatlichen Schlösser, Gärten und Seen, Munich)

from shortly after the accident shows a chapel in this location.[57] In time, upper and lower rooms were both used as dining rooms.

Max Emanuel pushed work on Schleissheim during the following years. By 1704, when he was forced to flee Bavaria, the corps-de-logis had been completely built and roofed, while its interior remained unfinished. Work on Schleissheim was suspended during the Austrian administration.

Nymphenburg

Simultaneously with the construction of Schleissheim, the first expansion of Nymphenburg, neglected during the early years of Max Eman-

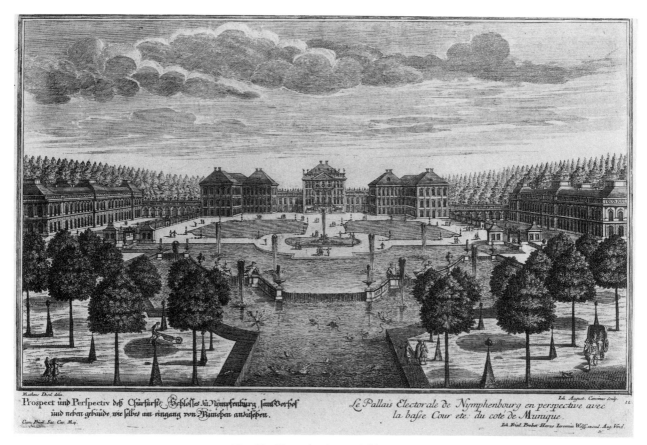

Fig. 28. Nymphenburg, Schloss, view of court (east) facade by Matthias Diesel, engraving, ca. 1720. (Staats- und Stadtbibliothek, Augsburg)

uel's reign, was undertaken. Zuccalli was directed to begin planning in
April 1701.[58]

Perhaps for sentimental reasons, Max Emanuel chose not to demolish
his mother's villa (fig. 19), but instead to add onto it.[59] Four cubical pavilions reflecting the existing building in form, but deferring to it in their
lower rooflines, were planned (fig. 28). They were placed at a respectful
distance from the central pavilion, joined to it by narrow galleries, and
set slightly in advance of it, to create at least the impression of a shallow
cour d'honneur.

The two inner pavilions were intended to contain apartments; the outer
north pavilion was reserved for the chapel, the outer south pavilion for
kitchens, pantries, Dirnitz, and other offices. In the central pavilion, ma-

jor changes were planned in the Saal. In order to better light the space, as well as to articulate the facades, it was decided to reduce the five middle bays to three bays of superimposed arched windows. Whether this was actually carried out during this building campaign is not known, although according to building accounts the Saal did undergo redecoration during 1701–3.[60]

By 1704, work on the new pavilions had brought the galleries and inner pavilions to completion. The outer south pavilion stood to the second floor. Construction of the outer north pavilion continued under the Austrian administration, and by 1716 it was complete.[61]

The Country Houses during the Late Reign of Max Emanuel, 1715–1726

Although the years of exile in Belgium and France offered Max Emanuel scant opportunity to exercise his love for building, they brought him into close, direct contact with French art and architecture. In 1705, he commissioned from Germain Boffrand designs for a hunting lodge, Bouchefort; they came to nothing, as Max Emanuel was forced to abandon Brussels in 1706.[62] It was probably also Boffrand to whom Max Emanuel entrusted the architectural training of Joseph Effner, the talented young son of the court gardener at Dachau, who was sent to Paris in 1706 to complete his education.[63] In September 1713, Max Emanuel acquired a house in St. Cloud, where he lived until his return to Bavaria in March 1715. He hired Boffrand to design the renovation of this house; Effner supervised construction.[64]

As soon as the Peace of Rastatt was ratified on March 7, 1714, Max Emanuel began preparing to resume work on Nymphenburg and Schleissheim. Wishing to consult with experts in Paris regarding the completion of his palaces, he wrote to Munich on June 8, 1714, requesting plans of Nymphenburg and Schleissheim and reports on their current condition.[65] He enlisted the services of Robert de Cotte, who prepared two projects for Schleissheim; neither, however, had any direct influence on the future work there.[66]

On his return in 1715, Max Emanuel's building activities widened in scope to encompass not only the continuation of work begun before the exile, but also totally new projects. At Nymphenburg, where work resumed almost immediately, the pavilions were finished, capacious service wings were planned and begun, and a vast park was laid out west of the palace. Two diminutive *maisons de plaisance,* the Pagodenburg and the Ba-

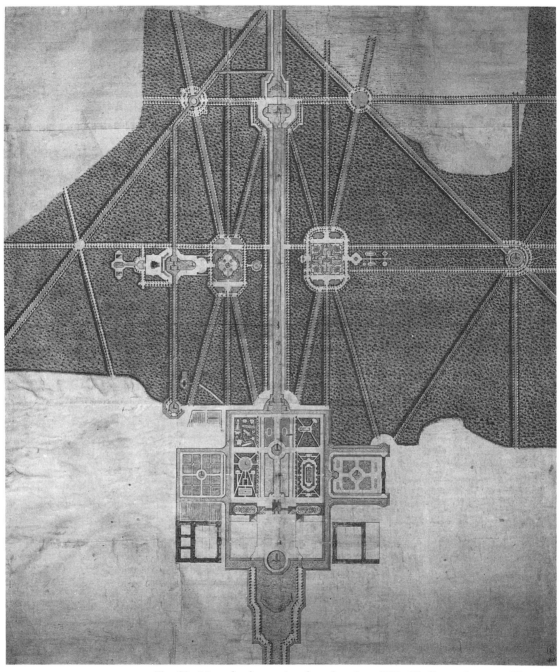

Fig. 29. Nymphenburg, site plan, drawing, 1715–20. East at bottom. (Plan-sammlung 5875, Bayerisches Hauptstaatsarchiv, Munich)

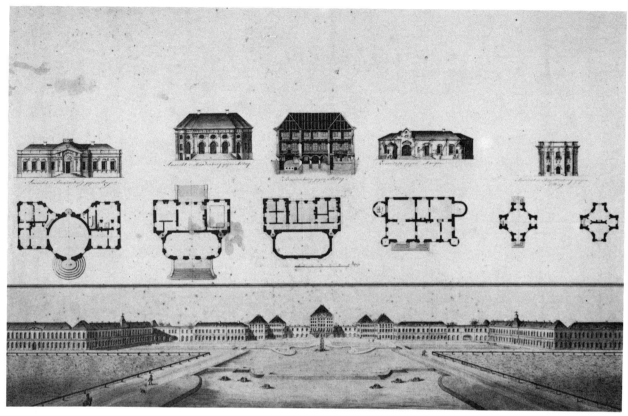

Fig. 30. Nymphenburg, plans and elevations of the Parkburgen and perspective
view of court (east) facade of Schloss by J. C. Altmannshofner, drawing, 1812.
(Bayerische Verwaltung der staatlichen Schlösser, Gärten und Seen, Munich)

denburg, as well as a hermitage, the Magdalenenklause, were set within
the park (fig. 29, plate 4 and fig. 30). At Fürstenried (figs. 31, 32), south
of Munich, a new house arose within the astoundingly short time of
two years. Renovation work was also pursued on several other country
houses. At Dachau (fig. 16), the corps-de-logis was given new facades
and a new staircase, and the Festsäle were redecorated. At Lichtenberg
am Lech (fig. 33), which had been substantially renewed by Zuccalli beginning in 1691, further modernization was undertaken.[67] Schleissheim
was at first neglected in favor of the other projects, but in 1719 work

Prospect und perspectiv deß Churfürstl. Schlosses zu Fürstenried, wie selbes von selten deß Gartens anzusehen.

Le Pallais Electorale de Fürstenried du coté de jardin.

27.

Fig. 31. Fürstenried, Schloss, view from garden by Matthias Diesel, engraving, ca. 1720. (Staats- und Stadtbibliothek, Augsburg)

there began again. New plans to complete the palace as a multiwinged structure did not come to fruition, but the interior of the corps-de-logis was decorated, the garden parterre laid out, and work pursued on the gallery behind Lustheim.[68]

To better oversee this activity, the Hofbauamt was reorganized to include a new department expressly responsible for the *kurfürstliches Lustbauwesen* (electoral building program for country palaces). Effner was made de facto chief of Lustbauwesen, while Zuccalli, who remained at the head of the Hofbauamt, retained effective control only over routine operations.[69] Effner's mandate was broad, and he orchestrated the contributions of an international corps of artisans assembled by the elector. At the end of his reign, Max Emanuel had a galaxy of country houses in the

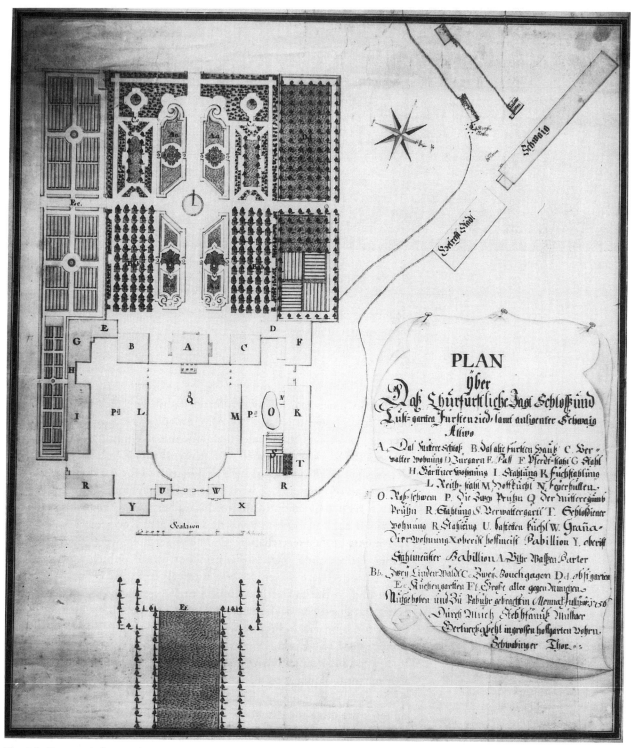

Fig. 32. Fürstenried, site plan, drawing, 1756. (Plansammlung 8217, Bayerisches Hauptstaatsarchiv, Munich)

Fig. 33. Lichtenberg am Lech, Schloss, view by Michael Wening, engraving, ca. 1700. (Österreichische Nationalbibliothek, Vienna)

vicinity of the capital in which he, his family, and his court could be accommodated in style.

Fürstenried

In August 1715, Max Emanuel purchased a manor located a short distance south of Munich from Graf Ferdinand Joseph von Horwarth, who had built a small house there in 1707. Max Emanuel commissioned Effner to prepare plans for its immediate enlargement into a hunting lodge (figs. 31, 32), and the work was pursued with great alacrity. On June 11, 1717, the elector slept in his new apartment at Fürstenried for the first time.[70]

The plan of Fürstenried, with its detached pavilions, was in many respects a reduced version of that of Nymphenburg. The central pavilion contained Säle on both ground floor and piano nobile, as well as the apartments of the Herrschaften. On the upper floor were rooms for gentlemen and servants. Two lateral pavilions, one of which was the earlier manor house, were placed at short intervals from the central pavilion.[71] According to the earliest description of Fürstenried, one of these contained the apartment of the electoral prince and the other contained apartments for courtiers and the concierge ("Gouverneur").[72] Other detached pavilions and stable wings were grouped around the *cour d'honneur,* closed by a wrought-iron gate, and the lateral *basses cours.* The gatehouse and its pendant building were flanked by two further pavilions for court officers; on a 1756 plan (fig. 32), one is labeled "Oberisthoffmeist[er] Babillion"; the other, "OberistStahlmeüster Babillion."

The courtyard, which was described in 1728 as "une espèce d'amphi-theatre," was ideally suited as a rallying point for the hunt.[73] Fürstenried was frequently visited by the court for this purpose and could be reached quickly from Munich by means of an allée laid out on axis with the twin towers of the Frauenkirche. In subsequent reigns, the house became the Witwensitz for Electresses Maria Amalie and Maria Anna Sophia.[74]

The Completion of Nymphenburg

The further expansion of Nymphenburg and the final design of the garden and park were carried out according to a comprehensive plan prepared by Effner and Dominique Girard. A site plan dating from 1715–20 (fig. 29) gives an idea of this project.

The five pavilions were framed by two service blocks, reminiscent of those at Vaux-le-Vicomte, which were set in advance of the pavilions to create a broad forecourt. Construction began in 1715 and extended over a period of almost forty years. Neither of the two blocks was finished exactly in accordance with the scheme seen in the site plan. In the north block, the salient corner pavilion (on the southeast), which housed a waterworks, was finished by 1716; the south wing, containing an orangery on the ground floor and a Comödiensaal or Concertsaal above, was completed by 1723. In that year the east wing was begun. Under Karl Albrecht, this wing was the home of the convent of the Augustine canonesses of the Congregation of Our Lady, which the elector had called to Munich from Luxembourg in 1730. The extension of this wing to the north, for which Max Emanuel had laid the cornerstone in 1718, housed a Capuchin monastery and hospital.

The east wing of the south service block, with stables and a carriage house on the ground floor and lodgings for gentlemen upstairs, was built from 1716–1719. Simultaneously, three small courtyards were laid out at the south end of the block to accommodate the estate farm. The north wing facing the great forecourt was begun in 1733 and finished in 1747; here there were additional stables and apartments for officials and gentlemen.[75]

In 1723, narrow wings, not foreseen in the site plan of 1715–20, were built to connect the service blocks with the pavilions (fig. 30).[76] The north wing was the Passgebäude (Pass building), where Pass, a game not unlike hockey or croquet, was played in a covered court.[77] The corresponding building on the south was the Comedihaus, which in 1749–50 was transformed into the court kitchen.[78]

Effner created pedimented frontispieces for the central pavilion. Arched windows lighting the Hauptsaal, if not built in 1702–4, were built now.

The original four bays to either side of the frontispiece were consolidated into three—a step that prompted a shift in the enfilade of the apartments toward the exterior wall, in order to align the doors with the corner windows. The interior of the central pavilion was extensively redecorated.[79]

In the inner north pavilion, two apartments were furnished for Max Emanuel. The piano nobile (fig. 35, right) was completely taken up by the rooms of his summer apartment (the Neue Sommerzimmer; plan E, 12–16). Above this was a smaller apartment for the elector, facing the garden (fig. 36). On the ground floor (fig. 34), the garden side was occupied by the Spiegel-Saal (mirror hall; called Sala Terrena on this plan), which served as a setting for social functions.[80] Next to this, in the southeast corner of the pavilion, was the Neues Tafelzimmer, or new room with tables (for dining). On the three floors of the inner south pavilion, called the Prinzenbau (fig. 35, left; plan E, 18–23), there were apartments for Max Emanuel's children.[81]

The plan of the garden devised by Effner and Girard (fig. 29) was followed in execution.[82] Of all Max Emanuel's gardens, it is the one most thoroughly in keeping with the French tradition of Le Nôtre. In the bosquet compartments flanking the great parterre, there were *cabinets verts,* a bowling green, a labyrinth, a "wild" garden with serpentine paths, and an open-air theater—all features that had become de rigueur in French aristocratic gardens—as well as clearings for the Pass-Spiel and Kegel-Spiel (skittles). Immediately adjacent to the side pavilions, oriented perpendicular to the parterre, there were two small Kabinettsgärten, isolated by dense hedges.

Beyond the parterre, the forested park, shot through with a network of radial allées, spread out to the west. The crowning features of the park were the two *maisons de plaisance* (fig. 30) set along the cross axis of the grand canal, each contained within its own garden domain.

The Nymphenburg Parkburgen

Max Emmanuel's Parkburgen include the two *maisons de plaisance* and a hermitage (figs. 29, 30). The Pagodenburg, the first of these houses to be finished, was erected in 1716–19 to Effner's designs.[83] According to several contemporary sources, Max Emanuel sketched the parti for the building himself.[84] The interior abounded with exotic materials and motifs—lacquer paneling, wallpaper, Delft tiles. The ceilings were painted with chinoiseries, including the *Pagoten* that seem to have lent the building its name.[85] The plan of the building, an octagon with four sides extended out into a Greek cross, was itself exotic. The ground floor was

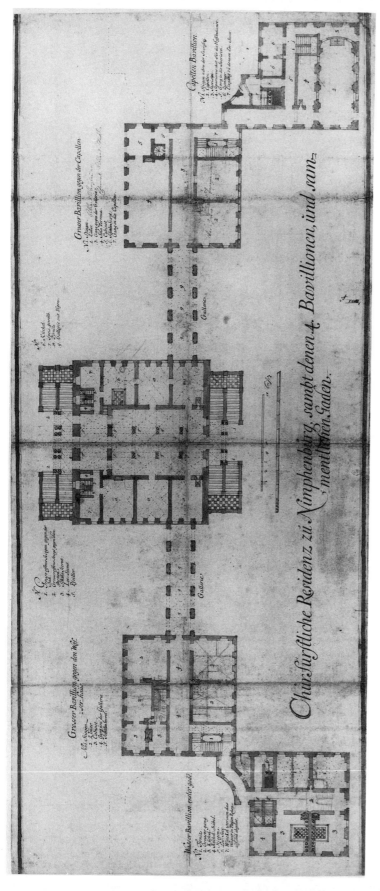

Fig. 34. Nymphenburg, Schloss, plan of ground floor, drawing, early eighteenth century. East at bottom. (Bauamt, Bayerische Verwaltung der staatlichen Schlösser, Gärten und Seen, Munich)

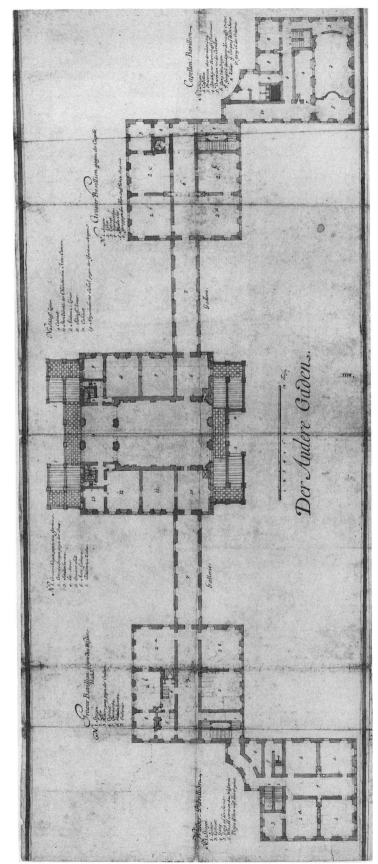

Fig. 35. Nymphenburg, Schloss, plan of piano nobile, drawing, early eighteenth century. East at bottom. (Bauamt, Bayerische Verwaltung der staatlichen Schlösser, Gärten und Seen, Munich)

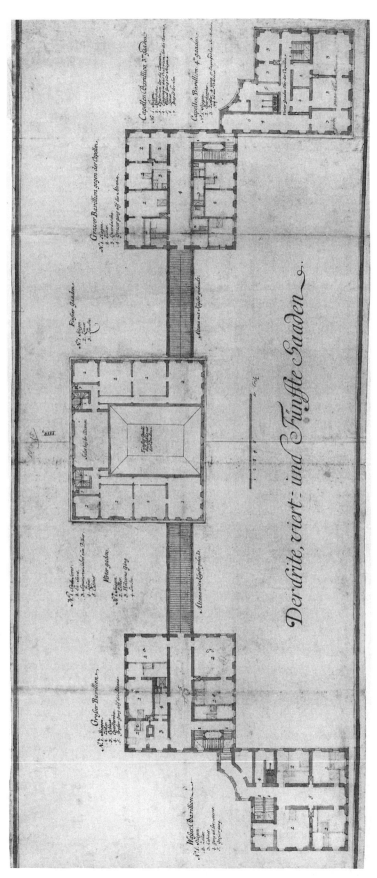

Fig. 36. Nymphenburg, Schloss, plan of upper floors, drawing, early eighteenth century. East at bottom. (Bauamt, Bayerische Verwaltung der staatlichen Schlösser, Gärten und Seen, Munich)

occupied by a single salon, the upstairs by an apartment of three oddly shaped rooms—antechamber, cabinet, and Cammer zu ruhen (room for rest).[86] Part of the novelty of this extraordinarily tiny Lustschloss seems to have been that it was, in effect, a complete house in miniature. The author of the protocol on the Elector of Trier's state visit in 1728 wrote that "on the second floor one is surprised to find a whole apartment."[87]

The Pagodenburg served, we are told, as a place to rest after playing pall-mall on one of the two alleys that flanked the water parterre in front of the house.[88] It was also a favored spot for intimate suppers and soirées: "Not far away in the woods is the place for the kitchen, as one often dines in the Saal—at a table where thirty to forty persons can sit. The pages and lackeys serve through the windows, so that one need not be inconvenienced by servants."[89] Preysing records frequent supper parties at the Pagodenburg. On August 6, 1720, for example, "a supper for forty, without the second Tafel, was taken at the Pagodenburg. Illumination of the basin, the amphitheatre [facing the house across the basin], and a part of the pall-mall, where the elector played two rounds by torchlight. On the other side of the pall-mall there was dancing. At 2:30 the party broke up."[90]

The Badenburg, erected in 1718–21, was a slightly more substantial house than the Pagodenburg.[91] Here it was possible to spend the night in comfort and even to accommodate a small suite. The house was divided into two distinct sections: a forestructure containing an oblong *salle à l'italienne* and, behind this, a block housing the apartments and the bath chamber that gave the building its name. The bath itself, situated in a corner of the rear section, was of two stories, with the basin in the basement and a gallery on the main floor. The rest of the main floor was occupied by the elector's apartment (antechamber, bedchamber, cabinet, and garderobe). The second floor contained, apart from rooms for gentlemen and servants, a smaller "fürstliches Appartement" (bedchamber and cabinet). In the basement there were two additional bath apartments, as well as the kitchen and boiler room.

A bathing pavilion with a bath sizable enough that more than one person could use it at once was a rarity in the early eighteenth century. The only other roughly contemporary examples are French—Robert de Cotte's bathing pavilion at Saverne and that at the Prince de Conti's Château d'Issy of around 1705. The latter pavilion also contained a Festsaal and limited living quarters; its bath chamber, however, was not nearly as large as that of the Badenburg.[92] This was also true of Louis XIV's *ap-*

partement des bains at Versailles (1671–77), where the basin was hardly larger than a modern bathtub. The Badenburg may also have been inspired by Turkish thermae, which Max Emanuel would undoubtedly have become acquainted with during his campaigns in Hungary.[93]

The third and last of Max Emanuel's Parkburgen was the Eremitage, or Magdalenenklause, begun in 1725. Max Emanuel did not live to see it finished; it was dedicated in 1728 by Karl Albrecht. Concealed in a "wild," wooded area north of the great parterre, the Eremitage was an artificial ruin on the exterior. Inside there was a chapel designed as a grotto, as well as a small, four-room apartment furnished *à la Capucinne,* in dark oak paneling.[94]

The Completion of Schleissheim

Work on Schleissheim recommenced in 1719. The terminal pavilions alongside the canals were completed according to Zuccalli's designs (fig. 27, lower left and right; fig. 37, right and left background). In 1723, the south pavilion (or Herkules-Pavillon, after the statue of Hercules in the south broderie compartment of the parterre) was finished and a beginning made with the interior work; in the winter of 1724–25, the apartment on the upper floor was furnished. The north pavilion (Pallas-Pavillon) was built from 1724 to 1728; the Pass-Spiel was located here (fig. 27, bottom left), as well as a water reservoir and pump for the fountains and a complete apartment upstairs.[95]

The interior plan of the corps-de-logis was altered only slightly (fig. 27). Space was found for the palace chapel in the southwest corner, convenient to the apartment of the elector. On both piani nobili, the rooms along the court facade were formed into a corridor or gallery communicating between the staircase and the chapel. In the area of the north wing corresponding to the chapel, small apartments were installed on both floors. These were likewise approached by means of corridors along the court facade.

The decoration of the interior proceeded from 1722 to 1726 and was essentially complete by the time of Max Emanuel's death. The only major item left undone was the staircase; the walls were decorated, but the stairs were built only provisionally in wood and were not replaced with the present stone staircase until 1848.

Plans to complete Schleissheim as a multiwinged structure enclosing a *cour d'honneur* were not abandoned. Effner produced a new project for this, which survives in a large-scale wooden model constructed in 1725.[96]

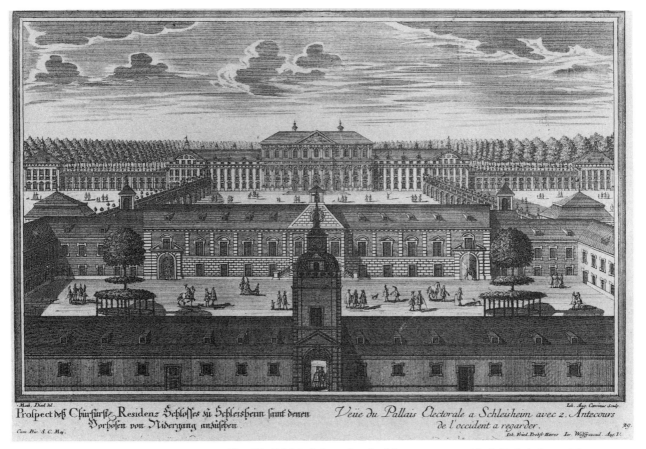

Prospect deß Churfürstl. Residenz Schlosses zu Schleisheim samt denen
Vorhofen von Nidergang anzusehen.

Veüe du Pallais Electorale a Schleisheim avec 2 Antecours
de l'occident a regarder.

Fig. 37. Schleissheim, view looking east across Alt-Schleissheim to Neu-
Schleissheim by Matthias Diesel, engraving, ca. 1720. (Staats- und Stadtbibliothek, Augsburg)

The model shows the Altes Schloss encased in new, more elegant facades
and extended outward into square terminal pavilions. The connection
between the two palaces was accomplished by means of closed galleries
supporting terraces at the level of the piano nobile. Attached to each gallery were three pavilions of two or three stories, the purpose of which
may be gleaned from various memoranda of 1723 and 1724.[97] The gallery on the elector's side, which would have provided covered access
to the chapel, had pavilions for gentlemen, for a kitchen, and for the
concierge. On the other side were pavilions for gentlemen and ladies.
Needless to say, this project never materialized. Views from the early
1720s (e.g., fig. 37) show the space between the two palaces enclosed

along the sides by simple arcades with terraced roofs. Whether these were ever erected remains unknown.[98]

The Country Houses under Max Emanuel's Successors

Karl Albrecht inherited his father's political ambitions and love of representation. The need to economize, however, resulted in the curtailment of large-scale building. This remained true under his two successors, Max III Joseph and Karl Theodor. It is interesting to note that in 1756 a petition submitted by François de Cuvilliés the Younger for the post of Unterbaumeister was denied; the reason stated was that he was experienced less in the practical side of building than in the development of grandiose projects, which in light of the financial situation were no longer desired. The only large-scale court projects of the second half of the century, Cuvilliés's and Verschaffelt's Residenz projects, grew out of the need to replace the ruined Neuveste.[99]

Karl Albrecht did not continue work on Schleissheim. The interior, in any case, had been largely finished by the time of Max Emanuel's death. All thoughts of carrying out Effner's project for the subsidiary pavilions along the courtyard were dropped.

At Nymphenburg, the country residence preferred by the court in the eighteenth century, work on the service blocks progressed; by midcentury, they were essentially filled out. Under Karl Albrecht, plans were developed for finishing the open area in front of the palace. This took the form of an expansive semicircular forecourt, known as the Rondell, bounded by a wall punctuated with ten small, two-story pavilions (fig. 38, center).[100] The center of the Rondell is occupied by a water parterre, into which the park canals flow; from the water parterre, a canal dug in 1728–29 flows eastward on axis with the palace. Bordered on both sides by allées, it creates a formal approach to the palace.

The Rondell pavilions, begun in 1728, were erected by the Hofbauamt and then presented to court officials. The first house to be finished (the center house in the south quadrant) belonged to Hofkontrollor Hieber, who in 1730 received a patent to operate a tavern in it.[101] Three further houses were completed probably in 1729; the southernmost house belonged to the keeper of the coursing hounds (Wärter des chiens courants), the one next to it to Vizeobriststallmeister Baron von Mayerhofen, and the northernmost house—originally intended as barracks for the Hartschier guard, to the Schlossverwalter (palace administrator). Most of the remaining houses were built over the course of the 1730s. The last, the center pavilion in the north quadrant, was put up in 1758 and served as

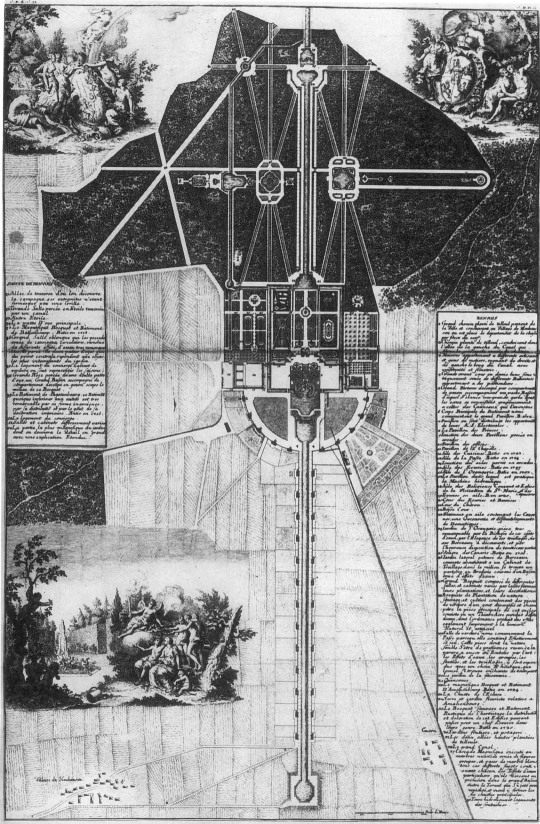

DELINEATIO GENERALIS AEDIFICIORUM, HORTORUMQUE NYMPHENBURGAE ARCIS ILLIUS PRAESTANTISSIMAE PER HORAE UNIUS
SPATIUM A MONACHIO DISTANTIS UNA CUM PARTE REGIONUM ADIACENTIUM DEDICATA SERENISSIMO AC POTENTISSIMO PRINCIPI
MAXIMILIANO IOSEPHO UTRIUSQUE BAVARIAE DUCI AC ELECTORI &c.   A Franc: de Cuvilliés Rhe · 1772 ·   Ioseph. Raltner Sculp:

headquarters for the Nymphenburg porcelain manufactory. Court servants were lodged in these houses, and the advantage in having the pavilions in private ownership was undoubtedly that the elector was spared maintenance costs.[102]

Along the canal, Karl Albrecht planned the foundation of a new town, to be called Karlstadt; it would feature small, regularly spaced houses, simpler than those of the Rondell, lining the canal in perfect symmetry. The purpose of the town, as stated in the draft of a patent for its foundation, was the encouragement of commerce and industry—which had been "allowed, sadly, to languish during the recent war [of the Spanish Succession]."[103] Settlers—artisans and tradesmen—were to be induced to locate here by granting them land, the protection of the court, and freedom from taxation and other duties, provided only that within three years they erect a house in conformity with Effner's guidelines. Although a number of persons took up residence, by the 1740s the town's growth had come to a halt, for reasons that have never been investigated. In the second half of the century, even the name Karlstadt was lost. The town thus never developed into one capable of supporting the court on a more or less permanent basis. The citizens of Munich, as Johann Georg Keyssler reported in 1729, had feared that because of electoral favor Karlstadt would prosper and eventually eclipse the capital in importance; but their fears were unfounded.[104] In any case, judging from the plans (fig. 38)—which show nothing more than a double row of widely spaced houses, each with a generous garden behind it—Karlstadt seems to have been conceived of as a decidedly pastoral community from the beginning.

Karl Albrecht's most notable contribution to Nymphenburg was small in scale: the Amalienburg, fourth of the Parkburgen, built in 1734–39 as a present for Maria Amalie and one of the preeminent Rococo buildings in Europe. Justly famous for the refinement of its decor as well as for the disarming simplicity of its highly sophisticated floor plan (fig. 30), it was the creation of François de Cuvilliés the Elder, who gradually replaced Effner as arbiter of architectural taste at the Bavarian court.[105]

The Amalienburg was planned as a pendant to the Eremitage and was placed in the center of an enclosed pheasant garden that was redesigned as a setting for the house. In plan, the building is a rectangular block whose central feature, a circular salon, pushes the garden facade into a convex pavilion and pulls the opposite side in to create a shallow, concave "cour d'honneur." Along the garden, there are two rooms on each side

Fig. 38. Nymphenburg, site plan by François de Cuvilliés, drawing, ca. 1770. East at bottom. (Bayerische Verwaltung der staatlichen Schlösser, Gärten und Seen, Munich)

The Country Houses

of the salon, the entire sequence forming a single apartment en enfilade. A *chambre* with an alcove bed in the south wing is balanced on the north by a room of identical breadth, called the Jagdzimmer (hunt room) after the paintings of court hunting parties on the walls.[106] Both ends of the enfilade are occupied by small cabinets. Ancillary rooms are located on the "court" side. Behind the *chambre* are a Retirade with a closestool, a garderobe, and a curious room lined with built-in dog houses and gun cabinets called the Hundszimmer (dogs' room). This room was apparently the idea of Maria Amalie, who was renowned for her prowess as a huntress in an age when everyone was well practiced in this sport; she liked to have her hunting dogs close at hand.[107] Behind the Jagdzimmer is the kitchen, its walls covered in colorful Dutch tiles; it may have been used occasionally as a dining room.[108] Two mezzanine rooms above the Hundszimmer served as a lodging for the concierge. A second staircase leads to a circular platform on the roof, "from which the elector can shoot pheasants without having to leave the building."[109]

Under Max III Joseph, Schleissheim experienced a minor renaissance. In 1756–57, he had the salon adjacent to the Sala Terrena on the north (today called the Musik- oder Billiardsaal; plan F, ground floor 16) redecorated by Johann Baptist Zimmermann. In 1772–74, the Garde-Saal underneath the Viktoriensaal was transformed into a dining room (on J. C. Altmannshofner's 1812 plan [fig. 27], this room is labeled "Neue Speise-Saal" [plan F, ground floor 3]).[110] Plans drawn up by architect Franz Anton Kirchgrabner to complete the staircase, however, remained unrealized.[111]

In the eighteenth century, Schleissheim was known chiefly as the palace in which the electoral picture collections were housed. Under Max Emanuel, large numbers of paintings were already hanging in the palace; they were concentrated in the Schöne Gallerie and in the Flemish Painting Cabinet of the elector's apartment.[112] In 1762, Bianconi noted that "at Schleissheim there is located the marvelous picture collection of the Bavarian court, which after that of my royal master [the King of Poland] is the choicest in all of Germany. The gallery connected to the imperial apartment [the Reiche Zimmer of the Residenz] is in comparison only a modest beginning."[113] Even after Karl Theodor opened the art gallery along the Hofgarten of the Munich Residenz in 1780 and transferred part of the collection from Schleissheim, large numbers of pictures remained in the palace and continued to be accessible to a limited number of interested visitors.[114]

Nymphenburg was also the scene of much interior work during Max III Joseph's reign. The crowning achievement was the redecoration of the

Hauptsaal (including the Gartensaal and musicians' gallery that precede it on the garden side) in 1755–57. Although directed by Cuvilliés, the work was the creation of Johann Baptist Zimmermann, who executed the paintings (on the theme of pastoral life) and the spirited rocaille work framing them.[115] The establishment of the apartments of the elector and the electress in the inner south pavilion (on the ground floor and the piano nobile, respectively) resulted in extensive renovation of these rooms in the 1750s and 1760s.[116] Above the orangery in the north service block, the old Comödiensaal of Max Emanuel was transformed into the Hubertus-Saal, named after the banquet held there on the day of the annual hunt of St. Hubert. Next to this was a "Salettl oder Caffée-Zimmer," which was decorated in 1758.[117] One of the last undertakings of Max III Joseph's reign was the installation of a dining room for gentlemen and officers in the upper story of the Küchenbau, begun in 1777 and finished the following year.[118]

The Campagne

In the eighteenth century, Nymphenburg enjoyed a preferred status among the country houses as the regular summer residence of the court. The completion of the service blocks, the connecting wings, and the Rondell pavilions made it possible to accommodate a large household, not to speak of necessary services such as stables and kitchens or of desirable appurtenances such as theater and assembly halls, Passgebäude, and orangery that could not easily fit into the central pavilions. The foundation of two religious institutions in the north service block lent Nymphenburg a certain additional legitimacy as a residence. Their presence was more immediate than the remote hermitages at Schleissheim. If the Karlstadt project never achieved commercial success, the establishment of the electoral porcelain manufactory in the Rondell offered at least some compensation.

The principal attraction of Nymphenburg as a residence was undoubtedly the garden (fig. 38). With its lively pattern of openness and enclosure, of symmetry in overall plan and irregularity in the details, it was clearly the most appealing of all the gardens available to the Bavarian court. It offered diverse possibilities for promenade and recreation and enjoyed the intimate relationship with the palace that one associates with small summer houses. By comparison, the garden at Schleissheim seems monotonous and distant.

The court's annual summer sojourn at Nymphenburg, which first became an institution during Max Emanuel's late reign and which remained such through the eighteenth century, was known as the Nymphenburg Campagne. Normally, the Campagne began in late April or May and ended in early October.[119] It seems likely that there were traditional dates set for the transfer of residence to and from the country that weren't necessarily always followed in practice. A letter of February 14, 1750, from the Schlossverwalter at Nymphenburg regarding the maintenance of stoves and fireplaces in the palace, mentions that the Herrschaften "were in the habit of" taking up residence at Nymphenburg on May 12 and ending it on October 4.[120] Sometimes the decision to begin or end the Campagne seems to have been made on the spur of the moment. Felix Andreas Oefele, tutor to Karl Albrecht's nephew Clemens, wrote in his diary on October 1, 1739: "Everybody made ready to return to town, but since the favorite [Karl Albrecht's mistress] did not wish to, we didn't do it. The foolish master of the stables, who had given the orders to send the baggage into town, had to have it brought back." On October 7, he wrote: "Today it was decided that we would return to town tomorrow, Thursday the eighth."[121] It is clear that the Munich court was not run with the clockwork precision for which Louis XIV was renowned.

The elector brought a considerable household with him when he and his family moved to Nymphenburg for the summer.[122] Statistics on the lodging of the court at Nymphenburg are available only for the period around 1770. From that year we have a list of more than 166 persons who were to make the move to Nymphenburg that summer—high court officers, personnel of the elector's own household, and personnel of the households of the two other Herrschaften then living directly at court (the electress and the widowed Margravine of Baden-Baden).[123] There is also a list that the Schlossverwalter compiled in 1766 of all personnel living permanently in the palace, the estate farm buildings, and the Rondell pavilions—290 in all, of whom only 94 lived in the palace itself. The majority of the 290 were persons involved with the upkeep of the buildings and gardens, farm servants, and workers in the porcelain manufactory.[124] Neither document includes the personnel of the kitchen, cellar, linen, and silver offices, who would certainly have formed an integral part of the household necessary to support a prolonged stay in the country. About 260 persons, plus the staffs of the kitchen and related offices, must therefore have been lodged in the palace, including the five pavilions, the service blocks (but not the estate farm buildings or the convent wing), and the connecting wings.[125]

At Nymphenburg, accommodations had to be provided for a broader range of officers and servants than in the Residenz, as in Munich a considerable portion of the household lived in town and not in the Residenz. Thus, although the household having direct, active service at Nymphenburg was smaller than that having service in Munich, Nymphenburg could accommodate a comparable number of personnel. Whereas only servants, pages, and ladies-in-waiting lived in the Residenz, at Nymphenburg lodging was also provided for the court officers and the members of the elector's personal household (of whom only several, at most, lived in the Residenz). The list of persons moving to Nymphenburg in 1770 includes thirteen court officers (who altogether have forty servants of their own), two pages (and one servant), and thirty persons (plus seven servants of servants) to wait upon the elector. All of these were lodged in the palace. Of the twenty one female members of the electress's household listed in the 1769 Hofkalender (from the Obristhofmeisterin and Kammerdamen down to the maids), fourteen had lodgings in the Residenz, according to the 1771 inventory. Ten or eleven were taken to lodge at Nymphenburg in the summer of 1770.[126] Of the eighteen male members of the electress's household listed in the Hofkalender (from her Obristhofmeister down to the Portiers and the lowest rank of servant, the Kammerknecht) only the Kammerknecht lived in the Residenz, whereas seven (plus five servants) were taken along to Nymphenburg. In 1771, twenty servants belonging to the kitchen staff, all from the lower ranks, lived in the Residenz. The 1769 Nymphenburg furniture inventory indicates that at least twenty-seven menial kitchen servants slept in the palace.[127]

Officers and servants were housed in virtually every part of the palace. Close personal servants slept in the dégagements and back rooms of the apartments themselves. In the electress's apartment for example, there was a room for the Kammerfrauen (female chamber attendant) with two beds and a room for the Kammermensch (lowest-ranking male chamber attendant) above the Retirade. The upper three floors of the central pavilion contained mostly apartments for ladies and female servants. On the ground floor of this pavilion, where in Henriette Adelaide's old villa court offices were already located, there were rooms for the Hartschier guard, the Silberkammer, the Zuckerbäckerei (confectionery), the Somelerie, the Apotheke, and the Leinwandkammer. The outer south pavilion, which was called the Dirnitz Pavillon in the late eighteenth century, had housed the court kitchen and its related offices until 1750, when the Comedihaus was renovated into the Küchenbau. In 1769, the Zergaden (pantry) and Dirnitz were still located here on the ground floor, along with lodgings for a small number of kitchen personnel. The upper floors were entirely devoted to apartments for court officers and rooms for the households of the Herrschaften living in the adjacent inner south pavilion. On the piano nobile, there were apartments for the Obristhofmarschall and for the electress's Obristhofmeisterin and Obristhofmeister. Lesser officers and servants were lodged on the upper floors; the Pagerie, for example, was on the fourth floor. Certain members of the household of the margravine, who lived on the third floor of the inner north pavilion, were housed in the adjacent Kapellenpavillon.[128] Above the stables in the south service block, there were lodgings for court officers and gentlemen. The 1769 furniture inventory lists one lodging here for a cabinet secretary; no rooms in the palace, however, were set aside for the chancellery or councils.[129]

While officially in residence at Nymphenburg, the elector made frequent trips to Munich to preside at council meetings, to grant audiences to foreign envoys, and to attend church services, theatrical performances, and social functions. Other members of the family did likewise. Sometimes they spent the night in town; sometimes they returned to Nymphenburg in the evening. No rigid weekly schedule was adhered to, although one seems to have existed—at least in theory.

Two or three times a week, the court held "Appartement" (see chap. 5), a social function at which the Herrschaften and their guests played cards, listened to music, and took refreshment, usually in the elector's apartment. In the summer months the Appartement was often held out-of-doors, becoming a "Hofgarten." Once a week or so during the Campagne, the Hofgarten was held at Nymphenburg, and the ladies and gentlemen having entrée drove out from Munich to attend. The ladies were then invited to stay for supper and returned to Munich in the evening.[130] The garden at Nymphenburg lent itself well to this social function—better, perhaps, than the Hofgarten or Residenzgarten in Munich. Johann Jakob Moser wrote of Max Emanuel's court around 1720: "When the court was in residence at Nymphenburg, everything was conducted almost as at the Orangerie [in the Hofgarten at Munich], except that one promenaded more often at Nymphenburg, and the ladies could avail themselves of this pleasure with greater ease."[131] Pöllnitz wrote in 1735: "Those who prefer promenading to cards find open calèches pulled by two horses waiting every evening at the foot of the perron. One gentleman drives the calèche, with two ladies below and another gentleman behind. Those who wish to promenade on the canal find gilded gondolas at their disposal. Nothing is lacking; every pleasure is to be had in this enchanted place."[132]

During the Campagne, the Herrschaften also spent much time at the other country houses within easy riding distance of Nymphenburg. The activities of the Herrschaften as they moved from city to country and from one house to another may be followed closely in Preysing's diaries from 1717 to 1760. During the period 1719–22, he made entries in his diary almost every day of the year, painting a detailed picture of annual itineraries (see apps. 2, 3). Preysing was then a Kämmerer attached to the service of the electoral prince and seems to have followed him almost everywhere (on his accession in 1726, Karl Albrecht appointed Preysing Obriststallmeister), but he also conscientiously recorded the activities of Max Emanuel.[133]

Under Max Emanuel and Karl Albrecht, Schleissheim was usually visited for an extended period of two weeks or more during June. This pattern may also have obtained under Max III Joseph, whose renovation work at Schleissheim bespeaks a continued interest in using the house as a secondary summer residence.[134] While staying at Schleissheim, the Herrschaften likewise went into town frequently, usually returning in the evening. Occasionally we read in Preysing of a Hofgarten held there, sometimes followed by supper in the Saal at Lustheim.

Schleissheim was also capable of accommodating a sizable household. In 1735, Schlossverwalter Gillet renovated one of the mezzanines in order to provide more rooms. In letters accompanying the invoices he submitted for this work, he boasted of what he had accomplished: "Out of twelve rooms I have had thirty-one made, big enough both for masters and for household servants, by means of partitions. . . . It should be noted that out of one room, which was more like a tennis court, I have made four."[135]

The 1761 furniture inventory lists beds for 151 officers and servants in the Neues Schloss and for 196 in the Altes Schloss. Almost no one other than ladies, gentlemen, and personal servants lived in the Neues Schloss. The lower mezzanine was reserved for ladies, gentlemen, and servants having immediate service who needed to be on hand. On the north side were the "mezzanines for the ladies of the electoral court"; on the south, those for the gentlemen.[136] The lower mezzanine was convenient, of course, to the apartments on both piani nobili; this was particularly important in cases where the same person had apartments both upstairs and downstairs. Max Emanuel planned to have a summer apartment for himself on the ground floor on the south side, in addition to his principal apartment on the main floor above. The upper mezzanine was devoted mostly to rooms for servants, although there were also lodgings for ladies and gentlemen. All other personnel were lodged in the Altes Schloss, where there were also apartments for certain court officers.[137]

The other houses around Munich—Dachau, Berg and Starnberg, and

Fürstenried—were visited mostly in the course of hunting expeditions. The court also hunted from Nymphenburg and Schleissheim. Hunting took place year-round, and sometimes—especially in summer and fall—the Herrschaften hunted every day of the week. Max Emanuel and his sons often hunted separately, which entailed considerable expense: Johann Jakob Moser noted that it required the use of almost four hundred horses every day.[138] Fürstenried was used almost exclusively for hunting deer in the surrounding forest. The hunting party would often assemble there for the midday meal before setting off and would return there for supper. Sometimes the night was spent; otherwise, the party returned to Munich or Nymphenburg late in the evening. Once or twice a year, usually in July, August, or November, the Campagne was punctuated by longer hunting trips of one to three weeks' duration, notably to Lichtenberg, Haag, Schwaben, or Landshut.

4

Apartments and Säle: Issues of Program and Plan

I n an examination of the functional composition of palace plans, the sovereign may be seen to embody three roles: head of state, private individual, and leader (or at least host) of court society. Rooms were needed as settings for state acts or public appearances of the sovereign, such as audiences, investitures, the opening of the Estates, or the administration of oaths of allegiance; for private functions that all share in common; and for receptions, assemblies, banquets, and balls. The importance of these three roles relative to one another varied from court to court. At some courts, the sovereign's role as leader of society was negligible. At others, public and private functions, or public and social functions, became so intimately wedded that they were barely distinguishable.

Court Ceremony: Versailles and Vienna

Once Louis XIV had consolidated royal authority, the French court became the center for the social life of the court aristocracy. Large numbers of courtiers were present at court on a more or less permanent basis. At Versailles, many occupied apartments in the palace itself, while others erected hôtels in the town that grew up in front of the palace. The king barred his nobles from holding ministerial posts, molding them into eager participants in the ceremonies that surrounded the events of his daily life. At his Lever and Coucher, which are perhaps the best-known court ceremonies of the absolutist age, the king was ministered to and observed by a multitude of courtiers. During the later years of his reign, he dined in public nearly every day when he was in residence at Versailles. Although the public nature of the royal regimen did not originate with Louis XIV, he imbued these mundane events with the solemn character of acts of state through the gravity of his monarchical demeanor and through the fastidiousness with which he elaborated their ritualistic niceties.

Foreign commentators often expressed shock at the lack of privacy enjoyed by the king, at the crowds thronging the antechambers, and at the ease with which strangers had access even to the king's bedchamber. Louis XIV accepted this situation with equanimity and never attempted to limit the publicity surrounding his person. In his instructions for the dauphin he identified the accessibility of the king as one of the distinguishing traits of the French monarchy: "There are nations where the king's majesty consists in not permitting himself to be seen, and that may be reasonable among those who think that one can govern only through fear and terror; but this is not our genius as Frenchmen, and if there is any special character in this monarchy, it is the free and easy access of the subjects to the prince."[1]

The king also entertained his court. The renowned *fêtes* held at Versailles between 1663 and 1674, with their cycles of ballets, plays, balls, and banquets, were an exception at Louis XIV's court. These were all held before Versailles became the seat of government; no *fête* on such a lavish scale was ever produced during the later years of the reign.[2] What remained was an annual calendar of receptions, theatrical performances, and balls. Theatrical performances (mostly comedies and tragedies; opera was less popular at the French court than elsewhere) were a weekly occurrence. Balls, often in masquerade and usually accompanied by banquets, were less frequent, although they increased in number and intensity during the carnival season. The centerpiece of the social schedule was the Appartement, an evening reception held two or three times a week at which the king entertained the court with cards, music, dancing, and refreshment. These were held whether the king was present or not. After 1691 he preferred to spend his evenings quietly with Madame de Maintenon, but liked to hear that the Appartements were well attended.[3] Even at his country houses, where ceremonial was relaxed, the king usually played host to not inconsiderable followings of courtiers.

The imperial court in Vienna was arranged along radically different lines. Here the Spanish ceremonial that had first been introduced in Austria under Charles V and that had gradually come to pervade court life under his sixteenth-century successors guaranteed the emperor and his family a considerable measure of privacy in their daily lives.[4] The public appearances of the emperor were strictly limited to certain occasions. Daily events such as the Lever, Coucher, dinner, and supper were ritualized, but these were domestic rituals that involved only officers and servants of the immediate household. Nor did the emperor entertain or play host to his nobility on a regular, continuous basis.

As Johann Küchelbecker tells us in his account of the court of Charles VI (1711–40), the emperor and empress appeared in public only on Sundays, days on which the rites of the Order of the Golden Fleece were celebrated, and gala days (birthdays and name days of the imperial family).[5] On these days, the emperor and empress dined in public and were waited on by the court in full court dress (spanische Kleidung). Once dinner was over, however, "it is usually totally quiet again in the Hofburg, or the imperial Herrschaften pay each other visits and in this way pass several hours."[6]

Little expense was spared on the festivities produced at the imperial court, which attracted wide acclaim for their lavishness and for the high quality of the music and theater. The tradition of festivals reached back at least as far as the reign of Ferdinand II (1619–37) and remained strong until well into the eighteenth century. In 1625, Ferdinand introduced Italian opera in Vienna. This, in conjunction with the ballet (another Italian import) soon became the central element in the standard festival cycle.[7] Older elements—tournaments, masked balls, theater, Bauernwirtschaften (see p. 25), parades, and sleigh rides—took on more magnificent forms.[8] These festivals were produced to celebrate state occasions such as coronations, births, and marriages.

On the other hand, regularly scheduled festivities and divertissements were sparse. Under Charles VI, only two operas were presented per year—one on the empress's birthday, the other on the emperor's name day.[9] Carnival was celebrated modestly, usually with little more than a repetition of one of the operas, a Bauernwirtschaft, and a comedy.[10] There was no equivalent of the French Appartement. Gambling, one of the most pervasive aristocratic pastimes of the period and the chief attraction of the Appartement, was forbidden at Charles VI's court; Küchelbecker noted that the emperor played only for very low stakes, with his family and a few invited guests, and then only during the long winter months.[11] Both Moser and Florinus, in their treatises on Hofwesen, describe a festivity that seems to have been unique to the imperial court. This was the so-called Cammer-Fest, at which dancing, music, and comedies were put on by the court pages. These affairs were very exclusive; nobody had entrée other than the Herrschaften and the inner circle of highest-ranking persons.[12]

Küchelbecker was prepared to approve of the imperial court's ceremoniousness and austerity. He felt that the grandeur of Spanish ceremonial befitted the court of the ranking monarch of Europe, and he interpreted the lack of amusements as an indication of the emperor's serious-minded devotion to affairs of government. The Habsburg territories, he concluded, were very fortunate in having a ruler who "placed his own pleasure after the good of the state."[13] Most other writers, however, while they gladly granted the imperial court first place in terms of magnificence, could not help finding it stiff and old-fashioned. Pöllnitz, who visited most of the courts of Europe during his extensive travels in the early eighteenth century, wrote:

> One cannot deny that the Court of Vienna is the largest and the most magnificent court in Europe, in terms of the great number of princes and lords who compose it. Nevertheless, the ceremonies and the etiquette, which is the name given to ancient customs, give it an air of constraint that is not seen anywhere else. Everyone cries out against this etiquette; even the emperor sometimes seems to be irritated by it, and nevertheless it is observed like a point of religion or as if it would need an ecumenical council to reform it.[14]

As if to compensate for the court's lack of conviviality, Viennese society seems to have been quite lively. Pöllnitz wrote that the nobility of all ranks gave frequent receptions, to which it was remarkably easy for a foreigner, once introduced at one house, to gain universal entrée.

Court Ceremony: Bavaria

The Bavarian court ultimately combined elements of the Habsburg and French models. Bavarian ceremonial was patterned closely on that of the imperial court; the Kammerordnungen of Albrecht V and Wilhelm V reveal elements of Spanish ceremonial in Munich as early as the late sixteenth century. Daily rituals were conducted in private, and public appearances of the duke/elector were limited to specific occasions. By the eighteenth century, however, social institutions and usages had developed that made the court the nucleus of the social life of the court aristocracy, a characteristic attributable largely to French influence.

The court of Maximilian I had a reputation for ceremonious magnificence. The aura of remote dignity in which Spanish ceremonial clothed the sovereign suited Maximilian's conception of himself as a bulwark of political strength within the empire. State occasions were commemorated with festival cycles that rivaled those produced in Vienna in their artistic brilliance and generous hospitality. The new Residenz that Maximilian built, which far outdistanced the contemporary Hofburg in size and splendor, was calculated above all to provide a suitable setting for princely representation.

Magnificence, however, was tempered with austerity. Firmly convinced of the sacred nature of his mandate as a sovereign, Maximilian wished his court to be known as a citadel of virtue. Himself diligent and pious, he demanded the same qualities of his entourage. There was little place at his court for self-indulgent amusement.[15] The statue of the Madonna was not placed in the center of the Residenz facade without good reason.

Under Dowager Electress Maria Anna's influence, austerity continued to dominate the court of her son and daughter-in-law. In 1657, a French visitor, Monsieur de Coulanges, compared the Bavarian court to a monastery: "There is no cloister where one lives a more regular and severe life than in this court." One rose at six in the morning, he noted, and went to bed no later than ten in the evening; after supper, at six, nobody remained in the palace other than "a few necessary servants." This assessment of the court was echoed in the report of another, anonymous French traveler in 1661.[16]

As Henriette Adelaide's influence grew—the birth of a daughter in 1660 and the long-awaited arrival of an heir two years later brought her considerably more authority—so her taste for festivities and entertainment came to prevail. After Maria Anna's death in 1665, the young electress had a free hand, as Ferdinand Maria deferred to his wife in most matters. Festivities became more frequent—no longer staged only for state occasions, but also for the birthdays of the electoral family.[17] Carnival came to be celebrated with great fanfare and was made the excuse for a steady round of amusements lasting for weeks on end. An annual schedule of festivities developed that persisted with greater or lesser intensity through the eighteenth century. Italian opera, introduced by Maximilian in 1651, became a regular feature of court life. In 1671, a troupe of French comedians was engaged. They were dismissed in 1676, by Ferdinand Maria (who sharply reduced the volume of festivities after Henriette Adelaide's death), but not before French comedy had threatened to supplant the German theater. Max Emanuel reintroduced French comedy on his return to Bavaria in 1715. This and the Italian opera remained the dominant theatrical genres at court until the end of the eighteenth century.[18]

Although ceremonial remained unchanged and undiminished, the style of court life under Henriette Adelaide's influence acquired an easier tone and a certain Gallic polish. She had grown up at a court ruled by the *galant* manner of the court of Henri IV, where women played a more prominent social role than their counterparts in Germany and where the opportunities for social interaction between the sexes were greater. Differences in social behavior between Germanic and "Welsch" cultures are tellingly illustrated in an imperial diplomatic report of 1670. In it the author praises the intellectual accomplishments of Electoral Prince Max Emanuel, but deplores his precocious flirtations with his mother's ladies-in-waiting and the familiarity with which he treats the foreign-born pages of his suite.[19] The inner circle of courtiers surrounding the electoral couple included many Italians, who established themselves in Bavaria under the electress's patronage. The presence of foreigners of standing at the Bavarian court remained constant through the eighteenth century.[20] While her initial contempt for Germanic culture later softened, Henriette Adelaide always remained a Savoyard first and foremost and she succeeded in instilling something of the Gallic temperament in her children.[21] In the eighteenth century, the character of Bavarian court society, like that of many other German courts, was overwhelmingly French. If the Bavarian court was more Gallic than most, this was undoubtedly due to the strong influence of Max Emanuel's mother and to his long exile in France, where he (and those who followed him into exile) sampled French culture at the source, both in the court of the aging Louis XIV and in the emerging salon society of aristocratic Paris.

No information has been uncovered on patterns of day-to-day social life under Ferdinand Maria and Henriette Adelaide; presumably, however, this reign paved the way for the central social role the court assumed in the eighteenth century. Under Max Emanuel, regular social functions became permanent fixtures at court. In the mid-1680s, he began the custom of holding Appartements very similar to those at Versailles two or three times a week; in 1685, apparently in honor of his Habsburg wife, Maria Antonia, he introduced the institution of gala on the birthdays and name days of the electoral family and its relatives.[22] Another type of reception, or assembly, was the Accademie, to which a wider circle of persons had entrée than to the Appartement; it appears with regularity as early as the 1720s. In the eighteenth century, moreover, the electoral family dined regularly in company with their courtiers, in addition to dining privately and, on occasion, in state.

In 1774, Max III Joseph instituted certain reforms in court ceremonial. They did not affect the ceremonial observed on state occasions, which continued undiminished, nor did they reduce the exclusivity of private life. Instead, their primary goal was to ease the constraints on social interaction at court. The number of gala days, which had been considerable, was reduced to only a handful. This meant that it was no longer necessary to appear at court in full gala dress at the frequent birthday and name-day celebrations. The elector also introduced the custom of *pêle-mêle* at the dinner table on a regular basis, in order to eliminate disputes over precedence and to increase opportunities for the exchange of visits between the ruling houses of Germany (see chap. 5).

The description that Pöllnitz left of Karl Albrecht's court in the 1730s contrasts vividly both with his contemporary description of the imperial court and with the seventeenth-century descriptions of the Bavarian court. Although the ceremonial in effect followed that of the imperial court, Pöllnitz found life in Munich otherwise very different.

> The court of Bavaria observes almost the same etiquette as the court of Vienna, so far as ceremonies are concerned. Otherwise, they live very differently: they have more ease and more diversion. The court of Bavaria is without question the most gallant and the most polished court in Germany. We have here at the moment French comedy, dance, and gaming every day. Three times a week there is a concert [accademie]. Everyone attends masked. After the concert they game and dance. . . . Besides these noisy pleasures, we have more tranquil ones—that is, those that a relaxed social life provides. That is what one finds here more than in other German cities.[23]

By certain standards, the sociability of the Bavarian court even figured as excessive. Imperial diplomats, used to the more sedate routine of the Hofburg, apparently sometimes had difficulty carrying out their missions in Munich. On July 4, 1751, the imperial resident, Baron von Widmann, reported to Maria Theresia: "Although, in accordance with the local manner of life and the daily amusements, business is discussed less than never, I did not neglect to speak with Graf Preysing and Graf Seinsheim regarding the matter in question immediately upon my arrival." The situation was even worse during the early part of the year, when the entire city was gripped by carnival fever. On January 18, 1754, Widmann wrote, "As affairs here are set up so that nothing is undertaken during carnival, I find myself unable to report anything by today's mail."[24] Like Max Emanuel during the early years of his reign, Karl Albrecht enjoyed a reputation for profligacy while electoral prince. The abandon with which he threw himself into the carnival celebrations in 1721 prompted his uncle, Joseph Clemens, to write Baron von Malknecht, Bavarian resident in Vienna, expressing fear that wind of Karl Albrecht's excesses of pleasure would reach the emperor and compromise the negotiations then under way for the hand of Archduchess Maria Amalie.[25] Karl Albrecht later proved to be a ruler who took his responsibilities seriously, and his amusements acquired a more measured pace.

Court Ceremony and Palace Plans: France

The critical factor influencing the planning of the principal rooms of palaces was the distinction between the public and private spheres of life. At German courts, where this distinction was sharply maintained, the typical apartment was fundamentally different in plan than the king's apartment in the French royal palaces. Before turning to an examination of the Munich Residenz, it is worthwhile taking a look at the situation in France.

The blurring of the public and private realms at the French court is reflected in two characteristics of the apartment plan. The major room—the climax of the apartment—was the bedchamber, which functioned as the focus of public representation. In this room it was virtually impossible, in fact, for the king to enjoy any privacy at all. The bedchamber was preceded by a relatively small number of anterooms.

In the king's apartment in the Louvre, which had been installed under Henri II (1547–59) and which was occupied by Louis XIV before the permanent move to Versailles, the anterooms consisted of a *grande salle,* or *salle des gardes* (reached by the staircase in the central pavilion of the west wing of the square court), and an antechamber. The *chambre de parade,* the next room in the sequence, occupied most of the king's pavilion at the southwest corner of the courtyard. Behind it to the east was a private bedchamber, which had access to the inner rooms of the queen's apartment through a small cabinet. On the other side of the *chambre de parade* was the king's grand cabinet, which adjoined the round Salon du Dôme located at the north end of the Galerie d'Apollon. Other than various cabinets on the floor above, this was the extent of the king's apartment.[26]

The first of Louis XIV's apartments at Versailles was finished in 1673 and overlooked the Parterre du Nord; it preserved exactly the same number and sequence of anterooms, the only difference being that they were now laid out en enfilade (fig. 2).[27] The Salle de Mars (preceded by a vestibule, later the Salle de Venus, at the head of the staircase) was the guard chamber; the Salle de Mercure, the antechamber; and the Salle d'Apollon, the bedchamber. The grand cabinet, later the Salon de la Guerre, was at the corner of the palace, overlooking the great parterre. Behind it were various private rooms, which gave on to the terrace in the center of the principal wing. Directly behind the king's grand cabinet was his private bedchamber.

When Versailles became the permanent seat of the court approximately a decade later, Louis XIV decided to move into rooms along the south and west sides of the Cour de Marbre, leaving the apartment along the Parterre du Nord as a state apartment and a suite of reception rooms. The Appartements continued to be held here. The new apartment differed from the earlier apartments in having not one but two antechambers. The second of these, a relatively small, dark room that received light only from the interior courtyard of the south wing, was enlarged in 1701 by combining it with the adjacent bedchamber to create the Salle de l'Oeil de Boeuf. The bedchamber was then installed in the central room (formerly the Salon du Roi) facing the Cour de Marbre; it was now not only the functional focus of the apartment, but also the physical centerpiece of the entire palace complex.

The bedchamber was the principal room of audience. Here the king received ambassadors, minor sovereigns, and other members of regnant families. Here he received the addresses and remonstrances of the *parlements* and performed many other state acts. Certain state acts, such as the ceremony of the washing of the feet on Maundy Thursday, took place in the guard chamber.[28] Although the king actually slept in the state bedchamber only in the second apartment at Versailles, it was in this room that he held his public Lever and Coucher.[29] Louis XV and Louis XVI gave up sleeping here, preferring the comfort of their private bedchambers; but they continued to fulfill their ceremonial duties in this room. In the bedchamber, Louis XIV dined at midday *au petit couvert* (the small service) in the presence of a group of ranking nobles and court officers, who stood in respectful silence while the king ate.

The king dined *au grand couvert* (the large service) in his antechamber. In the second apartment at Versailles, this took place in the first antechamber, which was called the "antichambre du grand couvert" or the "salle où le roi mange" (the hall where the king eats). In the later years of the reign, the king seldom dined at midday *au grand couvert* but he supped here every evening with the members of the royal family, in the presence of the court (with the ladies also in attendance).

The room in which the king lived and worked was the grand cabinet, or *cabinet du conseil,* located behind the bedchamber (in the second apartment, this room was separated from the bedchamber by the Salon du Roi until 1701). In the mornings, between mass (which followed the Lever) and dinner, the councils were held here on five days of the week. Here the king granted private audiences to his nobles and to foreign envoys, received ministerial reports, and heard the remonstrances of the *parlements* when they were delivered by deputy.[30] Courtiers of both sexes were presented to the king in this room.

A certain number of ranking courtiers enjoyed the right of entrée into the grand cabinet. They might follow the king into the room at certain points during the day in order to speak with him. When the Lever was over, the king passed into the grand cabinet and found his court officers, who had been present at the Petit Lever, waiting there. He gave them the orders of the day, spoke with anyone who asked, and then proceeded to mass. After dinner he once again entered the grand cabinet, and the very few distinguished persons who had the courage to follow him had the privilege of watching him feed his dogs and then change his clothes before going hunting or promenading. After supper the king installed himself for several minutes in front of the balustrade in the bedchamber and exchanged compliments with the courtiers who had been present at supper before bidding them good-night. He then went through the grand cabinet, where he gave the orders for the following morning to his officers, and into the next room—the Cabinet des Perruques, or Cabinet des Termes. There he spent approximately an hour in the company of his family before retiring to the bedchamber to hold his Coucher. During this family gathering, the door to the grand cabinet remained open; in the latter room, the ladies waited for the princesses.

Louis XIV's other cabinets located along the north side of the Cour de Marbre, included a billiard room and various rooms in which he kept his collections and library; he seems not to have used these rooms much. In the eighteenth century, they were destroyed to make way for the private rooms of Louis XV, who did in fact spend much time here. Louis XV's rooms included a private bedchamber; a private dining room, where he held intimate supper parties; and a great variety of cabinets (on the two upper floors as well as on the piano nobile), where he worked, studied, and pursued his avocations. By means of small back staircases he could reach the apartments of his mistresses. Louis XV retained the grand cabinet of his predecessor; it continued to serve for councils, private audiences (although "secret" business was conducted in the private cabinets) and court presentations.

In the later years of his reign, the only real privacy that Louis XIV allowed himself at Versailles he enjoyed not in his own apartment, but in that of Madame de Maintenon, where nobody had the right to follow him. He came here in the evening before supper (at ten) and often worked with his ministers in front of the fireplace in her bedchamber.[31] Here he could relax in the company of the few persons with whom he chose not to play the king.

What most distressed many foreign visitors about the French court, as it affected them personally, was the fact that no distinctions in rank were observed in the king's antechamber, which was the only place of waiting for the court. All persons of standing had the right to enter this room to wait on the king, although in the (second) antechamber of the second apartment at Versailles, those of lesser rank were usually politely urged by the portiers to pass on into the Galerie des Glaces. It was the congestion in the antechamber that prompted Louis XIV to enlarge it in 1701. In French royal apartments, not more than two anterooms—the guard chamber for servants and the antechamber for their masters—were necessary.[32]

The palace was accessible to a vast public—in fact, to all persons who were decently dressed and could afford to rent a sword at the gate. Even the king's bedchamber could be seen when he was not in it, and a valet was on duty to make sure that no one sat on the balustrade or touched the king's bed. Connoisseurs of art could obtain permission to view Louis XIV's collections housed in his cabinets.[33] A significant difference between Louis XVI and Marie Antoinette was that while the king's petits cabinets were opened to the public, the queen refused to open hers. Arthur Young noted this on his visit to Versailles in 1787 and felt that it did the queen no credit.

> In viewing the King's apartment, which he had not left a
> quarter of an hour, with those slight traits of disorder that
> showed he *lived* in it, it was amusing to see the blackguard
> figures that were walking uncontrouled about the Palace,
> and even in his bedchamber; men whose rags betrayed them
> to be in the last stage of poverty. . . . One loves the master
> of the house who would not be hurt or offended at seeing
> his apartment thus occupied if he returned suddenly. . . . I
> desired to see the Queen's apartment, but I could not. Is Her
> Majesty in? No. Why then not see it as well as the King's?
> *Ma foi. Mons., c'est une autre chose.*[34]

Court Ceremony and Palace Plans: Bavaria

Marie Antoinette's behavior would have aroused no unfavorable comment in Munich. In the Munich Residenz, as in other German Residenzschlösser, the inner rooms of an apartment—including the bedchamber—were strictly private. The bedchamber was shielded by a lengthy sequence of anterooms to which entrée was increasingly restricted as one approached the bedchamber. All public functions took place in the anterooms. In Germany, Louis XIV's apartment would have been sufficient only for a prince of very minor rank.[35] In addition to the guard chamber and antechamber, the basic German princely apartment contained an audience chamber and a grand cabinet, which was located in front of the bedchamber (in contrast to the French arrangement). Most princes had at least one further antechamber.[36] Few had as many anterooms as Joseph Clemens, however, whose apartment in the Residenz in Bonn must figure as the outer limit to which an apartment could grow. It contained two antechambers after the guard chamber, a dining room (somewhat to the side of the sequence of rooms leading to the bedchamber), and two antechambers in front of the audience chamber and grand cabinet.[37]

Entrance into the Munich Residenz itself was highly restrictive. This was generally true at the German courts. Julius Bernhard von Rohr wrote, "In the princely palaces in Germany, a stranger may not look around with the same freedom as in France."[38] This situation attracted comment from French travelers particularly. The anonymous Frenchman who visited Munich in 1661 was indignant at the difficulty he experienced in gaining admittance to the Residenz: "One cannot even enter the courtyards of the palace without permission." He and his party toured the apartments of the Kaiserhofbau but were not permitted to enter the apartments of the elector and electress, which they had heard were also worth seeing.[39] Coulanges had the same problem. He wanted very much to wait upon Henriette Adelaide, but the opportunity was denied him; he had to content himself with seeing her from a distance during a mass at the Carmelite church. He later learned that Obristhofmeister Graf Max Kurz, intent on keeping Bavaria on a pro-Habsburg course, had expressly ordered the guards to refuse entrance to suspicious Frenchmen.[40] For a stranger, it was not enough to be respectably dressed; one had also to identify oneself and state one's business at the gate. On the day of the procura wedding of Maria Antonia Walburga in 1747, it was thought desirable to have larger numbers of persons of quality at court than usual. The order was issued that "at the gates and all entrances guards are to be posted to ensure that no common people enter the Residenz. Strangers of good appearance, however, may be permitted to enter without too much inquiry—but not into the chapel, where only nobles who belong at court may enter."[41] In the diary he kept during 1651, Graf Kurz made specific note of the foreigners of standing to whom the apartments of the Residenz had been shown. On June 17, for example, "several citizens of Hamburg arrived here and, after Most Gracious permission was obtained, toured the Residenz."[42] The private rooms of the Herrschaften were rarely shown, even when they were not occupied. Hainhofer considered it a great honor that he was allowed to see the Reiche Kapelle in

1611, as it was opened only on high holidays and was normally shown only to "nobles and diplomats." In 1636, he wanted to see Maximilian's Kammergalerie, but this was not possible; he was on a tight schedule and there was no time to request permission from the elector, who was then at Starnberg.[43]

In examining the principal apartments in the Residenz, the first distinction to be noted is that between the Garde-Saal and the Ritterstube, on the one hand, and the apartment proper—which may be considered to begin with the antechamber—on the other. The Saal and Ritterstube formed a public zone within the sequence of rooms leading to the bedchamber; the apartment was the personal realm of its occupant.

The elector's Garde-Saal, the Herkules-Saal (plan B, 3), was the focus of public representation in the Residenz; It was open to all persons of standing who had or could obtain entrance to the Residenz. Persons who were privileged to enter one of the inner rooms left their liveried servants behind in the Saal, so that under normal circumstances it seemed to be given over to lackeys. In the Ritterstube (plan B, 4) a smaller, but by no means exclusive, body of persons was permitted to wait.

Certain traditional public acts took place in the Herkules-Saal. "Usually," wrote Wening, "public festivals are held in this room."[44] On the wedding days of family members, ceremonial balls were held here. These were very stiff affairs, at which the attendance of the court was strictly regulated by ceremonial and the dancing began in order of rank. At some ceremonial balls, such as those held for Maria Anna Josepha in 1755 and Josepha Antonia in 1765, only the Herrschaften danced. The only surviving early illustration of the Herkules-Saal, the engraving by W. P. Zimmermann from 1614 (fig. 39), depicts just such a ceremonial ball in progress—the one held at the marriage of Maximilian's sister, Magdalena, to Pfalzgraf Wolfgang Wilhelm von Neuburg in 1613.[45] At the wedding of Violante Beatrix in 1688, the marriage ceremony itself took place in the Herkules-Saal, at an altar set up in front of the fireplace; and later in the day the Herrschaften dined there in state.[46] The Erbhuldigungen of Karl Albrecht (in 1727) and Max III Joseph (in 1747) were held not in the Herkules-Saal but in the Munich city hall (Rathaus), although after the ceremony the elector rode back to the Residenz with the representatives of the Estates and treated them to a state banquet in the Ritterstube.[47] At the Bavarian court, as at many German courts, the investiture of vassals was handled purely as a bureaucratic matter during this period and was not solemnized in any ceremonial act.[48]

Moser noted that at virtually all courts there were certain Säle "dedicated from time immemorial to a particular public purpose"; he cited as

Fig. 39. Munich, Residenz, view of Herkules-Saal by W. P. Zimmermann, engraving, 1614. (Prestel Verlag, Munich)

an example what he termed Ritter-Säle, in which the Estates heard the Proposition of the ruler before the opening of the territorial diet and in which dynastic ceremonies such as weddings might take place.[49] The Ritterstube in the Munich Residenz (plan B, 4) was the room where the elector dined in public. Here also deceased electors were laid out in state prior to the funeral service in one of Munich's churches.[50] Not all Residenzschlösser had Ritterstuben. This room type seems, in fact, to have been somewhat rare, and it is not mentioned in the theoretical literature on Hofwesen.[51] In most Residenzen, the room in which the prince dined in public was designated simply as an outer antechamber. The term was difficult to translate into French; in his critique of Zuccalli's Schleissheim project of 1700 (figs. 23, 24), Joseph Clemens called this room "the first antechamber, referred to as the Ritterstube."[52] The emperor's apartment in the Leopold wing of the Hofburg had a Ritterstube, in which the emperor dined in public on a certain few ceremonial occasions. Probably most of the ranking princes of the empire, or at least the electors, also had them.

If the Herkules-Saal served as the most frequent setting for public ceremonies, it played a less important role in the staging of festivities. Large banquets and balls were more often than not held in the Kaisersaal (plan B, 20) and the adjoining Vierschimmelsaal (plan B, 22). When an imperial guest occupied the Kaiserzimmer, the Kaisersaal functioned, as a guard chamber and the Vierschimmelsaal as a public dining room. In the eighteenth century, the Accademies were often held in the Kaisersaal. These assemblies (like the more exclusive Appartements) featured music and cards. The 1769 furniture inventory lists thirty-seven card tables and a platform for an orchestra in this room.[53] Florinus distinguished two types of Säle in his discussion of the rooms necessary in a palace. Haupt-Säle are those which "serve for magnificence and for large, solemn assemblies." What he calls Kleine Säle serve as public dining rooms and as places for holding festivities such as balls.[54] There were thus, at least in the larger Residenzen, Säle dedicated principally to ceremonies and others dedicated principally to festivities. Equipment such as card tables, in any case, could not very well have been set up permanently in the Herkules-Saal.

Within the apartment itself, there was likewise a division between public rooms (the antechamber and audience chamber) and private rooms (the bedchamber and cabinets). Entrée to the antechamber was a prerogative enjoyed by a privileged few. Entrée to the audience chamber was enjoyed by even fewer, and then only on certain days. There was, however, no entrée to the bedchamber or cabinets. One entered these rooms by invitation only. Only family, close companions, one or two of the highest court officers and ministers (who were more than likely also companions), and the handful of Kämmerer and valets who at any given time were doing their tours of personal service could claim any rights of access.[55] The Kammerordnungen and Aufwartungs-Ordnungen are quite insistent on the matter of privacy in the inner rooms. The Kämmerer who waited on the elector had explicit instructions to wait in the antechamber until their services—at the Lever, Coucher, or private Tafel— were called for. If some urgent matter required that they see the elector, they were always to knock first and wait until the elector had given a sign to enter.[56] A memorandum detailing procedures to be followed during the visit of Marie Antoinette in 1770 contains a lengthy proviso that when, on the second day of the visit, she returned from the opera with the electress to the latter's bedchamber (where compliments would be exchanged before the dauphine proceeded via the Reiche Zimmer (plan D, 3–11) to her own bedchamber (plan D, 17) in the old electress's apartment), only her ladies were to be permitted to accompany her into the bedchamber. The officers of her suite were to pass through the chambermaids' room next to the Cäcilienkapelle (plan D, 28) and the remainder of her gentlemen were to be conducted to the elector's antechamber (plan D, 24) by a Bavarian Kämmerer via the palace corridors.[57]

The bedchamber inevitably acquired a certain mystique. To be admitted was an exceptional honor for those who were not in a position to expect this privilege. When one of Maria Antonia Walburga's maids of honor was to leave court service to enter a convent, Maria Theresia von Gombert noted in her diary that Maria Amalie "was Most Gracious enough to permit Fräulein —— to enter Her Most High bedchamber, and honored her with a Most Gracious address."[58] The widowed Margravine of Baden-Baden recounts a curious incident in 1774 involving one of the ladies-in-waiting of the visiting Princess Taxis. The Herrschaften and ladies were on one occasion compelled to take their coffee after dinner not in the electress's bedchamber, as planned, but in her audience chamber, because "this lady-in-waiting did not dare to enter the bedchamber."[59]

Since the anterooms of the apartment served as places of waiting for the court and since state acts, notably public audiences, took place there, the plan of the anterooms bore a very direct relationship to ceremonial usage and evolved in step with ceremonial. Such requirements did not apply, however, to the private rooms. The type of cabinets found in an apartment depended largely on the personal inclinations of the prince and was susceptible to architectural fashion. The appearance of the Holländisches Cabinet (plan C, 9) among the private rooms of Max Emanuel's Alexanderzimmer can be attributed to the fashion for exotic cabinets that was then in its early stages. That this room could later be transformed without qualms into a private chapel is indicative of the freedom that one had in planning the private zone of the apartment. A serious problem with Zuccalli's 1700 project for Schleissheim, as noted by Joseph Clemens, was the dearth of private rooms behind the bedchamber. Zuccalli had provided only one small cabinet (in the outer corner of the end pavilion), as well as a small private chapel directly accessible from the bedchamber. In his critique of the project, Joseph Clemens suggested that each principal apartment should have, in addition to the grand cabinet, a "cabinet des affaires" (room for business affairs), a "petit cabinet" (dressing room), a "chambre pour le billard" (billiard room), a "chambre où l'on peut mettre la musique" (music room), and a "chambre pour manger lorsqu'on veut être en particulier" (room for eating in private), not to speak of the necessary service rooms.[60] In order to be suitably housed in his Residenz in Bonn, he wrote to Robert de Cotte, he would need, in addition to a "secret room," the following private rooms behind the bedchamber: "several rooms with mirrors, collections of antiquities, medals, and curiosities, a room for storing documents, a library, a private chapel, a gallery, and a place for a billiard table."[61]

In the private zone, the linear sequencing of the apartment often broke down and patterns of circulation became more flexible, whereas in the public zone there was a single, unavoidable path of approach leading from one room to the next. In a palace in which the apartments extended outward from a centrally placed Saal, it was inevitable that the private rooms would be located at the ends of the building. As at Schleissheim (fig. 27), they were often grouped centrifugally in the corner pavilions or wrapped around the ends, while the anterooms were laid out en enfilade. Florinus recommended laying out the apartments of a palace to either side of a central Saal (a drawback to the parti that was noted by Joseph Clemens; see p. 87) and allowing the rooms to extend around the corners. The last rooms were not to be placed in a row, but instead "next to one another so that one is free to go from one to another as one wishes."[62]

No documentation survives on the earliest apartments in the Residenz. The apartments in the Neuveste are first described in later accounts, long after they had ceased to serve as principal apartments.[63] The plan of Wilhelm V's apartment above the Antiquarium is unknown. The first apartment for which we have any information on the component rooms is the apartment that Maximilian built for himself in the Grottenhofbau around 1600.

The 1638 furniture inventory mentions the following rooms belonging to Maximilian's apartment: AntiCamera, Audienz-Zimmer, Gallaria, and Schlafcammer, (plan B, 5–6, 8–9), as well as various subsidiary rooms.[64] It becomes clear in examining seventeenth-century plans (plans A, B, C) that not all the rooms of the apartment have been included in the inventory, which lists the contents of the Residenz not room by room but by type of object inventoried. The Kammerordnungen of 1589, 1597, and 1628 mention three of the duke/elector's rooms: Vorcammer or AntiCamera, Zimmer, and Cammer or Schlafcammer.[65] The Zimmer, like the Cammer, was a room to which access was strictly limited, and it must be counted among the private rooms of the apartment. It was in the Zimmer, according to the 1628 Kammerordnung, that Maximilian held his Lever and Coucher (at this early date, these ceremonies were known by the less pretentious German terms *Ankleiden* and *Abziehen*).[66] When he was ready to be dressed in the morning, Maximilian went into the Zimmer from his Cammer and rang for the Kämmerer, who were waiting in the antechamber to assist him in dressing.

The description of the Coucher in the 1628 Kammerordnung permits us to locate the bedchamber. When the Coucher was over in the evening, one of the attendant valets accompanied the elector to the bedchamber, "lighting the way for him through the gallery." The location of the bedchamber at the far end of the gallery is confirmed by the report of an audience Maximilian gave to a Danish envoy in 1643. The elector held the audience in bed, as he wasn't feeling well, and we read that the envoy was led "through the gallery to the bedchamber."[67]

Based on this information, the most likely reconstruction of the elector's apartment is the following: The antechamber (plan B, 5) and audience chamber (plan B, 6) were the two rooms along the east side of the Grottenhof. The next room—the small, square room with a door onto the altana, at the head of a service staircase, was probably a passage that may also have served as a waiting room for the Zimmer (plan B, 7).[68] The latter was at the east end of the gallery (plan B, 8). The bedchamber (plan B, 9) was located either directly at the west end of the gallery, overlooking the garden, or behind this, at the west end of the altana.[69]

The electress's apartment, as inventoried in the 1638 furniture inventory, contained a Tafelstube (plan B, 11), two further rooms (second and third Kurfürstin-Zimmer; plan B, 12–13), and the Schlaf-Cammer (plan B, 14). These composed the flight of rooms facing the street. In addition, two cabinets, or Schreibstübl, are mentioned, as well as the Gallaria (Plan B, 15) at the west end of the Residenzgarten; the Gallaria, like the elector's gallery, was a private room.[70] The rooms along the garden that were furnished for Maria Anna in 1638–40, with their scagliola wall paneling (one of them was the Grottenzimmer, with its wall fountain), are not mentioned in the inventory. Unfortunately, the layout of the electress's apartment before the transformations undertaken for Henriette Adelaide in the 1660s has not been the object of serious study, and it is not possible to draw any firm conclusions regarding the effect that the work in 1638–40 might have had on the plan of the apartment.[71]

The sequence of anterooms seen in the electress's apartment, with two rooms between the Ritterstube and the bedchamber, was standard for the apartments in the Residenz. In the first half of the seventeenth century, only the elector's apartment had more anterooms. Even the imperial apartment (plan B, 22–28) conforms to this pattern. Two rooms—antechamber (plan B, 23) and audience chamber (plan B, 24)—intervened between the Vierschimmelsaal or Ritterstube (Plan B, 22) and the bedchamber (Plan B, 25).[72] The apartments of the Trier wing likewise had only two anterooms (plan B, 29–35).[73] When the Margravine of Baden-Baden occupied the north half of the Trierzimmer in 1761–76, the Weisser Saal served as her Ritterstube. This was followed, according to the 1769 furniture inventory, by an antechamber, audience chamber, bedchamber, and cabinet.[74] The south half of the Trierzimmer, which was entered directly from the Herkules-Saal, had the disadvantage that there was no intermediate room that could serve as a Ritterstube. Either the first anteroom had to double as Ritterstube and antechamber or the audience chamber had to be sacrificed. Wening in 1700 gave the sequence of rooms as antechamber, audience chamber, and bedchamber; the 1769 furniture inventory, however, lists them as Ritterstube, antechamber, and bedchamber.

The remodeling of the electress's apartment for Henriette Adelaide (plan D, 12–18) brought the insertion of one further room in front of the bedchamber. We are on firmer ground in discussing the plan of this apartment, as the two earliest descriptions—Pallavicino of 1667 (or Schmid of 1685) and Wening of 1700—both list the rooms in sequential order. The first room of the apartment was no longer a Ritterstube, but had become a guard chamber—the Hartschiersaal, "where the electoral Hartschier guard keep watch."[75] The Ritterstube was now the next room, followed by the antechamber and audience chamber. The audience chamber was located at the end of the flight facing the street, directly before the gallery with its two end cabinets. The next room, overlooking the garden, was the Grottenzimmer, which attracted much comment from all three authors on account of its exotic decoration. Pallavicino and Schmid tell us nothing about the purpose of this room. Wening terms it the Grosses Cabinet and states that it was "dedicated to private audiences."[76] He notes further that the wall fountain made it a pleasant place in which to escape the summer heat. A wall fountain is not the sort of architectural feature that one would expect to find in a Grosses Cabinet; it was, of course, a survival from the previous reign, when this room had presumably functioned as an inner cabinet. The Grottenzimmer was followed by the bedchamber (Alkovenzimmer), the Herzkabinett, and various service rooms. Along the opposite side of the garden was the electress's library, which was reached via the gallery.

The electress's apartment seems to have expanded at the expense of the elector's apartment. Although Pallavicino's description of the latter is somewhat scant (he concentrated his attention on Henriette Adelaide's new rooms), we can infer from it that the elector's bedchamber was no longer located at the west end of the gallery, but at the east end. At the west end there seems to have now been a "picciolo gabinetto" containing antique medals and other treasures.[77]

The construction of the Alexanderzimmer (plan C) in 1680–85 increased the area of the elector's apartment significantly. It did not, however, increase the number of anterooms beyond that of Maximilian's or Henriette Adelaide's apartment. Both Schmid and Wening give detailed descriptions of the elector's apartment. The antechamber (plan C, 3) and audience chamber (plan C, 4), along the east side of the Grottenhof, were not changed in plan. They were followed by an interior, or private, Audienz-Zimmer (plan C, 5); here, as Schmid writes, "the elector is in the habit of lending an ear to his own kind."[78] This room was the successor to Maximilian's Zimmer. It not only served for private audiences, but also conferences, dining in private (particularly privately in company), and holding small family social gatherings, to which an inner circle of courtiers might be invited. Called also the Grosses Cabinet, Conferenzzimmer, and Wohnzimmer, it was in effect both an official study or workroom and a private living room. In the Kammerordnungen, the Kämmerer are explicitly forbidden to rummage among the elector's books and papers when duty requires that they enter this room during the elector's absence.[79] Florinus tells us that a Cabinet was the room "where the Herrschaften congregate in private or hold private audiences."[80]

In 1684, Max Emanuel granted Prince Eugene of Savoy a private audience in the Grosses Cabinet and afterwards treated him to a private dinner in the same room, at which the pages and valets served.[81] Preysing reported on February 15, 1719, the day of the arrival of Duke Ferdinand's bride in Munich, that the Herrschaften, after dining in public, "conversed together *en cercle* in the Grosses Cabinet of the elector until 10 P.M."[82] On March 5, 1719, he noted a "concert de music" in the elector's Grosses Cabinet, at which the elector played the gamba and Duke Ferdinand the flute; "the ladies sat around in a circle." The Alexanderzimmer also included a Geheimes Cabinet (plan C, 7), located behind the bedchamber and reached from the alcove in which the bed stood. In this room Max Emanuel handled affairs "which should remain concealed until their time has come."[83]

In apartments that did not have cabinets in front of the bedchamber, intimate social gatherings were held in either the audience chamber or the bedchamber. Which room was chosen depended on the occasion and the company present. Dinner could be, and was, taken in any of the anterooms of the apartment, with an ascending degree of privacy and exclusivity as one approached the bedchamber (see chap. 5). In the eighteenth century, when it was customary to drink coffee after a meal, one retired to an inner room to do so. The incident described above involving the lady-in-waiting who had reservations about entering the electress's bedchamber took place in Maria Anna Sophia's apartment above the Antiquarium, which did not have a cabinet between the bedchamber and audience chamber. In July 1776, during the visit (presumably at Nymphenburg) of a Prince Radzivil, who was invited to dine at midday with the Herrschaften on each day of his visit, coffee was taken not in the bedchamber but in an outer room. This deviation from normal practice was made in order to circumvent a problem of etiquette.[84]

What was new about the Alexanderzimmer was the suite of rooms— the Sommerzimmer (plan C, 10)—erected simultaneously on the site of the altana. Schmid and Wening describe these rooms, but give no indication of their purpose. Other evidence suggests that it was in the Sommerzimmer, possibly in conjunction with the antechambers and the Kammergalerie, that the newly instituted Appartements were held (see chap. 5).

We may assume that the sequence of anterooms in the Alexanderzimmer fully suited the requirements of ceremonial at the time and use the sequence as a criterion in examining the apartments seen in the various projects for Schleissheim. Although only the project of 1700 has a room legend, on several earlier plans the bedchambers have been identified by means of lightly drawn beds. On the earliest project for a new palace at Schleissheim, the bedchambers of the twin apartments along the garden facade are shown as the fourth rooms from the central Saal.[85] On one of the later projects for a quadrangular palace, the bedchambers of the ground-floor apartments are likewise the fourth rooms in the sequence, in this case with access from the hypostyle vestibule. These are, however, either summer apartments or apartments of minor Herrschaften; lacking a plan of the piano nobile, we cannot know whether the principal apartments were provided with the same or a greater number of anterooms.[86] With only three anterooms after the Saal or vestibule, these apartments would have been inadequate as state apartments. The apartments of the elector and electress in Zuccalli's 1700 project, however (fig. 23), however, have a sequence of anterooms corresponding exactly with that of the Alexanderzimmer. The apartments of the piano nobile and the summer apartments directly underneath are identical. Each has, according to

Zuccalli's legend, two Anticamere, a Camera d'Udienza, and a Gran Gabinetto, followed by the Camera da Dormire. The Gran Gabinetti were the last rooms in the flight before the corner pavilions; the bedchambers were the sizable square rooms in the pavilions. Although in some of the later drawings the Gran Gabinetti have become excessively small because of the insertion of service staircases directly behind them, this basic configuration of rooms was preserved through the subsequent planning phases, and the palace was built according to this plan.

When work recommenced on Schleissheim in 1719, the bedchambers and Gran Gabinetti were switched in position. This necessitated enlarging the *gabinetti* toward the rear in order to accommodate the beds.[87] No archival evidence has been uncovered to document the reasons behind this change. As we have already seen, Zuccalli had made scant provision for private cabinets behind the bedchambers. The most compelling reason that can be deduced from the plan drawings is that the rooms in the corner pavilions were inconvenient as bedchambers, in that the placement of the doors (en enfilade from one end of the building to the other) did not permit space for a balustrade in front of the bed. In any case, that this change in the sequence of rooms could be made is a strong indication that Max Emanuel, despite his determined efforts to complete Schleissheim, no longer seriously regarded the palace as a major residence.

With the construction, completed in 1737, of the Reiche Zimmer in the Residenz, the sequence of anterooms in the elector's apartment reached its greatest extent. The Grosses Cabinet (plan D, 6) retained its function as a room for conferences, private audiences, and intimate social affairs; but it was moved into the south wing of the Grottenhofbau where formerly the Kammergalerie and the Sommerzimmer had stood. Behind the Grosses Cabinet were a new bedchamber (plan D, 7) and two inner cabinets—the mirror room (plan D, 8) and the cabinet for miniature paintings (plan D, 9). The Grüne Galerie (plan D, 10) became the setting for the Appartements. In 1764, a dining room was attached to the gallery. This is the first instance of a dining room in the Residenz that did not also function as an antechamber. It was not a public dining room, but a social dining room, where the elector and his family dined in company.

A Grosses Audienzzimmer (plan D, 5) now occupied the site of the former Grosses Cabinet at the point of juncture between the three tracts of the apartment. The room that was new in function, which stood on the site of the former audience chamber, was variously called the second Antechamber or first Audience chamber (plan D, 4). There was now one more place of waiting for those persons privileged to enter the antechamber (plan D, 3), and further distinctions in rank could be made. A new

Aufwartungs-Ordnung was published in 1739 to take advantage of the increase in the number of anterooms (app. 4). Distinctions could now be made among foreign envoys by granting audience in the Grosses Audienzzimmer to envoys of higher standing (see chap. 6).

The Grosses Audienzzimmer served another, very specific function that may well have played a role in the decision to create this sort of exalted audience chamber. It has to do with the Order of the Knights of St. George, founded by Karl Albrecht in 1729 as a Bavarian order dedicated to defending the doctrine of the Immaculate Conception. The knights of the order, over which the elector presided, held celebrations in the Georgskapelle (until it burned in 1750) on two days of the year— St. George's Day (April 24) and the Day of the Immaculate Conception. Conferences to nominate and elect new knights were held shortly before the celebrations, apparently in the Grosses Audienzzimmer.[88]

Von Rohr, writing in 1729, identified the multiplicity of anterooms as a sign of the times. "At the beginning of the past century, one didn't know as much as today of the many antechambers that follow one after the other."[89] He attributed this phenomenon to the "tremendous increase" in numbers experienced by princely households during the previous half century. Whether this increase figured as a reason in the creation of the Reiche Zimmer is not easy to determine. It is interesting to note, however, that whereas Louis XIV increased the space available for waiting by enlarging his antechamber, Karl Albrecht did so by creating more antechambers.

The increase in the number of anterooms may be seen as a significant architectural testimonial to Karl Albrecht's political ambitions. Not only did the new apartment sport interiors of dazzling magnificence and serve to advertise the august lineage of the House of Wittelsbach through its iconography, but it also now had more anterooms than the emperor's apartment in the Hofburg.[90]

Karl Albrecht expanded the private realm of the elector's quarters through the construction of the Gelbes Appartement (ground floor, beneath plan C, 10; see also fig. 9). This apartment, which consisted of two antechambers, a bedchamber, and a cabinet, is the first instance of a complete private apartment in the Residenz. It seems to have been used by Karl Albrecht as a retreat within the palace where he could enjoy almost total isolation from the court. In 1739, Preysing reported that the elector was confined to bed by severe pains in the feet and legs that seem to have prevented him from making public appearances. On February 9, Preysing wrote, "Mass held in the Gelbes Schlafzimmer at 12 o'clock, then he dined on the *lit de repos*." On the fifteenth, "Serenissimus had himself carried to the electress's chapel in order to hear mass, and then dined in the Gelbes Zimmer." On March 25, the elector, still not better, held an audience here: "The Duca Miranda, a Neapolitan of the House of Carraccioli, was presented in the Gelbes Zimmer."[91]

Although it did not function as a retreat, Max III Joseph's apartment above the Antiquarium was also a private apartment (plan D, 23–28). Entrée to the antechambers of this apartment was highly restrictive. The antechambers of the Reiche Zimmer continued to function as places of waiting, and public audiences were still held in the two Reiche Audienzzimmer (plan D, 3–5). The Grüne Galerie (plan D, 10) retained its role as the setting for the Appartements. The Reiche Zimmer, or at least the former private rooms along the Residenzgarten, acquired the designation Parade-Zimmer (plan D, 6–9).[92] Conferences, on the other hand, were now held in the audience chamber of the private apartment (plan D, 25), which was located directly in front of the bedchamber. In the 1769 furniture inventory, this room is called an Audienzzimmer, "in which conferences are also held." In the waiting room behind it, there was an armoire in which supplies necessary for the conferences—paper, pens, ink, etc.—were kept.[93]

Under Max III Joseph, the elector's apartment reached its greatest extent, making considerably more rooms available to him than to his predecessors. Life at court had undergone changes since the time of Maximilian I. The court had more than doubled since the early seventeenth century and now included a multitude of officers whose duties were purely honorific. Its ceremonies were—at least in the case of public dining—less frequent but no less magnificent than before; and diplomatic receptions were much more elaborate. The demographic growth of the court and the increasing complexity of state ceremonial had impelled a gradual distention of the public zone of the apartment. Under Max III Joseph, state ceremonies continued to take place in the anterooms of the Reiche Zimmer, to which the Grosses Audienzzimmer and the Grosses Cabinet provided a stately culmination. The court had become not only more ceremonious, but also more sociable. Individuals belonging to the upper echelons of court society were now guests of the elector at a regular round of receptions and dinners. This custom, unknown under Maximilian (whose role as a host was limited to the extraordinary festivities occasioned by state and dynastic events) resulted in the appearance of a suite of social rooms—an integral, although distinct, component of the apartment. The picture gallery, which under Maximilian had been reserved for the elector's personal enjoyment, assumed a new function as a reception room. Throughout the period, private life remained secluded.

The installation of a complete private apartment, its rooms more intimate in scale and decor than the adjacent state anterooms, affirmed the sanctity of the distinction between public and private. The three spheres of life—public, private, and social—may be seen to be well balanced in the plan of Max III Joseph's apartment.

As state acts did not as a rule take place in the country houses, it was not vital to maintain a prescribed number and sequence of anterooms in their apartments. Rooms served combined functions. Moser wrote that in Landschlösser where it was not possible to accommodate the "number of rooms desired by today's standards of pomp," one often found that the "antechamber, dining and audience room" were one and the same.[94] At Nymphenburg, in any case, the pavilionated plan precluded long, linear flights of anterooms. In country houses, a greater proportion of space could be devoted specifically to private and social purposes. Nymphenburg was well provided with social rooms. The entire ground floor (fig. 34) of the inner north pavilion served as a reception suite, with the Appartements hall along the garden and the dining room facing the court. Large banquets were held in the main hall in the middle pavilion. In the principal apartments on the piano nobile of the inner side pavilions, there were smaller rooms that served for dining and social gatherings. For extraordinary festivities, there were the Comedihaus (the south wing building) and the orangery and Hubertus-Saal in the north service block.

The two inner side pavilions at Nymphenburg were the major residential pavilions of the palace (figs. 34–36). They had the advantage of long views of the garden and forecourt, and if an entire floor of a pavilion was arranged as one apartment, it could be quite spacious. Although the apartments in the middle pavilion offered adequate accommodations for country residence, they permitted only uninspiring views toward the sides. Through much of the eighteenth century these apartments either were unoccupied or served to lodge guests.[95]

Originally, the plan of the inner side pavilions featured corridors running through the pavilions from side to side, forming part of the path of circulation from one end of the palace to the other. Pairs of apartments on each floor were arranged on either side of the corridor. In the inner south pavilion, there were six apartments on the three floors, for Max Emanuel's children. These were the most basic apartments imaginable. Along the garden facade there was space for three rooms—antechamber, bedchamber, and cabinet—as well as one or two very small service rooms. Along the court facade there was less space, because of the presence of staircases in the outer corners. A cabinet could be accommodated only by reducing the size of the bedchamber. Direct comparison between the lodgings of minor Herrschaften in the Residenz and at Nymphenburg is possible in the case of the Margravine of Baden-Baden. In the Residenz, according to the 1769 furniture inventory, she had a Ritterstube, antechamber, second antechamber, bedchamber, and cabinet. At Nymphenburg, where she occupied the apartment facing the garden on the third floor of the inner north pavilion, she had, according to the inventory of the same year, a Ritterstube, antechamber, bedchamber, and two cabinets.[96]

When Max Emanuel decided to establish the inner north pavilion as his lodging after his return from exile, he created a single apartment on the piano nobile by having the corridor cut back to create a large anteroom in the inner corner on the court side (plan E, 11–16). In the *Ausführliche Relation* of 1723, this room is called the Saal.[97] The elector had an antechamber, bedchamber, and cabinet, facing the garden, and the Geheimes Rats-Zimmer in the center of the court side.[98] This last room was the equivalent of the Grosses Cabinet. Upstairs, Max Emanuel had another apartment of four rooms along the garden (the apartment later occupied by the margravine).

When on occasion an ambassador was granted a public audience at Nymphenburg, the gallery, the first anteroom of the apartment in the middle pavilion, and the main hall could be brought into play to function as additional anterooms. In 1741, a French ambassador, the Maréchal de Belle-Isle, was received in public at Nymphenburg. Belle-Isle was lodged in the palace (a rare honor) and was conducted by the Obristhofmarschall from his guest apartment on the third floor of the inner south pavilion through the south gallery and the main hall and into the north gallery. Here he was greeted by the Obristkämmerer, who in the Residenz normally greeted ambassadors in the Ritterstube. The Obristkämmerer led him into the antechamber of the elector's apartment, where the elector greeted him and conducted him into the Grosses Cabinet der Malereien (large cabinet of paintings) for the audience. The Hartschier guard stood at attention in the galleries and the Trabanten guard in the Hauptsaal during the audience.[99]

The main floor of the inner south pavilion underwent a similar renovation to make a single apartment out of the earlier pair of apartments. This change was probably made under Karl Albrecht, when the electress apparently occupied this part of the palace.[100] Maria Anna Sophia lived here during the following reign. The arrangement of rooms was much the same as that of Max Emanuel's apartment on the opposite side of the palace. The large corner room was called the Ritter-Sällel in the 1751 furniture inventory; the center room on the court side was called the Grosses Cabinet or mirror room in the 1751 inventory and the music room in the 1769 inventory. Along the garden were an antechamber, bedchamber, and cabinet.

A frustrating feature of the Nymphenburg furniture inventories is the lack of consistency in room designations. In the 1751 inventory, for example, the first room of the north apartment in the middle pavilion is called Vorzimmer or Ritterstube, while the corresponding room of the south apartment is called Claines Sällel vor dem Apartament (small room in front of the apartment). In the 1769 inventory, both rooms are called Saletl. The 1719 inventory lists the rooms of Max Emanuel's upper apartment as antechamber, audience chamber, bedchamber and cabinet; in the *Ausführliche Relation* of 1723, however, the audience chamber is described as a room for music. This inconsistency probably results not from any uncertainty about the purpose of these rooms nor from radical changes in function over short periods of time, but instead from the fact that in the country houses—more than in the Residenz—rooms served multiple functions.

The sanctity of the private realm is reflected architecturally in another characteristic of the apartments in the Residenz. Virtually all of them are organized into pairs, in such a way that the private rooms of the two component apartments are contiguous, meeting in most cases in the center of a linear building tract. The two apartments are approached from opposite ends, via the Säle or guard chambers located more or less at the points of juncture between building tracts. In this way, private communication between the apartments of a married couple could be maintained without the necessity of passing through a Saal, which might at any time be crowded with persons of all ranks. Karl Eusebius von Liechtenstein wrote in his *Werk von der Architektur* that it was imperative that the apartments of the family head and his spouse should be continuous. "Communication must not be impeded by a staircase or a place for servants. The owner and his wife should be able at all times to meet without being observed by others." [101]

This parti is most evident in the Trierzimmer (plan B, 29–35), the rooms above the Antiquarium (plan D. 23–36), and the Charlottenzimmer, all of which Wening describes as double apartments. It is also seen in the apartments of the elector and electress, where the private rooms meet back-to-back along the Residenzgarten (plan B, 4–14). The construction of the Alexanderzimmer resulted in the separation of the inner rooms through the insertion of the Sommerzimmer, a suite of assembly rooms serving as the setting for relatively exclusive receptions (plan C).

The back-to-back parti was later restored with the construction of the Reiche Zimmer (plan D, 3–18). In this context we should also take note of the passage along the north side of the Grottenhof (plan B, 18), by which the elector could proceed to the Hofkapelle without having to pass through the R.tterstube and Herkules-Saal.

This parti was not unique to the Munich Residenz. In the Hofburg, the apartments of the emperor and empress met back-to-back in the center of the Leopold wing. This characteristic is also seen in many, although by no means all, Residenzschlösser elsewhere in Germany.

In the course of the seventeenth century, the scheme of planning houses with a Saal in the center and apartments to either side—an idea whose derivation is both French and Italian—took hold in Germany. The advantage of the scheme was primarily architectural. A monumental interior space in the center allowed an accent on the exterior capable of asserting its presence over axially planned surroundings. Small country houses in which the program called for only one Saal and one or two apartments could hardly be planned otherwise. In houses such as Alt-Schleissheim, the original villa at Nymphenburg, or Lustheim, the Saal in the center posed no functional problem. Entrée to these houses was restricted, and these Säle were not guard chambers frequented by lackeys, but Festsäle in which the Herrschaften and their guests banqueted and danced.

The scheme could present problems when applied to a larger house. Neu-Schleissheim is a case in point. As the project grew in size and assumed the dimensions of a major residence, the central Saal of the early phases—which was probably chiefly an architectural response to Lustheim and Alt-Schleissheim—was retained. In Zuccalli's project of 1700, the Saal had become, at least in Joseph Clemens's opinion, problematic. The further modifications to the plan of the corps-de-logis seen in subsequent drawings may be interpreted as an attempt to rectify the situation.

In his critique of the project, Joseph Clemens pointed out that the Saal, which extended through the entire depth of the corps-de-logis and formed the only means of approach to the apartments of the elector and electress, interrupted communication between the apartments. The Saal would be a room always filled with "a thousand different persons"; and it was a pity, in his opinion, that the best view of the garden should be enjoyed by lackeys. He therefore proposed certain changes, with the intention that "the whole facade facing the garden . . . will be entirely for Your Electoral Highness and for Madame the Electress." Sketches attached to his letter have apparently been lost, and we can only attempt to reconstruct his proposals by reading between the lines. He did not specifically suggest creating the gallery that appears in the later drawings, but wrote that he had left the salon "so that Your Electoral Highness may use it for yourself and for those you are pleased to admit, and when you wish to give some fête." He proposed pulling Zuccalli's two staircases in from the corners of the courtyard and placing them adjacent to the salon or at least nearer to it. Before the anterooms of the apartments he placed a "large salon that opens to the apartment": one on one side for the elector and "a similar salon for the apartment of Madame the Electress" on the other.[102] Space for these two large salons would seem to exist only on the court side of the corps-de-logis.

Two slightly later plan drawings of the piano nobile (fig. 26) seem to reflect Joseph Clemens's intentions. On both plans it is possible to enter the antechambers of the apartments directly from large rooms at the head of the staircases on the court side. Along the garden there would then be only antechambers—rooms to which entrée was highly exclusive—while along the court would be rooms to which entrée was more general. The installation of a gallery in front of the Saal on the garden side would seem to be an obvious next step in the creation of a suite of rooms at the center of the palace that could be used for festivities and social functions. Versailles may have served as inspiration. From around 1680, when the Galerie des Glaces was built on the site of the earlier terrace, to 1701, when Louis XIV moved his bedchamber onto the axis of the palace, a similar configuration of central salon and gallery existed at the French royal residence.[103]

A pair of lateral Säle along the court facade did not form part of the plan of Schleissheim as executed. It was not possible to enter the apartments without passing through the main hall. This suggests that the main hall was intended to function as a guard chamber, as well as a Festsaal. Flanking the main hall on the north was a dining room (the Viktoriensaal), through which it was possible to enter the north apartment. The gallery would have had to serve as a shared outer antechamber for the two apartments.

There is evidence of a continued desire to keep servants out of the central Säle. In his estimate of April 6, 1719, detailing the work necessary to complete the corps-de-logis, Effner mentioned a room that he called "antechamber for liveried servants." He noted that a partition wall was to be erected in this room and that part of the room was to be turned into a staircase (with an iron railing) extending through all floors.[104] This description fits the small staircases adjacent to the main staircase on the south and to the dining room on the north, and suggests that the rooms in these locations were meant to function as waiting rooms for servants.[105]

As things turned out, the problem identified by Joseph Clemens was hardly critical, since Schleissheim was never used much. Under Karl Albrecht and Max III Joseph, the elector's apartment was located not in the south wing on the piano nobile, where Max Emanuel had planned it, but in the north wing on the ground floor. This meant that anyone waiting on the elector had no need to climb the stairs to the upper floor. Until 1772, when it was redecorated as the new dining room, the ground-floor Saal flanking the vestibule on the north functioned as a guard chamber. The adjacent north garden hall (which is today called the music or billiard room) is labeled Hartschier-Stube on Altmannshofner's plan of 1812 (fig. 27). The electress's apartment was directly above the elector's on the piano nobile, so that private communication existed between the two apartments via back staircases.[106]

Chapter Four

5

Elements of Everyday Life

Julius Bernhard Von Rohr—who, like other eighteenth-century writers on Hofwesen, found it expedient to approach his subject by creating exhaustive taxonomies—divided the courts of Europe into two types in terms of day-to-day existence: orderly courts and disorderly courts. At the former, fixed schedules prevailed that allowed ample time for the conduct of state business. At the latter, the pursuit of pleasure ruled the day and intruded on business to an unpardonable degree. "Night is turned into day, and day into night; and one spends a large part of the time that should be devoted to rest in eating, drinking, gambling, dancing, and other divertissements, often sleeping until midday." Von Rohr gives examples of the first type. The imperial court was a model of orderliness, particularly under Ferdinand II and Leopold I, as was the court of Louis XIV. Among the minor princes of the empire, Joachim of Anhalt and Ernst of Saxe-Gotha had distinguished themselves. The court of Bavaria was not among those von Rohr mentions. Of the second type, the only example is one so distant in time that its citation could have offended nobody: Emperor Domitian, who spent hours on end locked in his room, absorbed in the pleasure of killing flies with a silver dagger.[1]

The full and vigorous social schedule that prevailed at the Bavarian court in the eighteenth century did, as we have seen in previous chapters, sometimes take precedence over business. The evidence for this comes not only from foreign observers, but also from internal sources. A weekly order of business issued by Karl Albrecht in 1743 concluded with the blanket disclaimer that if and when—on holidays and gala days or when there was a hunt or other "obstacle"—conferences and meetings could not be held, changes would be promptly announced.[2] The round of festivities and receptions did not, however, create such chaos that certain generalizations about daily schedules cannot be drawn.

In the seventeenth century, the day began and ended somewhat earlier than it would in the eighteenth. The first fixed point of the day was the elector's Lever (although he might have been up for several hours before this event), after which he went directly to mass. Morning mass was held every day of the year, whether the court was in residence in Munich or in the country. When illness prevented him from attending mass in the court chapel, the elector heard it in his room or in his private oratory. Mass was followed almost immediately by dinner, the first substantial meal of the day. In the early-to-mid seventeenth century, mass was normally held at nine and dinner at ten.[3] In a decree of 1688 regarding the daily schedule at court, Max Emanuel fixed the hour for mass at eleven on ordinary days and ten on Sundays and holidays (presumably because the service was more elaborate). The dinner hour was set at 11:30; this pertained whether dinner was taken in public or in private.[4]

In the eighteenth century, the dinner hour became still later, usually around one in the afternoon.[5] Dinner might last for several hours—particularly if the elector dined in company with the gentlemen of his suite or with male guests, when there was sometimes heavy drinking.[6] The morning mass was held either immediately before dinner or somewhat earlier in the day, leaving several hours that could be devoted to conferences, audiences, or a short hunt.[7] On Sundays, holidays, and gala days, dinner was usually held in public, and the court assembled beforehand in the anterooms to wait on the Herrschaften before accompanying them to the table. This assembly was known as the Cour-Zeit.

The hour of the evening meal was also fixed. In the early to mid-seventeenth century, supper was held at six.[8] It was preceded by the evening vesper service. Coulanges wrote in 1657 that vespers were held every day. In the eighteenth century, evening services were held less frequently, usually only on Sundays and holidays. During Lent, these services were often very time-consuming. Under Maximilian and during the early reign of Ferdinand Maria, when the schedule of festivities and social functions at court was sparse, the hour for retiring was eight to ten.[9] The 1589 Kammerordnung tells us that the duke's Coucher took place at nine in summer and eight in winter.[10]

In the eighteenth century, however, eight to ten was the normal supper hour.[11] The afternoon was more often than not spent in hunting or riding. During certain seasons, the Herrschaften hunted every day of the week. On more ambitious hunts, which might last the whole day, dinner was often taken in the field. Afternoon conferences and audiences were usually held late, around four or five. The evening hours, from five or six until supper, were the time for festivities and social functions—

theater, opera, Appartements, and Accademies. The court gathered beforehand in the anterooms, where a short Cour-Zeit was held, and then proceeded to the function. Afterwards, supper was taken in company, usually with the ladies dining at the table of the Herrschaften and the gentlemen at a table nearby. On days when no festivity or assembly was held, the Herrschaften spent the evening quietly, together with the members of their immediate suites, and supped in private. During the carnival season, balls and banquets might last until all hours, and the following day would not begin until the afternoon.

Court Attendance

For the officers and gentlemen of the prince's household, attendance at court was the most fundamental activity of the day. Waiting in the antechambers monopolized the time of the zealous courtier. This was one of the less enviable aspects of court life. "I know courtiers," wrote the philosopher Christian Wolff, "for whom time passes very slowly in the antechambers of their lords. If life weren't made moderately tolerable by conversation, billiards, riding, and cards, they would surely die of boredom. It is a bad *métier* to be a *pilier de l'antichambre*." [12]

The courtiers who waited on the prince were dependent on his whim. If he was not inclined to be punctual, or if he chose to sleep late in the morning, then they had no alternative but to wait. Max Emanuel seems often to have imposed on the good will of his suite in this way. The decree of 1688 mentioned above calls attention to the fact that the Kämmerer had recently become very disorderly in their attendance. They were not to blame for this, however, as the elector had himself not been keeping regular hours. He resolved to do better in the future and wished the Kämmerer to follow suit. [13] Conte Lantery reported to Turin that on Ash Wednesday of 1683, Max Emanuel slept so late after a wild ball the evening before that the gentlemen in the antechamber began playing cards in order to pass the time. When the elector finally appeared, he joined in, and the company became so absorbed in the sport that the games were continued until well into the evening. [14] Karl Theodor, on the other hand, had a reputation for punctuality in all things. "One could be certain," wrote Stephan Freiherr von Stengel, "never to have to wait long in his antechambers. Only in extraordinary circumstances would one have to waste even a quarter of an hour waiting for him." [15]

Courtiers waited on the prince to perform the services expected of them by virtue of the offices they held. On ceremonial occasions—either state ceremonies (Huldigungen, investitures, public receptions of envoys or visiting princes, weddings, baptisms, funerals) or domestic ceremonies (public dinners)—they were required to appear to perform particular ceremonial duties or simply to lend the proceedings greater luster by their presence. State occasions might require the attendance of not only the court nobility—the nobility in the prince's service—but also his vassals.[16]

The officers of the elector's personal household, the Kämmerer, were required to wait on him at certain points during the day, to participate in his Lever and Coucher, to accompany him to and from chapel, and to be present at dinner and supper, whether public or private. The office of Kämmerer conferred a particularly privileged rank on its bearer and distinguished him from the mass of courtiers.[17] It was the highest distinction that the elector could grant a courtier, other than one of the high court offices. As the Kämmerer were responsible for the elector's daily service, the office offered them direct access to his person, as well as entrée to the antechamber—the privileged place of waiting in the hierarchy of anterooms. The symbol of their office was the golden Kammer key, which they were expected to wear when they had court service.

The elector could confer the office of Kämmerer as freely as he wished. Over the course of the seventeenth and eighteenth centuries, as the idea took hold that a numerous court was a reflection of the magnificence of the prince, the ranks of the Kämmerer swelled, reaching a peak in the second half of the eighteenth century—which Moser termed "this Cammer-Herrn-Seculo."[18] A list of the Bavarian household from 1615 has 12 Kämmerer; in 1667, Pallavicino noted that the elector had 130.[19] The annual Hofkalender list 236 Kämmerer in 1738, 332 in 1769, and 415 in 1781.[20] The majority of them were merely "titular" Kämmerer, whose names fill the Hofkalender like a Who's Who of the southern German nobility. For these, the title was purely honorary, with neither service nor salary attached. As their number increased, the title lost prestige. Moser noted that at the imperial court it was very easy to obtain the Kammer key, as long as one was of gentle birth and reasonably well-to-do; he quotes a Viennese adage to the effect that although it was a disgrace not to have the golden key, it was also no honor to have it.[21] In 1668, Conte Galeazzo Gualdo Priorato listed 20 Kämmerer at the Bavarian court, so that we may assume that of the 130 listed by Pallavicino, approximately 110 were "titular."[22] Of the 236 Kämmerer in 1738, only 97 are listed as actually in service. In 1782, Lorenz Westenrieder noted that the elector had 96 Kämmerer.[23] The Kämmerer served on a rotating basis. In the eighteenth century, the tours of duty changed each week. At all times there were two Kämmerer in "primary service" as well as a certain number in "secondary service." On important occasions, all the Kämmerer in service were summoned to appear.[24]

For the Kämmerer having service, attendance in the antechamber was a duty and not a pastime. They were expected to appear punctually—in fact, often well in advance of the time that their services were required—and to maintain an attitude of dignified attentiveness: "In Our Anticamera, no one shall have his hat on . . . excepting Fürstenpersonen. . . . In the presence of Our Obristhofmeister and Our Obristkämmerer, but especially when nobility are in attendance, Our Kämmerer, as also all others who have Accessum, should refrain from walking up and down; should never turn their backs to Our high officers, much less to the nobility; and should never sit down."[25] The 1739 Aufwartungs-Ordnung contains the explicit provision that the tabourets that had "crept into the antechamber" were to be immediately removed (the banquettes could stay). The Kämmerer often played cards in the antechamber, despite the fact that this was forbidden. When the elector, visiting princes, or their envoys passed through the antechamber, the Kämmerer stood in two lines forming a lane.[26]

On Sundays, holidays, and gala days, as well as regularly on certain other days of the week, the court appeared in full force in the anterooms at appointed hours—normally before dinner or before a comedy, opera, Appartement, or other evening divertissement. All those who were *hoffähig* (including, of course, "titular" Kämmerer) might appear, and foreigners of standing were presented to the elector and the other Herrschaften. These days were called Aufwartstagen; the appointed hour was known as the Cour-Zeit or simply "the hour." Moser wrote that the ordinary meaning of *Cour* was "the daily attendance of the court at the usual hour, normally just before dinner. Nobles and others who have some purpose in appearing may attend. . . . When the prince appears, he has the foreigners presented to him and speaks with this and that person; and after about half an hour, the Cour is at an end."[27] The Herrschaften and court then proceeded to the public dinner or to the evening's divertissement. Before a special ceremony—a wedding or baptism in the Hofkapelle, for example, or a ceremony outside the Residenz (such as a service in one of the city churches)—the court assembled in the anterooms in order to accompany the Herrschaften in procession to the place where the ceremony was to be held. At the wedding of Maria Antonia Walburga in 1747, the ladies were ordered to assemble in the elector's rooms above the Antiquarium and the ministers, gentlemen, and councillors in the Reiche Zimmer, "each in the place appropriate to his *Caracter*."[28] The Saxon ambassador was to wait in the Grosses Cabinet of the

Reiche Zimmer, where the two younger princesses and the two duchesses were also to appear. The elector and the other Herrschaften would assemble in the elector's room with the ladies. The entire assembly then processed via the Herkules-Saal, the corridor in the story of the Hofdamen, and the Hartschiersaal to the Hofkapelle, the Herrschaften preceded by the court. When the ceremony was over, everyone returned to the elector's room, where the ladies and gentlemen paid their compliments and were permitted to kiss the hands of the bride and the other Herrschaften.[29] The company stayed there until it was time to attend the state dinner in the Ritterstube; then everyone returned to the Reiche Zimmer before proceeding to the Herkules-Saal for the ceremonial ball.

On Sundays, holidays, and gala days that occurred on the birthdays and name days of the electoral family and its relatives, as well as at special ceremonies, the court appeared in full court dress. The institution of gala on birthdays and name days was introduced by Max Emanuel in the mid-1680s, following the practices of the imperial court. The pretext for this was probably the arrival in 1685 of Max Emanuel's Habsburg wife, Maria Antonia.[30] In the eighteenth century, gala days were more numerous in Munich than in Vienna, as the Bavarian court observed not only the birthdays and name days of the immediate family, but also those of its relatives by marriage, particularly those of the imperial family. Keyssler wrote in 1729: "Because the family is so extensive and because of its connections with the imperial house, there are at present thirty three gala days at the Bavarian court. The number is increasing, much to the dismay of those who do not wish to appear often in the same clothes, but who are not in a position to lay out great sums of money for such things."[31]

In 1774, Max III Joseph sharply reduced the number of gala days, apparently in the expectation that easing the dress code would make it possible for courtiers of slimmer means to appear at court more frequently. The Margravine of Baden-Baden recorded in her diary on December 20, 1773, that the electress had told her that "except for Christmas, Easter, Pentecost, Corpus Christi, the two festivals of the order [of St. George], and New Year's Day, all festival celebrations will be abolished next year."[32] Eventually, it was decided to limit gala days even further, to only New Year's and Corpus Christi, as we learn in an imperial diplomatic report of June 7, 1774.[33] The relaxation of the dress code did not apply to all courtiers. A memorandum regarding the abolition of gala contains the recommendation that unmarried ladies should continue to appear at the Appartements on Christmas, Easter, and the two celebrations of the order in court dress, but that elderly and pregnant ladies, as well as those who had no court dress, might be permitted to appear in less elaborate Appartements dress.[34]

During Cour-Zeiten and at other times when he passed through the anterooms, the elector made himself accessible to persons who wished to speak with him, although it was necessary to request a private audience through the proper channels if one wished to speak with him privately. On the way to and from chapel in the morning, the elector heard petitions from a wide variety of persons. Hainhofer noted during his 1612 visit in Munich that Maximilian "hears mass every morning and . . . takes Supplicationes from his poor subjects on the way."[35] On September 27, Hainhofer had a private audience with the duke and told him, among other things, of a friend "waiting outside" who was eager to offer Maximilian his services as an expert in mining. Maximilian replied that the friend should hand him a memorial the next morning on his way to mass.[36] It was clearly not always easy to approach the elector in the crowded Ritterstube or Herkules-Saal, and the temptation to avail oneself of one's connections at court to procure a more favorable introduction must have been great.[37] The Kammerordnungen are replete with stipulations forbidding the Kämmerer to present petitions, either for themselves or for others, during their weekly service, or to attempt to introduce persons to the elector—particularly in the back rooms of the apartments (where, in fact, the Kämmerer themselves had entrée only when they had service). All persons desiring audience with the elector were directed to request it through the Obristkämmerer and no one else. The 1769 Kammerordnung contains the following provision:

> SCD has observed with great displeasure that for some time
> all sorts of *Sollicitanten* and other persons have been intro-
> duced into the small corridor or Retirade leading to his Pu-
> derzimmer [one of the back rooms of the Kurfürstenzimmer],
> or have found their way there alone; therefore SCD orders
> His Obristkämmerer to take the greatest care in the future
> that no one, except when expressly ordered, is to be permit-
> ted to enter this corridor, particularly at times when it
> pleases SCD to be present in his Puderzimmer.[38]

In 1777 Mozart spent several months in Munich attempting to secure a position at Max III Joseph's court and was fortunate in having friends to present him.

> At nine o'clock today [September 30] I went as arranged
> with M. Woschitka to Court. . . . I might have gone there

yesterday evening, but I did not want to tread on the toes of
M. Woschitka, who of his own accord had offered to procure me an audience with the elector. At ten o'clock he
showed me into a little narrow room [probably the irregularly shaped corridor leading from the small Ritterstube to
the Ritterstube of the Reiche Zimmer] through which the
elector was to pass on his way to hear Mass before going
to hunt.

The elector spoke very amiably with the composer, but the desired position was not forthcoming. Mozart was not immediately discouraged.
"M. Woschitka has advised me to put in an appearance at Court as often
as I can." [39]

Unlike the French court, with its tradition of grande entrée to the
king's antechamber, the German courts, including the imperial court,
based entrée on a hierarchy of rank corresponding to the hierarchy of
anterooms. Moser wrote: "With us, entrée presupposes a classification
and rank at court, by which entrance into the various rooms is permitted
according to their degree of dignity. Such regulations are fastidiously
observed at the large courts, and, indeed, at all well-organized courts." [40]

In France, all distinctions in rank were considered to disappear in the
presence of the sovereign. Distinctions existed, of course, and were clev-
erly fostered by Louis XIV to achieve political ends. They manifested
themselves not in spatial terms, however, but in such matters as the right
of the tabouret or the right to perform certain actions during court
ceremonies. Baillie suggests that rank at the French court tended to be
temporal rather than spatial in nature. The king's Lever and Coucher
proceeded in stages; while a wide range of courtiers had entrée to these
events, only those of higher standing participated in the preliminary
stages of the former and the advanced stages of the latter. [41]

The German princes, on the other hand, were themselves members of
a hierarchy, standing on various steps of the ladder of rank. In the Hofburg, they took their places in the Ratsstube (the highest place of waiting) along with the ranking officers of the imperial household and envoys
of the first class. [42] When the emperor paid them a visit, they were in
effect reduced to the status of courtiers in their own residences. A memorandum regarding the ceremonial to be observed on the emperor's visit
to Munich in 1653 contains the provision that on each morning during
the visit, the elector was to inquire when the emperor had been dressed
and then wait upon him in the antechamber (of the Kaiserzimmer) along
with the imperial officers and privy councillors. He was to go no farther

than the antechamber and was to wait there until the emperor called for him.[43] Matters of rank and precedence affected the German princes personally on many and various occasions and often created insurmountable difficulties in arranging meetings between them. This, as well as the principle of limited, selective access to the prince's person, undoubtedly contributed to the pervasiveness of distinctions in rank at the German courts. Here rank had a strong spatial presence in addition to its other manifestations.[44]

The most basic distinction in rank at the Bavarian court was that which granted the Kämmerer the exclusive privilege of entrée to the antechamber. Only they and those higher in rank—the Herrschaften, the high court officers, and the nobility—had entrée to this room. This is evident as early as the late sixteenth century, in the earliest existing Kammerordnungen from that period.[45] In 1667, Pallavicino called the elector's antechamber the "anticamera di Cavalieri della chiave d'oro."[46] The Kämmerer were not permitted, however, to proceed farther than the antechamber without being summoned. This was a privilege reserved for the Herrschaften, certain high court officers, and the Kämmerer and personal servants having weekly service.

Persons not holding the office of Kämmerer waited in the Ritterstube (plan B, 4) and the Herkules-Saal (plan B, 3). In the former room, wrote Hainhofer in 1611, the councillors (Räte) and officers waited until the duke came out of his room to accompany him to mass.[47] The lackeys—court lackeys, as well as those of courtiers, envoys, and foreign visitors—were forbidden to mingle with the officers waiting in the Ritterstube. A decree of 1717 states, "On days of attendance, the lackeys are no longer to appear in the Ritterstube, where it is fitting that only the electoral Truchsesse, councillors, and better persons shall enter."[48] This decree is to be interpreted not as a change from previous usage, but as an indication that the lackeys had been taking liberties.

By the eighteenth century, most German princes had begun issuing Aufwartungs-Ordnungen that spelled out in detail the hierarchy of entrée to the sequence of anterooms. Some of these Aufwartungs-Ordnungen were quite elaborate, none more so than that published by Joseph Clemens in 1717 for his Residenz in Bonn; Moser cites it as a model of explicitness.[49] In it, the body of attendants was pedantically divided into four groups—clerics, court officers and servants, military personnel, and foreign travelers—and distributed among six places of waiting: the vestibule under the staircase, the Vorsaal at the top of the staircase, the main (or guard) hall, the Ritterstube, the antechamber, and the audience chamber.[50] The Portiers stationed at the doors to each of the anterooms were responsible for seeing that no one entered farther than he should. If this happened, the portiers were to politely request that the offending person remove himself, and they were instructed to use force if necessary.[51]

The preface to this Ordnung states that it was based on the usages of the imperial and Bavarian courts. Unfortunately, no Aufwartungs-Ordnungen have survived from the reign of Max Emanuel or his predecessors. The most we have is the decree of 1688 mentioned above, which is addressed specifically to the Kämmerer. It states only that the Kämmerer were to wait in the antechamber (plan C, 3) and were not to enter the audience chamber (plan C, 4), but that those having weekly service should wait in the Grosses Cabinet, or inner audience chamber (plan C, 5).[52]

In 1739, shortly after the completion of the Reiche Zimmer, Karl Albrecht issued an Aufwartungs-Ordnung designed to take into account the increase in the number of anterooms. It constituted a continuation of previous practice in that it allowed the Truchsesse and councillors entrée to the Ritterstube (plan D, 2) and forbade the lackeys to associate with them in this room. The insertion of an additional room between bedchamber and antechamber (plan D, 3–7) prompted an innovation in the order of entrée to the antechambers: "It has most graciously pleased ICD, for the greater order of his court and the better arrangement of the Hof-Etikette, but principally for the greater splendor of His antechambers and the greater honor of those who enter them, to institute a fourfold division."[53]

This fourfold division regulated entrée to the first antechamber, second antechamber, Grosses Audienzzimmer, and Grosses Cabinet. The "increase in honor" affected above all the Kämmerer; they were granted entrée to the second antechamber, leaving the first antechamber for an unspecified body of gentlemen who had been "favored with the entrée."[54] The Grosses Audienzzimmer was reserved for court officers holding major posts, state ministers, noble privy councillors (non-noble privy councillors waited in the second antechamber with the Kämmerer), and the two Kämmerer having primary service. The Grosses Cabinet could be entered only by the Herrschaften, the most highly placed ministers (the Conferenz-Minister), and the holders of the four high court offices, as well as the Obristhofmeister of the other Herrschaften. Distinguished nobility—both those in electoral service and visiting or foreign princes—might also enter here.

This order of attendance was in effect, however, only on Sundays, holidays, and gala days. On ordinary days, the Grosses Audienzzimmer and the Grosses Cabinet were not opened, and the places of waiting were reduced to the two antechambers. Persons who had entrée to the latter two rooms were then to wait together in the first antechamber, and those having entrée to the Grosses Audienzzimmer and the Grosses Cabinet waited in the second antechamber.

Max III Joseph reiterated the provisions of this Ordnung in one of his own issued in 1747.[55] In 1756, he published a new Aufwartungs-Ordnung, in an attempt to coordinate the order of attendance with the new physical circumstances of the elector's apartment.[56] A fourfold division was retained in name, but it was pushed back to the Ritterstube, the two antechambers, and the audience chamber. The Grosses Cabinet no longer had any relevance as a place of waiting for the inner circle of persons surrounding the elector. Entrée to the Ritterstube remained as before, but the previous fourfold division was effectively reduced to a threefold division—achieved by assigning to the first antechamber both the group that had previously had entrée to the second antechamber and the group having entrée to the first antechamber. The first antechamber functioned as an antechamber to the private apartment via a door that gave it direct access to the small Ritterstube.[57] It thus made sense to reassign the Kämmerer to the first antechamber (although the Kämmerer having weekly service waited in the second antechamber). The audience chamber continued to be kept closed except on Sundays, holidays, and gala days; on ordinary days, those who had entrée to this room waited in the second antechamber. In the 1766 republication of the Aufwartungs-Ordnung, this rule was extended to the second antechamber as well.[58] On ordinary days, the entire court now waited in the Ritterstube and first antechamber. Only on special days, when receptions were held in the Parade-Zimmer, were the two additional places of waiting available.[59]

Lever and Coucher

Little information exists on the practice of the Lever and Coucher at the Bavarian court. Graf von Preysing, who as a high court officer was in a position to attend the Lever and Coucher, rarely mentioned these events in his diary. Sparse evidence need not surprise us, however. At the Bavarian court, as at many German courts that adhered to the principles of Spanish ceremonial, these were private ceremonies; they were attended only by officers and servants of the personal household, who had services to perform, as well as by a limited number of other high court officers.

The missing element—by contrast so predominant a characteristic of the Lever and Coucher of the French king—is the spectator.[60] The

Ankleiden (Lever) and Abziehen (Coucher) described in the late sixteenth-century and seventeenth-century Bavarian Kammerordnungen are extremely modest affairs. If we discount the presence of the Obristkämmerer and the Kämmerer, they have all the appearance of the toilette of a wealthy gentleman being assisted by his servants. The earlier Kammerordnungen (1589, 1597, and 1628) do not make it clear whether all the Kämmerer participated or only a certain few having service. Later, however, with the increase in the number of Kämmerer, the participants were limited to those having weekly service. This is the case in the 1654 Kammerordnung. The servants in attendance were valets (Kammerdiener), the barber (Leibbarbierer), the doctor (Leibmedico) if called for, pages (Kammeredelknaben), and wardrobe personnel. The Kammerordnungen do not specify which, if any, of the other court officers (who did not belong to the Kammer group) might have been present, perhaps to receive the orders of the day.

These ceremonies, however modest, were highly ritualized. The Kammerordnungen spell out in detail who was to perform which service at what point in the proceedings. According to the 1589 and 1597 Kammerordnungen, the duke's Ankleiden took place as follows: When the duke was ready to be dressed, the participants, who were waiting in the antechamber, entered the room together. The Obristkämmerer (or, in his absence, the eldest Kämmerer present) began by removing the duke's nightdress. After this, the barber, or one of the valets, massaged the duke with towels, while at the same time the Obristkämmerer handed him his comb so that the duke could comb his own hair and beard (presumably he also shaved at this point, if necessary). The Obristkämmerer then took the shirt from a valet, one of the Kämmerer took the stockings and shoes from another valet, and they helped the duke put on these articles of clothing. The Kämmerer then presented the basin, pitcher, and towels, and the duke washed his hands and rinsed his mouth. When he had finished, these items were returned to one of the valets. The Obristkämmerer then presented the doublet, which was tied by two Kämmerer. The dressing concluded with the coat, which was likewise presented by the Obristkämmerer; he also handed the duke the sword, belt, and Order of the Golden Fleece. If the duke demanded his tooth powder and hand soap (presumably while he was washing), they were also presented by the Obristkämmerer, who received them from the barber. Once dressed, the duke passed into his antechamber and from there to the chapel to hear mass. He was accompanied by the Kämmerer, who preceded him, and the Obristkämmerer, who followed. The Lever described in the 1628 and 1654 Kammerordnungen differs from the above only in minor details. The elector was not waited on by any of his officers before he had risen from bed; and, in fact, it was not until he had gone into the Zimmer or cabinet that the ceremony began.[61]

In the eighteenth century, some German princes, following the example of Louis XIV, refashioned their Levers and Couchers into ceremonies that were more elaborate and more public. Von Rohr, writing in 1729, noted that practices varied greatly from court to court.

> At some courts, [certain officers] are permitted to be present at the Lever once the prince has risen from bed, whereas others may enter only after he is half or completely dressed. Many princes are surrounded by lots of pages and valets while they dress, with a Cammer-Herr or Cammer-Junker also in attendance. Others have only a single servant on hand. Occasionally one finds persons of lower station whose service is more involved than that of great princes.[62]

The Kammerordnung published by Joseph Clemens in 1698 describes a fairly elaborate Lever and Coucher. Like its French model, the Lever, which was held in the bedchamber, began with the attendance of certain high court officers while the elector was still in bed and then proceeded in two stages. The entrées, however, were not as generous as at Versailles. Entrée to the Grand Lever was not open to all persons of standing who might wish to attend, but only to a specified list of court officers (who were not already present at the Petit Lever) and to all Kämmerer actually in service, privy councillors and the cathedral canons of Joseph Clemens's several bishoprics.[63] Emperor Charles VI's Lever, on the other hand, remained a very private ceremony.

> After His Imperial Majesty has risen from bed, he betakes himself, dressed in his nightgown, from his bedchamber into the next room. Here he is dressed by the valets and the Kämmerer having service, or by those in attendance. The valets perform the lesser services of putting on the shoes and stockings; the Kämmerer assist His Majesty with the shirt, clothes, and wig. It should be noted that no one may attend the Lever other than those who have this right, which in France is open to almost everyone, even as concerns the Petit Lever.[64]

No descriptions of the Lever of the Bavarian electors in the eighteenth century have been found. Preysing mentions a Petit Lever in two instances in 1719 and 1720, at Nymphenburg and when Max Emanuel was staying at Landshut.[65] In a memorandum (undated) containing a list of unresolved matters of etiquette during the summer Campagne at Nymphenburg, the question is raised whether the gentlemen should be given the opportunity to attend when the elector holds a Grosses Lever and not a Petit Lever, and whether this attendance should occur daily or only on certain days of the week.[66] These indications are not substantial enough to tell us whether there might now have been a two-part Lever (after the manner of Joseph Clemens's Lever) held at least in the Residenz, if not also in the country houses, or whether the Petit Lever was simply a reduced version (with a more exclusive entrée) of the Grand Lever, the former being the norm during the Campagne or on ordinary days of the week.

The "Entrée au Lever" published by Max III Joseph in the 1766 Aufwartungs-Ordnung and the 1769 Kammerordnung—an indication of usages obtaining only in the Residenz, not in the country houses—does not distinguish between a Grand Lever and a Petit Lever.[67] The list of officers granted entrée to the Lever is certainly greater than the number who would have been present at Maximilian's Lever. Included are the high court officers (down to the Vice-Obristfalkenmeister), all councillors at conferences (Conferenz-Räte) and all privy councillors who were Kämmerer in service, certain military officers, the officers of the Trabanten and Hartschier guards, and the two Kämmerer having primary service. Although somewhat more exclusive, this list corresponds generally to the list of officers having entrée to Joseph Clemens's Grand Lever.

We are also permitted no firm conclusions regarding where the Lever was held. The presence of a dressing room (Ankleidezimmer; plan C, 8) behind the bedchamber of the Alexanderzimmer may indicate that the Lever was held there, although the Ankleidezimmer may also have been a room in which the elector dressed or changed clothes without ceremony at other times of the day. The Reiche Zimmer also seem to have included a dressing room behind the bedchamber (plan D, 7).[68] The decree of 1688 addressed to the Kämmerer makes it clear, however, that the Lever did not take place in the Grosses Cabinet (plan C, 5), as the Kämmerer having primary and secondary service are instructed to wait in this room until the elector calls for them.[69] This leaves only the bedchamber (plan C, 6) or the Ankleidezimmer. The 1769 Kammerordnung suggests that the Lever took place in the bedchamber.[70]

Under Karl Theodor, the Lever became minimal, as we learn from Ludwig I's diaries.[71] Only a "kleines Lever" was held. Karl Theodor (who occupied the Kurfürstenzimmer; plan D, 23–28) went almost completely dressed into his dressing room, where the Obristkämmerer presented to him the last items of clothing. Then the actual Lever took place in an adjoining room; presumably there was nothing left to accomplish, other than to don his decorations, choose a handkerchief, or give the orders of the day. Under Max IV Joseph, a Lever was no longer possible, as the elector rose very early in the morning.[72]

Dining in Public and Private

"One must let the Germans eat and drink," wrote the Marquis de Villars, in describing to Louis XIV the difficulties he was encountering in securing Max Emanuel as an ally for France. "This is the only way to win their friendship and their esteem. It is an absolute necessity to maintain a lavish table."[73] Although it is wise to be suspicious of anything a Frenchman writes about Germany, we are compelled to take remarks such as this seriously. Similar observations regarding German gourmandism may be found in a wide variety of sources both native and foreign. Pöllnitz's accounts of the interminable drinking bouts he had to endure at Würzburg and Fulda are only the most colorful among the many descriptions of the excessive devotion to food and drink at the German courts.[74] We will concentrate here, however, not on the quantity or quality of food consumed, but on the manner in which one dined.

Dining was the only daily activity that, at least at the Bavarian court, spanned all three spheres of life—public, private, and social. The elector and his family dined privately in their rooms on ordinary days or when they were ill. On holidays and days of assembly, they dined in public, either alone in state or in company with their courtiers. At courts governed by Spanish ceremonial, dining was the only domestic event that was, on occasion, elevated to a public act. When the elector dined in state, the highest court officers waited on his table, and the persons privileged to watch were expected to maintain a reverent silence. Great variety existed in the pattern of dining—in the service, in the company, and in the place where dinner was taken. Depending on the circumstances, dinner could be, and was, taken in almost every room of the palace.

In the sixteenth century, as in previous centuries, it was the custom at the German courts for the prince to board his entire household in the Residenz.[75] In a pre-monetary economy, the provision of food and drink, as well as of shelter and clothing, was the only way in which retinue and servants could be recompensed for their services.[76] By the seventeenth century, the court had come to be somewhat conservative in this regard, as institutions and employers in other sectors of society began substituting a fixed salary for other kinds of compensation.[77]

Boarding several hundred persons every day involved considerable expense and offered abundant opportunity for corruption and abuse. In an attempt to keep things under control, the princes of the sixteenth century issued Speiseordnungen, specifying which persons were entitled to dine at court and the quantity and quality of the dishes they were to receive. Other typical stipulations provided that the Residenz gates were to be locked during meals, to prevent unauthorized persons from attaching themselves to the tables, and that access to the kitchens and cellars was to be strictly regulated, to curb the removal of provisions.[78]

Typically, three meals a day were provided—breakfast (Frühsuppe), dinner (Morgen- or Mittagsmahlzeit), and supper (Abendmahlzeit). Only dinner and supper, the two main meals of the day, were taken together by the prince and his household. Breakfast was eaten privately, the Herrschaften in their rooms and the personnel in their places of service—stables, chancellery, kitchen, cellar, etc.

The Speiseordnungen divided the mass of persons to be fed at dinner and supper into a hierarchy of tables, according to rank and occupation; the lower-ranking tables had eight to ten places each. A Bavarian Speiseordnung of 1589 specified by name and position the diners at twenty-one tables in the Neuveste and eight in the Alter Hof; four additional tables in the Neuveste were for persons who are named but whose professions are not stated.[79] In the Neuveste, there were tables for the Herrschaften, the duke's children and their Hofmeisterinnen, the Kämmerer, the ladies and female servants (three tables); the Kammer servants, the lackeys, the dwarfs, the singers, the pages, the chaplain, the guards, and the servants who cared for the silver. In the Alter Hof, the councillors, personnel of chancellery, stables, and hunt, and other kitchen officers and servants were boarded. Those who waited on the tables ate after the others and were known as Nachesser. One of the eight tables in the Alter Hof was a Nachesser table at which Truchsesse, servants who waited table, guards, and others ate. Often the Nachesser received only what remained from the regular tables.[80]

The quantity and quality of the food varied from table to table. When the duke and his family dined in public, with or without guests, "twenty four warm dishes in two courses" and a third course of cold dishes, as well as whatever wine was called for, were to be served to him. In a long paragraph, the Speiseordnung directs the kitchen head to take particular care that no "unclean or badly cooked dishes" appear at the duke's table. The table for the Kammer servants was provided with only seven warm dishes, in addition to cheese and fruit, and for each person "a half measure of wine." The Nachesser table in the Alter Hof received four dishes and for each person "his measure of beer."

By the late sixteenth century, many princes had begun to provide at least part of the household with a food allowance (Kostgeld) in place of board at court.[81] This novelty—which does not seem to have found favor with the retainers and servants, who were spoiled by the court's largesse—was introduced in Mecklenburg, for example, in 1574, for the greater part of the household; and somewhat later in Pomerania, where a Hofordnung of 1624 stipulated that from then on, only servants standing in the duke's direct service were to be boarded at court.[82] Kostgeld was introduced in Bavaria in 1607. In a decree of April 14, 1606, Maximilian announced his decision that "beginning on May 1 of next year, with the exception of the Herrschaften, other nobility, the ladies, pages, some of the Kammer servants, and a certain few other persons, no one, whoever he might be, is to be boarded at court, but is instead to receive an allowance."[83] That this decision was actually carried out is indicated by Hainhofer, who noted in 1611 that Maximilian gave his household an annual sum, "from which each of them must provide for himself." He remarked further that for this reason one saw very few tables set in the Ritterstube and the Dirnitz.[84]

When the court ate together at dinner or supper, the main body of servants ate in the several Dirnitzen.[85] The ladies and female servants of the Herrschaften had their separate dining rooms near their living quarters.[86] The officers privileged to dine at court also dined in a separate room devoted to this purpose. In 1700, Wening described a room in the upper story of the Neuveste (on the level of the Georgs-Saal; plan A), "where the court officers tend to dine."[87] At Nymphenburg (plan E), where it was necessary to board the entire household from the court kitchen during the summer Campagne, the officers' dining room (the Grüner Saal) was installed in the upper story of the kitchen in 1777–78.[88] The tables for the officers included the so-called Marschalls-Tafel—a table for miscellaneous officers, as well as officers and gentlemen belonging to the suites of visiting Herrschaften. Johann Jakob Moser, in his life of Karl Albrecht, wrote that the elector discontinued the institution of the Marschalls-Tafel on his accession, presumably in the interest of economizing.[89] This change probably did not apply to the country houses or during festive or ceremonial occasions. Graf Friedrich Ulrich Lynar, a Saxon who left an account of a day he spent at Nymphenburg in 1762, wrote that he dined at noon at a Marschalls-Tafel set for forty persons.[90]

Two modes of dining for the Herrschaften are distinguished in the late-sixteenth-century and seventeenth-century Speise- and Kammerordnungen. On certain days, the duke/elector dined privately in his bedchamber, alone or in the company of his family and guests. The Kämmerer and Kammerdiener waited on the table and ate afterwards.[91] Despite the private nature of dining in the Cammer, the service, like that at the Lever and Coucher, followed a prescribed ritual. On other days, the duke/elector dined "in publico," again either alone or with his family and visiting princes. The Kämmerer accompanied him to the table, waited until he had seated himself, and then went to their own table. Other court officers had service. The Kämmerer were expected to reappear when the duke/elector was ready to rise from the table and accompany him back to his room.

By the late sixteenth century, public dining at the Bavarian court had come to be regulated by a ceremonial based on the Spanish-imperial model.[92] This prescribed an elaborate, stately ritual, conducted with all the solemnity of a high mass. Once the dining table and the buffet had been prepared and set—acts that were performed, or at least supervised, by the high court officers—the dishes were brought in procession from the kitchen and placed on the buffet. The announcement was then made to the prince that all was ready, and he proceeded forth from his room. The highest court officers performed the services of carving the meat, tasting the dishes, decanting the wine, and pulling back the chair, as well as presenting the finger bowl and napkin, the dishes for the prince to inspect before each course was served, and his goblet when he gave a sign that he wished to drink. Most of these presentations were made on bended knee. At a certain point during the meal, usually when the prince sat down or when he took his first drink, those in attendance who had the right to dine at court retired to their own dinner in another room, returning to wait on the prince when he rose from the table. Those who were permitted to watch the prince dine, but not to dine at court, remained standing silently in the room through the entire meal. Normally there was dinner music, and the arrival of each course was accompanied by trumpet fanfares and drum rolls.

The details of this ritual, its elaborateness, and the status of the officers who had service varied from court to court and depended on the occasion. In Vienna, for example, the emperor dined in public in his Ritterstube only four times a year—on Christmas, Easter, Pentecost, and St. Andreas, in the company of the Knights of the Golden Fleece. On Sundays, other holidays, and gala days, he dined in public at midday with the empress, in the Ratsstube. The dishes were carried by Truchsesse and served by Kämmerer. When ambassadors were present, they left after the first drink. Nobody, not even an elector, dined at the emperor's table under these circumstances. Only when the emperor dined in public in the evening in the empress's apartment were other princes (as well as the young imperial Herrschaften) permitted to share the emperor's table.[93]

Watching the prince dine in public was a privilege enjoyed by all persons, both domestic and foreign, who were *hoffähig,* although on certain occasions the body of spectators might be restricted. Normally, however, foreigners of birth had only to announce themselves to the appropriate official (usually the Obristhofmarschall) in order to gain entrée. They were expected to be properly dressed and might not appear in overcoats (presumably for reasons of security). Sickly or deformed persons—whose revolting appearance, as von Rohr put it, might ruin the prince's appetite—were denied entrance.[94]

Although the Bavarian Spiese- and Kammerordnungen of the late sixteenth and seventeenth centuries state only that the duke/elector dined publicly "in front," we know from other sources that the public dining room was the Ritterstube. In 1611 Hainhofer wrote that from the Herkules-Saal (plan B, 3), "one enters a large Stube, the Ritterstube [plan B, 4], in which there is a long table under a baldachin at which the duke dines."[95] Hainhofer describes a public dinner that he witnessed there:

> On the third day [of my visit] I saw Duke Maximilian dine, together with his consort, his brother Duke Albrecht, and his sister Duchess Magdalena, as I was being shown around the Residenz in the morning. Twelve trumpets and two drums are sounded in the inner courtyard [probably the Brunnenhof] to announce dinner. In the room, various Trabanten stand at the two sides of the table; three noblemen who were expecting to be made Truchsesse waited on the table. Each princely person has his own cupbearer (Mundschenk); everything proceeds with great stillness. The pages who bear the dishes [wear blue and white uniforms]. The last place at the table was occupied by Wölfflein, an elderly fool, who sat on a painted chair.[96]

The Ritterstube remained the traditional public dining room through the eighteenth century, although it came to be used for this purpose only on extraordinary ceremonial occasions. During the wedding festivities of Maria Antonia Walburga in 1747, a ceremonial dinner was held in the elector's Ritterstube on the day of the wedding (June 13). We are fortunate in having a protocol that describes in detail the ceremonial observed.[97] The entire electoral family and the Saxon ambassador—nine persons in all—dined at a long table, the center third of which was elevated on a dais for the bride, the elector as procura groom, and Dowager

Empress Maria Amalie. Two buffets—one for the higher-ranking Herr-schaften, the other for the lower-ranking ones—were set up, and the orchestra was stationed at the opposite end of the room (toward the Herkules-Saal). The highest court officers, as well as the Kämmerer and their servants, had service. The Kämmerer, who were to change the plates during the entire meal of three courses, stayed in the room until the end. The high court officers and the spectators were free to leave after the first drink, if they wished. Similar "Ceremonientafel" were held in the Ritterstube at the procura weddings of Maria Anna Josepha in 1755 and Josepha Antonia in 1765.[98] On the day of his Erbhuldigung in 1727, Karl Albrecht dined in the Ritterstube after the ceremony in the Munich Rathaus. Thirty-six persons dined at a long, rectangular table; the representatives of the Estates sat on one side, the electoral officers on the other. The elector sat alone at the head of the table under a baldachin. The dinner held at Max III Joseph's Erbhuldigung in 1747 was exactly the same.[99]

Dining with this degree of solemnity, which was known in the eighteenth century as "Speisen en ceremonie," was rare.[100] On most days when public dining was held—Sundays, holidays, and gala days—one dined in lesser state, usually in the antechamber (plan B, 5) or audience chamber (plan B, 6). There are records from the 1630s and 1640s of Maximilian dining in his antechamber with visiting princes. Regarding a visit of the Duke of Württemberg in 1640, for example, we read, "When this prince was present at the elector's dinner in the Antecammer, the gilded bowls for sweets were used, and each time there was music." In 1645, the Bishop of Eichstätt dined once during his two-day visit, "with the elector, the electress, Duke Albrecht, and his son [probably Duke Albrecht Sigmund] in the Anticammer, whereby the Kämmerer had service."[101]

A memorandum of 1749 regarding the manner in which the name day of Empress Maria Theresia had been observed the year before states that in the evening "one had dined, as otherwise daily, in the elector's Anti-Cammer" (plan D, 24).[102] On May 13, 1756—the birthday of Maria Theresia—Maria Amalie was not feeling well and could not participate in the gala celebrations, she granted the imperial resident, Baron von Widmann, a private audience so that she could present him her compliments. Widmann reported home that "she excused herself that her indisposition prevented her from appearing at the Appartement and from dining in public in her audience chamber" (plan D, 32)."[103] A daily record of events kept during the double Saxon-Bavarian marriage in June and July of 1747 permits us to gain an idea of where public dining was held, as the protocolist was careful to note this information not only on the days of the major ceremonies, but also on the days in between.[104] A large number of public dinners were held during these two months, more than under normal circumstances. Most were held either in the elector's antechamber (plan D, 24) or in Maria Amalie's antechamber or audience chamber (plan D, 31–32). Only on the wedding days (June 13 and July 9), when ceremonial dinners were held in the Ritterstube (plan B, 4), and on the day of Max III Joseph's Erbhuldigung (July 17), when the Estates banquet took place at midday in the Ritterstube and a public Souper was held in the Kaisersaal (plan B, 20), did one dine in greater state.

The service was less elaborate when dinner was taken in the antechamber, and the body of persons having entrée to observe this event was probably more limited. In his Hofinstruktionsordnung of 1726, Clemens August of Cologne specified that although "all respectable people of both sexes" should be permitted to watch when he dined in public at midday, only those who otherwise had entrée to the antechamber should be admitted when he dined "in public in the evening in the usual manner."[105]

The Herrschaften dined in the antechambers either together ("en famille") or in company with their courtiers and eligible foreigners (Moser terms the latter case "open table").[106] Dining in company was very common in the eighteenth century and seems to have been what Preysing meant when he recorded a meal taken "à l'ordinaire."[107] The memorandum of 1773 or 1774 regarding the abolition of gala argues that the elector gave the nobility plenty of opportunity to appear around him at the "daily afternoon meal" (as well as at the Appartements, Accademies, and summer ladies' days).[108]

After an evening Appartement or theatrical performance, supper was always taken in company, at one or more tables. In his account of Max Emanuel's court around 1720, Johann Jakob Moser wrote that after such events, "the company went into another room, where there was a large and well-laden table. The elector, the princes, and the ladies took their places; and when places were left over, the gentlemen, foreigners, and sometimes even those having service could take them. No rank was observed at these meals, and the princes took the best places they could find."[109] A second table (Nebentafel) might also be set up for the gentlemen, as at supper it was almost always the ladies who had the right to dine at the elector's table. After an Appartement, one might also dine directly at the card tables. The Herrschaften dined privately with their suites, as well as publicly. J. J. Moser noted that on ordinary days they dined privately ("auf der Serviette") both at midday and in the evening, often admitting the ladies and gentlemen to their tables.[110]

The institution of *pêle-mêle* (also called *bonderie* or *bunte Reihe*), whereby observance of rank in the order of seating at the dinner table was suspended, afforded welcome relief from the strictures of ceremonial when dinner was taken in company. The dinner guests either sat down at the nearest place or drew lots beforehand. Although *pêle-mêle* seems to have been frequent, it was observed on a case-by-case basis and normally did not apply to the Herrschaften, who reserved the places of honor for themselves.[111] In 1774, however, Max III Joseph made *pêle-mêle* permanent and extended it to himself and his family. The Margravine of Baden-Baden was very upset when the elector announced this to her in advance, as she confided in her diary.[112] As a widowed sibling, her status at court was somewhat peripheral, and she seems to have been morbidly sensitive about slights to her dignity. Envoys sometimes neglected to pay her their compliments, and courtiers took liberties in entering her bedchamber; now she might have to sit at the bottom of the dinner table. But the elector took the trouble to explain his reasons. He revealed to her that the electors of the empire had made a pact among themselves that they would not yield precedence to other regnant princes when the latter visited them, but would seek to avoid disputes over precedence by "offering each visiting prince a *pêle-mêle*." This ruse was easily seen through, however, with the result that the princes were very reluctant to visit the electoral courts. Max III Joseph hoped that a permanent *pêle-mêle* including the Herrschaften as well as the court would solve the problem. He reassured the margravine by offering to arrange things during the first weeks so that she could sit as near him as possible. The permanent *pêle-mêle* was introduced on January 9, 1774.[113]

The custom of dining publicly in company in the Residenzschloss was the mark of a smaller court. Neither the emperor nor the French king ever dined in company in the Hofburg or at Versailles. Louis XIV dined in company (with the ladies of his court) only in his *maisons de plaisance*—at Marly or the Trianon. The supper parties that Louis XV held in his petits cabinets at Versailles were strictly private affairs.[114]

In the country houses, even Nymphenburg, public dining was exceptional.[115] In fact, we occasionally read in Preysing of the elector's traveling from the country to the Residenz to dine in public, just as he went in to hold audiences, and then returning later in the day.[116] When the Herrschaften were in residence in the country, the usual manner of dining was either "auf der Serviette" or in company. The service was less elaborate than in the Residenz, and a greater variety of persons might be invited to dine with the Herrschaften at their table. At Nymphenburg, the elector normally dined at midday with the gentlemen and supped two or three times a week with the ladies who had come out from Munich to attend the Appartement or Hofgarten.[117]

The first rooms that were specifically devoted to dining appear in the country houses. The inclusion of a dining room (Tafelzimmer) behind the Appartements-Saal on the ground floor of the inner north pavilion at Nymphenburg made perfect sense, as supper was always taken in company after the Appartements.[118] When the company was large enough or when the occasion demanded it, dinner or supper was taken in the Hauptsaal (plan E, 1) in the central pavilion.[119] The two smaller Säle of the principal apartments on the piano nobile were also used as dining rooms (plan E, 2, 6) The Viktoriensaal at Schleissheim (plan F, 3) was clearly in a position to function as an anteroom; and it was probably intended for public, as well as social, dining. That it was ever used for public dining is, of course, highly unlikely.[120]

The coupling of a reception room and a social dining room occurs in the Residenz with the construction of the Grüne Galerie (plan D, 10). An estimate of 1731 regarding work necessary to finish the Reiche Zimmer refers to one of the end salons of the gallery as Speise-Saal (plan D, 11).[121] The dining room erected next to the gallery in 1764 is called "the ordinary dining room" in several late-eighteenth-century sources, leaving us to conclude that it was here that Max III Joseph normally dined in company.[122]

Of all the Säle in the Residenz, the Kaisersaal (plan B, 20) and the Vierschimmelsaal (plan B, 22) figured most prominently as the setting for banquets and public dining on festive occasions, and not only when visiting princes were lodged in the Kaiser- or Trierzimmer. This remained the case throughout the two centuries of their existence, until they were demolished in 1799 to make way for the Hofgartenzimmer. The advantage they offered in the staging of festivities was that they could be used together. After a banquet in the Vierschimmelsaal, for example, one could proceed directly to a ball in the adjacent Kaisersaal.[123] Only seldom do we read of banquets held in the Herkules-Saal (plan D, 1) or the Schwarzer Saal (plan D, 29), although these rooms were probably used more frequently for this purpose before the erection of the Kaisersaal.[124] There are occasional records of a public dinner or banquet in the Antiquarium in the seventeenth century, but none in the eighteenth century.[125]

Certain ceremonial banquets traditionally took place in particular Säle. Wening describes a Tafelstube in the Neuveste (on an upper floor in the structure immediately east of the Hoher Stock; plan A) in which the Bavarian Estates were dined once a year.[126] The rites of the order of St.

Fig. 40. Munich, Residenz, a marriage ceremony in the Georgs-Saal of the Neuveste by Nikolaus Solis, engraving, n.d. (Bayerische Verwaltung der staatlichen Schlösser, Gärten und Seen, Munich)

George included an annual banquet in the Georgs-Saal (plan A, 2; fig. 40) immediately after the Ordensfest in the Georgskapelle (plan A, 3).[127] After the Georgs-Saal burned in 1750, these banquets were held in the elector's Ritterstube.[128]

During marriage celebrations or state visits of foreign princes, when the festivities often lasted as long as several weeks, one strove to introduce variety in the pattern of dining. Thus we read in a memorandum regarding the state visit of the three ecclesiastical electors of Mainz, Cologne, and Trier in 1665 or 1666 that "one had thought that dinner would be held once in the Kaisersaal, once in the Antiquarium, once by the Corallen Brunnen [in the Grottenhalle], and frequently in the Grosser Garten [Hofgarten], weather permitting."[129] Much of the variety was afforded by excursions to the country houses, where dinner could be taken in the Saal at Lustheim, at one of the Nymphenburg park pavilions, on board the Bucintoro, or on board barges on the canals at Nymphenburg or Schleissheim. During the state visit of the Elector of Trier in 1728, supper was held one evening at Nymphenburg on an enormous barge, which floated down the canal while the court dined at two tables—one set with eighty places, the other with thirty. A temporary kitchen had been set up in the bosquet alongside the canal. When the barge arrived at the far end of the canal, the company alighted and inspected a triumphal arch that had been erected around the cascade in honor of the visitor. Meanwhile, the barge was quickly converted into a ballroom, and the company danced while being transported back down the canal. On one morning during the visit the Herrschaften breakfasted at the Pagodenburg, on another at the Badenburg. Trips to Schleissheim, Lustheim, Fürstenried, and the Starnbergersee were also made the occasion for dining in ever-changing settings. On one of the evenings spent in Munich, a surprise supper was served in the opera house during the performance. At a certain point in the second act, there was knocking on the doors of the boxes, and servants carried in little tables and hampers of food and wine. A huge, laden table was lowered from the ceiling of the house for the spectators in the parterre. Once everyone had finished eating, the opera resumed.[130]

Festivities and Receptions

In the late seventeenth and eighteenth centuries, the social life of the court revolved around the series of divertissements—Appartements, Accademies, comedies, and operas—that occupied four or five evenings of the week and continued unabated year-round. Only during Lent was this social schedule curtailed drastically. On extraordinary state occasions and during carnival, court festivities increased in both variety and intensity.

The reigns of Ferdinand Maria, Max Emanuel, and Karl Albrecht constituted the great age of festival cycles staged for dynastic events and state visits of foreign princes.[131] The main features of these festivals were lavishly produced operas, ballets, and tournaments, which were usually thematically related to one another. These were only the high points in an agenda of balls, banquets, comedies, receptions, hunts, illuminations, parades, and, in winter, sleigh rides—as well as excursions to the country houses for more of the same. The Herrschaften and the court took an active role in the dramatic productions, often performing in the ballets themselves. The tournaments were held either in the Turnierhaus erected in 1661 at the west end of the Hofgarten or in one of the courtyards of the Residenz. They were no longer merely demonstrations of knightly sportsmanship, as in previous centuries, but elaborate allegories conducted according to a precise scenario, on such themes as the victory of princely virtue.[132]

The magnitude of these celebrations, which might last as long as several weeks, corresponded roughly to the importance of the event. Imperial visits and births and marriages of male heirs were celebrated with the greatest extravagance; visits of fellow princes of the Empire, births and marriages of younger children, and family birthdays occasioned somewhat less fanfare.[133] Festival cycles on state occasions became less frequent and less lavish in the second half of the eighteenth century. The tournament disappeared completely from the repertoire.[134] The last festival on a grand scale was that staged in 1765 for the marriage of Josepha Antonia with the future Emperor Joseph II.

In the late seventeenth and eighteenth centuries, carnival in Munich was celebrated from Twelfth Night (January 6) to Ash Wednesday (in February or March). The round of festivities at court was intense. In 1678, Conte Lantery reported to Turin that the carnival schedule that year included a ball every Sunday and a theatrical presentation twice weekly. A Bauernwirtschaft was celebrated and the carnival opera was repeated three times. When there was snow on the ground, sleigh rides were frequent.[135] The Margravine of Baden-Baden noted in her diary on January 9, 1774, that the weekly carnival schedule foresaw a ball on Sundays and Wednesdays, an opera on Mondays, an Accademie on Tuesdays and Thursdays, and a German comedy on Fridays.[136] Banquets and balls, which might last until dawn, were often held after these events. As the elector was the principal host to Munich society, most of the festivities took place in the Residenz; but the nobility also held balls, banquets, and Accademies in their homes, which the electoral family often attended.[137] The Redoutenhaus in the Prannerstrasse was another focus of carnival activity.

The festivities were held mostly in costume or at least masked, in order to circumvent ceremonial. The Bauernwirtschaft or Bauernhochzeit, a traditional German court festivity, was a regular feature of the carnival. At this, the elector and electress, costumed as an innkeeper and his wife, played host to the court, which appeared dressed as peasants (shepherds, farmers, hunters, millers, gardeners, etc.). The Bauernhochzeit was a variation on the Bauernwirtschaft in which two courtiers were chosen by lottery to play the roles of a peasant bride and groom. After a parade through the streets of Munich, the company returned to the Residenz for the wedding dinner and ball.[138] Carnival opened each year with the Königsmahl festival (also called the Königreichfest) held on Twelfth Night

(Dreikönigstag), a festivity that afforded relief from court ceremonial while at the same time parodying it. Several days beforehand, the Herrschaften and courtiers drew lots for the roles they were to play in the make-believe royal household. The elector usually ended up as a page or Kämmerer, while one of his gentlemen played the king. Like the Bauernhochzeit, the Königsmahl opened with a parade or sleigh ride through the city. The dinner that followed was conducted with the strictest observance of Spanish table ceremonial. Everyone played his role; the elector performed the services expected of him as a Kämmerer or page.[139]

The Appartements that Max Emanuel began holding in the mid-1680s were patterned quite closely on those held at the French court. There, as the Duc de Saint-Simon tells us in 1692, Appartements took place three times a week in winter; on three other evenings, plays were presented; and on Sundays there was nothing.

> What they called Appartement was a reception for the entire Court in the great suite of rooms that runs from one end of the long gallery to the ante-chamber of the chapel. It lasted from seven until ten in the evening, when the king sat down to supper. At first there was music, and then tables were prepared for all kinds of games. There was one for lansquenet, which Monseigneur and Monsieur always played, and another for billiards; in a word there was freedom to do as one pleased, to make up card-parties and to call for more tables when necessary. Beyond the room used for billiards there were refreshments, and each room was beautifully illuminated.[140]

The atmosphere was relaxed. Persons not ordinarily permitted to sit in the presence of the king and queen could do so if they were playing at one of the card tables: "The king, the queen, and all the royal family descend from their greatness to play with many people in the assembly who have never had that honor. The king goes from one table to another, and wishes no one to rise or to stop playing at his approach."[141]

What must be one of the earliest surviving descriptions of an Appartement at the Munich court was written by Conte Lantery on January 25, 1686:

> We see five or six rooms, one after the other, all beautifully adorned and illuminated, with various tables for gaming, while at the same time there is dancing in another room. Besides the ladies of the court, those of the city are also present, and all the gentlemen. This *conversazione* is held three days a week—Sunday, Tuesday, and Thursday. Large trays

of drinks of all sorts are carried around. On other evenings there is Italian comedy.[142]

In later years, the Appartements were held on different days of the week; in 1719 and 1720, according to Preysing's diaries, they occurred on Mondays and Thursdays. They were held during the winter season, when the court was in residence in Munich—normally from October or November to March. During the remainder of the year, Hofgärten replaced the Appartements. Hofgärten were merely Appartements held out-of-doors, in the Residenzgarten or the Hofgarten or at Nymphenburg. Often a Hofgarten was held in Munich when the Herrschaften were staying in the country, and they came into town to attend. Occasionally, Preysing gives a few details about an Appartement. On November 14, 1720, for example, he tells us that three rooms had been set up; in one there was music and in the other two, cards. On December 11, he noted that there had been seven "ombra" tables, one "Landsknecht" table, and two "pharaon" tables.[143]

The Appartements were held in the elector's apartment. This becomes clear from Preysing's diaries, where he occasionally notes that an Appartement was held elsewhere—"on the Kurfürstin's side," for example, or "with the duchess."[144] A list of stoves and fireplaces prepared in 1750 mentions that although under normal circumstances eleven stoves and two fireplaces were in operation in the elector's apartment, "when there is an Appartement, two additional fireplaces are lit."[145] Lantery describes the Appartements as taking place "in five or six rooms, one after the other." The suite of rooms that best meets this description is the Sommerzimmer (plan C, 10), a flight of four rooms facing the Grottenhof.[146] These rooms could well have been used in conjunction with the antechambers and the gallery facing the Residenzgarten. Preysing occasionally refers to rooms that he calls the Appartements-Zimmer. On February 12, 1719, for example, he recorded a "midday meal in the Appartements-Zimmern with the ladies." On January 5, 1721, he noted that there was card playing in the evening "on the side of the Appartements." The diaries also document the existence of what Preysing calls an Appartement-Stiege (Appartement staircase).[147] This can probably be identified as the staircase located between the audience chamber and the Grosses Cabinet on the overlay of the plan of 1616–30 (plan C, 5). This staircase was clearly in a position to provide access to the Sommerzimmer, although why such an Appartement-Stiege was necessary is not certain.

The erection of the Sommerzimmer provided Max Emanuel with a

Plate 1. Conversation Piece: The Electoral Families of Bavaria and Saxony at Various Amusements, by Peter Jakob Horemans, oil on canvas, 1761. (Bayerische Verwaltung der staatlichen Schlösser, Gärten und Seen, Munich)

Elector Max III Joseph, on the viewer's right at the red-draped table, playing cards.

Electress Maria Anna Sophia, sister of Friedrich Christian of Saxony, on the right at the coffee table, pouring coffee into a saucer.

Archbishop-Elector Clemens August of Cologne, uncle of Max III Joseph, playing the bass viol.

Cardinal Johann Theodor, uncle of Max III Joseph, playing cards.

Maria Antonia Walburga, sister of Max III Joseph, married to Friedrich Christian of Saxony, at the coffee table to her brother's left.

Electoral Prince Friedrich Christian of Saxony, in wheelchair.

Maria Anna Josepha, sister of Max III Joseph, playing the cembalo.

Josepha Antonia, sister of Max III Joseph, future wife of Emperor Joseph II, playing cards to her brother's right.

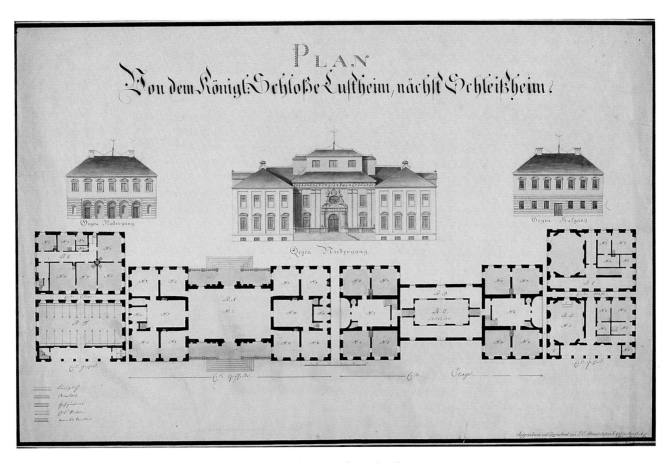

Plate 2. Schleissheim, Lustheim, plans and west elevations by J. C. Altmannshofner, drawing, 1812. (Bayerische Verwaltung der staatlichen Schlösser,
Gärten und Seen, Munich)

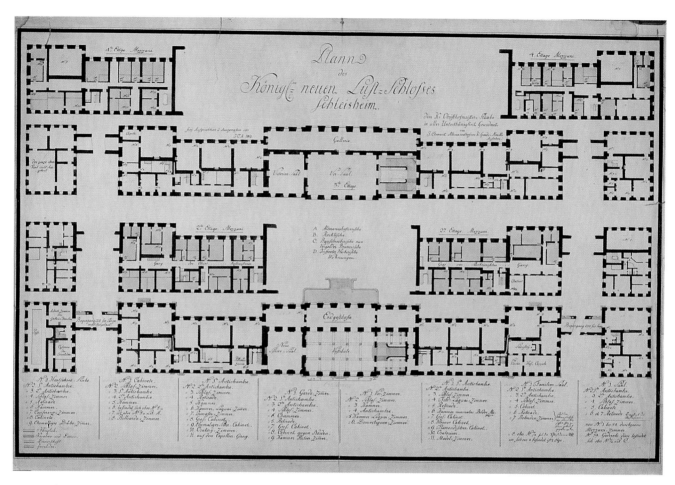

Plate 3. Schleissheim, Neu-Schleissheim, plans by J. C. Altmannshofner, drawing, 1812. East facade at top. (Bayerische Verwaltung der staatlichen Schlösser, Gärten und Seen, Munich)

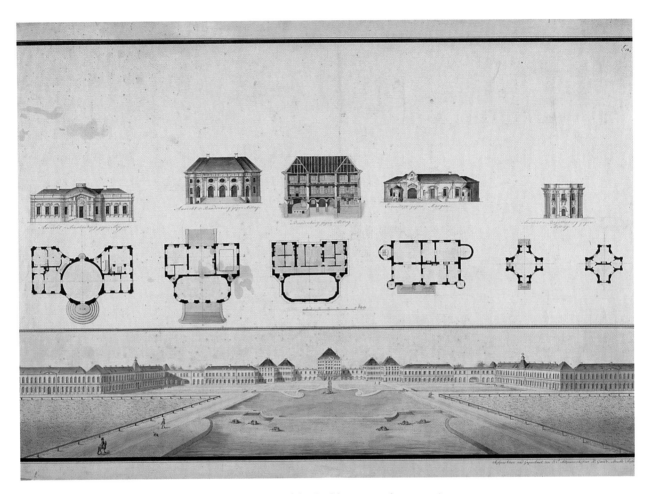

Plate 4. Nymphenburg, plans and elevations of the Parkburgen and perspective
view of court (east) facade of Schloss by J. C. Altmannshofner, drawing, 1812.
(Bayerische Verwaltung der staatlichen Schlösser, Gärten und Seen, Munich)

suite of reception rooms distinct from both the antechambers and the private living rooms of the apartment. The situation is analogous to that at Versailles after Louis XIV moved into the apartment along the south and west sides of the Cour de Marbre. The significant difference was that the Sommerzimmer were located in the private zone of the palace along the Residenzgarten, whereas the state apartment at Versailles was part of the path of circulation from the ambassadors' staircase and the chapel to the Galerie des Glaces.

When the Sommerzimmer were destroyed to make way for the private rooms of the Reiche Zimmer, the Grüne Galerie (plan D, 10) became the setting for the Appartements. The imperial staircase next to the gallery would probably have assumed whatever functions were served by the Appartement-Stiege. In 1781, Gottfried Edler von Rotenstein described the Grüne Galerie as the room where "the gentlemen and ladies assemble on gala days."[148] Other rooms were also opened during the Appartements, at least when they were held on gala days or on special occasions. After Max III Joseph established his private apartment above the Antiquarium, the entire suite of Parade-Zimmer along the Residenzgarten (plan D, 6–9) was often opened. In 1741, an Appartement held during the embassy of the Maréchal de Belle-Isle began with an inspection of the "downstairs gallery," which excited much admiration.[149] In 1752, at an Appartement during the state visit of the Elector and Electress Palatine, "all the rooms up to the Schatzkammer were magnificently illuminated. The empress's card table was set up . . . in the beautiful Grüne Galerie. The Schatzkammer was opened and shown to everyone from the Palatine entourage."[150]

Entrée to the Appartements was restricted generally to those gentlemen and ladies who were *kammermässig*—that is, those who had entrée to the antechambers of the elector and electress. Certain gradations of entrée also applied during the Appartements; the atmosphere seems to have been not quite as free as at Versailles. In the 1769 Kammerordnung, we read that gentlemen who did not have the rank of Kämmerer but did have entrée to the antechamber, and thus also to the Appartements, were not permitted to play cards and should not enter the "innermost chamber" where the Herrschaften were playing.[151] Under Karl Theodor, the privilege of attending the Appartements was extended to the Truchsesse, councillors, and certain additional military officers—who were likewise, according to the 1794 Kammerordnung, neither to play cards nor to enter the room where the Herrschaften played.[152]

Unlike the Appartement, the Accademie did not have its origin in court practices. Instead, it originated in the Italian cities—notably Venice, where public gambling casinos, called *ridotti,* offered entertainment not only to the nobility, but also to the middle classes. These were a special feature of the carnival season. In France, according to Florinus, such institutions were called *redoutes* or *accademies.*[153]

The Accademies that were held once or twice a week in winter during the eighteenth century were similar to the Appartements in that they featured gambling and music.[154] Music played a much greater role, however, and for this reason they were sometimes called *accademies de musique.* Baron von Widmann described this function to Maria Theresia in 1753 as "nothing more than an Appartement with continuous music throughout."[155] Karl Albrecht and his family were gifted musicians, and during his reign and that of Max III Joseph, the Herrschaften often performed in front of the court. At an Accademie held during the visit of the Elector of Trier in 1728, for example, the musical program (which followed the card playing) consisted of a lute duet played by the elector and electress, a flute solo by Duke Ferdinand, a lute solo by Ferdinand's young son Max, and a cantata sung by an Italian virtuoso.[156]

Entrée to the Accademies was more liberal than that to the Appartements. The 1794 Kammerordnung states that all persons of quality might appear (although only those having the key, as well as foreign envoys, were permitted to play cards).[157] For this reason, the Accademies were held not in the elector's apartment, but in one of the Festsäle, apparently most frequently in the Kaisersaal (plan B, 20). They were often held masked.

An excellent description of an Accademie is given by Freiherr von Hertling, a Palatine minister who kept a journal of his trip to Munich in 1785.

> At the appointed hour, my brother and I appeared at the Accademie. It was held in a very large Saal decorated *à l'antique.* The assembly was very numerous and consisted of thirty eight card tables, at which we counted some seventy ladies. We placed ourselves near the orchestra not far from the table where the elector was playing with the widowed electress [Maria Anna Sophia], the duchess [Clemens], the Fürstin von Fürstenberg, and the Gräfin von Riaucour. At a break in the game, the elector was so gracious as to approach us, and inquire after my indisposition. After a brief conversation, he returned to his game. We then spoke with Graf von Seeau [Intendant of the opera], whom I begged to secure us an audience with the duchess. Shortly thereafter, he

brought the duchess to us and she spoke with us most graciously for quite a while.[158]

The first Accademies in Munich were probably held not in the Residenz, but in the ballrooms established in the late 1680s by a Monsieur Dannet. Here one could gamble and dance, and admission was open to anyone who could afford the price.[159] Dannet's establishment was followed by the Redoutenhaus, erected in the Prannerstrasse in 1719 by another Frenchman, Duclos.[160] The Herrschaften visited the Redoutenhaus frequently, particularly during carnival. The earliest Accademies recorded by Preysing, in 1720 and 1721, were held here. On January 21, 1721, he wrote:

> At six o'clock, the *accademie de music* in the Redoutenhaus began. Here are admitted not only the nobility, but also officers and others, who come masked but must identify themselves at the door. There were three games of *pharon,* three of *ombra,* and one of *Landsknecht* whereby the music played continuously. This lasted until nine. At ten, the electoral prince gave a supper for fifteen persons in one of the downstairs rooms of the Redoutenhaus. This was over at one in the morning.[161]

Gaming tables were set up in the Redoutensaal itself, as well as in the balcony that ran around three sides of the room. Here balls and masquerades were also held. Light operas and ballets were presented on a stage attached to the Saal, while elsewhere in the building there were dining rooms, refreshment rooms, and drawing rooms (Gesellschafts-Zimmer). Serious dramatic works were seldom performed in the Redoutenhaus. Leopold Mozart, who was in Munich in 1774–75 during the production of Wolfgang's *La finta giardiniera,* complained to his wife:

> "Once the carnival is in full swing, only light and short operettas are performed on a small stage, which is rigged up in the Salle de Redoute. Here people gather in masks, here there are numbers of gaming tables and there is perpetual noise, conversation, and gambling. Nothing sensible is ever performed there, because nobody pays any attention."[162]

Verschaffelt's 1799 design for a "salle d'académie de musique, et de bal" for the Residenz—with its side galleries, apsidal podium, and subsidiary social rooms (a "salle de rafraîchissement" and two "parloirs")—clearly provided much the same accommodations as the Redoutensaal.[163] The

"salle d'académie" remained a project, but the destruction of the Kaisersaal made it necessary to find a new location for the Accademies. The
Herkules-Saal, which had lost its importance as a guard chamber, came
to be used for this purpose, or at least for the large Accademies. In
1814–16, it was redecorated and a spectators' gallery was installed at
one end.[164]

6

State Acts: Diplomatic Receptions and Audiences

Diplomatic receptions and audiences were the most common of the state ceremonies that took place at court, ceremonies that also included such acts as coronations, weddings, funerals, the rendering of homage, and the reception of visiting princes. The German princes, more than the sovereigns of major states, were in the habit of conducting diplomatic business through special, rather than permanent or resident, envoys; and they received in person representatives from a wider spectrum of political entities, even those as lowly as free imperial cities or cathedral chapters. This meant that public audiences were a frequent event at court.

A diplomatic reception utilized the spatial setting of the apartment more fully than most other ceremonies. Dining in public could be very elaborate, but it took place in only one room. When the Bavarian elector received princely visitors, he proceeded forth to the carriage at the bottom of the staircase or at least to the top of the staircase to greet them. This he did without regard for the status of the visitor relative to himself. When he received envoys, he proceeded forth a shorter distance or remained in the audience chamber and delegated the task of greeting the envoy to his high court officers. The status of the sovereign represented, the classification of the envoy, and the importance of the mission played a role in determining the exact agenda of the reception. The number of officers employed to greet the envoy and the places at which each greeted him were adjusted to reflect these factors. The court could be either fully or partially summoned to appear in the anterooms. The seventeenth and eighteenth centuries witnessed a tremendous increase in the elaboration of the reception and in its capacity to differentiate nuances in status and meaning. At its most ceremonious, the ritual of greeting was spread out over the entire path of approach from the staircase to the antechamber.

International Diplomacy

The importance of international diplomacy in the political world of seventeenth- and eighteenth-century Europe cannot be overestimated. Diplomacy was both an alternative and a complement to warfare, inasmuch as it could be an instrument for keeping the peace or for gaining political advantage. In either case, the nations of Europe, whether at war or peace, engaged in diplomatic interaction with an intensity unknown before. It was an age of congresses convened for years on end, of intricate networks of alliances, of diplomatic adventurers and secret agents, and—especially in the eighteenth century—of bedroom intrigue.

The urgency of all this is reflected in the inordinate interest taken in diplomatic ceremonial, which governed the public side of diplomatic exchange and was understood as a tangible expression of the formal relationships between sovereigns of widely varying rank. Ceremonial interaction obeyed its own imperatives—it was possible, for example, for two sovereigns technically at war with one another to exchange compliments through special ambassadors—and could have grave implications for international equilibrium. A case in point: Marie Antoinette's initial reluctance to address a few customary pleasantries in public to Madame du Barry so annoyed Louis XV that the continued existence of the *renversement des alliances* was jeopardized. Theoretical writers on diplomatic ceremonial took care to stress its importance. Friedrich Carl von Moser, in introducing the chapter on diplomatic audiences in his *Teutsches Hof-Recht* (1754–55), wrote, "This subject is among those that come up at court most frequently, that brings with it the most punctilios, and where it is most easy to offend or to compromise one's dignity, or to augment this by shrewd innovation."[1]

Most courts kept voluminous records regarding the reception of envoys, and there is probably more information to be had on this than on any other aspect of court life. Since the ruler was less free to tamper with tradition in his dealings with foreign princes than in dealings with his subjects, diplomatic ceremonial remained relatively resistant to arbitrary change.[2] Under Max III Joseph, whose reformist intentions prompted him in 1774 to simplify court etiquette by abolishing ranked seating at the dinner table and restricting the wearing of gala dress to only a few holidays, diplomatic receptions were nonetheless as elaborate as ever.

In the Western world, diplomacy as a political institution experienced its first florescence in Italy during the period 1200–1500.[3] In a country where numerous small, hostile states vied constantly for hegemony, the arts of negotiation, conspiracy, and espionage proved to be a less costly means of maintaining political stability than warfare. Diplomacy and warfare came to be held in equal regard as tools for achieving political ends; and the negotiator or agent, like the soldier, became a permanent figure at the Italian courts. Venice took much of the initiative in refining diplomatic techniques and practices; through its commercial contacts, it had profited from close observation of the highly sophisticated diplomatic machinery of the Byzantine Empire, with its set regulations for the conduct of envoys abroad and its elaborate codes of ceremonial for the reception of foreign embassies in Constantinople.[4]

Diplomacy took on a pan-European dimension toward the end of the fifteenth century, when France's violent intervention in Italian affairs threatened to have far-reaching consequences for the stability of the entire continent. Other countries, whose initial exposure to the diplomatic skills of the Italians came as a revelation, began to recognize the efficacy of diplomacy in regulating their affairs. France assumed the lead. Louis XI (reigned 1461–83), who appears in the memoirs of Philippe de Commnes as a skilled (though unscrupulous) tactician, is generally recognized as the first French ruler to have exploited diplomacy's possibilities as a political instrument. Under Louis XI's sixteenth- and seventeenth-century successors, organs of government were evolved to handle foreign affairs with relative efficiency; and a tradition arose of using literate, well-educated men in the diplomatic service—men who could bring a knowledge of history and jurisprudence to bear on their talents as negotiators and who could influence people by their cultivated manner. Several centuries of experience thus stood behind Louis XIV, who assigned his ambassadors central roles in his determined pursuit of a politics of magnificence and prestige. Under his reign, French diplomats successfully personified France's self-assurance abroad and took every opportunity to capitalize on the fascination of other princes with the image of the *Roi Soleil*. French diplomacy eventually replaced Italian as the model for the rest of Europe.

France's diplomatic superiority, which began to wane only in the first decades of the eighteenth century, was all the more striking in comparison to the situation at most other courts. In Brandenburg-Prussia, the admirable beginnings that the Great Elector, Frederick William (reigned 1640–88), made toward a competent diplomatic service were not continued by his two successors. It was not until the reign of Frederick the Great (1740–86) that Prussian diplomacy once again became active. At the imperial court, foreign affairs were directed by a cumbersome structure of committees, whose authority often overlapped and whose members were notoriously susceptible to bribery.[5] Austrian diplomacy first challenged French supremacy only toward mid-century—notably in the figure of Graf Kaunitz, a statesman of the highest caliber who began his career as a diplomat and masterminded the *renversement des alliances* in 1752. Kaunitz was a diplomat in the French manner—polished, articulate, grandiose. Although he was an exceptional figure, he was by no means alone. In the second half of the century, many courts were sending envoys fully the equals of their French colleagues.

Medieval diplomacy was characterized by the sending of special embassies to resolve problems on a case-by-case basis. Beginning in the fifteenth century, however, as contact between states increased, diplomacy came to be regarded as a continuous process serving the state's interests. Envoys and agents were relied upon to keep channels of negotiation open on a sustained basis and to provide a steady supply of information on the internal affairs of foreign courts. The volume of diplomatic missions increased dramatically during the late fifteenth and sixteenth centuries, and permanent embassies appeared. Certain historians have seen this latter development as the central issue in the formation of modern diplomacy, and there have been several authoritative German studies devoted to localizing the inception of this practice and charting its development.[6] Italy was the forerunner. Around the middle of the fifteenth century, the Italian states began to exchange permanent envoys among themselves; by 1500 several were sending such missions to countries north of the Alps.[7] Only very gradually was the practice adopted by other states. Permanent embassies did not become the norm until the nineteenth century. Even in the eighteenth century, states that had long been in the habit of exchanging permanent residents or agents still relied on special envoys for a wide variety of purposes.[8]

The amplified self-consciousness of rulers in the sixteenth and seventeenth centuries forced diplomacy into a representational mode, a development that coincided roughly with its emergence as a permanent institution. The diplomat became a public figure. If in the Renaissance he had been an agent—a "broker," in effect—in the seventeenth century he existed to personify the power and majesty of his master abroad.[9] In the conspicuous display of the ambassador, the absolutist state found its confirmation. "It is beyond dispute," wrote Abraham de Wicquefort, "that a good ambassador is also a theatrical personage; in order to succeed in this career, one must be something of an actor."[10] François de Callières, whose *De la manière de négocier avec les souverains* (1716) is the major state-ment of French diplomatic theory of the period, was of the same opinion:

> In order to maintain the dignity of this charge, he who holds
> it must cut a liberal and splendid figure. . . . His magnifi-
> cence should manifest itself in his entourage, his livery, his
> horses and carriages. At his table, cleanliness, abundance,
> and good taste should reign. He will give frequent recep-
> tions, at which the most important court officers, as well as
> the prince himself when he is so inclined, will appear. He
> should strive to appear in the prince's company as often as
> possible, but without importunity and with the most pleas-
> ant manner.[11]

Callières also claimed that abundant hospitality was a way of seducing the foreign court. Political ends could be achieved through a lavish table, since "the warmth of the wine often unravels important secrets."

More attention was now paid to social status in the selection of envoys. In the Middle Ages and up to the mid-sixteenth century, almost all dip-lomats had been middle-class in origin. Now, in cases where representa-tion was of concern, rulers chose men of noble birth and financial means—men who possessed dignity and social savoir faire and who were prepared to use their own resources to equip themselves with fitting magnificence. Where representation did not count, men of lower rank were favored for diplomatic posts. One might send lawyers or scholars to lesser potentates and republics, and rich merchants or Jews to free imperial cities.[12]

As the range of subjects handled through diplomatic channels ex-panded, greater differentiation developed in the nature and purpose of diplomatic missions. This had a bearing on the choice of envoys. The significant distinction, which by the eighteenth century had become a cliché in the theoretical literature, was that between political missions and ceremonial missions.[13] The former encompassed all matters that might be negotiated between two states, from mundane commercial agree-ments to dynastic alliances. The latter involved solely the exchange of courtesies between sovereigns. Envoys were dispatched with some fre-quency to announce or congratulate on the birth of an heir, an engage-ment or marriage, accession to a throne, or the conferment of an honor; or to present condolences on a death in the family. Ceremonial embassies were normally entrusted to envoys of high rank; political matters could often be better handled by lawyers.

The diplomatic reception, which was the central act in the interchange between envoy and host, became more and more a public event, divorced from the business of negotiation.[14] The reception was regulated by ceremonial usage, which gradually acquired fixed forms and became increasingly intricate. Each court developed its own usages. There were general patterns in such basic elements of the reception as notification of arrival, escort to the audience, and manner of greeting during the audience; but usages could vary considerably in detail.[15] A ceremonial emphasizing outward displays of courtesy and respect—meticulously calculated in its nuances to render visible the relative status of the two sovereigns involved—developed first in the Romance lands and somewhat later in the territories of the Holy Roman Empire.

German theorists of the eighteenth century took the view that the preoccupation with ceremonial, by then universal, was a foreign importation that had only begun to make inroads into German Hofwesen in the not-too-distant past.[16] They saw this as an onerous inevitability, something essentially alien to the German character. "The customs of our princes," wrote Moser, "were still very modest and ordinary at a time when our neighbors were already conceited and pompous. The craze for magnificence, waste, and comfort has come to us only lately."[17] Von Rohr quotes a passage from Leibniz's *De jure suprematus ac legationis principum Germaniae* of 1677, in which the latter noted that he had encountered councillors at many German courts who did not know the difference between an *ambassadeur* and an *envoyé*. This prompted von Rohr to suggest that seventeenth-century publicists would have been appalled at the solemnity with which ceremonial matters were disputed in his day, "as if it were the Laws of Moses in question."[18]

Although Spanish ceremonial had been current at the imperial court since the time of Charles V and had gradually filtered down to the smaller German courts, particularly the Catholic courts, real impetus for the adoption of an elaborate ceremonial came in the seventeenth century. The protracted negotiations that ended the Thirty Years' War in 1648 first brought many German princes into contact with foreign ambassadors well versed in ceremonial niceties.[19] Furthermore, the humiliations suffered by the German princes at the French court in the seventeenth century impelled them, as Moser wrote, "to begin asserting their prerogatives, in order to distinguish themselves from the mass of their peers in as conspicuous a manner as possible."[20]

Over the course of the late seventeenth and eighteenth centuries, the German princes made periodic attempts—largely unsuccessful—to agree upon a common ceremonial among themselves. The first efforts in this direction originated with the non-electoral princes of the empire, who were annoyed at the pretensions of the electors. Resolutions were adopted at the Fürstenvereine of 1662 and 1693 (between Pfalz-Neuburg, Braunschweig, Württemberg, and Hessen-Kassel) to the effect that "the [non-electoral] Fürsten should stand together and guard against any encroachment on their rights and prerogatives, either at Reichsversammlungen or at imperial, royal, or electoral courts . . . in matters that concern the Titulatur [proper forms of titles for address] and treatment of their ambassadors."[21] The electors responded with similar measures. A letter of 1671 from the Elector of Brandenburg lamented the lack of a common ceremonial among the electors, "particularly now that so many fine distinctions are being drawn between ambassadors, envoyés extraordinaires and ordinaires, and residents." The letter concluded by proposing that this matter be taken up by the deputies at the Perpetual Diet in Regensburg.[22] Rarely did concrete results materialize from these good intentions, as resolution followed resolution.[23] In 1700, however, the princes of the imperial diet convened in Nürnberg and issued a work on ceremonial entitled *Protocollum Particulare das Ceremonial betreffend de anno 1700,* which set forth detailed guidelines for the reception of envoys.[24]

An undated memorandum from the second half of the sixteenth century makes it clear that at that time diplomatic ceremonial at the Bavarian court was still for the most part undetermined. The memorandum, titled "List of various points to be researched regarding the arrival of envoys," is a detailed catalog of questions for which answers were needed. Should someone be sent to meet envoys outside the capital? Should a distinction be made between envoys in offering them accommodations either in the Neuveste or in town? Should the duke meet envoys in person, and if so, how far should he go out from his room? Or should he delegate this task to someone else?[25] Another memorandum prepared in 1581 under Wilhelm V is still couched in rather equivocal terms; it is less a body of regulations than a sort of policy statement. It begins by making a distinction between German and foreign envoys and seems to be an attempt to establish basic regulations (a General-Regel) for all German envoys, at least. German and foreign envoys, we read, have different expectations. Germans do not expect many of the ceremonial flourishes that Italians take for granted during the audience, but are easily impressed by the material aspects of hospitality—not least an invitation to dine with the duke. With Italians, on the other hand, one needs to be very particular about titles—and the author of the memorandum suggests that it would be advisable to have an interpreter on hand.[26] By the 1630s, from which time we have extensive and continuous documentary evidence for the conduct of diplomatic receptions, diplomatic ceremonial at the Bavarian court had assumed a generally fixed pattern. It will be our task in the following pages to examine the historical developments that can be extracted from this body of material.

As the states of Europe came into increased contact with one another, the matter of rank among their rulers came to be a problem whenever they or their representatives met in person. In theory, it seemed self-evident that greater princes deserved precedence over lesser ones.[27] In practice, it was seldom so easy. No one disputed the pope's right to first place or the emperor's right to second, but beyond that there were no rules, and individual cases had to be resolved on their own merits. Disputes over precedence often resulted in two states' having no choice but to avoid formal contact with each other. Since sovereigns did not often meet in person the perennial struggle over precedence unfolded largely in the arena of diplomacy.

The classification of envoys into different ranks arose as diplomacy became a permanent institution and as differentiation was established in the social status of envoys and in the purpose of missions.[28] Rulers sought to lend certain of their representatives greater dignity by providing them with lofty titles. These titles might or might not reflect the political significance of the mission and they came to have relevance principally in the realm of ceremonial. By the seventeenth century, classification was commonplace among theorists. Normally, diplomats were divided into two classes. Callières distinguished between envoys of the first and second order. "Those of the first Order are Ambassadors Extraordinary and Ambassadors Ordinary; those of the second Order are Envoys Extraordinary, and Residents."[29]

Although Callières chose not to recognize further distinctions within the second class in his theoretical hierarchy, elsewhere he made it clear that there was a difference between envoys extraordinary and residents. The latter title, he tells us, had begun "to be in disrepute," particularly now that a distinction was made between envoys and residents at the French and imperial courts.[30] Wicquefort, who remarked that the title envoy extraordinary was more modern than resident, suggested that it arose when princes began sending gentlemen of high rank—for whom the title resident would have been an indignity—on missions that did not merit sending an ambassador.[31] The appeal that the new title quickly acquired prompted most of the sovereigns who maintained residents at the French court to transform them into envoys extraordinary.[32]

The traditional dual classification of envoys retained its validity, however, since only ambassadors were classified as having character—that is, the diplomat represented the person of his sovereign and had the right to all ceremonial prerogatives due the latter (in practice, of course, ambassadors were received with less pomp than princes). Envoys who did not possess Character were received with less ceremony and had to defer to ambassadors—even those sent by lesser sovereigns—in matters of precedence. Residents were received with a minimum of ceremonial; at some courts, such as in France, they did not even have the right to an audience with the sovereign, but instead dealt exclusively with his ministers.[33]

These distinctions in rank were not academic. On the contrary, the advantages of having lower ranks of diplomats were very real. The overwhelming majority of envoys who appeared at the Bavarian court were of lower rank. Sending an envoy was, first of all, a way of avoiding the cost of equipping an ambassador, who almost by virtue of his title was expected to comport himself with the utmost splendor. The lower status of envoys and residents had no necessary correlation with their role as political operators. In conducting negotiations, they were sometimes at an advantage, in that they were less constrained by ceremonial than ambassadors.

The most important advantage was quite simply that sending an envoy was a way of evading disputes over precedence and ceremonial. If a ruler anticipated that his ambassador might not be received at a foreign court with the honors he felt were due to himself, he could send an envoy instead. Because of the possibility of such a slight, the Reichsfürsten were very wary about sending ambassadors to electoral courts. An exchange of letters from 1666 between the Elector of Brandenburg and Ferdinand Maria opened with a request from Brandenburg: An extraordinary Gesandter sent to Berlin by the King of France had refused to appear before the elector until he was assured that the latter would allow him the right hand during the audience. The elector was in a quandary, as he did not customarily allow any Gesandter, no matter how exalted his principal, this distinction; and he asked for information about how such matters were handled at the Bavarian court. Ferdinand Maria replied that usage at the Bavarian court was exactly the same and that "when an ambassador insists too strongly, it is arranged beforehand that he shall appear not as a formal Gesandter [ambassador], but as an Abgeordneter [envoy of lower rank] or even as a private person."[34]

Receptions in Bavaria

The Bavarian court, like most other courts of the time, kept laborious records regarding diplomatic ceremonial. For each embassy that arrived in Munich, a protocol detailing the manner in which the envoy had been received was written up and kept for future reference. Questions often arose on particular points of ceremonial, and it was necessary to know how envoys from the sovereign in question had been received in the past.[35] In 1726, for example, on the arrival of the imperial ambassador, Graf von Sinzendorf, a memorandum was prepared to document the fact that imperial ambassadors in 1635, 1638, 1667, and 1679 had been met by the elector at the door to the Ritterstube.[36] It was undoubtedly from these individual protocols that officials of the Obristkämmerer's office compiled a compendium with abstracted descriptions of embassies, as well as visits of foreign princes. Various copies of this compendium, covering the period 1633–1702, are extant.[37]

We have occasional short memoranda that sketch in general terms the procedures to be followed at a diplomatic reception. The earliest of these, from the sixteenth century, have already been mentioned. The next was prepared for Conte Tarini Imperiale, a Savoyard diplomat, and probably dates from shortly after Max Emanuel's return to Bavaria in 1715. It details the usages of the Bavarian court regarding envoys of the second rank from crowned heads of state.[38] The last was issued under Karl Theodor, sometime between 1777 and 1790, and pertains to "imperial, royal, or electoral envoys (Gesandte) of the second rank."[39]

In these protocols, the basic agenda of the diplomatic reception was outlined, with particular attention paid to those elements of the reception that were critical from the point of view of ceremonial. The general format was the same for all receptions, but they varied considerably in the details, according to the class of the envoy, the status of his principal, and the purpose of the mission (whether political or ceremonial). Rigid guidelines did not exist, and it is clear that there was room to manipulate ceremonial to reflect political and dynastic policies. Augmenting the honors with which an envoy was received could be a significant demonstration of friendship for a fellow ruler. This was easy to do, although there was the danger of establishing a precedent that could be taken advantage of by other rulers of comparable station. Diminishing the honors, however, clearly could be done only upon careful consideration of the consequences.[40]

The high point of the embassy was the initial public audience with the elector, which was usually held several days after the envoy had arrived in Munich and after his credentials had been presented and accepted. It was not customary at the Bavarian court for envoys to make a formal entry into Munich; this was planned only for embassies of exceptional moment. On the day of the audience, the envoy was picked up at his hostelry and escorted to the Residenz by a cortege composed of electoral officers and liveried servants. Once at the Residenz, he was greeted in the elector's anterooms by a succession of court officers, with the court either fully or partially in attendance. He was then conducted to the audience chamber, where the audience itself took place in private. Afterwards, he was conducted to the apartment of the electress, who received him in much the same manner, and thence possibly also to other members of the family. After all audiences were over, he was given a return escort—either back to the inn, or to new quarters in the Gesandtenhaus or one of the noble houses of Munich, where he was kept at electoral expense. Only ambassadors from the emperor (and occasional royal ambassadors) were lodged in the Residenz. Before his departure from Munich, the envoy requested and received a departure audience from the elector; it was conducted in exactly the same manner as the initial audience. The significant variables in all this—the size and composition of the escort, the elaborateness of the reception in the anterooms, the manner in which the envoy's rooms were furnished, the number of officers and servants delegated to wait on his table—were carefully recorded in the protocols.

With the exception of ambassadors lodged in the Residenz, who were usually taken there directly, envoys arranged their own accommodations on their arrival in Munich. Most, along with the members of their suites, put up at one of the city's better inns.[41] As soon as he was settled, the envoy paid a visit to the Obristkämmerer (or sent his legation's secretary) in order to announce his arrival, present a copy of his credentials, request the honor of an audience with the elector, and arrange a date and time for this.[42] It was also customary before the audience to visit the other court officers, as well as the Hofmeister of the other Herrschaften, who would then return the visit. A commissary (Commissarius), usually of the rank of Truchsess, was delegated by the Obristhofmeister to wait upon the envoy during his stay in Munich, to escort him to and from the audience, and to supervise the arrangements for his new lodging after the audience.[43]

Standard procedure for the escort (Abholung) to the audience called for the commissary to pick up the envoy at his lodging shortly beforehand in a carriage drawn by six horses. Two lackeys marched alongside the carriage. Very often a second carriage, drawn by only two horses, was sent to carry the envoy's gentlemen, if there were any, or his secretary. The envoy's carriage was permitted to drive into the Residenz and discharge its passengers before the principal staircase. This honor was not accorded the second carriage, whose passengers were required to alight outside the Residenz and proceed by foot to rejoin the envoy and commissary at the bottom of the staircase.[44]

Entry to a Residenz was gained through the guarded gates of a passageway that led into an interior court, as at the Munich Residenz, or of a fence closing the open side of a forecourt, as at the Würzburg Residenz. In either case, additional courtyards used for ceremonial purposes might lie further within the building complex. Apparently baffled by the great variety in the palace architecture of Europe, neither Moser nor Florinus in their treatises on Hofwesen gives a conclusive prescription for the plan of a Residenzschloss or the configuration of courtyards. Both writers discuss the formal characteristics of courtyards, and both stress the advantages of open forecourts in presenting the palace. Implicit in their discussions is the idea that multiplicity of courtyards was a distinguishing trait of a Residenzschloss.[45]

Courtyards were not only an architectural feature to be used to aesthetic benefit, but also a functional necessity. The subject was of considerable importance; Moser devotes an entire chapter to "Squares and Courtyards of Palaces and Castles." As the home of the ruler, whose personal security was a matter of grave concern, and as the seat of the court, where rights of entrée were one of the principles of existence, the Residenzschloss needed to be well guarded. Control at the gates was strict (see chap. 4). The major advantage of multiple courtyards was flexibility in regulating access to the building. Moser wrote:

> The palace courtyards and squares have their various purposes and uses. Outer courtyards serve (1) for magnificence and to enhance the visibility of the building; and (2) for the security of the owner, as by custom the right of entry may be refused to commoners, foreigners, or otherwise suspicious persons. Inner courtyards serve (3) for the maintenance of peace and quiet and for the convenience of the owner, insofar as permission to drive into these in carriages is very limited. For this reason, (4) the division into separate courtyards has an influence on rank and ceremonial.[46]

The right to drive or ride into a Residenz was reserved to ranking courtiers and carefully fixed in court regulations.[47] If the layout of courtyards in a particular palace permitted, this privilege could be hierarchized in a manner analogous to the privilege of entrée to the anterooms of the resident prince's apartment. An order issued in 1727, which probably constituted a continuation of previous practice, granted the right to drive into the Munich Residenz to the high court officers, the Obristhofmeister of other family members, the captains of the two corps of guardsmen, a certain few ministers and generals, ranking foreign ambassadors, and the court ladies. All other persons, including the Kämmerer, were required to alight from their carriages or dismount from their horses outside the gates. This was also demanded of the lackeys of courtiers permitted to drive in; the lackeys were expected to rejoin their masters on foot.[48] An order of 1748 makes it clear that the privilege of driving into the Residenz corresponded roughly to entrée to the elector's audience chamber and Grosses Cabinet, the two innermost places of waiting in the apartment. The body of persons having the privelege was then divided into two groups. The first group was permitted to descend at the Breite Treppe (plan B, 1); a smaller group of lesser rank was required to descend at the Kapell- oder Kanzlei-Stiege (chapel or chancellery stairs; plan B, near 16) at the foot of the Kapellenhof. The court ladies could descend at the far end of the Brunnenhof, at the entrance to the electress's apartment (plan D, near 29).[49] The Kämmerer first acquired the right to drive into the Residenz in the late 1760s. A regulation published as part of the 1769 Kammerordnung permits them to descend at the Kapellenstiege.[50]

Cases not clearly addressed in the regulations had to be decided on an individual basis. This sometimes led to controversy. On the occasion of Marie Antoinette's visit in 1770, Graf Podstasky, imperial resident in Munich, wrote home on April 6 that he was engaged in negotiations as to whether the *garde noble* accompanying the future dauphine should be allowed to ride into the Residenz with the rest of the cortege, as Podstasky demanded, or should ride only as far as the gate, as Max III Joseph wished. He reported later in the month that despite his best efforts, the elector had prevailed.[51]

An elaborate Abholung was staged for the audience of the Saxon ambassador in 1747, at which he formally sued for the hand of Princess Maria Antonia Walburga, who was to wed the Electoral Prince of Saxony. The details of this audience were carefully worked out beforehand between the two courts, as was often the case in these matters. The ambassador, who was the Saxon resident in Munich, received special credentials granting him Character for several days, in order that the engagement ceremonies could be conducted in a fitting manner. The procedures agreed upon for the Abholung, as well as for the other engagement ceremonies, were outlined in a series of lengthy memoranda. Three electoral carriages—two with six horses and one with two horses—were ordered for the Abholung. A cortege consisting of a Kammerfourier, a Hoffourier, two footmen, four court lackeys, four Heiducken (light-armed guards), four Trabanten, and two pages (who would march beside the ambassador's carriage) was to accompany the procession of carriages. Two Truchsesse, as well as the commissary, were to ride with the ambassador and his suite in the carriages. The carriages drove first to the commissary's house and proceeded from there to the ambassador's quarters. Several minutes earlier another commissary, riding in a two-horse carriage, had come to announce the arrival of the cortege to the ambassador. When the principal commissary arrived, the ambassador met him at the carriage and took him up to his room, where they exchanged compliments. They then went back down, and the cortege was formed to drive to the Residenz. There were five, possibly six carriages in all: first, the commissary's own carriage, with six horses, which traveled empty; second, an electoral two-horse carriage, carrying the two Truchsesse; third, an electoral six-horse carriage, with the Saxon gentlemen from the ambassador's entourage; fourth, the electoral ceremonial carriage carrying the ambassador, who sat in the privileged position facing forward, and the commissary, who sat opposite him; fifth, the ambassador's own carriage, traveling empty (this carriage was optional); and finally, a two-horse carriage belonging to the ambassador, for his legation's secretary. Upon reaching the Residenz, the ceremonial carriage drove into the building and stopped at the principal staircase. This honor was to be extended to the ambassador's empty carriage if it was included in the cortege; if not, the second carriage carrying the Saxon gentlemen could follow the ceremonial carriage into the Residenz. All other carriages stopped before the main gate.[52]

When the participants in a diplomatic audience had left their carriages and assembled at the prescribed staircase to the piano nobile, the envoy and his commissary, preceded by the entourage, went up the stairs and through the anterooms to the audience chamber. The members of the entourage, both Bavarians and guests, took their places in the rooms appropriate to their station.[53] At the Saxon audience of 1747,

> the electoral lackeys, footmen, and Heiducken, as also those of the ambassador, wait outside in the Guarde-Saal [Herkules-Saal]; the electoral pages, the ambassador's pages, and the other officers enter the Ritterstube and wait there until the audience is over. If the ambassador has cavaliers with him, they will be presented to Serenissimus after the audience and allowed to kiss his hand.[54]

In the anterooms, members of the court, who had been expressly summoned to appear at the appointed hour, were waiting. From at least the 1670s, it was customary to call out the entire court—Kämmerer, Truch-

sesse, councillors, and pages (Edelknaben), as well as the entire Trabanten and Hartschier guards. The Kämmerer waited in the antechamber
(Plan D, 3); the Truchsesse, councillors, and pages in the Ritterstube
(Plan D, 2). As we learn from the memorandum prepared for Conte
Tarini, in each room they stood in two groups, probably in two lines
forming a pathway through which the envoy and his escort passed.[55] The
Trabanten guard stood in parade formation in the staircase, lining the
stairs on either side, and the Hartschier stood in the Herkules-Saal
(plan D, 1). The Hartschier were often deployed from the top of the
staircase up to the door of the Ritterstube. For envoys representing lesser
principals (non potentates such as imperial cities, imperial prelates, cathedral chapters, or imperial counts), the body of courtiers in attendance
was reduced; usually, councillors and pages were left out. The guards
were either only partially mustered or limited to those having routine
sentry duty.

As he passed through the anterooms, an envoy was met and greeted
by either the elector or the high court officers. A host greeted visitors of
superior or comparable station by going out a certain distance to meet
them and escorting them back to his room. The distance involved was
calculated to reflect the difference in rank between visitor and host. In-
feriors were not greeted in this way, except as a mark of friendship or
affection; instead, they were allowed to come to the host. This also applied to envoys, although the honor bestowed in this way on an envoy—even one with character—was never as great as that proper for his
principal.

The greeting of envoys is fairly extensively addressed in the protocols.
In order to make historical patterns intelligible, this material has been
tabulated in appendix 8.[56] The chart reveals two trends. First, the role of
the elector in receiving envoys diminished in importance over time,
while that of the high court officers increased; by the second half of the
eighteenth century, it was normal to greet an envoy with three officers.
Second, once the court officers began to take over the task of greeting
envoys, it became possible to augment the honors with which envoys
were received. Envoys from lesser principals, who formerly were not
specially met in the anterooms, were now granted this distinction.

Under Maximilian I, envoys either were greeted by the elector in person in one of the anterooms or were not greeted at all. Maximilian met
envoys from the emperor, from other regnant members of the imperial
family, and from foreign crowned heads in either the Ritterstube (plan B,
4) or the antechamber (plan B, 5); there was a total of four possible meet-

ing points—the doors to these rooms and in the middle of them.[57] Other envoys—from fellow electors, other Reichsfürsten, and lesser powers—made their way to the audience chamber (plan B, 6), escorted by the commissary.[58]

Maximilian's successors proceeded forth to greet envoys only very rarely. This came to be a distinction reserved for imperial envoys of the first class and for ceremonial embassies of great importance. In 1679, for example, Graf von Nostiz, who had been sent by the emperor to proffer condolences on the death of Ferdinand Maria, was received by Max Emanuel at the door to the Ritterstube.[59] The Marchese Corsini arrived in 1688 to escort Princess Violante Beatrix, newly wed to the Hereditary Prince of Tuscany, to Florence; he was met "ten steps outside the Hercules-Saal" (plan B, 3) by the Obristkämmerer and "three steps outside the antechamber" by the elector.[60]

The Obristkämmerer took over the function of receiving envoys in the anterooms. The first recorded instance of the elector's delegating this responsibility was in 1644, at the reception of an Abgesandter from the archduchess in Innsbruck. "Aforesaid envoy had one audience with ICD, who awaited him in the room. His Grace the Obristkämmerer received the envoy a couple of steps before the antechamber in the Ritterstube."[61] Under Ferdinand Maria and Max Emanuel, second-class envoys from all sovereigns (including Reichsfürsten), as well as the occasional envoys sent by imperial cities and cathedral chapters, were greeted by the Obristkämmerer in either the Ritterstube or the antechamber. By the reign of Karl Albrecht, it had become standard procedure for two officers—the Obristhofmarschall, in addition to the Obristkämmerer—to meet the envoy. Both officers might meet him in the Ritterstube; or the reception might be spread out to include the antechamber as well, with the Obristhofmarschall meeting him in the former room and the Obristkämmerer in the latter. Under Max III Joseph, the diplomatic reception reached new heights of elaboration, as yet a third officer, the Obristhofmeister, joined his colleagues in greeting envoys. It is clear that the possibilities for differentiating nuances of meaning in the manner of greeting envoys were now considerably greater than ever before. The memorandum prepared between 1777 and 1790 under Karl Theodor specifies a standardized three-part reception for imperial, royal, and electoral envoys of the second class: the Obristhofmarschall was stationed at the door to the Ritterstube, the Obristkämmerer at the door to the first antechamber, and the Obristhofmeister in the middle of the first antechamber. The latter officer escorted the envoy to the door of the audience chamber.[62]

At the audience of the Saxon ambassador in 1747, a more elaborate three-part reception, at which the officers went out farther than usual, was planned.

> His Excellence the Ambassador . . . will be met at the carriage by two electoral Kämmerer, Graf Daun and the young Baron von Neuhaus. At the top of the staircase, the Obristhofmarschall, Baron von Lerchenfeld, will receive him; in the middle of the Ritterstube, the Obristkämmerer; and in the Antecamera, the Obristhofmeister, who in approaching the middle of the second Antecamera will go somewhat ahead in order to announce the ambassador's arrival and will then introduce him to the Audienzzimmer.[63]

In 1755, Baron von Gemmingen, an envoy from the Margrave of Baden-Baden who had come to request the hand of Princess Maria Anna Josepha for his master, was granted a similar, though somewhat reduced, reception. He was not met at the carriage by specially appointed Kämmerer, but instead was escorted up the stairs by his commissary.

> At [or immediately in front of] the door to the Ritterstube, the Obristhofmarschall received him and accompanied him up to the door of the Anti-Camera, where he was received by the Obristkämmerer. At the door of the second Anti-Camera, he was taken over by the Obristhofmeister; he was led through this room by both officers, who conducted him into the Audienzzimmer after first announcing him.[64]

Private and Public Audiences

Private audiences were granted when an envoy requested it, when he arrived incognito or without proper credentials, or when he required further meetings with the elector after his initial public audience. A private audience could take place totally without ceremonial, in which case the envoy would be escorted into the elector's cabinet by a Kammerfourier or Kämmerer via a back staircase. It could also be conducted with a minimal ceremonial. No courtiers would be expressly appointed to wait in the anterooms, but the envoy would be met in the antechamber by a Kämmerer on duty, who would lead him into the cabinet.[65] Baron von Leonroth, Abgeordneter from the Bishop of Eichstätt, was received in this manner in 1738. As he had applied for the post of Kämmerer at the Bavarian court, the elector gave him the choice of being received with or without ceremony. He chose the latter, apparently thinking that this decision would be construed as a gesture of fealty.[66] Imperial envoys who requested private audiences were sometimes received with slightly more distinction than this. In 1765, the imperial resident, Graf Podstasky—who, unlike Leonroth, was permitted to drive into the Residenz—was met by two Kämmerer at the carriage, in the first antechamber by a Kämmerer on duty, and in the second antechamber by the Obristhof-meister, who led him to the elector.[67]

The protocols are overwhelmingly silent about the audience itself. This act, which rarely lasted more than a quarter of an hour, took place behind closed doors, with no one present in the room other than occasionally the Obristkämmerer. For this reason, protocolists may not have often had access to detailed information.

It is nonetheless possible to gain a general idea of how diplomatic audiences were conducted at the Bavarian court. There were two possible modes for the audience: it could be conducted with both parties either standing or seated. Which mode of audience to grant was, in theory at least, entirely at the prince's discretion.[68] There are, however, strong indications that the standing audience was the rule among the German princes. Callières noted that the "temporal electors" received envoys from the King of France (Louis XIV almost never sent ambassadors to the German princes) standing and bareheaded.[69] Moser (whose *Teutsches Hof-Recht* is limited to describing German circumstances) wrote, "Regarding sitting or standing, so much may be said: solemn audiences of envoys always occur standing; at least, I have encountered no case where it is mentioned that the person receiving audience was sitting."[70] Both these sources make it clear that the standing audience followed the practices of the imperial court, where the emperor received a wide range of envoys standing. The memorandum for Conte Tarini describes a typical Bavarian audience:

> In the audience chamber, SA the Elector awaits the envoy standing on a dais underneath a baldachin, and, seeing the envoy approach, he removes his hat.
>
> After the envoy has made his reverences, he proceeds up to the foot of the dais, where he stops without mounting, and delivers his proposition. When the envoy begins to speak, SAE covers his head.
>
> The envoy having heard the response and the audience being finished, he (the envoy) again makes the above-mentioned reverences and retires with the same formalities as in coming, and SAE again takes off his hat.[71]

The envoy would have approached with his head bare, and—although it is not mentioned here—after the elector covered his own head, he normally gave a sign to the envoy that he should do the same.[72] The 1747 audience of the Saxon ambassador is one of the very few that are described in detail in the protocols:

> At the entrance of the ambassador, ICD stands under the baldachin and, after the ambassador's reverence, takes his hat off; he puts it back on as the ambassador approaches the baldachin, whereupon the ambassador also covers his head. ICD takes the Creditiv [accrediting document] and puts it unopened in his pocket. After the ambassador has finished his address, the elector gives his answer.[73]

Seated audiences were granted on extraordinary occasions. Permitting an envoy to sit in one's presence was a more generous gesture than standing up for him in a situation where he was expected to stand. Particularly in the context of a private audience, it could also be construed as a mark of friendship.[74] Even during seated audiences, however, there were ways of making distinctions in station tangible. The elector would more than likely sit on a fauteuil more elaborately carved and upholstered than that provided for the envoy. His chair would stand in the privileged position underneath the baldachin and facing the door. The *Protocollum Particulare* of 1700 specified that "if the audience takes place sitting, the chairs will be different in color and the envoy will sit with his back to the door."[75] The Obristkämmerer would be on hand to pull the elector's chair back from the table, whereas the envoy would probably be expected to do this for himself. In 1727, the Margravine of Ansbach granted the imperial plenipotentiary, Graf Wurmbrand, a seated audience:

> The audience took place sitting, and His Excellence the Count and ID the Margravine sat on black velvet, gilded fauteuils. And although they sat opposite one another (excepting that the envoy's chair stood somewhat away from the wall and to the side), the envoy nonetheless pulled his chair back from the table himself, such that he was sitting lower than ID and with his back completely toward the door.[76]

In 1741 a French envoy, the Maréchal de Belle-Isle, arrived in Munich and, prior to appearing at court, submitted a memorandum demanding preferential treatment for himself. He based his claims on the treatment accorded the Duc de Gramont in 1658 and noted, among other things, that on that occasion the elector had offered Gramont a chair of the same form and style as he himself had sat on. Belle-Isle made it clear in no equivocal terms that he expected the same, despite the fact that he did not enjoy the rank of ambassador, as had Gramont: "As SAE always remains standing and uncovered during audiences, he must accord [Belle-Isle] this treatment; and if the conversation drags on, SAE will sit down with [Belle-Isle] without ceremony, on equal chairs."[77]

In determining in which rooms audiences were held, we are dependent on sources other than the protocols, where this information is seldom recorded. Prior to the construction of the Reiche Zimmer in the 1730s, there were two places for audiences in the elector's apartment. Private audiences were held in the Grosses Cabinet (plan C, 5), which Joanne Schmid described as the inner Audienzzimmer.[78] Wening called this room the inner or private Audienzzimmer. Public audiences were held in the audience chamber, which Wening calls the outer Audienzzimmer (plan C, 4).[79] In 1684, Max Emanuel gave an audience to Prince Eugene of Savoy in the Grosses Cabinet. Although on this occasion the reception in the anterooms had all the marks of a public reception, the audience itself had a more private flavor. It was conducted sitting and bareheaded, and afterwards a private dinner, at which the pages and Kammerdiener waited, was served in the same room.[80]

With the construction of the Reiche Zimmer, there were now two places for public audiences: the first audience chamber (plan D, 4), which Küchel called the prince's in his travelogue of 1737; and, following this, the Grosses Audienzzimmer (plan D, 5), which Küchel called the imperial audience chamber. Rotenstein, in his 1781 description of the Residenz, noted three places for audiences in the elector's apartment. The first antechamber (plan D, 3) was an "Audienzzimmer for the residents"; the next room he describes as the "second Audienzzimmer or Antecamera for the envoys" (plan D, 4). This is followed by the "third Audienzzimmer, where imperial and royal ambassadors receive audience" (plan D, 5).[81]

This left the Grosses Cabinet (plan D, 6) as the place for private audiences and meetings with fellow princes. In 1739 Freiherr von Wachtenthan, an envoy of the Elector Palatine who happened to be passing through Munich on his way from Vienna to Mannheim, requested an audience with the elector. Since he was not accredited to the Bavarian court, it was decided to treat him as a Minister de la maison, and the elector received him in the Grosses Cabinet.[82] In 1741 Conte Montijo, ambassador from the King of Spain, was likewise received in this room, the elector going out as far as the center of the Grosses Audienzzimmer to meet him. The reason given was that he was considered to represent a sovereign standing in close "friendship by family lineage" with the electoral house and thus deserved "familiar treatment."[83]

The 1769 furniture inventory documents the presence of a baldachin

and an *audience fauteuil* in the audience chamber (plan D, 25) of Max III
Joseph's private apartment above the Antiquarium. There is, however,
no record of audiences having been held there. The only audiences during his reign for which the location is noted in the protocols took place
in the Reiche Zimmer (plan D, 3–11), which remained very actively in
use as a state apartment for public functions.

Once the audience with the elector was over, the envoy was taken
immediately to audiences with the electress and possibly other family
members as well. In theory, it was left to the envoy to decide whether he
wanted public audiences with these persons; if so, he was required to
request this expressly through their Hofmeister. Courtesy dictated, however, that he not neglect to do so, or he risked offending the person
involved.[84]

Audiences with female Herrschaften tended to be held in outer anterooms (very often in the antechamber) with ladies-in-waiting present.
The 1747 audience of the Saxon ambassador with Dowager Empress Maria Amalie, the mother of the bride, serves to illustrate this.

> Once the audience with the elector is over, the ambassador
> proceeds to his audience with Her Majesty the Empress.
> The procession goes through the Garde- or Hercules-Saal,
> through the Lange Gallerie, and through the so-called Leder-
> ner Saal [Hartschiersaal] up to HM Ritterstube, to which
> point the Obristhofmarschall also accompanies the ambassa-
> dor. At the entrance to the Ritterstube [where several Käm-
> merer from the elector's antechamber have come to await the
> ambassador's arrival there], the ambassador is received by
> HM Obristsilberkämmerer, Graf von Hund. In the middle
> of the Ritterstube, HM Obristhofmeister receives the ambas-
> sador and leads him to the audience [which, we are told else-
> where, takes place in the empress's antechamber]. Both parts
> of the door are opened by a Kammerdiener and remain open
> during the audience.
>
> HM stands under the baldachin. The court ladies who are
> present stand according to their rank on the window side,
> such that the last is next to the door and the first toward the
> baldachin. In front of the baldachin stands the Fräulein-
> Hofmeisterin, as well as Madame Freyberg, and in the first
> position the Obristhofmeisterin.
>
> Her Highness the Princess Maria Antonia, bride-to-be,
> stands next to HM. After the ambassador enters the room,
> he first delivers his courtship address to HM and then asks

HH for her hand. The latter, after requesting permission of HM and making a deep curtsey, gives her acceptance in the appropriate terms.

If there are gentlemen from the ambassador's suite present, these—but no others—will be admitted to kiss the hands of HM and HH.

The ambassador was then received by the two younger princesses; he was met at the door of their antechamber by the Kämmerer on duty and at the door of their audience chamber by their governess. Once all audiences were finished, the ambassador, preceded by the entire cortege, returned to the staircase. The Obristhofmarschall took his leave at the head of the stairs, where he had first received the ambassador. The two Kämmerer who had met him at the carriage accompanied him back to that point and remained standing until the carriage had pulled away.[85]

Lodging and Dining Diplomats

After his audience, an envoy was driven directly to the new quarters that had been made ready for him. There he was provided for at electoral expense for the duration of his visit or, in the case of permanent or long-term embassies, for a short period of time.[86] Only imperial, royal, and electoral envoys of the first rank were lodged in the Residenz, where there were several apartments available for this purpose in the Neuveste.[87] The most prestigious of these, in which imperial and royal ambassadors lodged, was that in the Mittlere Rundstube (plan A, 1). Here three rooms, hung with tapestries and specially furnished for the occasion, were usually placed at the ambassador's disposal—a bedroom and two anterooms. The first anteroom served as his Tafelstube; the second, fitted out with a baldachin, as his audience chamber. After the 1750 fire that destroyed the greater part of the Neuveste, these rooms no longer existed, and there was now considerably less space in the Residenz in which to house guests and ambassadors. In 1765, Graf Podstasky, the imperial resident in Munich—who received special credentials on the occasion of the wedding of Princess Josepha Antonia to Joseph II—was lodged in the Maxburg, as the presence of five princely wedding guests precluded putting him up in the Residenz, "where it would have been fitting to lodge him."[88]

When an ambassador dined in public in his Tafelstube, Truchsesse and pages were delegated to wait on his table. Electoral Trabanten often stood guard at the entrance to the apartment. In 1679, the imperial ambassador, Graf von Nostiz, who had three rooms next to the Katherinen-kapelle (where he heard mass), was treated with unusual liberality: "At his table. five Truchsesse served. Herr von Pfitten poured; Herr von Heimhausen carved; and the others, along with four pages, carried the dishes. Six Trabanten stood at attention in his rooms at all times, and a Portier had service."[89]

It was customary for the elector to pay a return visit to imperial and royal envoys lodged in the Residenz. The visit to Graf von Nostiz took place two days after his initial audience with the elector: "The ambassador went out to receive the princely persons [Herzog Max Philipp, serving as administrator during Max Emanuel's minority, accompanied him] at the St.-Catherina-Capelle and, ceding them the right hand, led them back to his room. . . . The entire electoral court was in attendance. The Trabanten stood at attention along the Langer Gang until the visit was over."[90]

For other envoys there was, until the early eighteenth century, the Ge-sandtenhaus—an electoral building in the Theatinerstrasse that contained several apartments for envoys and limited accommodations for their suites.[91] Here, as in the Residenz, rooms were specially furnished as necessary. At the beginning of Karl Albrecht's reign, the tradition of lodging envoys in the Gesandtenhaus came to an end. On April 30, 1726, two months after the death of Max Emanuel, the building was presented to Graf von Piosasque de Non, who commissioned Cuvilliés to erect a town palace on the site.[92] The following year, the elector issued a decree that envoys were no longer to be lodged and boarded in electoral buildings.[93] This measure was undoubtedly part of the general program of reducing expenditures that Karl Albrecht, who had inherited enormous debts from his spendthrift father, instituted at the beginning of his reign.[94] Envoys were also lodged in the town palaces of the court nobility.[95] Envoys from lesser principals and those who arrived incognito or without accreditation were taken back to their inns after audiences. The protocols sometimes report that an envoy voluntarily chose to remain at his inn after having been offered quarters in the Gesandtenhaus. Although the reason for the choice is never stated, it was probably a way of avoiding ceremonial disputes.

Wherever they were accommodated, envoys received food and drink from the court kitchens and cellars and were waited on at table by court lackeys. The Obristhofmeister or the Obristhofmarschall had the responsibility for seeing that inns and other non-electoral buildings, came temporarily under electoral jurisdiction.[96] One or several court officers—Truchsesse, councillors, or Kämmerer—might be delegated to dine with the envoy and keep him company. An agenda prepared in 1740 for the embassy of Baron von Kesselstadt, Abgesandter from the Elector of Mainz, tells us that the Obristhofmarschall was to arrange a dinner party of eight of the highest court officers for the first day Kesselstadt spent in his quarters (with Baron von Neuhaus). On subsequent days, he was free to invite any dinner guests he might choose.[97]

This practice of boarding envoys seems to have often led to abuse. A decree issued by Max Emanuel in 1682 expressed concern that all too often, after an envoy had been transferred to the Gesandtenhaus, unauthorized—sometimes even disreputable—persons attached themselves to the envoy's table. It also noted great disorder and laxity on the part of the lackeys in the transfer of food from the court kitchens, resulting in considerable waste. The elector ordered that as a rule no more than four guests, carefully picked for their circumspection, were to be appointed to dine with an envoy.[98]

After his initial audience, an envoy was free to appear at court on all occasions when the court was in attendance. The memorandum for Conte Tarini states: "In the court chapel and on all occasions where it is customary to appear in full dress, the envoys [those of Tarini's status] have their place immediately after the Obristhofmeister. When they appear at court on other occasions or in the Anticamera at the appointed hours, they are left to mingle with the gentlemen without order."[99]

In the seventeenth and eighteenth centuries, an invitation to dine at the elector's table was a rare honor. According to the above memorandum, an envoy dined with the elector only when his audience had taken place in the country; the invitation included also the gentlemen from his suite. On October 3, 1750, the imperial resident, Baron von Widmann, reported that he had been invited to dine the day before; with obvious satisfaction, he noted that this was "a gesture of exceptional politeness not usual here."[100] Later in the century, such invitations became more frequent. The memorandum prepared under Karl Theodor tells us that when the audience took place in the morning, an invitation to dine the same day was forthcoming, and it was left to the envoy to decide whether to return to his quarters beforehand or remain at court. In the case of an afternoon audience, he was invited for the following day.[101]

Envoys were, as a routine courtesy, shown the sights of the Residenz—especially the Schatzkammer and the Antiquarium—during their stay in Munich. Less often, they were taken to tour the country palaces. In 1733, a Saxon envoy, Graf von Watzdorf, was invited to go deer hunting with the elector and afterwards dine with him at Nymphenburg. Several days later, when the elector went to Schleissheim, Watzdorf was driven there in a berlin along with several court officers. He toured the palace and gardens and dined there at midday.[102]

The diplomatic reception, and the audience to which it was the immediate prelude, carried the most ceremonial weight within the agenda of the diplomatic mission. This becomes clear from the protocols, which normally outline the elements of the reception in detail while only briefly noting the honors and courtesies bestowed upon the envoy during the remainder of his visit. It does not surprise us that this point of initial encounter should be the object of such elaboration in an age that placed great emphasis on the external expression of a real or imagined order and in which public life was deeply imbued with the quality of theater. Stairs, public rooms, and antechambers of the sovereign's apartment served as settings for these acts of greeting and welcome.

Appendix 1
The Bavarian Wittelsbachs, 1500–1800

This information has been compiled from Haeutle, *Genealogie,* and Rall, *Wittelsbacher Lebensbilder.*

With the exception of Max II Emanuel's son Joseph Ferdinand, only children who survived their tenth year have been included here. Unless otherwise noted, births and deaths occurred in Munich; in a few sixteenth-century instances, the sources do not list places of birth or death. The bishoprics and cardinalates held by the ecclesiastical princes of the family have been listed, but none of their lesser offices (abbacies, priorates, canonicates, etc.).

Wilhelm IV (b. Nov. 13, 1493; d. Mar. 7, 1550). Reigned from Mar. 18, 1508.
Consort:
Jakobaea Maria of Baden (b. June 25, 1507; d. Nov. 16, 1580). Daughter of Margrave Philipp of Baden. Married 1522 (wedding in Munich, Oct. 5).
Children:
Albrecht V (b. Feb. 29, 1528).
Mechtilde (b. July 12, 1532; d. Nov. 1, 1565, Baden-Baden). Married 1557 to Margrave Philibert of Baden.

Albrecht V (b. Feb. 29, 1528; d. Oct. 24, 1579). Reigned from Mar. 7, 1550.
Consort:
Anna of Austria (b. July 7, 1528, Prague; d. Oct. 16, 1590). Daughter of Emperor Ferdinand I. Married 1546.
Children:
Wilhelm V (b. Sept. 29, 1548).
Ferdinand (b. Jan. 20, 1550, Landshut; d. Jan. 30, 1608). Married Maria Pettenbeck, daughter of the ducal Landrichter at Haag, morganatically in 1588. Ferdinand was the founder of the cadet line of the Counts of Wartenberg, which became extinct in 1736.
Maria (b. Mar. 21, 1551; d. Apr. 29, 1608, Graz). Married 1571 to Archduke Karl II of Austria.
Maximiliana Maria (b. July 4, 1552; d. July 11, 1614).

Ernst (b. Dec. 17, 1554; d. Feb. 17, 1612, Arensberg in Westfalen). Elected Bishop of Freising, 1566; Bishop of Hildesheim, 1573; Bishop of Liège, 1581; Archbishop-Elector of Cologne, 1583; Bishop of Münster, 1585.

Wilhelm V (b. Sept. 29, 1548, Landshut; d. Feb. 7, 1626). Reigned from Oct. 24, 1579, to Oct. 15, 1597, when he abdicated in favor of his son Maximilian.
Consort:
Renata of Lorraine (b. Apr. 20, 1544, Nancy; d. May 22, 1602). Daughter of Duke Franz I of Lorraine. Married 1568 (wedding in Munich, Feb. 22).
Children:
Maximilian I (b. Apr. 17, 1573).
Maria Anna (b. Dec. 8, 1574; d. Mar. 8, 1616, Graz). Married 1600 to the future Emperor Ferdinand II.
Philipp Wilhelm (b. Sept. 22, 1576; d. May 18, 1598, Dachau). Elected Bishop of Regensburg, 1595; appointed Cardinal, 1597.
Ferdinand (b. Oct. 6, 1577; d. Sept. 13, 1650, Arensberg). Elected Bishop of Hildesheim, 1612; Archbishop-Elector of Cologne, 1612; Bishop of Liège, 1612; Bishop of Münster, 1612; Bishop of Paderborn, 1618.
Albrecht der Leuchtenberger (b. Apr. 13, 1584; d. July 5, 1666).
  Consort:
  Mechtilde (b. Oct. 15, 1588; d. June 1, 1634). Daughter of Landgrave Georg Ludwig of Leuchtenberg. Married 1612.
    Through Mechtilde, Albrecht came into possession of the landgraviate of Leuchtenberg, which he exchanged in 1650 for the Reichsgrafschaft Haag. After the death of his son Maximilian Heinrich, Haag reverted to Bavaria.
  Children:
  Maria Renata (b. Aug. 3, 1616; d. Mar. 1, 1630).
  Karl Johann (b. Nov. 10, 1618; d. May 19, 1640).
  Maximilian Heinrich (b. Oct. 8, 1621; d. June 3, 1688, Bonn). Elected Archbishop-Elector of Cologne, 1650; Bishop of Hildesheim, 1650; Bishop of Liège, 1650; Bishop of Münster, 1683.
  Albrecht Sigmund (b. Aug. 5, 1623; d. Nov. 4, 1685, Freising). Elected Bishop of Freising, 1652; Bishop of Regensburg, 1668.
Magdalena (b. July 4, 1587; d. Sept. 25, 1628, Neuburg). Married 1613 to Pfalzgraf Wolfgang Wilhelm of Pfalz-Neuburg (wedding in Munich, Nov. 11).

Maximilian I (b. Apr. 17, 1573; d. Sept. 27, 1651, Ingolstadt). Reigned jointly with his father from Dec. 1, 1594, alone from Oct. 15, 1597. Named Elector of Bavaria, Feb. 25, 1623.
Consorts:
Elisabeth Renata of Lorraine (b. Oct. 9, 1574, Nancy; d. Jan. 4, 1635, Ranshofen bei Braunau). Daughter of Duke Karl II of Lorraine. Married 1595. The marriage was without issue.
Maria Anna of Austria (b. Jan. 13, 1610, Graz; d. Sept. 25, 1665). Daughter of Emperor Ferdinand II. Married 1635.
Children:
Ferdinand Maria (b. Oct. 31, 1636).

Maximilian Philipp (b. Sept. 30, 1638; d. Mar. 20, 1705, Türkheim). Married Mauritia Febronia (1652–1706), daughter of the Duc de Bouillon, in 1668. The marriage was without issue. Maximilian Philipp was invested with the landgraviate of Leuchtenberg in 1650; it reverted to Bavaria on his death.

Ferdinand Maria (b. Oct. 31, 1636; d. May 26, 1679). Reigned from Sept. 27, 1651.
Consort:
Henriette Adelaide (b. Nov. 6, 1636, Turin; d. Mar. 18, 1676). Daughter of Duke Victor Amadeus I of Savoy. Married 1652 (wedding in Munich, June 25).
Children:
Maria Anna Christina (b. Nov. 17, 1660; d. Apr. 20, 1690, Versailles). Married 1680 to Louis of France, Grand Dauphin (procura wedding in Munich, Jan. 28).
Maximilian II Emanuel (b. July 11, 1662).
Joseph Clemens (b. Dec. 5, 1671; d. Nov. 12, 1723, Bonn). Elected Bishop of Freising, 1685; Bishop of Regensburg, 1685 (resigned 1716 in favor of his nephew, Clemens August); Archbishop-Elector of Cologne, 1688; Bishop of Liège, 1694; Bishop of Hildesheim, 1714.
Violante Beatrix (b. Jan. 23, 1673; d. May 29, 1731, Florence). Married 1689 to the future Grand Duke Ferdinand III of Tuscany (procura wedding in Munich, Nov. 21, 1688).

Maximilian II Emanuel (b. July 11, 1662; d. Feb. 26, 1726). Reigned from May 26, 1679.
Consorts:
Maria Antonia of Austria (b. Jan. 18, 1669, Vienna; d. Dec. 24, 1692, Vienna). Daughter of Emperor Leopold I. Married 1685.
Therese Kunigunde of Poland (b. Mar. 4, 1676, Warsaw; d. Mar. 10, 1730, Venice). Daughter of King Johann III Sobieski of Poland. Married 1695.
Children of the first marriage:
Joseph Ferdinand (b. Oct. 28, 1692, Vienna; d. Feb. 6, 1699, Brussels).
Children of the second marriage:
Maria Anna Karolina (b. Aug. 4, 1696, Brussels; d. Oct. 9, 1750). Entered the Convent of the Clarissines in Munich in 1720 under the name of Sister Therese Emanuele.
Karl Albrecht (b. Aug. 6, 1697).
Philipp Moritz (b. Aug. 5, 1698, Brussels; d. Mar. 12, 1719, Rome). Elected Bishop of Paderborn and Bishop of Münster posthumously in 1719.
Ferdinand Maria Innocenz (b. Aug. 5, 1699, Brussels; d. Dec. 9, 1738).
Consort:
Maria Anna Karolina (b. Jan. 30, 1693, Reichstadt in Bohemia; d. Sept. 12, 1751, Ahaus in Westfalen). Daughter of Pfalzgraf Philipp Wilhelm of Neuburg. Married 1719.
Children:
Maximilian Joseph (b. Apr. 11, 1720; d. Apr. 28, 1738).
Clemens Franz (b. Apr. 19, 1722; d. Aug. 6, 1770).
Consort:

Maria Anna Charlotte (b. June 22, 1722, Schwetzingen; d. Apr. 25, 1790). Daughter of Hereditary Prince Joseph Karl Emanuel of Pfalz-Sulzbach. Married 1742. The marriage was without issue.

Therese Emanuele (b. July 22, 1723; d. Mar. 27, 1743, Frankfurt).

Clemens August (b. Aug. 17, 1700, Brussels; d. Feb. 6, 1761, Coblenz). Elected Bishop of Regensburg, 1716 (resigned 1719 in favor of his brother Johann Theodor); Bishop of Münster, 1719; Bishop of Paderborn, 1719; Archbishop-Elector of Cologne, 1723; Bishop of Hildesheim, 1724; Bishop of Osnabrück, 1728.

Johann Theodor (b. Sept. 3, 1703; d. Jan. 27, 1763, Liège). Elected Bishop of Regensburg, 1719; Bishop of Freising, 1727; Bishop of Liège, 1744; appointed Cardinal, 1743.

Karl Albrecht (b. Aug. 6, 1697, Brussels; d. Jan. 20, 1745). Reigned from Feb. 26,
1726. Elected King of Bohemia, 1741. Elected Holy Roman Emperor (Karl VII), Jan. 24, 1742 (crowned on Feb. 12).

Consort:

Maria Amalie of Austria (b. Oct. 22, 1701, Vienna; d. Dec. 11, 1756). Daughter of Emperor Joseph I. Married 1722.

Children:

Maria Antonia Walburga (b. July 18, 1724; d. Apr. 23, 1780, Dresden). Married 1747 to the future Elector Friedrich Christian of Saxony (procura wedding in Munich, June 13).

Therese Benedicte (b. Dec. 6, 1725; d. Mar. 29, 1743, Frankfurt).

Maximilian III Joseph (b. Mar. 28, 1727).

Maria Anna Josepha (b. Aug. 7, 1734; d. May 7, 1776). Married 1755 to Margrave Ludwig Georg of Baden-Baden (procura wedding in Munich, July 10). After the death of her husband in 1761 (their three children died in infancy), Maria Anna Josepha returned to the Munich court to live permanently.

Josepha Antonia (b. Mar. 30, 1739; d. May 28, 1767, Vienna). Married 1765 to the future Emperor Joseph II (procura wedding in Munich, Jan. 13).

Maximilian III Joseph (b. Mar. 28, 1727; d. Dec. 30, 1777). Reigned from Jan. 20,
1745.

Consort:

Maria Anna Sophia (b. Aug. 29, 1728, Dresden; d. Feb. 17, 1797). Daughter of King Friedrich August II of Poland and Elector of Saxony. Married 1747 (wedding in Munich, July 9). The marriage was without issue.

Max III Joseph was succeeded as Elector of Bavaria by:

Karl Theodor (b. Dec. 11, 1724, near Brussels; d. Feb. 16, 1799). Reigned from Dec. 30, 1777. Reigned as Elector Palatine from 1742.

Consorts:

Elisabeth Auguste (b. Jan. 17, 1721, Mannheim; d. Aug. 17, 1794, Weinheim). Daughter of Hereditary Prince Joseph Karl Emanuel of Pfalz-Sulzbach. Married 1742. The marriage was without issue.

Maria Leopoldine (b. Dec. 10, 1776, Milan; d. June 23, 1848, near Wasserburg am Inn). Daughter of Archduke Ferdinand of Austria-Modena-Este. Married 1795. The marriage was without issue.

Karl Theodor was succeeded as Elector of Bavaria by:

Maximilian IV Joseph (b. May 27, 1756, Mannheim; d. Oct. 13, 1825). Reigned from Feb. 16, 1799 (as Elector of Pfalzbayern). Reigned as Duke of Pfalz-Zweibrücken from 1795. Named King of Bavaria (Maximilian I Joseph), Jan. 1, 1806.

Consorts:

Auguste Wilhelmine (b. Apr. 14, 1765, Darmstadt; d. Mar. 30, 1796, near Heidelberg). Daughter of Landgrave Georg Wilhelm of Hessen-Darmstadt. Married 1785. Three children of this marriage survived their tenth year, among them Max I Joseph's heir, Ludwig I (1786–1868; reigned 1825–48).

Karoline Friederike (b. July 13, 1776, Karlsruhe; d. Nov. 13, 1841). Daughter of Hereditary Prince Karl Ludwig of Baden. Married 1797. Six children of this marriage survived their tenth year.

Appendix 2
Excerpts from the Diary of Graf von Preysing, 1719

The following excerpts from Maximilian Graf von Preysing's diary of 1719 (BStB, HsAbt, Cod germ 5456) serve to illustrate the kinds of information he provides on day-to-day life at the Bavarian court.

Information not pertinent to court life has been omitted from the transcribed passages. Punctuation has been altered somewhat to render them more intelligible, but orthography has been changed only minimally.

Sunday, January 15. Mittags Taffl mit denen Dames. Abents Vesper, darauf die erste franzosische Comedie, eine piece serieuse genandt Iphigenie, nebst dem Nachspill Le port de mer. Die Comedie wurde in dem Opera Hauss gespillt, und wegen des ceremoniel, so man mit dem Comte Charolais evitieren wolle, das kleine Theater bey Hoff gar nit aufgemacht. Die Stund zur Comedie ware nach d. Vesper gegen $\frac{1}{2}$7 Uhr abents. Nachts so dan redoute.

Monday, January 16. Das appartement bey Hoff, wobey auch die Churfürstin.

Tuesday, January 17. Mittags wurde mit denen Dames gespeist. Abents giengen die Printzen in die teutsche Comedie. Gegen 9 Uhr zum General Rechberg, wo auch d. Churfürst und Comte Charolais nebst 3 Hoff- und 4 Stadt-Dames sich eingefunden, allda zu nacht gespeist und darauf dem masquierten bal, so bis 4 Uhr gethauret, beygewohnt. Masqueren waren nur gegen 30 da.

Wednesday, January 18. [Nothing pertinent.]

Thursday, January 19. Abents das gewöhnliche Appartement. Darauf Redoute.

Friday, January 20. Vormittags Ambt bey Hoff. Abents Vesper und Anticamera.

Saturday, January 21. War d. Churfürst nebst denen Printzen auf d. Reittschuel, d. Aufzug zum Carousel zu probieren. Nachmittag umb $\frac{1}{2}$4 Uhr geheimer Rhat, darauf Littaney, und Anticamera.

Sunday, January 22. Speiste d. Churfürst mit denen Dames bey Hoff. Abents ware frantzosische Comedie Andromaque, mit dem Nachspill Le mariage forcé. Darauf redoute.

Monday, January 23. Ware Appartement, darauf Soupé, und bal bey Grafen Costa. Bey dem ersteren waren d. Churfürst und die gdste Printzen nebst Comte Charolais, dan 4 Hoff- und 3 bis 4 Statt-Dames, bey dem letzteren aber ware jed. masque sich einzufinden erlaubt. Ware zimlich eng, da man nur 2 ordinari Zimmer zum dantzen gehabt.

Tuesday, January 24. Geheten die gdste Prinzen abents in die teutsche Comedie auf das Rath haus, so umb 5 Uhr anfangt. . . . Nachts ware das Soupé bey dem Obristcammerer, wo d. Churfürst und die Printzen nebst denen Hoff- und 4 bis 5 Statt-Dames sich eingefunden. Darauf d. masquierte Ball, so bis 5 Uhr frueh gethauert, und über 500 masqueren dabey zu sehen geben.

Wednesday, January 25. Gienge d. Churfürst, so in seinem Retirade mittags gespeiset, abents auf d. Hirsch anger, gegen die nacht aber umb 6 Uhr in die frantzosische Comedie, in d. nur ein petite piece als Le menteur reprasentiert wurde, ursachen solches ein Stuckh von 5 acten ist.

Thursday, January 26. Mittags Taffl mit denen Dames. Nach solch probierte man auf d. Reittschuel d. Auf- und Abzug des Carousel. Nachts Appartement.

Friday, January 27. Das mittag mahl zu Fürstenried, darauf Reh Jagd im Parc. Nachts Anticamera bey Hoff und Gesellschafft in d. Statt bey Closen.

Saturday, January 28. Prob im Reutthaus des Auf- und Abzugs. D. Hoff allenthalber in d. Retirade gespeist. Nachts Anticamera.

Sunday, September 3. Die Hl. Mess [at Nymphenburg] ein wenig vor 12 Uhr ohne music, darauf die Taffl à l'ordinaire. Anstatt d. Comedie, hat d. Sailtantzer umb 6 Uhr zu spillen angefangen, darauf ein nachspill beym fackhln gemacht, so bis 8 Uhr gethauret. D. Spill platz war auf d. offnen Theatro. Darauf ware assembleé, folgents soupé mit 2 gleichen Taffln, und 12 Uhr aber alles aus.

Monday, September 4. Frueh in Nimph à l'ordinaire. Mittags zu München mit denen Dames, umb $\frac{1}{4}$ nach 2 in die Jesuiten comedie. Nach solcher grosser Hoffgarten. Und blibe d. Hoff über nacht zu München.

Tuesday, September 5. Umb 11 Uhr die Hl. Mess. Vorhero geheimber Rhat. Darauf nach Fürstenried zum Fruehstuckh. Nach solchem Hirsch iagt, so abermahl gefählt worden. Nach solcher d. Churpr. nach München zum Sailldantzern, umb $\frac{1}{2}$10 nach Nimphenb., wo alles zu nacht gespeist, auch die Hertzogin [Ferdinand] hinkommen.

Wednesday, September 6. Umb 11 Uhr d. Churf. nach Schleissh. Alldort mittags gespeist, und abents Huener geschossen. D. Churpr., Comte Charolais und Hertz. Ferdt seynd frueh morgens in ihren wild bahn, haben zu Gelting mittags gespeist, und d. gantzen tag gegen 80 Stückh zu sammen geschossen. Nach d. Jagt giengen sie zum sail dantzer und umb $\frac{1}{2}$10 Uhr nach Nimphenb. zum soupé.

Thursday, September 7. D. morgen und mittag à l'ordinaire. Abents . . . [Preysing apparently did not finish this entry.]

Friday, September 8. Umb 12 Uhr die Hl. Mess ohne music. Abents spilten die Herrschaften auf d. Pass, und gegen 7 Uhr fahrten sie grad zum Augustinern in die Littaney. Nach solcher d. Churf. nach Fürstenried, allwo er zu nacht gespeist, und geschlaffen. Die Printzen bliben zu München, und folgten erst am Sambstag frueh hinach.

Saturday, September 9. Umb ½8 Uhr die Hl. Mess zu Fürstenr. Darauf auf die Hirsch iagt, weillen man aber keinen gefunden, kame alles zu ruckh zum mittagmahl nach Fürstenr. D. gantz abent wurde mit Huenerschiessen zu gebracht, und wurden 114 Stückh geschossen. Ds nachtmahl ware zu Nimphenb., wohinn auch die Hertzogin komen.

Sunday, September 10. Die Hl. Mess nach 11 Uhr, darnach alles nach München, wo mittags mit denen Dames in d. Schwartzen Sällerl gespeist worden. Abents geheimber Rhat. Nach solchem d. Churf nach Fürstenried, die Printzen aber zu München gebliben, und erst folgenten morgen gefolgt.

Monday, September 11. Die Hl. Mess gegen 9 Uhr. Darauf auf die Hirsch iagt, wo wid. keiner gefunden, und bis 2 Uhr [illegible] worden. Umb halb 3 Uhr kame die Herrschaft nach Hauss, wo die Printzen ds mittag mahl eingenommen, d. Churfürst aber gar nit, sondern erst umb 6 Uhr gespeist. Nach d. Taffl auf Huener schiessen, d. Churf. gegen d. nacht nach Nimph., die Prinzen aber nach München, wo grosser Hoffgarten.

Tuesday, September 12. [sometime after 9 A.M.] d. Churpr. zum [illegible] mahler [for a portrait sitting] gefahren, umb ½12 Uhr aber nach Nimph. zur Hl. Mess und Mittagmahl. Nach solchem gegen 3 Uhr d. Churpr. auf Huener schiessen bis gegen 7 Uhr. D. Churfürst aber nach Neuhauss. Gegen d. nacht ware music, folgents wurde noch vor dem essen beym [torchlight?] auf d. Pass gespilt.

Wednesday, September 13. D. morgen und mittag à l'ordinaire. Abents weillen es starckh geregnet wurd die iagt eingestellt. D. Prinzen fahrten in die Statt zum Sail dantzer, so aber nit gespilt, destwegen wurde d. kleine daschen spiller . . . nach Hoff zu denen Hoff Dames hinauf beruffen, und nach solchem von d. Singerin etliche Arien gesungen. Umb ½9 giengen die Prinzen wid. zurück nach Nimph.

Thursday, September 14. Frueh à l'ordinaire, wo d. Churpr. auf Huener schiessen. Nach d. Taffl geheten alle Herrschaften auf die iagt bis 6 Uhr. Ware so dan grosser Hoffgarten zu Nimphenb. und soupé mit denen Dames.

Friday, September 15. In d. frueh à l'ordinaire. Mittags zu Nimphenb. Gegen 4 Uhr nach München zur ersten Prob d. gantzen Opera in dem Schwartzen Sällerl. Folgents nach Fürstenried nach 9 Uhr, wo man gespeist und geschlaffen.

Saturday, September 16. Die Mess umb 9 Uhr. Darauf hirsch iagt, wurde gefangen, und zwahr d. erste in diser saison. D. retour zu Fürstenried umb 2 Uhr. Folgents ist d. Churfürst nach Schleissheim, d. Churpr. aber nach München sich mahlen zu lassen, umb 8 Uhr aber auch nach Schleissheim gefolgt.

Sunday, November 26. Umb 11 Uhr die Predig bey Hoff, und Hochambt. Die Taffl mit denen Dames. Darauf geheimber Rhat umb ¼4 Uhr bis gegen 6 Uhr, wo d. Churf. nach Fürstenr. Die Prinzen aber erst umb 8 Uhr nachgefahren, daraus gespeist, und geschlaffen.

Monday, November 27. Die Hl. Mess nach 10 Uhr, darauf ds Fruehstuckh. Nach solchem geklopft im brandt, so lang man gesehen. Wurden 13 Fuchs und etliche haasen geschossen. Umb 9 Uhr so dan gespeist, folgents bis nach 11 Uhr auf d. Pass gespilt, dan zur ruhe gangen.

Tuesday, November 28. Die Hl. Mess umb ½11 Uhr, darauf ds Fruehstuckh. Nach solchem gegen Gauting zum klopfen. . . . Dan umb ⅓3 Uhr widerumb nach Fürstenr. gefahren, d. abent auf d. Pass zugebracht, umb 9 Uhr gespeist, und nach 11 Uhr zu böth gangen.

Wednesday, November 29. Wegen starckhen Wind und schnee wetter wurde die Hirsch iagt eingestellt. Umb ½12 Uhr die Hl. Mess gehört, dan ds fruehstuckh genommen. Folgents d. Churfürst in die berline gesessen und nach Nimph. gefahren. Die Prinzen aber nach München, wo sie gespeist, d. Churpr. aber zum schlaffen wid. nach Nimph. kommen.

Thursday, November 30. Die Hl. Mess ohne music gegen 12 Uhr. D. Churf. blibe im Schloss d. gantzen abent. D. Churpr. aber hat etliche haasen und Huener gesuecht. Ds nacht mahl und nacht lager ware zu Nimph.

Friday, December 1. Die Hl. Mess umb ½11 Uhr. Darauf ds Fruehstuckh, folgents zur Hirsch iagt. Weillen aber wegen starckhen Wind kein hirsch [illegible] worden, kame man gleich wider zuruckh nach Nimph. und wurde die iagt auf morgen aus gesetzt.

Saturday, December 2. Umb 9 Uhr in die Hl. Mess, wo vorher die Procession umb die Capelle mit den Hochwürdigsten in Begleittung des Hoffs und 14 Caputziner gehalten. . . . Darauf nach Fürstenr. zum Fruehstuckh, folgents Hirsch iagt. Die jagt theilte sich auf 2 Hirschen und wurde keiner gefangen. D. retour ware zu München.
NB. Heuth abents ist ds winter quartier zu München bezogen und die Nimphenburg. campagne geendet worden.
NB. Heuth ware vor heur die letzte hirsch jagt.

Sunday, December 3. Die predig umb 11 Uhr bey Hoff, so dan ds Hochambt. Darauf die Taffl mit denen Dames. Nach solcher auf die Pass. Umb 5 Uhr Vesper. Nach 6 Uhr spilten vil Statt Dames bey d. Hertzogin, wo auch music gemacht wurde. Nachts speisten die Herrschafften iede auf ihrer Seitten.

Monday, December 4. Weillen wegen gestern eingefallnen ersten Advent Sontag ds fest des St. [Francis Xavier] auf heuth verschoben worden, gienge d. Churfürst umb 11 Uhr über die gang zum Jesuitern, wo er nebst denen Printzen und Hertzogin 2 Hl. Messen gehört. . . . Mittags speiste d. Churfürst allein und gienge zum ersten mahl vor dise Zeit auf d. hirsch anger, wo er 11 ändten geschossen. D. Churpr. speiste auf d. Hertzogin Seitten. Abents gegen 7 Uhr spilte d. Churfürst bey d. Hertzogin, und ware zugleich music.

Tuesday, December 5. Heuth als Geburthstag des Churfürst von Cölln ware angesagt. Galla. Umb 11 Uhr gienge d. Hoff offentlich über in die Hoff Capelle, ware ds ambt mit trompetten und paukhen. Darauf offentliche Taffl, wo die Cavaliers speisen getragen. . . . Umb ½6 Uhr Vesper. Nach solcher gienge d. Churf., Churpr. und Hertzog Ferdt zu d. Ctsse Albert, wo die Casolana gesungen und d. Churf. und Pr. Ferdt mit musiciert von 8 bis 10 Uhr. Bey d. Hertzogin waren nur die Hoff Dames, so gespilt, von der Stadt waren keine darin.

Wednesday, December 6. Umb 11 Uhr zum Carmelittern über d. gang, wo ein Hochambt gewesen. Mittags die Taffl mit denen Dames. Umb 3 Uhr geh. Rhat. Nach solchem d. Churf. nach Fürstenried. Die Printzen aber erst umb 11 Uhr nach gefahren und vorher musiciert bey d. Hertzogin.

Thursday, December 7. Solte hirsch iagt seyn. Weillen aber so starckh gefrohren, wurde solche eingestellt, und darvor ds rech geiagt. Ds fruehstuckh ware zu Fürstenr. Nach d. jagt kame alles nach München, ware Vesper und Littaney mit 2 Hl. Seegen.

Friday, December 8. Die Predig umb 11 Uhr. Darauf ds Hochambt. Mittags speisten alle Herrschaften auf ihrer Seitten iede allein. Abents die Vesper umb ½6 Uhr, darauf die Littaney. Folgents zur Hertzogin, wo ein Spil, und music à l'ordinaire.

Saturday, December 9. Ds Englambt umb 12 Uhr. Die Herrschaften speisten iede auf ihrer Seitten. Umb 6 Uhr die Littaney, die Prinzen folgents zur Hertzogin gangen, und aldort musiciert.

Appendix 3
Annual Court Itineraries, 1719 and 1720

The information on annual court itineraries contained in Maximilian Graf von Preysing's diaries of 1719 and 1720 (BStB, HsAbt, Cod germ 5456) has been diagrammed on the following two calendar tables. During the period 1719–22, Preysing made entries in his diary almost every day of the year, so that a fairly complete picture of the movements of the court is possible. Preysing was at that time attached to the household of Electoral Prince Karl Albrecht (and seems to have been a close companion of the latter), but he also conscientiously recorded the daily activities of Elector Max Emanuel and gave frequent indications of the activities of the other family members who participated in court life in these years. This did not include Electress Therese Kunigunde, who spent most of her time in semiretirement at Blutenburg or Lichtenberg am Lech, making only occasional appearances at court. The elector and his children often went their own separate ways. During the summer they might, for example, be together at dinner, supper, or an evening Appartement or Hofgarten in Munich or at Nymphenburg; but the elector might then spend the night at Nymphenburg, while Karl Albrecht slept in town. The calendars show where the elector spent the night, as this was recorded by Preysing.

Preysing noted the following dates for the beginning and end of the Campagne: 1719, April 26–December 2; 1720, May 31–November 24.

On days for which Preysing did not record where the elector slept, the date has been left blank. This usually meant that Preysing was not in Munich. From April 29 to May 26, 1719, for example, he accompanied Karl Albrecht and three of his brothers on a tour of Italy. He spent the month from September 5 to October 8, 1720, at his country estates. In April 1719, he seems to have been in Munich (at least some of the time), but he made very few entries in his diary.

The "Other" category indicates a few nights spent at Dachau and Starnberg, but mostly trips farther afield (to Landshut, Ingolstadt, Haag, Schwaben, Wasserburg, Altötting, etc., primarily for purposes of hunting).

1719

JANUARY

S	M	T	W	T	F	S
1	2	3	4	5	6	7
8						

FEBRUARY

S	M	T	W	T	F	S
		14				

MARCH

S	M	T	W	T	F	S
				8		
19	20	21				
				29	30	31

APRIL

S	M	T	W	T	F	S
						1
		4	5	6	7	8
9	10	11	12	13	14	15
16	17	18	19	20	21	22
	24	25	26	27	28	29
30						

MAY

S	M	T	W	T	F	S
	1	2	3	4	5	6
7	8	9	10	11	12	13
14	15	16	17	18	19	20
21	22	23	24	25	26	

JUNE

S	M	T	W	T	F	S
				1	2	3
	5	6			9	10
		13	14	15	16	17
	20	21	22	23	24	
	27	28	29	30		

JULY

S	M	T	W	T	F	S
						1
		4	5	6	7	
	10	11			14	15
16	17	18	19	20	21	22
23	24	25	26			

AUGUST

S	M	T	W	T	F	S
		1	2	3	4	5
6	7	8	9	10	11	12
13	14	15	16	17	18	
	21	22	23	24	25	26
	28	29	30	31		

SEPTEMBER

S	M	T	W	T	F	S
					1	2
3		5	6	7	8	9
10	11	12	13	14	15	16
17		19	20	21	22	23
24	25	26	27		29	30

OCTOBER

S	M	T	W	T	F	S
1		3	4	5	6	7
8	9	10	11	12	13	14
15	16	17	18	19	20	21
		24			27	
	30	31				

NOVEMBER

S	M	T	W	T	F	S
			1	2		
5	6	7	8	9	10	11
12		14	15	16	17	
	20		22	23	24	
26	27	28	29	30		

DECEMBER

S	M	T	W	T	F	S
					1	
			6			
		12	13			
			20	21		

1720

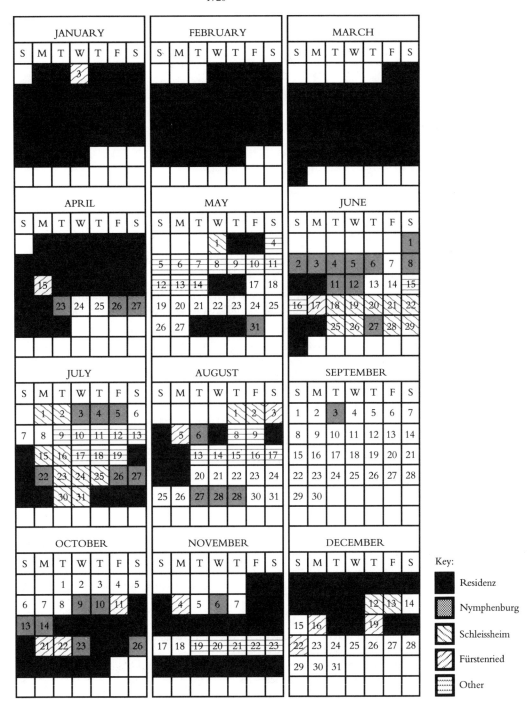

Appendix 4
Aufwartungs-Ordnung 1739

Source: HStA, HR1 34/17.

Publication der Churfrtl. Gdisten Verordnung betr. die churfrtl. AntiCammern und Entrée hierzue, den 4ten 9ber 1739.

Die churfrtl. AntiCamera, und derselben Neuen einrichtung betreffente Puncten, welche den 2ten Decemb. 1739 zur gdisten Resolution kommen seind.

Demnach Ihro Churfrtl. Drtl. sich genädigist gefallen lassen zu mehrer Ordnung Ihres Hofs, und besserer einrichtung selbigen Ethiquets, forderist zu mehreren Splendor Ihrer AntiCamera, und grosseren Ehr deren, so sye betretten, selbige zu vermehren, in der That aber eine vierfache abtheillung vorzunemen, welche nachgestaltsambe der Hof Chargen, Dienst, und Ämbter von Inländisch- und frembden Ministern, Cammerer, und Cavalieren mögen besuecht werden, Als wirdet sothanne ab- und Vertheillung hiemit vorgetragen bestehent.

1mo.   In der Ersten AntiCamera.

2do.   In der Zweyten AntiCamera.

3io.   In dem Grossen Audienz Zimmer.

4to.   In dem Grossen Cabinet.

Weillen aber sich nit schicklen noch erlaubt sein will, dass jeder, da Er nacher Hoff zur Aufwarttung kommet, in iedes obernanter Vier Orthen freyen Eingang nach seinem belieben nemme, als hat sich ieder nach folgenter austhaillung selbst auszumessen, nach solcher sich zu halten, und nit Ursach zu geben, dass Er darüber ankommen, und dahin wohin Er gehörig, zu selbsten seiner Unlust, angewisen werden müsste.

1.   Erste AntiCamera. In solche haben einzutretten, und in solcher Ihre aufwarttung zu machen alle Cavaliers, oder andere Churfrtl. bediente, so mit dem zuetritt begnadet seynd.
2tens.   Alle Staabsofficiere als Obrist, ObristLieut. und Majors, wann schon sye den Cammerschlissel nit haben.

2. Zweyte AntiCamera. Dise können besuechen
1mo.   Alle churfrtl. Cämmerer.
2do.   Auch alle Geheimbe Räthe von der gelehrten banckh.
3io.   Alle Generalen, wann Sye auch nit Cammerherren seind.

3. Grosses Audienz Zimmer. In solchen derffen sich einfünden
1mo.   Alle Geheimbe Räthe und Ministri, so Cavaliers seind.
2do.   Alle in churfrtl. Hofämter stehente Cavaliers Als
der ObristJägerMaister
    die 2 Garde Haubtleuth
    der ObristFalckhenmaister
    der ObristSilberCammerer
    dess ChurPrintz UnderHofmeister
    der Intendant der Music
    der Intendant der Fest
    der ObristKuchlmaister
    Eines Jungen Prinzen Oberhofmr.
3io.   Die wurckhlichen in Haubtdienst bey Ihro Churfrtl. Drtl. sich befündente
2 Cämmerer.

4. Grosses Cabinet. Solches ist forderist vorbehalten denen gdisten Herrschafften, das jedoch die Conferenz- dann Staabs-Ministri darinnen sich gleichfals einfinden mögen. Warunter auch deren Churfürstin, Churprinzens, und übriger Churfrtl. Herrschafften ObristHofmeister verstandten, wie nit weniger die in churfrtl. Diensten stehente oder auch andere sich hier einfindente Vornemme Fürsten Personen zur besonderer Distinction in solches einzufuehren seynd.

Weitter gdiste Verordtnungen.

1mo.   Ist mit dem Stockh in der AntiCamera, und noch mehr in denen innern Gemächen sich einzufinden allen verbotten, welche keine Hofstaabs Vorgesezte, auch keine Gral [General] seynd.

2do.   Seynd zu Vermeydung viller Indecenz die in der Anticamera eingeschlichene Tabouretten, so vor disem nie gebräuchig gewesen, weeder annoch bey anderen Höfen seind, mit Gestattung iedoch der banqueten, abgeschafft.

3io.   Ist angeschafft worden, dass täg- und gemeiniglich nur die 2 Anticameren geöffnet, und besuecht werden sollen, dergestalten, dass was der obigen Repartition nach in der ersten und zweyten Anticamera sich einfinden darff, zusammen in der ersten, und was in das dritte dann vierte Piece oder Gemach verthailt worden, in der zwayten sich versamblen möge.

4to.   Dass an denen Galla Sonn- und feürtägen hingegen alle 4 Zimmer eröffnet, dan [entry incomplete]

5to.   Jedes wenigistens Vormittag mit einem Portier oder Thürsteher besezt, und die gebuehrente Instruction von dem Cammerfourier ihme beygebracht werden solle.
Gleich aber wie schon gemeldet, gemeiniglich, als Werckhstäge nur 2 Zimmer oder Anticamern zu eröffnen kommen, als kommen auch gemeiniglich mehr Portier nit dann zwey anzustellen.

6to. Zu Abstellung eingeschlichener grosser Unehrbiettigkeit bey dem vorgehenten Gottesdienst in der chl. Hof Capelle ist ultimator und fürnemblich genädigist verordtnet worden, dass wehrenten Gottesdienst der H. Mess, Hochambt, Predig, Vesper, oder Littaney, wobey Gdiste Herrschafften sich selbst anwesend findet, iederzeit zwey Hartschier die Wacht an den Thüren dess Oratorij halten, und darob seyn sollen, dass alles ohne geschwätz mit gebuehrenter Ehrnbiettigkeit, und andacht abgehe, niemand, ausser Vesper, und Predig zeit, sich niedersize, und noch minder der H. Mess sich anders als kniend von dem Sanctus an bis nach der Sumption einfinde, widerigens jener, so in einem oder anderen sich vergisset, das erst- oder andere mahl zu seinem Unlust wurde gemahnt, und da es öffters geschechete, zu seiner selbstigen Prostitution ihme, wer immer Er sein möchte, schärffer und allenfahls mit hinweckhschaffung wurde begegnet werden.

Appendix 5
Kammerordnung 1769

Transcribed from the copy in BStB: 2. Bav. 1400. V. 3.

Churbajerische Kammerordnung.

Demnach Se. churfürstliche Durchlaucht &c. &c. zu höchstem Missfallen mehrfältig einsehen müssen, wie das sowohl bey höchstdero, als Ihro Durchlaucht Churfürstin, und anderer durchläuchtigster Personen Antekammern und ordinari Wohnzimmern, dann in der schuldig respectvollesten Bedienungsform alle Ordnung gänzlich abzunehmen und ausser Acht gesetzt zuwerden anfange; als haben höchstermelt Se. churfürstliche Durchlaucht &c. &c. die nöthige Verfassung nachstehend- selbst gnädigst ratificierter Kammerordnung dero Oberstkammerherren übertragen, und selbe der genauesten Darobhaltungswillen zum öffentlichen Druck zu befördern gnädigst anbefohlen.

1. Es haben alle churfürstliche Kämmerer, Kammerdiener, Kammerportier und andere nach Ordnung des Hofkalenders unter dero Staab befindliche Personen dem Oberstkammerern als vorgesetzt ihre Obrigkeit zu erkennen, und dessen Befehle so, wie dessen Verboth auf das genaueste zu befolgen, oder zu unterlassen: und obschon die churfürstl. Kammerknaben, Leibmedici, Leibchirurgi und mehr andere, die bey der churfürstlichen Kammer und denen Wohnzimmern Dienste zu verrichten haben, immediate unter dem Oberstkammerer nicht stehen, so haben sie jedannoch dessen Befehlen in so lang gehorsam nachzukommen, als lange ihre wirkliche Dienstverrichtung hierinnen andaueret.

2. Die Kammerdienste sollen friedlich, getreu und fleissig, dann mit Beybehaltung des schuld- unterthänigsten Respects jederzeit verrichtet werden. Dahero man sich all anstössigen Vexirens, Spottens, Zankens und handgemeinen Scherzens, sonderheitlich aber aller Thätlichkeiten, bey Vermeidung höchster Straffe und Ungnade, zuenthalten; massen, so jemanden was missfälliges begegnen würde, man sich dessen bey dem Oberstkammerer zubeschwären, und von ihme hierinnen billigen Bescheid und Handlung zuerwarten hätte.

3. Imgleichen solle sich niemand unterfangen, die Briefe, Schriften, Anlangen, Bücher und anders, so in denen churfürstlichen Zimmern auf denen Tischen ver-

deckt, oder offen lieget, noch minder die Kästen und Schreibtische zuerforschen und einzusehen, oder wohl gar hievon etwas zuentziehen: im Gegentheil mehrers jederzeit beflissen seyn, auch das, was man währender Dienstverrichtungen siehet, höret, oder erfährt, verschwiegen und geheim bey sich zubehalten.

4. Wenn einem churfürstlichen Kammerer durch den auch churfürstlichen Kammerfourier, auf folgenden Sonntage zum Kammerdienst ordentlich angesagt wird, so hat sich derselbe längstens bis vorgehenden Mitwoch Mittags zu Annahm des Dienstes zuerklären, oder im wichtigen Hindernissfall bey dem Oberstkammerer hierumen zuentschuldigen.

5. Die wirklich dienende Kammerer haben in ihre ordentliche Kammerdienstwechslung alle Sonntage nach dem Gottendienst einzutretten, und so diese Zeit versaumet wird, so ist die ganze Diensttour versaumet, indeme zu accurater Beybehaltung der eingeführten Ordnung, auch kein Vertauschen gestattet wird. Desgleichen haben sich auch die Kammerdiener, und Portiers an die zwischen selben eingeführte Ord- und Wechslung genau zu halten.

6. So jemanden wehrend wirklicher Dienstwoche eine Unpässlichkeit, oder sonstig wichtige Hinderniss aufstosset, hat selber solches dem Oberstkammerer ohngesäumt zuinsinuiren, um noch in der Zeit nöthige Veranstalung vorkehren zulassen.

7. In der churfürstlichen Kammer oder Schlafzimmer, hat sich ausser dem An- und Abkleiden, oder sonstiger Diensterforderniss, niemand, auch kein Kammerer vom Dienst oder Kammerdiener, um Sr. churfürstlichen Durchlaucht nicht beschwerlich zu seyn, aufzuhalten, sondern letztere in dem nächst daranstossenden Vorzimmer, bis auf gnädigstes Rufen, oder sonstiges Zeichen, zuzuwarten.

8. Es gebühret sich auch nicht, wehrender Dienstwoche die gnädigste Herrschaften mit eigenen Gesuch und Sollicitationen zu beschweren, dahero Se. churfürstl. Durchl. fernershin denen im Wochendienste stehenden Kammeren und Kammerdienern um so mehr die Annahm und Ubergab fremder Memorialien, gleich auch die Fürsprache für andere, ausser gnädigsten Specialbefehl, alles Ernsts verbothen haben wollen: da im übrigen jedannoch ohnverwehrt bleibet höchstdieselben müheselig-betrangter Personen, oder sonst wichtiger Umstände wegen bescheiden zuerinnern.

9. Und damit höchsternennt Se. churfürstliche Durchlaucht für das künftige auch des vielen unnöthig und importunen Angehens entübriget seyn mögen, so solle fernershin keinem in Dienst stehenden Kammerern, noch minder einem Kammerdiener, ausser auf besondern churfürstlichen Befehl, oder in Fällen, wo Gefahr ob dem Vorzug haftet, mehr erlaubet seyn, jemanden bey Sr. churfürstl. Durchlaucht zumelden, als jene Ministers und Räthe, so in höchst-herrschaftlichen Diensten unterthänigst zu raportiren haben, noch weniger aber jemanden voroder aufzuführen, sondern sie sollen all und jede, die immer eine gnädigste Audienz zuerbitten gedenken, an dem churfürstlichen Oberstkammerer gebührend anweisen, als von deme die Ansuchende sonach das weitere zugewärtigen haben.

10. Es haben Se. churfürstliche Durchlaucht ferners sehr unbeliebig ersehen, dass einiger Zeithero in das zu Dero Buderzimmer führende kleine Gängl, oder

Retirade, verschiedene Sollicitanten und andere Personen, so die kleine Entrée nicht haben, eingeführet worden, oder selbst dahin zu kommen, sich unterstanden haben, höchstdieselben befehlen dahero Dero Oberstkammerern künftighin genauest darob zu seyn, dass sich Niemand ohne Unterschied, ausser auf gegebenen Specialbefehl, sonderbar zur Zeit wo höchstdieselbe sich inbesagten Buderzimmer aufzuhalten geruhen, in erwehnt kleinem Gängl betretten lasse.

11.   Die in Kammerdiensten stehende Kammerer bedienen die höchste Herrschaften mit an der Seite hangenden Degen, und beyseit gelegten Hut, den sie aber, so die gnädigste Herrschaften ausser Ihre Zimmer zugehen geruhen, jedesmalen zu sich zu nehmen haben: die Kammerdiener legen Degen und Hut beyseit.

12.   Ubrigens sollen fernershin alle Kammerer ohne Unterschied den churfürstlichen Kammerschlüssel, jederzeit so oft sie immer den churfürstlichen oder herzoglichen Hofe betretten, an der Seite tragen, ausser dem sie sich selbsten beyzumessen haben werden, wenn ihnen als unerkannt die gebührende Honeurs nicht bezeiget werden.

13.   Mit dem Stock in die Antekammern und churfürstlichen Wohnzimmer einzugehen wird alleinig denen Staabsministers, Generalfeldmarschallen, Generalfeldzeugmeistern, Generaln von der Cavallerie, und Officiers deren beeden churfürstlichen Leibguarden zugestanden.

14.   Da sich auch keineswegs gebühren will in der churfürstlichen Antekammer eigener Gelegenheit- und Zeitverkürzungswillen, sich (wie bishero öfters geschehen) ordentliche Spieltische setzen, und zurichten zu lassen, als solle solches bey unbeliebiger Ahndung unterbleiben.

15.   Wenn Se. churfürstliche Durchlaucht mit dem Corteggio offentlich über die Galerien zu gehen pflegen, so gehen die im Dienst stehende Kammerer vor, der Oberstkammerer aber nach Dero höchsten Person, wobey ernstlich zu erinnern kommet, dass fernershin das allen Respect entgegenstehende Lermen und Geschwätz unterbleiben, auch alle Kammerer, so nach, wie vor der Kirchen sich zahlreicher einfinden, und nicht wie bishero zuweilen geschehen, halben Weege anticipieren, oder gar durch andere Galerien gehend, ihrer Schuldigkeit ausszuweichen suchen sollen. So der Zug in Gala offentlich durch die Strassen der Stadt geschiehet, haben hiebey auch alle Kammerdiener, und nicht wirklich diensthabende Portiers in ihrer Ordnung zuerscheinen.

16.   Wenn einem Kammerer ein Dienst zum Himmel- oder Speisentragen, so andern angesagt wird, so hat sich keiner mit der Ausrede, dass jüngere zugegen seyen, zuentschuldigen, immassen die Ursachen derley Disposition dem Oberstkammerer bekannt seyn müssen.

17.   Bey offentlichen Tafeln in der churfürstlichen Residenz, ausser denen Ritterfesten, gebühret dem ältesten von denen wirklich dienenden Kammerern die Ehre des Schenkens, und dem jüngsten das Vorschneiden, wobey zu erinnern, das den eersten Trunk Sr. Durchlaucht Churfürstens, der Oberstkammerer, und die erste Speise der Oberstkuchenmeister, bey denen andern gnädigsten Herrschaften aber die Kammerer vom Dienst credenziren. Auf dem Land entgegen stehet das Schenken und Vorschneiden den erst und letzt im Wochendienst stehenden Kammerern zu.

18. Wenn die gnädigsten Herrschaften eine Reise über Land vorzunehmen geruhen, wo die Kammerer vom Wochendienst nicht mitzugehen pflegen, und solche Reise vor dem Mitwoch oder auch Mitwochs vor der Mittagstafel anzutretten beliebet wird, so bleibet der Dienst stehen, und tretten bey der Zurückkunft der gnädigsten Herrschaften die zurückgebliebene Kammerer in ihren vorigen Platz des Kammerdienstes ein: so die Abreise aber erst Mittwochs nach der Mittagstafel, oder die folgenden Täge geschiehet, so werden die zwey Kammerer vom Hauptdienst ausstehen, und bey der Wiederkunft der höchsten Personen die andere vorrucken, und neue zwey einstehen.

19. So ein churfürstl. Kammerer von dem Hoflager verreisen will, stehet demselben zu, wie gleichfältig bey dessen An-oder Zurückkunft sich bey dem Oberstkammerer hierumen gebührend melden zulassen.

20. Fernershin solle kein Kammerer vor Jahr und Tage von Zeit des erhaltenen churfürstlichen Schlüssels angerechnet, um die gnädigste Erlaubniss Kammerdienste machen zu dörfen, sich melden.

21. Ob zwar Se. churfürstliche Durchlaucht jenen Cavalieren und Standespersonen, welche sich, ob sie schon keine churfürstliche Kammerer sind, der Entrée in die churfürstliche erste Antekammer zu erfreuen haben, auch die sogenannte Appartements frequentiren zu dörfen, gnädigst zugegeben haben: so sollen sich dieselbe jedannoch nicht allein des Spielens, sondern auch des Eintritts in das innerste Gemach, wo die höchste Herrschaften zuspielen pflegen, allerdings enthalten.

22. Geschiehet, dass denen in den churfürstlichen Antekammern anwesenden Cavaliers, oder andern, Ausrichtungen zu machen sind, so haben selbe die Kammer- und nicht die Ritter-Portiers, oder wohl gar die Livereybediente zu machen.

23. Gleichwie auch zu Abstellung eingeschlichen- grosser Unehrenbietigkeit bey denen in der churfürstlichen Hofkapelle vorgehenden Gottesdiensten schon in vorigen Jahren gnädigst verordnet worden, dass wehrend dem Gottesdienst der heil. Mess, Hochamts, Predig, Vesper, oder Litaney, wobey die gnädigste Herrschaften sich anwesend befinden, jederzeit zwey Hartschier die Wache an denen Thüren des Oratorii halten, und darob seyn sollen, dass alles ohne Geschwätz mit gebührender Ehrerbietigkeit und Andacht abgehe, auch niemand ausser der Vesper- und Predigzeit, sich niedersetze, noch minder bey der heil. Mess anderst als kniend von dem Sanctus an bis nach der Sumption sich einfinde, widrigens jenem, so in ein oder andern sich vergisset, das erst- oder anderemal mit Ermahnen, und da es öfters geschehete, noch schärfer, auch allenfals zu nicht geringer Prostitution mit Hinwegweisung wurde begegnet werden; als hat es anmit noch ferners sein unabänderliches Verbleiben, und sind deme gemäss die churfürstliche Hartschier neuerdings erinneret worden.

24. Damit nun schlüsslichen der churfürstliche Kammer- und Hoffourier, als denen die Aufsicht der jeden gebührenden Entrée am meisten oblieget, ihrer Schuldigkeit gesichert, auch die Kammer- und Ritterportiers ihrer Obliegenheit hierinfals genugsam informieren, und bey Versehen erinnern: annebens jedermänniglich die ihme nicht zuständige Plätze vermeiden, und solchermassen einer

unbeliebigen Ahndung unausgesetzt seyn könne; so solle die gnädigst ratificierte Entrée-Ordnung hiemit zu mäniglicher Einsicht vorgetragen, und hierauf zufolge churfürstlicher schärfesten Befehle genauest attendieret werden.

Die Ritterstube betreffend.

Haben selbe zu betretten die churfürstl. Truchsess und Räthe.

Die churfürstl. Oberofficiers bis auf den Oberstlieutenant inclusivé, wenn sie nicht wirkliche Kammerer sind, oder ihnen der Zutritt in die erste Antekammer sonderbar bewilliget ist.

Die Dechani und Canonici von denen Collegiatstiftern.

Die Rectores, Priores, Guardiani und dergleichen geistliche Vorstehere.

Nicht weniger alle churfürstl. Oberbeamte und Secretarien.

Auch können sich die churfürstl. Meisterjäger, so sich Dienst halber auzufragen haben, dann die churfürstl. Hoflaquais, doch nur jene, so in dem Wochendienst stehen, alda aufhalten. Wobey denen churfürstl. Ritterportiren ernstlich aufgetragen wird, genauest darob zu seyn, dass sich ausser obangeführten niemand, besonders weder der Cavaliers noch andere Livereybediente alda betretten lassen, als welche allein in dem Vor- oder Herculessaal zuwarten haben.

Die erste Antekammer belangend.

In solche haben einzutretten, und hierinnen ihre Aufwartung zu machen:

Alle churfürstl. Kammerer, Cavaliers und andere, so mit dem Zutritt specialiter begnadet.

Die churfürstl. gelehrte wirkliche und Titular-geheime Räthe.

Die von fremden Höfen am hiesig churfürstl. Hofe nicht accreditierte Ministers und Residenten.

Die Generalwachtmeistere und Oberste, wenn sie schon auch den Kammerschlüssel nicht haben.

Die churfürstl. Canzler und Directores, auch wirklich characterisierte Vicecanzler und Vicedirectores deren Dicasterien.

Die fünf Rentmeister.

Die Prälaten und Pröbste.

Die insulierte Dechani von denen Collegiatstiftern.

Die zweyte Antekammer.

Diese können besuchen die wirkliche und Titular- geheime Räthe, so zugleich churfürstl. Kammerer sind.

Die im wirklichen Wochendienst stehende Kammerer.

Alle in churfürstl. hohen Hofämtern stehende Cavaliers: Als

Der Oberstjägermeister.

Die zwey Leibguarde-Hauptleute.

Der Oberstfalkenmeister, Oberstkuchenmeister, Oberstsilberkammerer, Vice-Oberststallmeister, Vice-Oberstjägermeister und Vice-Oberstfalkenmeister. Die Generalfeldmarschall-Lieutenants, und churfürstl. General-Adjutanten, dann die Lieutenants und Cornet von denen churfürstl. zwey Leibguarden deren Hartschier und Trabanten.

Das churfürstl. Audienzzimmer.

In dieses tretten ein die auswärtige und in churfürstl. Diensten stehende Fürsten und Prinzen.

Die vier Minister der churfürstl. Hofstäaben.

Der Obersthofmeister von Ihro Durchlaucht der Churfürstin &c. &c.

Die churfürstl. Conferenzministers.

Die Kaiserl. geheime Räthe.

Die am hiesig-churfürstl. Hofe accreditiert-auswärtige Gesandte zugleich Ministers.

Die churfürstl. Generalfeldmarschallen, Generalfeldzeug- und Oberstlandzeugmeister, dann

Die Generalen von der Cavallerie.

Wann aber obstehende zweyte Antekammer, nebst dem Audienzzimmer selten geöffnet zu werden pflegen, so haben diejenige, welche obiger Repartition nach in mehrbemeldt- churfürstl. Audienzzimmer und zweyten Antekammer sich einzufinden befugt seyn, solchenfals in der ersten Antekammer, oder aber in denen churfürstl. neuen Vor- und Wohnzimmern, die entgegen künftighin jemand anderer, der nicht sonderbarer Dienstverrichtungen halber hierinnen zu thun hat, ohne special gnädigste Erlaubniss nicht mehr betretten solle, zu verbleiben.

Die Entrée au Lever.

Solle fürohin zum Anziehen Sr. churfürstlichen Durchlaucht &c. &c. alleinig zugestanden und gestattet werden

Denen Ministers der churfürstlichen vier Stäaben, nebst Sr. Durchlaucht der Churfürstin Obersthofmeistern.

Denen churbaierischen Conferenz- und wirklichen geheimen Räthen, so Kammerer sind, und wem aus denen Ministers Se. churfürstl. Durchlaucht noch sonderbar zubenennen geruhen.

Denen zwey im Hauptdienst stehenden churfürstl. Kammerern.

Denen Generalfeldmarschallen, Generalfeldzeugmeister, und Generaln von der Cavallerie, wenn sie auch nicht churfürstliche Kammerer sind, dann denen Generallieutenanten und Generalmajoren, wenn sie churfürstliche Kammerer sind, wie auch denen churfürstlichen Generaladjutanten.

Denen zwey churfürstlichen Capitains, deren zwey Leib-Guarden Hartschier und Trabanten.

Dem churfürstlichen Oberstjägermeister, und Oberstfalkenmeister.

Einem churfürstlichen Oberstküchenmeister, Oberstsilberkammerer, Vice-Oberststallmeister, Vice-Oberstjägermeister, und Vice-Oberstfalkenmeister.

Denen Lieutenants deren zwey Guarden deren Hartschier und Trabanten, wie auch dem Cornet der Hartschierguarde.

Denen zwey churfürstlichen Kammerknaben.

Dem churfürstlichen P. Beichtvater.

Dem churfürstlichen Cabinetssecretär.

Denen churfürstlichen Leibmedicis.

All wirklich dienenden churfürstlichen Kammerdienern, sie mögen vom Wochendienst seyn, oder nicht.

Ordnung der Einfahrt in die churfürstliche Residenz.

In die churfürstliche Residenz können einfahren und bey der grossen Stiegen absteigen:

Auswärtige Fürsten und Prinzen.

Die Chefs von denen vier churfürstlichen Hofstäaben, als

Der churfürstliche Obersthofmeister, Oberstkammerer, Obersthofmarschall, und Oberststallmeister.

Alle churfürstliche Conferenzministers.

Der Obersthofmeister von Ihro Durchlaucht der Churfürstin &c. &c.

Die kaiserliche geheime Räthe.

Die accreditiert-auswärtige Gesandte und Ministers.

Die churfürstliche Generalfeldmarschallen, Generalfeldzeug- und Oberstland-zeugmeister.

Die Generals der Cavallerie.

Der churfürstliche Oberstjägermeister.

Der churfürstliche Revisionsraths-Director, Hofraths- und Hofkammerpräsi-dent.

Die Vicedommen deren churfürstlichen Regierungen.

Die churfürstl. wirkliche geheime Räthe.

Die churfürstliche Titular- geheime Räthe, so zugleich churfürstliche Kammerer sind.

Der Stadthalter in der obern Pfalz.

Die beede Capitains der Guarden derer Hartschier und Trabanten.

Sämmtliche Hof- und Stadtdamen, die auch an der hintern Stiegen im Brunnhofe absteigen mögen.

Dahingegen können zwar in die churfl. Residenz, jedoch mit eigener Equipage einfahren, sollen aber nicht bey der grossen Stiegen, sondern bey der Kapell- oder Canzleystiegen absteigen:

Die Commenthurn von dem hohen St. Georgii Ritterorden.

Die churfürstlichen Kammerer.

Die General-Lieutenants.

Der churfürstliche geheime Kanzler, und geheime Vice-Kanzler, wenn ihnen nicht ein mehrerer Character was anders zugeleget.

Ubrigens ist denen Lehen und all andern derley Wägen die Einfahrt schärfesten Ernsts verbothen.

Welchem allen sohin jedermänniglich gehorsamst nachzukommen, und sich von allenfalls ernstlicher Ahndung gleichwohl von selbsten zu hüten wissen wird. Gegeben München den 2. Jänner 1769.

Ex Commissione Serenissimi Domini Domini Ducis Electoris Speciali.

Franz Xaveri Menrad von Vorwaltern, churfl. wirkl. Hofrath und Kammer-fourier.

Appendix 6
Schedule of Ceremonies and Festivities at the Double Marriage between the Electoral Houses of Bavaria and Saxony, June–July 1747

This schedule has been compiled from the following two sources:

HStA, FS 772n, "Anzeig über das, so von morgen dem 10. Juny an bis 10. July der einstehent. Drtisten doppel heurath halber vorgehen wirdet," [June 9,] 1747. HStA, FS 777, "Austheilung deren verschiedenen Festins und Unterhaltungen, so bey nächst bevorstehenter ID Churfürstin Ankunft vom 9. bis 26. Juli (beyden inclusive) zusammen 18 Tage hindurch gehalten und vorgehen werden," n.d. [1747].
It should be noted that both sources describe what was planned and not necessarily what took place.

June 10. Public "Anwerbungs-Audienz" of the Saxon ambassador, 11–12 A.M., after which the ambassador leaves (see chap. 6). "Ganze Gala" observed. At midday, public dinner, whereby all members of the family dine alone in the apartment of Dowager Empress Maria Amalie, "in ihrer Anticamera."

June 11. Gala at court. Sermon and high mass. Midday dinner once again in the dowager empress's "Anticamera." In the evening, Italian comedy, "grosses Souper," and ball, all in costume dress, but without masks and without observance of rank.

June 12. The renunciation ceremony of Princess Maria Antonia Walburga. Midday dinner in the dowager empress's "Cammer."

June 13. The wedding ceremony around 6 P.M., then the Te Deum and "grosses Souper" in the elector's Ritterstube, at which the family and the Saxon ambassador dine (see app. 7). Then the "Ceremonienball."

June 14. Midday dinner "en famille" in the dowager empress's apartment, either in the "Cammer" or the "Spiegel-Zimmer" (audience chamber). In the evening, the ladies-in-waiting take leave of the princess. Supper "in der Cammer." Everybody retires early, as an early departure is planned for the following day.

June 15. Early mass "im Spital." From there, the departure of the princess and her retinue. Midday meal taken at Wolnzach, to which point the dowager empress accompanies the princess. Night quarter in Ingolstadt.

June 16. Night quarter in Neumarkt.

June 17. In Amberg.

June 18. Midday meal in Weiden. Night quarter in Waldsassen.

June 19. Arrival early in the morning in Adorf, the first stop in Saxon territory. Here the princess is taken over by her Saxon retinue. The Bavarian retinue returns to Waldsassen and spends the night there.

June 20 or 21. The princess arrives in Dresden. After the benediction, the wedding takes place. From the following day until July 2, various festivities are held in Dresden.

July 3. Princess Maria Anna Sophia leaves Dresden.

July 4. Arrival in Bavarian territory. Night quarter in Waldsassen.

July 5. Night quarter in Amberg.

July 6. In Neumarkt.

July 7. In Ingolstadt.

July 8. In Wolnzach. Here the dowager empress meets the princess and spends the night.

July 9. Arrival in Munich in the morning. The procession enters the city through the Neuhauser Tor (Karlstor) and proceeds to the Residenz "über den Platz" (Marienplatz). During the procession, there is a triple- gun salute and the garrison and citizenry stand in parade formation. The princess alights in the Brunnenhof at the foot of the staircase to the electress's apartment.

At midday, the dowager empress, elector, and electress dine in the elector's second antechamber. The Kämmerer have service. (This is the account given in FS 777. FS 772n, which must be regarded in this instance as a less reliable source, states that this dinner takes place "in der Cammer.").

Around 6 P.M., the court assembles in gala for the public procession to the Jesuit Church (Michaelskirche), where the benediction is held. From the "schöne Zimmer" one proceeds through the Herkules-Saal, the Lederner Saal, the Theatiner Galerie, and the Kaisersaal, then down the Kaisertreppe, and to the Kaiserhof, where one mounts. Then the procession passes through the Kaisertor and to the church via the "Obere Schwabingergasse" (Residenzstrasse) and the "Platz."

Upon the return to the Residenz, the "churfürstliche Parade-Zimmer" are illuminated and the "Stadtdamen" (wives of Munich patricians) are admitted "zum Hand-Kuss und Glückwunsch." Supper in the elector's Ritterstube exactly as on June 13. After this, a ball in the Herkules-Saal, "jedoch nur en famille." Early to bed because of the tiring journey.

July 10. Name day of the dowager empress, and therefore "grosse Gala." High mass with trumpets and drums. At midday, public dinner in the empress's apartment. In the evening, "Stunde," then card playing in the empress's Spiegel-Zimmer and public supper in the antechamber.

July 11. Midday dinner "en famille" in the Spiegel-Zimmer. The afternoon and evening are spent in touring the Residenz (Grüne Galerie, Antiquarium, etc.). Supper at Nymphenburg, where the night is spent. In this way the "Landleben" is begun.

July 12. Tour of the garden and the Parkburgen (Magdalenenklause, Pagodenburg, Badenburg) at Nymphenburg. For this purpose, the "Garten-Wägelein" are to be placed in readiness for the Herrschaften. Supper in the "Grosser Saal," during which a "Concert de music."

July 13. Midday at Nymphenburg. In the evening, Jesuit comedy. After this, the court returns to Nymphenburg for supper and to sleep.

July 14 or 21. One of these two days is a day of rest at Nymphenburg. On the other day the following will be undertaken. Breakfast at Nymphenburg. Then to the Starnbergersee for a "Hirsch- und Wasserjagd." Return to Schloss Berg. Then "beim Mondschein" (probably, "if there is moonlight") by boat to the landing dock (presumably at Schloss Starnberg); and from there, into the waiting carriages and back to Nymphenburg.

July 15. Day of rest at Nymphenburg. The evening is taken up with a concert, then cards.

July 16. The court goes early in the day to Munich. Around 11 A.M., to the Carmelites to attend the service and the "Scapulier-Fest." At midday, public dinner in the electress's Spiegel-Zimmer. Night quarter in Munich.

July 17. Day of the elector's Erbhuldigung. High mass in the Hofkapelle. At 9 A.M., public procession to the Rathaus, where the Erbhuldigung takes place. Then procession to the Frauenkirche, where a Te Deum is heard. Then procession back to the Residenz. At midday, the elector dines with the "Erbämter" (holders of the hereditary court offices), the ministers, and the "Landschafts-Verordnete" (representatives of the Estates), as well as two or three of the elder Kämmerer. Public supper in the Kaisersaal. Then an illumination and tour of the city.

July 18. Name day of Electoral Prince Friedrich Christian of Saxony. Therefore, high mass with trumpets and drums. At midday, public dinner in the elector's apartment. In the evening, opera. Supper "in der Cammer, au petit couvert."

July 19. Midday in the city "à l'ordinaire." In the evening, an illumination "bis zum canal." Then a pantomime in the "offenes Theatro" at Nymphenburg. Then Hofgarten and supper in the Hauptsaal, to which the Stadtdamen are invited.

July 20. Midday as otherwise at Nymphenburg. In the evening, to Fürstenried, where there is a "Nacht-Schiessen" and an illumination of the garden. After supper with the ladies and gentlemen, return to Nymphenburg.

July 21. Day of rest at Nymphenburg, in the event that the deer hunt at Starnberg was held on July 14.

July 22. First "Jahr-Markt" at Nymphenburg. The "Magdalena-Fest" is celebrated in the Hofkapelle and the Eremitage. In the evening, a "concert de music."

July 23. Midday at Nymphenburg. In the evening, a masked opera in the city. Then return to Nymphenburg, there to dine "in der Cammer" and to sleep.

July 24. At midday to Schleissheim, where the midday meal is taken. In the afternoon and evening, tour of the palace, and then a tour of the garden and Lustheim. Return to Nymphenburg for supper.

July 25. Illumination and supper at Amalienburg. Then a ball in the Hauptsaal, to which the Stadtdamen are invited.

July 26. Name day of the electress. Public dinner at midday at Nymphenburg. In the evening, "Grosser Hofgarten," supper, and fireworks.
"Womit also die Festins beschlossen werden."

Appendix 7
Ceremonial Observed at the Zeremonientafel Held on the Day of the Procura Wedding of Princess Maria Antonia Walburga, June 13, 1747

Source: GHA, Korr Akt 791.

Ceremoniel, so bey der nach erfolgter Trauung Sr. Hochht. der erstgebohrnen Kayl. Princessin Maria Antonia zu haltenden offentl. Tafel beobachtet werden solle, verfasst den 3ten Juny 1747.

1. Wirdet in der sogenannten grossen Ritter-Stuben Sr. Churfrtl. Drtl. unter einem anständigen Baldachin eine viereckhigtlänglichte Tafel auf einem mit galonniertem Sammet belegten Töppich, dan mit rothem Duech, oder türckhischem Töppich belegten Antritt an dem gewohnlichen Plaz aufgeschlagen.

2. Wann dise gedeckhet, solle vor Ihre Mayt. die Kayserin ein Fauteuil von schwarzem Sammet, vor beede durchleuchtigste Braut-Persohnen aber dergleichen Sessel von Cremoisin-Sammet mit reicher Galonnierung, dann gefüterten und mit Sammet yberzogenen Armlehnen gestellet werden. Des Herrn Cardinals durchleuchtigste Eminenz und beede kleinere Hochhten erhalten ihre Fauteuils von Cramoisin-Sammet mit goldenen Bordten, jedoch nicht so reichgeprämbt, und leediglich mit vergoldeten ungefüterten Armlehnen. Hingegen werden vor beeder Frauen Herzoginnen Drtl. Drtl. dann den Herrn Bottschaffter dergleichen Stühle mit etwas niderigeren Ruckhwänden und braunen Nussbaumenen Armlehnen gegeben.

3. Die 3 ersteren Sessel seynd sogleich auf den Antritt, die ybrigen 6 aber herunter des Antritts solchergestalten zu placieren, das die äusserste oder leztere vor deren Frauen Herzoginnen Drtlen. und den Herrn Ambassadeur in etwas vom Staffel entfremter als die erstere stehen.

4. Die Tafel wird mit zwey Gängen warmer Speisen bedecket und das drittemahl das Confect aufgetragen, so das die Tafel dopplet zu deckhen, und bey Auftragung des Confects das erstere Tischtuch abzunemmen ist, wo wohin die Mundbesteckhe mit porcellainenen Schalen gegeben werden.

5. Bey der zweymahligen Auftragung deren frischen Speisen bleibet der alte Surtout stehen, und wirdet mit keinem anderen ausgewechslet.

6. Die ganze Taffel wird mit vergoldetem Silber bedient. Augma, Serm. Sponsus et Sponsa, des Herrn Cardinalen Drtlgste Ez und beede Kayl. Hochhten haben Ihre Cadenats, deren Frauen Herzoginnen Drtlen. und der Herr Bottschaffter hingegen bekommen an deren Statt vergoldete Teller mit dem Brod, auf weissen Tischservieten, wo immitls die Mundbesteckhe Sr. Kayl. Mayt. und beeder Brauthpersonen von purem Gold seyn sollen, und beynebens allerhöchstgdl. Sr. Kayl. Mayt., Sponso, et Sponsa, dann beeden Hochten Servieten unter die Teller gebreithet werden.

7. Zur linckh. und rechten Hand nächst der Tafel an denen Pfeileren seynd zwey Schenkh Tische zu sezen. Von deren ersterem die vördersten 4 Herrschafften, von dem zweyten aber die ybrige benebst den Herrn Ambassadeur zu bedienen seynd.

8. Zwischen beeden Thuren nächst dem Ofen wirdet ein Orchester aufgericht, und hieraus währenden Soupierens Musique gemacht.

9. Nachdeme die Speisen unter Trompeten und Pauckhen Schall aufgetragen worden, saget solches der Churfrtl. Herr ObristHofMarschall mit den Staab an, und gehet sohin unter Begleithung des ObristKuchenmeister- und Obrist-SilberCämmerers-Staabs denen gdgsten Herrschafften voraus.

10. Allerhöchst. und Höchstderoselben werden die Eventails, respective Hüthe und Handschue durch dero ObristHofmeister, ObristCämmerer, dann Cämmerer abgenommen, von disen auch die Sessel geruckht, so bey dem Herrn Bottschaffter gleichfahls durchgehends zu beobachten.

11. Der Obrist-Hofmarschal, ObristKuchenmeister und ObristSilberCämmerer stellen sich (jeder mit seinem Staab) unten am Staffel Aug.ma, Ser.mo Sponso et Sponsa gerad gegen über, dero dass Handwasser von dem dienenden Cammerherrn, so das Beckhen zugleich haltet, aufgegossen, die Servieten aber durch die respective ObristHofmeister und ObristCämmerer prosentieret werden. Em.tmo und beeden Hochhten wirdet ein nasses Serviete auf einer Credenztaze, beeden Frauen Herzoginnen und dem Herrn Ambassadeur aber dergleichen auf einem vergoldeten ordinari Teller von denen Cämmereren gereichet.

12. Das Benedicite, wie auch nach der Tafel das Deogratias, wirdet von dem anweesenden ersten Insulierten, als nembl. dem Herrn Ordens Bischoffen, gesprochen, dem der HofCaplan, so sonsten vorbettet, respondieret.

13. Die dienende Cammerherren bleiben den ganzen Tisch yber hinter ihren Stühlen stehen, dahingegen sich die Churfrtl. Herren ObristHofmeister und ObristCämmerer nach Yberreichung des ersteren Trunckhs gleichwohlen retirieren mögen.

14. Zeiget die Anlaage die Austheilung des Sizens und deren Couverts. (This diagram was not found with the document, but see my reconstruction of the Tafel below.)

15. Die Churfrtl. Cämmerer haben die Teller zu wechslen. Die ObristHofmeister, und ObristCämmerer prosentieren den ersten Trunckh, der ihnen von Churfrtl. Pagen zugetragen wirdet, denen 3 ersteren allerhöchst und höchsten

Personen. Hinnach solle das Trinckhen von denen dienenden Cammerherren bey dem Credenztisch gehohlet, und an die höchste und hoche Behörden yberreichet werden.

16.   Zwey Churfrtl. Herren Cämmerer schneiden vor.

17.   Sobald mann zur Tafel gesessen, nimmet der erstere Vorschneider bey der ersten Tracht ein Stückhlein neugebackhene Brodmollen, fahret mit einer Credenzgabel yber alle Schüssel und Teller hin, berührt dieselbige mit der Molle, und credenzet hierauf.

18.   Eben derselbe bedienet Ihre Mayt. die Kayserin, und beede Durchleuchtigste Braut Persohnen jederzeit mit—tragung eines mit Yberteleren bedeckhtem Couverts, dahingegen all ybrige mit ohnbedeckhten Telleren von dem Plaz deren Vorschneideren aus bedienet werden.

19.   Bey der zweyten Tracht wirdet der Aufzug mit Trompeten und Pauckhen widerholet, bey dem Confect aber unterlassen.

20.   Die Kayl., Churfrtl., und Herzogl. Cammerdiener tragen die Speisen mit dem Huth auf dem Kopf, welcher denenselben bey dem Eintritt in die Ritterstuben von denen Portiers abgenommen wirdet.

21.   Bey Ihro Kayl. Mayt. und beeden Höchsten Brauthpersonen wirdet der Trunckh credenziert.

22.   Beeden Durchleuchtigsten Frauen Herzoginnen und dem Herrn Bottschaffter wirdet dero Trunckh auf vergoldeten ordinari-Teller, und die Gläser, wann Sye auch Deckhl-Gläser seynd, ohne Deckhl gereichet.

23.   Nachdeme Allergdgst. und Gdgste Herrschafften das erstemahl getrunckhen, stehet dem anweesenden Adel frey, längers zu verbleiben oder nach Gefallen sich nacher Haus zum Speisen zu begeben.

24.   Die Stühle werden beym Aufstehen von denen Churfrtl. Herren Cämmereren, respective Herren ObristHofmeister und ObristCämmerer (wann dise annoch zugegen) geruckht, welche auch die von denen Edlknaben zuzutragen seyente Eventails, Hüthe und Handschue zuruckhstellen, wohin sye gehören.

25.   Der vorige Insulatus verrichtet das Tisch- oder Dankhgebett wider, wie zuvor.

26.   Mit Prosentierung des handwassers wird alles wie vor der Tafel gehalten.

27.   Und gehet sohin alles in die ParadeZimmer zuruckh, doch ohne Vortrettung der MarschallsStäaben.

Reconstruction of the Tafel (see par. 14):

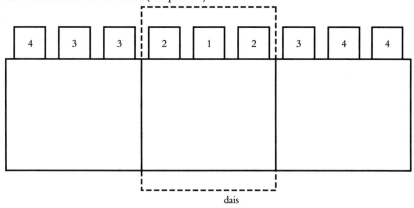

dais

1. Dowager Empress Maria Amalie

2. The bridal pair (Princess Maria Antonia Walburga and Elector Max III Joseph as procura bridegroom)

3. The cardinal (Johann Theodor) and the two princesses (Maria Anna Josepha and Josepha Antonia)

4. The two duchesses (Duchess Ferdinand and Duchess Clemens) and the Saxon ambassador

Appendix 8
Chronological Record of Diplomatic Receptions in the Residenz: The Greeting of Envoys in the Anterooms

This appendix tabulates all available information from Bavarian court records regarding the greeting of envoys at public audiences with the elector in the Residenz. The diagram shows in each instance which court officers met the envoy in which of the anterooms. The sequence of meeting points (columns 5–11) is as follows: 1A, at the carriage or the bottom of the staircase; 1B, at the top of the staircase; 2, in the Herkules-Saal; 3 door, at the door to the Ritterstube; 3 middle, in the middle of the Ritterstube; 4 door, at the door to the (first) antechamber; 4 middle, in the middle of the antechamber.

The officer greeting the envoy at a particular point then escorted him to the next meeting point, where he was taken over by another officer. The last officer to greet the envoy conducted him into the audience chamber. In the 1740s and 1750s, the records occasionally indicate that both the Obristkämmerer and the Obristhofmeister (the latter officer met the envoy in the antechamber) conducted the envoy to the audience chamber. In such cases, both these officers appear in column 11 (the two officers who appear in column 7 of row 132 met the envoy at different points in that room).

In examining the diagram, it is worth keeping in mind what is implied as standard procedure in the two extant memoranda outlining general programs for the diplomatic reception. The first of these, the memorandum prepared for Conte Tarini shortly after 1715 (StAM, Hoh Arch A685), specified that envoys of the second rank ("inviati") from crowned heads of state were to be brought to the door of the antechamber by the commissary. The Obristkämmerer met them there and led them to the door of the audience chamber. The second memorandum, issued between 1777and 1790 under Karl Theodor (HStA, KS 11817), outlined a standardized reception for imperial, royal, and electoral envoys of the second class. The envoy was met by the Obristhofmarschall at the door to the Ritterstube, by the Obristkämmerer at the door to the antechamber, and by the Obristhofmeister in the middle of the antechamber.

Although the Herkules-Saal was rarely used as a meeting point, a column for this room has been included in the diagram in order to keep the sequence of rooms intact. After the construction of the Reiche Zimmer (1725–37), the elector's apartment contained an additional or second antechamber. This room, in which audiences with lesser envoys were held, was almost never used as a meeting point (but see remark for row 129) and has not been included in the diagram.

The information was compiled from the numerous protocols of individual embassies found in the Bavarian state archives. The period 1633–1702 is covered by a compendium, or record book, containing abridged descriptions of embassies (two copies of this were used—one in HStA, FS 126½ and the other in HStA, KS 11824); the chronological record for this period is thus quite thorough. For subsequent decades, there are only the individual protocols found scattered throughout the archives (mostly in HStA, FS 126½ and HStA, KS 11760–11850). The record for these years is less complete, as witnessed by the relatively few entries on the diagram after 1702. It should be noted that not all protocols give information on the reception of the envoy in the anterooms. Only those that do are represented on the diagram.

Little attempt has been made to interpret the information contained in the protocols. For example, a statement that an envoy was "not a formal Abgesandter" has been entered on the diagram as it stands, although this certainly implies that the envoy was an Abgeordneter, or envoy of lower rank. The purpose of missions was seldom recorded. The exceptions are mostly ceremonial embassies—for example, to present congratulations on the birth of a child (e.g., row 11, "birth MP"), or condolences on a death in the family (e.g., row 33, "death HA"), or to fulfill various other ceremonial commissions (as given in column 4). Notation of the rooms in which audiences were held was equally rare. When an identifiable room is named, it has been entered on the diagram (column 12). Most records, however, state merely "Audienzzimmer," without specifying which audience chamber is meant.

Space did not permit giving the names of the envoys; this, however, is less important than the status of the sovereign represented and the diplomatic rank.

Blank rows have been left between reigns.

Abbreviations used in the diagram:

Abges	Abgesandter	Kab	Kabinett
antech	antechamber	Käm	Kämmerer
Anwerb Aud	Anwerbungs-Audienz	Kft	Kurfürst
Audz	Audienzzimmer	MA	Maria Amalie
bevoll	bevollmächtigter	MAC	Maria Anna Christina
Bf	Bischof	MP	Maximilian Philipp
FM	Ferdinand Maria	OHMl	Obristhofmarschall
HA	Henriette Adelaide	OHMr	Obristhofmeister
Herc-Saal	Herkules-Saal	OK	Obristkämmerer
JC	Joseph Clemens	Tru	Truchsess
KA	Karl Albrecht	VB	Violante Beatrix

	1	2	3	4	5	6	7
1	Year	Principal	Rank	Occasion	IA	IB	2
2	1635	King of Hungary	Abgesandter				
3	1635	Erzherzogin at Innsbruck	Abgesandter				
4	1636	King of Hungary and Bohemia	?				
5	1638	Duke of Modena	Abgesanter				
6	1638	King of Denmark	Abgesanter				
7	1638	Kurfürst von Sachsen	Abgeordneter				
8	1638	Herzog von Lothringen	not formal ambas				
9	1638	Herzog von Lothringen	Abgesandter				
10	1688	King of Poland	Abgesandter				
11	1638	Pfalzgraf von Neuburg	Abgesandter	birth MP			
12	1638	Kaiser	Abgesandter				
13	1639	King of Spain	Abgesandter				
14	1639	Kaiser	Abgesandter				
15	1639	Pope	nuncio				
16	1640	Kaiser	Abgesandter			Kft	
17	1641	King of Spain	ambassador				
18	1642	Kurfürst von Köln	Abgesandter				
19	1643	King of Denmark	Abgesandter				
20	1643	Kaiser	not formal Abges				
21	1644	Pope	Abgesandter				
22	1644	Erzherzogin at Innsbruck	Abgesandter				
23	1645	Kaiser	Abgeordneter				
24							
25	1658	King of France	ambassador				
26	1663	Kurfürst von Mainz	formal Abges				
27	1666	Kurfürst von Brandenburg	Abgesandter				
28	1667	Kaiser	formal Abges		Tru		
29	1667	Kaiser	formal Abges				
30	1675	King of France	Abgeordneter				
31	1675	King of Sweden	Abgeordneter				
32	1675	Switzerland	bevoll Abges			OHMl	
33	1676	Fürst von Neuburg	Abgeordneter	death HA			
34	1676	Erzbischof von Salzburg	Abgeordneter	death HA			
35	1676	Kürfust von Sachsen	Abgeordneter	death HA			
36	1676	Duchess of Savoy	Abgeordneter	death HA			
37	1676	Kaiser	Abgeordneter	death HA			
38	1676	Kurfürsten v Mainz & Sachsen	2 Abgeordneter				
39	1676	Fürst von Neuburg	Abgeordneter				
40							
41	1677	Herzog von Neuburg	Abgeordneter				
42	1677	Duchess of Savoy	Abgeordneter				
43	1677	Herzog von Württemberg	Abgeordneter				
44	1678	Herzog von Lothringen	Abgeordneter				
45	1678	Kaiser	Abgeordneter				
46	1678	Duchess of Savoy	Abgeordneter				
47	1679	Kurfürst von Sachsen	Abgeordneter				
48	1679	Herzog von Lothringen	Abgeordneter				
49							

8	9	10	11	12	13	
3 door	3 middle	4 door	4 middle	Audience	Remarks	
		Kft				1
		Kft				2
						3
			Kft		Kft went out 3 or 4 steps from dais in Audienzzimmer	4
	Kft					5
						6
					Kft did not go out from Audienzzimmer to meet him	7
					Kft did not go out from Audienzzimmer to meet him	8
	Kft				Kft did not go out from Audienzzimmer to meet him	9
						10
Kft					Kft did not go out from Audienzzimmer to meet him	11
Kft						12
						13
					Kft did not go out from Audienzzimmer to meet him	14
				in bed	Kft not felling well	15
Kft						16
						17
					Kft did not go out from Audienzzimmer to meet him	18
Kft						19
					Kft did not go out from Audienzzimmer to meet him	20
					Kft did not go out from Audienzzimmer to meet him	21
	OK				OK met him a couple of steps before antechamber	22
					Kft did not go out from Audienzzimmer	23
			Kft			24
	OK					25
					No one went out to meet him	26
					1st audience; Kft met him at door to Audienzzimmer	27
Kft					2nd audience	28
	OK					29
	OK					30
	OK					31
			OK			32
			OK			33
			OK			34
			OK			35
	OK					36
			OK			37
			OK			38
						39
	OK					40
			OK			41
			OK			42
	OK					43
	OK					44
		OK				45
		OK				46
			OK			47
						48
						49

	1	2	3	4	5	6	7
	Year	Principal	Rank	Occasion	IA	IB	2
50	1679	Kurfürst von Sachsen	Abgeordneter	death FM			
51	1679	Herzog von Neuburg	Abgeordneter	death FM			
52	1679	Bischof von Passau	Abgeordneter	death FM			
53	1679	Stadt Augsburg	2 Abgeordneter				
54	1679	Bischof von Straßburg	Abgeordneter	death FM			
55	1679	Herzog von Württemberg	Abgeordneter	death FM			
56	1679	Herzog von Lothringen	Abgeordneter	death FM			
57	1679	Erzbischof von Salzburg	Abgeordneter	death FM			
58	1679	Kaiser	formal Abges	death FM			
59	1679	Bischof von Eichstätt	Abgeordneter	death FM			
60	1679	Duke of Savoy	Abgeordneter	death FM			
61	1679	King of France	Abgeordneter	death FM			
62	1679	King of France	Abgeordneter				
63	1679	Kaiser	Abgeordneter				
64	1680	Herzog von Neuburg	Abgeordneter				
65	1680	King of France	Abgeordneter	(see col.13)			
66		King of Spain	Abgeordneter				
67	1680	Bischof von Passau	Abgeordneter				
68	1681	Bischof von Bamberg	Abgeordneter				
69	1681	King of Sweden	Abgeordneter				
70	1681	Kaiser	Abgeordneter				
71	1682	Kurfürst von Brandenberg	Abgeordneter				
72	1682	Stadt Hamburg	Abgeordneter				
73	1682	Kiing of France	Abgeordneter	(see col.13)			
74	1682	Herzog von Württemberg	Abgeordneter				
75	1682	Kaiser	Abgeordneter				
76	1683	King of Sweden	Abgeordneter				
77	1683	Herzog von Neuburg	Abgeordneter				
78	1683	Kurfürst von Sachsen	Abgeordneter				
79							
80	1683	Domkapitel von Regensburg	Abgeordnter	(see col.13)			
81	1683	Domkapitel von Augsburg	Abgeordnter				
82	1683	Fürst von Holstein	Abgeordnter				
83	1685	Herzog von Braunschweig	Cavalier				
84	1685	Deutschmeister at Mergenthal	Abgeordneter				
85	1685	Kurfürst von Sachsen	Abgeordneter				
86	1685	Erzbischof von Salzburg	Abgeordneter				
87	1685	Duchess of Savoy	Abgeordneter				
88	1685	King of France	Abgeordneter				
89	1685	Herzog von Lothringen	Abgeordneter				
90	1685	Bf von Dillingen & Augsburg	Abgeodneter				
91	1685	Bischof von Passau	Abgeordneter				
92	1685	Erzbischof von Salzburg	Abgeordneter				
93	1685	Kurfürst von der Pfalz	Abgeordneter	(see col.13)			
94	1688	Grand Duke of Tuscany	Abgeordneter				
95	1688	Kurfürst von Brandenburg	Abgeordneter	(see col.13)			
96	1688	Grand Duke of Tuscany	Abgeordneter				
97	1688	King of France	Abgeordneter				
98	1688	King of France	Abgeordneter				

8 3 door	9 3 middle	10 4 door	11 4 middle	12 Audience	13 Remarks	
	OK					50
	OK					51
	OK					52
			OK			53
	OK					54
	OK					55
	OK					56
	OK					57
Kft						58
	OK					59
	OK					60
	OK					61
OK						62
OK						63
	OK					64
OK					To escort MAC (bride of dauphin) to France	65
OK					Kft went out 2 steps from dais to met him	66
		OK				67
			OK			68
	OK					69
	OK					70
	OK					71
			OK			72
	OK				To announce the birth of a son to MAC	73
			OK			74
	OK					75
	OK					76
			OK			77
			OK			78
						79
					To congrat. JC on election as Koadjutor-Bf v Regensburg	80
			OK			81
	OK					82
		OK				83
	OK					84
	OK					85
	OK					86
	OK					87
	OK					88
	OK				Ok met him "außerhalb AntiCammer"	89
			OK			90
			OK			91
	OK					92
	OK					93
		OK			To negotiate marriage of VB and Hered. Prince of Tuscany	94
	OK					95
	OK				To present portrait of bridegroom to VB	96
OK						97
	OK					98

	1	2	3	4	5	6	7
	Year	Principal	Rank	Occasion	IA	IB	2
99	1688	Grand Duke of Tuscany	formal Gesandter	Anwerb Aud		OK	
100	1689	Kurfürst von Sachsen	Abgeordneter				
101	1689	Kurfürst von Brandenburg	Abgeordneter				
102	1689	Bischof von Münster	Abgeordneter				
103	1691	King of Spain	Abgeordneter				
104	1691	Bischof von Eichstätt	Abgeordneter				
105	1701	Bischof von Augsburg	Abgeordneter				
106	1701	Bischof von Freising	2 Abgeordneter				
107	1701	Herzog von Württemberg	Abgeordneter				
108	1701	King of France	Abgeordneter				
109	1702	Duke of Savoy	Abgeordneter				
110	1715	Kurfürst von Sachsen	Gesandter				
111	1724	Kaiser	Abgeordneter				
112							
113	1726	Erzbischof von Salzburg	Gesandter	(see col.13)			
114	1726	Kurfürst von Mainz	Abgeordneter				
115	1732	Pater General der Kapuziner	in person				
116	1733	Kurfürst von Sachsen	Gesandter				
117	1739	Pater General der Karmeliter	in person				
118							
119	1739	Kurfürst von Sachsen	Abgeordneter				
120	1740	Kurfürst von Mainz	Abgesandter		Käm	OHMl	
121	1740	Kurfürst von Sachsen	Abgesandter				
122	1741	King of Spain	Botschafter		2 Käm	OHMl	
123	1741	King of France	Gesandter			OHMl	OK
124							
125	1747	Kurfürst von Sachsen	Botschafter	Anwerb Aud	2 Käm	OHMl	
126	1750	Pater General der Karmeliter	in person				
127	1750	Kurfürst von der Pfalz	bevoll Minister			OHMl	
128	1752	Kurfürst von Sachsen	Gesandter				
129	1755	Margrave von Baden-Baden	Gesandter	Anwerb Aud			
130	1756	Kaiser	Gesandter			OHMl	
131	1757	Kaiser	bevoll Minister				OHMl
132	1765	Kaiser	Abgesandter	Anwerb Aud			OHMl OK

8	9	10	11	12	13	
3 door	3 middle	4 door	4 middle	Audience	Remarks	
	Kft				OK 10 steps before Herc-Saal; Kft 3 steps before antech	99
	OK					100
	OK					101
		OK				102
	OK					103
		OK				104
	OHMl					105
	OHMl					106
	OHMl					107
	OHMl					108
	OK					109
OHMl		OK				110
	OK					111
						112
OHMl		OK			To congralulate KA on his accession as elector	113
OHMl	OK					114
OHMl	OK				To Residenz on foot via covered gallery	115
OHMl		OK				116
OHMl	OK					117
						118
OHMl				Großes Kab		119
	OK	OK OHMr			Audience held "Im Großen Kab, wo reicher Baldachin"	120
OHMl	OK		OK OHMr	Großes Kab		121
	OHMr			Großes Kab	OHMl met him at 1st landing in staircase	122
	OK		OK OHMr	Großes Audz	Kft went out 2 steps from dais to meet him	123
						124
	OK		OHMr			125
OHMl			OK	Kaiser Audz	To Residenz on foot via covered gallery	126
		OK			Audience held "Im 3. Zimmer, wo reicher Baldachin"	127
OHMl	OK				Audience held "Im Großen Kab, wo reicher Baldachin"	128
OHMl		OK			OHMr met him at door to 2nd antechamber	129
	OK	OHMr			Audience held "Im Großen Kab, wo reicher Baldachin"	130
		OK	OK OHMr	3rd Audz	To Residenz on foot via covered gallery	131
OHMr	Kft					132

Appendix 9
Numerical Distribution of Court Personnel by Office in 1738 and 1781

According to the Hofkalender of 1738 and 1781, Bavarian court personnel were distributed among the court offices as listed below. Because some persons held more than one post, the number of individuals at court would have been somewhat lower (see chap. 1, n. 13).

Hofkalender 1738:
   Obristhofmeisteramt: 330
   Obristkämmereramt: 261
   Obristhofmarschallamt: 111
   Obriststallmeisteramt: 393
   Obristjägermeisteramt (incl. Obristfalkenmeisteramt): 64
   Household of Electress Maria Amalie: 55
   Household of Electoral Prince Max Joseph: 24
   Household of Duchess Maria Anna Karolina (in the Convent of the Clarissines): 1
   Household of Duchess Maria Antonia Walburga: 11
   Household of Duchess Therese Benedicte: 7
   Household (shared) of the two above duchesses: 8
   Household of Duchess Maria Anna Josepha: 5
   Household of Duke Ferdinand: 30
   Household of Duchess Ferdinand: 18
   Household of Duke Clemens: 13
   Household of Duchess Therese Emanuele (daughter of Duke Ferdinand): 6
      Total: 1,337
Hofkalender 1781:
   Obristhofmeisteramt: 905
   Obristkämmereramt: 468
   Obristhofmarschallamt: 261
   Obriststallmeisteramt: 354
   Obristjägermeisteramt in Munich: 27

Obristjägermeisteramt in Mannheim: 29
Household of Electress Elisabeth Auguste: 43
Household of Dowager Electress Maria Anna Sophia: 33
Household of Duchess Clemens: 19
    Total: 2,139

On the origins of the four-court-office system in the household of the Frankish kings, the transformations this system underwent at the court of Burgundy in the late Middle Ages to adapt it to a court regimen in which ceremonial played a preponderant role, and the adoption of the Burgundian system by the Habsburgs, see the short accounts in Ehalt (32–54) and Plodeck (90–98). Both these sources include references to the extensive literature on the subject. The smaller German courts were less elaborately structured; very few followed the four-office system, contenting themselves with fewer offices. Friedrich Carl von Moser notes, for example, that very few courts below the electoral level had Obristkämmererämter (2:106–7). The courts that maintained the closest cultural relations with the emperor (e.g., the Catholic courts) followed the imperial model the most closely in terms of the distribution of duties among the officers and the personnel over which each had jurisdiction.

Appendix 10
A Note on Staircases

The importance of the staircase for court ceremonial, particularly on state occasions, is well established; this was recognized by contemporaries (e.g., F. C. Moser, 2:286). It seems highly probable that the development of monumental staircases during this period was, partly at least, a function of the increasing emphasis on state ceremonial—although as meeting points within the continuum of anterooms, they played a larger role in the reception of visiting princes than of envoys. There is little doubt that the development of monumental staircases—particularly those of the imperial type or of the type of the Escalier des Ambassadeurs at Versailles, in which the stairs can be seen as a whole and thus approach the condition of a theater stage—was closely related to the increasing elaboration of state ceremonial. Very few Baroque palaces were without such a feature.

At the Bavarian court, as at many other courts, the guard was deployed in the staircase during the reception of foreign princes and envoys, and the elector or the high court officers often met visitors at either the top or bottom of the stairs (chap. 6). The fact that the staircase does not figure as a place of waiting in the eighteenth-century Bavarian Aufwartungs-Ordnungen, as it does in the Cologne Ordnungen, could be related to the lack of a truly monumental staircase leading to the elector's apartment (the Breite Treppe, erected under Maximilian, must have seemed very antiquated in the eighteenth century). The staircase erected under Karl Albrecht next to the Grüne Galerie may be considered an attempt to rectify this situation. Of the imperial type and generous in scale, the stair was decidedly monumental, but also something of an anachronism in its location at the "rear" of the apartment. It cannot have served a critical ceremonial function there, and it is never mentioned in diplomatic protocols. Its monumentality probably stemmed from the dissatisfaction that must have been felt with the Breite Treppe at the front of the apartment. Replacing the Breite Treppe with a larger staircase, however—one better designed to meet the heightened demands of ceremonial—clearly would have entailed major intrusions into the building fabric. If such a project was ever contemplated, it was probably dismissed as infeasible. It is tempting to see the staircase next to the Grüne Galerie as compensation for this—an architectural feature that had become de rigueur by this time, but that unfortunately was not in a position to fulfill the purpose so strongly suggested by its form. It is significant that the staircase survived only some thirty years, until Max III Joseph had it demolished in 1764 to make way for the new dining room. In this instance, program and plan seem to lack the close correspondence that we have been able to observe in most other areas of the palace.

Notes

Abbreviations

AM	*Altbayerische Monatsschrift*
BSV	Bayerische Schlösser-Verwaltung (Bayerische Verwaltung der staatlichen Schlösser, Gärten und Seen), Munich
BStB	Bayerische Staatsbibliothek, Munich
FS	Fürstensachen, HStA, Munich
GHA	Geheimes Hausarchiv (Abteilung III des HStA), Munich
Hoh Arch	Hohenaschauer Archiv
HR1	Hofamtsregistratur 1, HStA, Munich
Hs	Handschriften (manuscripts)
HsAbt	Handschriften-Abteilung, BStB, Munich
HStA	Bayerisches Hauptstaatsarchiv, Munich
JMG	*Jahrbuch für Münchener Geschichte*
Korr Akt	Korrespondenzakten, GHA, Munich
KS	Kasten schwarz, HStA, Munich
MF	Finanzministerium, HStA, Munich
MJBK	*Münchener Jahrbuch der bildenden Künste*
OA	*Oberbayerisches Archiv*
StAM	Staatsarchiv München
StV	Staatsverwaltung, HStA, Munich
ZBLG	*Zeitschrift für bayerische Landesgeschichte*

Preface

1. HStA, KS 8289–91, letter of January 4, 1705, Max Emanuel to Gräfin Arco.

2. Richard Sedlmaier and Rudolf Pfister, *Die fürstbischöfliche Residenz zu Würzburg* (Munich, 1923), 6–7.

3. Christian Wolff, *Vernünftige Gedanken von dem gesellschaftlichen Leben der Menschen* (1721; new ed., 1971), 500. On the idea that human beings understand only what they see, see also Elias, 117–18.

4. A further study of interest is Raschauer.

5. Adalbert Prinz von Bayern's two works on the Bavarian court (see the Bibliography) are primarily anecdotal and lack the scholarly apparatus of footnotes; they nonetheless provide useful information. Treusch von Buttlar and Voigt are valuable general works on German court life for a slightly earlier period. There are two studies of the German courts, also primarily anecdotal, by the French authors Fauchier-Magnan and Lafue. Both of these works treat their subject from a condescending, highly chauvinistic point of view; their validity is thus questionable. Vehse is valuable primarily for the documents published therein.

6. The closest thing to a definitive monograph for the Munich palaces is Hager, although this is by now somewhat dated. Elmar Schmid's studies of Nymphenburg and Schleissheim are reliable and fairly thorough, but are unfortunately without documentation. There is no good comprehensive, current work on the Residenz.

7. Only material found in the archives and libraries in Munich was used in the present work. Because of this limitation, the diplomatic records of other courts, a potentially invaluable source, were not searched for material pertinent to the Bavarian court. Only published diplomatic records were consulted; Sebastian Brunner's two volumes, which publish eighteenth-century imperial ambassadorial reports from Munich, deserve particular note.

8. Regulations and instructions are found throughout the Bavarian archives, mostly in HStA, HR1, and GHA, Korr Akt 1712. Accounts of ceremonies and festivities are scattered throughout the archives. References to specific documents appear in the following chapters.

9. Preysing's diary is in BStB, HsAbt, Cod germ 5456; Maria Anna Josepha's journal is in GHA, Hs 194. Two other, somewhat less useful diaries are those of Felix Andreas Oefele, tutor and later cabinet secretary to Duke Clemens (nephew of Elector Karl Albrecht), covering the years 1738–43 (BStB, HsAbt, Oefeleana 483); and Maria Theresia von Gombert for 1734 (published by F. X. Zettler in *AM* 5 [1905]). Gombert was attached to the household of Electress Maria Amalie.

10. Among the most useful such accounts are Hainhofer, Pöllnitz, and Lynar.

11. References to specific furniture inventories are found in the following chapters.

12. This is considerably less true of most German architectural treatises of the sixteenth to eighteenth centuries (e.g., Sturm/Goldmann, Furttenbach, Dieussart, Decker), which tend to present desiderata and often quite utopian projects.

Chapter One

1. "Die Residenz ist die ordentliche, beständige Wohnung des Regenten an dem Ort, wo der eigentliche Sitz des Hofs und der Collegien ist. Hier ist der Regent eigentlich zu Haus und bey Abmessung des Ceremoniels und Feststellung dessen Regeln ist eigentlich auf den in der Residenz gewöhnlichen Gebrauch zu sehen (Friedrich Carl von Moser [hereafter cited as Moser], 2:252)."

2. "Die Residenz ist diejenige Stadt, in welcher ein Potentat, oder Fürst sein Hoflager hält, daselbst auch die obern Collegia, als Regierung, Hofgericht, Cammer und andere, so die gemeinen Angelegenheiten des Landes zu besorgen haben,

verbleiben. Lat. Urbs regia; urbs, in qua princeps sedem fixit" (Johann Heinrich Zedler, "Residentz," *Grosses vollständiges Universal-Lexikon* [Leipzig/Halle, 1742], vol. 31, col. 717).

3. Moser, 1:274.

4. Ibid., 2:267–69.

5. Florinus, 2:861.

6. Ibid., 862.

7. Moser, 2:282–83.

8. On the types of regulations issued for the household at the German courts, see Kern, introductions to both volumes.

9. Hartmann, 68.

10. Föringer, "Hofstat."

11. Hüttl notes that at the end of the Thirty Years' War the household numbered around 450 (572 n. 129). He does not, however, cite a source for this number.

12. The 1705 description is in the Haus-, Hof-, and Staatsarchiv in Vienna (Bavarica 21 B, Libellum Hofstaat) and is transcribed in Hüttl, 572–74 n. 129.

13. *Chur-bayerischer Hofcalender* (Munich, 1738, 1781). Whereas the descriptions of 1615 and 1705 list the personnel of court and government together, the eighteenth-century Hofkalender list the two branches of the household completely separately. The directories in the Hofkalender are listings of posts, not persons. Since certain persons, particularly highly placed officers, held more than one post, the number of persons belonging to the court was slightly less than the figures given above. See appendix 9 for numbers assigned to each office.

14. See chapter 5 (section on court attendance) regarding the increase in the ranks of the electoral chamberlains.

15. The 1615 description lists 40 Trabanten (including officers) and 6 lackeys; the 1705 description, 91 Trabanten and 27 lackeys; the 1738 Hofkalender, 72 Trabanten and 39 lackeys; the 1769 Hofkalender, 129 Trabanten and 36 lackeys.

16. Moser, 1:32; Rohr, 17.

17. Baillie, 193. See also Straub, 117–46.

Chapter Two

1. Adalbert, *Residenz,* 346.

2. Wening, 8.

3. A detailed discussion of Maximilian's revisions to the Residenz is found later in this chapter.

4. Florinus, 2:861–62.

5. Riezler, vol. 3.

6. The definitive history of the Neuveste is Meitinger. The work is based not only on a thorough investigation of the primary external sources, but also on archaeological excavations undertaken during the reconstruction of the Residenz after World War II.

7. Schattenhofer, 1207.

8. This occurred after 1530, according to Meitinger (32, 34). He bases his assumption on the fact that several views of 1530 do not show the new buildings; they first appear on a view of 1559.

9. The Rundstubenbau is described by Wening (6).

10. This event, to which numerous princely guests were invited, was memorialized in two texts: Massimo di Trojano, *Die Vermählungsfeier des Herzogs Wilhelm des Fünften von Bayern mit Renata . . . von Lothringen, zu München in Jahr 1568* (1568; German ed., Munich, 1842); and Hans Wagner, *Beschreibung der Hochzeit Herzog Wilhelms und Renatas von Lothringen* (Munich, 1568). Early descriptions of the Georgs-Saal are contained in Wagner, Wening, and Hainhofer (1611 trip, p. 79). Its building history is discussed by Hartig (187–88) and Meitinger (34–37), both of whom also publish the two existing sixteenth-century depictions of the Georgs-Saal, by Wolfgang Muelich (1567) and Nikolaus Solis (1568).

11. Hartig, 178; H. Brunner, *Kunstschätze* 17.

12. Hartig (205–11) has reconstructed the building history of the Kunstkammergebäude and also gives a detailed description of the museum rooms based on an inventory of 1599 (BStB, HsAbt, Cod germ 2133) and on Hainhofer's lengthy description of 1611. The crowning feature of the building is the three-story arcaded courtyard. Since 1809 the building has been used as the Bavarian Münzamt.

13. Albrecht V's activities as an art collector, as well as the building history of the Antiquarium, are treated definitively by Hartig (200–225). Two later studies on the Antiquarium are also important: Erich Hubala, "Ein Entwurf für das Antiquarium der Münchner Residenz, 1568," *MJBK* 9/10 (1958/59): 128–46; and Heike Frosien-Leinz, "Das Antiquarium der Residenz: Erstes Antikenmuseum Münchens," in *Glyptothek München 1830–1980,* exhibition catalog (Munich, 1980), 310–21.

14. A preliminary plan drawing (HStA, Plansammlung 7939) shows the main entrance at the east end, with the principal staircase to one side of a rectangular vestibule. At the west end is a minor staircase. In a protocol of a conference with the architect from 1570 (published by Hartig, 223), we read, however, that the door was to be in the center of the south side, "gegen der Münch Garten." This protocol also indicates that the library floor contained small rooms at the two ends, presumably with a long hall between them, but gives no clear idea of number or disposition of these rooms.

15. The earliest plan depiction of the suite of rooms above the Antiquarium is that on the plan of the Residenz from 1616 to 1630, when these rooms were used as guest quarters. Whether this plan represents the arrangement during Wilhelm V's reign, and whether this apartment was a double apartment with rooms for both the duke and his consort, is not known.

16. The name Schwarzer Saal, which appears in the seventeenth century, is a reference to the original dark tones of the decor. The Saal was also called the Perspectivischer Saal, after the illusionistic painted architecture of the ceiling.

17. There are entries in the Hofbauamtsrechnungen for 1587 that refer to demolition of the vaults of the Antiquarium (Hartig, 224). The building history of Wilhelm V's Gartenbau has not been adequately addressed. In particular, information is lacking on the configuration of the second floor. Where Duchess Renata was lodged also remains unknown.

18. Haeutle, *Residenz,* 18. Anna enlarged the original site through the purchase of an adjacent property in 1580.

19. Busch, 404.

20. Pfister, 77.

21. The building history of the Erbprinzenbau has been reconstructed by Busch (399–404).

22. Thoma and Kreisel, 15 (hereafter cited as Thoma).

23. Busch, 403. Busch argues that the erection of the Hofdamenstock was probably at least planned under Wilhelm, as the structures framing the Jägergassl on the south and west and effectively transforming the street into a narrow court made its complete enclosure obvious.

24. The building history of the Ballhaus has not been studied by historians. Most sources place its origins under Wilhelm V (as Thoma, 9). Others assume that it was erected under Albrecht V (as Otto Meitinger, "Die baugeschichtliche Entwicklung der Münchener Residenz," *Bayerland* 63 [1961]: 365).

25. Thoma, 9.

26. On the reign of Maximilian, see Pfister.

27. The discrepancy in dates results from the fact that Hollar took his material from Tobias Volckmer's 1613 plan of Munich, on which the area of the Residenz was left blank—probably because of the substantial construction work then in progress. Presumably for the sake of consistency, Hollar drew the Residenz as it existed before the addition of the Kaiserhofbau, although it is not known what source he might have used (Knüttel, 187, 205 n. 1).

28. Hainhofer (1611), 69.

29. Busch, 400–401, 404. The demolition and rebuilding of the Erbprinzenbau was probably due to structural faults in the basement.

30. BStB, HsAbt, Cod germ 2123, "Inventarium der Tappezereyen . . . und andere Mobilien, so in Curfurtl. Haubt-Residenz München, Starnberg, und Schleissheim sich befunden, und beschriben worden, den 1. Jul anno 1638."

31. Thoma, 13, 106; Busch, 403.

32. Thoma, 13, 109–10.

33. Knüttel (187–94) provides a thorough discussion of the iconographical program of Maximilian's Herkules-Saal and also illustrates the only existing early depiction of the room (by W. P. Zimmermann, in 1614). On the tapestries, see Brigitte Volk-Knüttel, *Wandteppiche für den Münchener Hof nach Entwürfen von Peter Candid* (Munich, 1976).

34. Hainhofer (1611), 59. The letters *ID, ICD,* and the like are abbreviations for formal terms of reference or address such as "his electoral highness."

35. H. Brunner, *Kunstschätze,* 82; Diemer, 129–74. A Hausurkunde of 1607 regarding the formation of the Kammergalerie states that it was partly the desire that the paintings be better cared for that led Maximilian to take this step (HStA, HR1 24/67; quoted in Brunner, 82). Hainhofer noted in 1611 that because various objects had been stolen from the Kunstkammer, foreigners could not easily obtain permission to see the collections.

36. This description of the Kammergalerie is from the 1607 Hausurkunde cited in n. 35.

37. The building history of the altane has been reconstructed by Diemer (137). Hainhofer describes the early altana (1611, 73). The later altana can be seen in the engravings of Michael Wening (fig. 1) and Matthias Diesel (fig. 8).

It was probably also during the first decade of the seventeenth century that the facades of the Grottenhof received the fastidious embellishment of superimposed Corinthian pilasters, bas-relief panels, and statues in niches that may be seen in

Diesel's views of the courtyard (the descriptions by Hainhofer and Wening are in agreement with Diesel). Diesel's views indicate that while the eastern Grottenhalle, with its elaborate Mannerist "Korallenbrunnen," was left as it had been, the loggia opposite had by his time been reduced in size through the enclosure of the two outermost bays at each end. Hainhofer tells us that this loggia was meant for the court ladies: "[Under the Reiche Kapelle] hats noch eine loggia, darinnen dass Adelich Frawenzimmer stehet" (1611, 69).

38. Hainhofer (1611), 70. Hainhofer's description agrees with that given by Wening of five "Sommer- oder Gartenzimmer" having on the ceilings "painted portraits from the Kurhaus Bayern" (14). The garden rooms, as well as ground-floor rooms along the Residenzstrasse, were, as Knüttel argues, painted by Peter Candid in the first decade of the seventeenth century with portraits of Wittelsbach ancestors, in order to document the illustrious descent of the dynasty (194–200).

39. Hainhofer (1611), 74. Wening also records the presence of this loggia, which he calls Garten-Gallerie, noting that it featured "elf offene Bögen."

40. In the late eighteenth century this Saal, which was flanked by two Retirat-Zimmer, or cabinets, seems to have remained virtually unchanged; see the 1769 Residenz furniture inventory (HStA, HR1 22/58) and Maximilian von Verschaffelt's 1799 plan of the Residenz (fig. 12). Both Hainhofer (73–76) and Wening (7) offer thorough descriptions of the Residenzgarten itself, its parterres and fountains.

41. The fountain that gives the courtyard its name was also put up at this time (1610–13). It features a bronze statue of Otto von Wittelsbach, founder of the dynasty, on a high pedestal, surrounded by statues of river gods and allegorical figures of the four elements on the lip of the basin (Thoma, 13–14).

42. Thoma, 9, 14, 43, 187.

43. A letter of Max Emanuel written from St. Cloud on August 12, 1714, regarding his intentions for the accommodation of the electoral family in the Residenz upon their return, specifies that this apartment was to be assigned to Princes Ferdinand Maria Innocenz, Clemens August, and Johann Theodor and notes that they had lived here previously (GHA, Korr Akt 753/50, R4b/1,2,3).

44. Hainhofer (1611), 69–70. Herrschaften are members of ruling families.

45. Max Emanuel's occupancy of the apartment is recorded as early as 1667 in Pallavicino (122). In Max Emanuel's letter of August 12, 1714 (see n. 43 above), this apartment is assigned to Electoral Prince Karl Albrecht and his younger brother Philipp Moritz: "Vor den ChurPrinzen bleibet jenes Appartement, wo wür als ChurPrinz logiert, zuverstehen, ds der Eingang von unserer Ritterstuben her seye, und er seine Wohnung auf der seithen des Oval-Hofs habe. Der Herzog Philipp kan die 2 Zimmer auch auf selbiger seithen einnemmen, ds ist, die lesstere gegen dem Perspectiv-Sall, woher der Eingang zu seinem Appartement seyn solle; die Zimmer hingegen gegen dem Garten hinaus müssen lähr- und zu unserer disposition verbleiben."

46. Hainhofer (1612), 164.

47. The most authoritative treatment to date of the building history of the Kaiserhofbau is Knüttel (199–205).

48. Knüttel, 199.

49. The earliest appearance of the name Kaiserzimmer is in the 1638 furniture

inventory, where the apartment is called "khayl. Zimmer" (BStB, HsAbt, Cod germ 2123). Pistorini in 1644 calls it the "Appartamento dell'imperadore."

50. Pistorini calls the Trierzimmer the "Appartamento del Consiglio," after its iconographical program organized around the theme of the ruler as dispenser of justice. The widowed Margravine of Baden-Baden lived in the north half (HStA, HR1 22/58, Residenz furniture inventory, 1769).

51. Trautmann, "Aus alten Reisetagebüchern," 482.

52. HStA, FS 126½, "Beschreibung derenjenigen Gesandt-Schafften welchige sich bey dem churfürstl. bayerischen Hoff haben einbefundten . . . ," [1633–83].

53. HStA, FS 109, "Kurzer Begriff, wie es bey Ankunfft der kaiserlichen und königlichen Maytten zu Dachau und alhier zu haltten," [1653].

54. Ernst Bassermann-Jordan, *Die dekorative Malerei der Renaissance am bayerischen Hofe* (Munich, 1900), 137–42.

55. Burkard von Roda, ed., *Schloss Aschaffenburg und Pompejanum: Amtlicher Führer* (Munich, 1982), 31, 80. See also Arnulf Herbst, "Zur Ikonologie des barocken Kaisersaals," *Bericht des Historischen Vereins für die Pflege der Geschichte des ehemaligen Bistums Bamberg* 106 (1970): 207–345.

56. Bassermann-Jordan, 141–42.

57. The Weisser Saal was originally called, for reasons unknown, the Hall "beim schwarzen Hund" (Haeutle, *Residenz,* 54; HStA, HR1 22/58, Residenz furniture inventory, 1769).

58. Wening, 6.

59. Knüttel, 202.

60. The lower mezzanine also exists in parts of the tracts around the Grottenhof and Hofkapelle. Verschaffelt's plan of 1799 (GHA, Hs 64) shows mezzanine rooms along the south and west sides of the Grottenhof, parts of the palace radically altered under Karl Albrecht. I am unable to determine whether these mezzanines are older than those alterations. Diesel's two views of the Grottenhof of around 1720 (fig. 8 is one of them) do not show mezzanine windows on these facades.

61. On the garden of Albrecht V, see Hartig, 190–98. Wilhelm IV's garden was destroyed during the construction of the fortifications; the electoral arsenal went up on this site. According to Wening, the north pavilion (Albrecht V's pavilion), which was joined to the arcade running along the north side of the Hofgarten, contained a Festsaal and a "fürstliche Wohnung"; the central pavilion was used "zur Aufführung von Komödien"; and the south pavilion was used by the Hofgärtner as living quarters and for winter storage of plants (8–9).

62. Wening, 6–7; HStA, FS 126½, Compendium of embassies, 1633–83.

63. This information is from a contemporary diary quoted in Günter Brucher, *Barockarchitektur in Österreich* (Cologne, 1983), 93–94.

64. Pistorini, 6–7. In 1673, Chapuzeau reiterated the analogy with a city: "Le Palais ressemble plutôt à une Ville entière qu'à une seule Maison" (48).

65. Developments before the war are recounted in detail by Pfister (141–52, 157–75).

66. The Turnierhaus occupied the site of the present Bazargebäude (Leo von Klenze, 1824–26). There are two contemporary views of it in Melchior and Matthias Küsl, *Churfürstlich-Bayrisches Frewden-Fest . . . bey den Tauff-Ceremonien des . . . Max Emanuel* (Munich, 1662). Regarding its capacity, see Wening and the

travelogue of Nicholaus Galler from 1782 in Trautmann, "Aus alten Reisetagebüchern," 486.

67. On Bavarian politics under Ferdinand Maria and Max Emanuel, see Doeberl; and Strich, *Kurhaus*.

68. Eberhard Straub paints a certainly exaggerated portrait of Ferdinand Maria as little more than a simpleton (179–80).

69. Henriette Adelaide has been the subject of several biographies; see Claretta, Merkel, and Bary. See also Straub's very critical assessment of her personality and her cultural influence in Bavaria (174–79).

70. GHA, Korr Akt 631/5, "Bericht dessen was zu Ankunfft der churfrtl. Prinzessin und deren Bedienung abgeredt, verglichen und von Sr. Churf. Drtl. gnädigst placitirt worden," n.d. This memorandum states that Henriette Adelaide was to be treated as a guest of honor in the Kaiserzimmer for a maximum of eight days and that if and when the Herrschaften made an excursion to Schleissheim, she would move into her permanent quarters upon return.

71. Haeutle, *Residenz*, 77; Bary, 235.

72. The gallery is described by Wening, who notes that the ceiling featured allegorical paintings and that at the far end of the gallery there was a small cabinet containing paintings representing the wisdom of Solomon (6). The gallery may be seen in Wening's perspective view of the Residenz (fig. 7); it was first depicted in plan by François de Cuvilliés around 1760 (fig. 10).

73. On May 24, 1664, she wrote thanking Karl Emanuel for drawings of "sofites et alcoues" intended for her new bedroom and other rooms in the Residenz (Merkel, 374 n. 1).

74. Bary states that Maria Anna was living in the Witwenbau at the time of her death (236).

75. On the iconography of the Herzkabinett, see Cornelia Kemp, "Das Herzkabinett der Kurfürstin Henriette Adelaide in der Münchener Residenz," *MJBK* 33 (1982): 131–54.

76. Reinhold Baumstark, "Abbild und Überhöhung in der höfischen Malerei unter Henriette Adelaide und dem jungen Max Emanuel," in *Kurfürst Max Emanuel* 1:180.

77. Chapuzeau, 48.

78. On Pallavicino, see Bary (236–37).

79. The story of the fire is recounted in detail in Beauvau (424–34).

80. HStA, HR1 25/89/1, contains numerous memoranda and other documents relating to restoration work on the Kaiserzimmer from 1678 to 1687. The new ceiling for the Vierschimmelsaal was executed only in 1692–94 (Thoma, 20). The restoration work seems to have been finished by 1699; a letter of October 24 addressed to Max Emanuel from Zuccalli(?) states, "Havendo il Signor Rosa [court painter] ricercato de finire il residuo delle stanze del apparamento dell'Imperatore, ritrovo che sono tutte finite" (GHA, Korr Akt 753/42a [R220]). On the electress's rooms, see Haeutle, *Residenz*, 85. Joanne Schmid describes Henriette Adelaide's ceilings 58–62, but has probably merely taken this over from Pallavicino.

81. On Max Emanuel's reign, see the two recent biographies by Hüttl and by Rall and Hojer. See also Karl Otmar Freiherr von Aretin, "Die Politik des Kurfürsten Max Emanuel und die europäischen Mächte," in *Kurfürst Max Emanuel* 1:35–50.

82. Quoted in Hüttl, 268.

83. Pöllnitz, 2:16–17. Moser notes that the practice of adorning the front facade or front entry of a palace with an image of a saint or "Schutz-Patron" had been common "in olden times," when princely courts were more pious (2:258–59). The usual decorations in his day were coats of arms, inscriptions memorializing the builder, military devices, and statues of pagan deities.

84. To us, the elector's apartment seems to have been very favorably sited within the palace. Bridging various building tracts, various zones of the palace, the apartment enjoys views over more than one courtyard. Its component rooms have views that seem to correspond to their function. The Ritterstube, the most accessible of the anterooms, looks out over the Kapellenhof and Brunnenhof, the most public of the courtyards; the view of carriages driving into the Residenz must have been quite dramatic. The remaining anterooms look into the Grottenhof, and the private rooms into the Residenzgarten. By contrast, the rooms of the apartments facing the Brunnenhof and Kaiserhof all have exactly the same view. There is no indication in early commentary that this feature of the elector's apartment was appreciated at the time.

85. Joanne Schmid, who has given us the earliest description of the Alexanderzimmer, wrote, "[It has pleased the elector], seine fürstliche Wohnungen mit den tapffern Thaten Alexandri des Grossen zu beehren, damit er nemblich stäts sein selbst eygene Grossmütigkeit vor Augen haben möchte" (153).

86. Paulus, 71. For a brief biographical sketch of Zuccalli, see Samuel J. Klingensmith, "Zuccalli Family," *Macmillan Encyclopedia of Architects* (New York, 1983).

87. This drawing is published in Hojer, "Residenzen." It is found in a bound volume (Ms 1040) in the Bibliothèque de l'Institut de France in Paris, together with other drawings by Zuccalli for Schleissheim and Nymphenburg. These drawings were part of the legacy of Robert de Cotte and according to Petzet, were sent to Paris in 1714 to serve as a basis for the new designs that Max Emanuel had requested from de Cotte, "Nymphenburg," 202–3. Projects by de Cotte for Schleissheim survive; none do for the Residenz, however, and this drawing may have been intended merely as informational material.

The overlay on the drawing also contains a project for the renovation of the apartment over the Antiquarium. It is next to impossible to ascertain the plan of this apartment before its renovation in 1746–48 as a double apartment for the elector and electress, and thus we cannot know whether this project was carried out. It should be noted, however, that it is much easier to reconcile Wening's (somewhat problematic) 1701 description of this apartment with Zuccalli's new plan than with the pre-1680 plan, so that it is possible that at least some work was carried out here at this time.

88. Kalmbach, 153–246; Schmid, 153–246; Wening, 3–4.

89. Wening does not mention a dressing room. It is described by Schmid, however, as being adjacent to the Schlafzimmer: "[Ankleidezimmer] warinnen Ihro Churftl. Drtl. sich an- und abzukleyden pflegen" (201). The narrow, one-bay room that appears on the plan following the dressing room cannot be identified in the descriptions; Hojer speculates that it might have been omitted in execution and its area added to that of the dressing room, or that it might have served as a private chapel ("Residenzen," 143).

90. Hojer, "Residenzen," 166 n. 8; Peter Volk, "Die bildende Kunst am Hofe

Max Emanuels," in *Kurfürst Max Emanuel* 1:138 n. 42. As the Holländisches Cabinet was not furnished until 1693–94, Schmid does not mention it. Kalmbach and Wening are not in complete agreement regarding its location. From Kalmbach's description it can indeed be identified as the oval room at the end of the new wing. Wening describes it as being located directly behind the bedroom; Hojer suggests, however, that Wening was confusing the rooms in his memory. Whether this room was intended as an exotic cabinet prior to 1693 is not known.

91. The term Sommerzimmer was a contemporary designation; Wening, Schmid, and Kalmbach use it. The term Alexanderzimmer, however, was not; these rooms were known at the time simply as the "churfürstliche (neugebauten) Zimmer." Regarding the enclosure of the altana, see Heym, *Zuccalli,* 39.

92. The picture gallery of the Sommerzimmer is shown on the plan of 1616–30 as the third room of the sequence. Wening and Schmid, however, describe it as the second. On the 1616–30 plan, the space of the Kammergalerie has been divided by means of pencil lines into four rooms, reflected on plan C.

93. Hartmann, 107.

94. After Karl Albrecht's death in 1745, these rooms were occasionally called the Kaiserzimmer, a reference to his reign as Emperor Charles VII. They, or at least the private rooms along the garden, were also called the Parade-Zimmer (see chap. 4, n. 92).

95. Decree of January 25, 1725, quoted in Hauttmann, *Effner,* 156.

96. A memorandum of the Hofbauamt from August 20, 1726, notes "da die jetzt regierende kf. Dl. neben den obern auch die untern Zimmer zuzurichten Dero Hofkammerrat und Architetto Effner mündlich gnäd. anbefohlen, die Unkosten wohl auf etlich 20–30,000 Gulden kommen dürften." This is to be compared to the six thousand gulden that Max Emanuel had originally earmarked for the project (Hauttmann, *Effner,* 156).

97. Karl Albrecht himself is the principal witness for this catastrophe. He wrote in his diary on December 14, 1729: "Umb 6 Uhr in der fruhe ist eine grausambe brunst in meinen neu angebauten Zimmern in der Residenz entstanden, bei welchen trey Zimmer Völlig verbrunnen, Und der Haus Schatz kimerlich erettet worden" (GHA, Hs 256, Karl Albrecht, Eigenhändig geschriebene Denkwürdigkeiten seines Lebens bis 1730).

98. In order to accommodate these dégagements, the wall had to be moved out several feet into the area of the Grottenhof; and Cuvilliés designed new facades for the north and south walls of the courtyard. Somewhat later, probably around 1740, the open loggia on the ground floor along the west side of the Grottenhof was closed in, and the wall (only the lower level) was given the same treatment with pilasters (Thoma, 37; see also n. 102 below).

99. On the iconography of its ceiling frescoes, see Lorenz Seelig, "Ein Deckenbildentwurf für die Grüne Galerie der Münchner Residenz," *Weltkunst* 50 (1980): 3647–49.

100. HStA, HR1 25/89/2, Prod. 49, contains various documents from 1764 regarding the "neuer Kuchen- und Tafelzimmerbau" and the demolition of the "schöne Stiege." The decoration of this dining room—which also included next to it a Retirade (latrine) with a niche containing a fountain—is exhaustively described in the 1769 Residenz furniture inventory (HStA, HR1 22/58). It is first shown in plan by Verschaffelt in 1799 (fig. 13).

101. On the Ahnengalerie, see Seelig.

102. The 1769 Residenz furniture inventory (HStA, HR1 22/58) lists the following rooms as belonging to the Gelbes Appartement: Ritterstube (this would be the anteroom serving as point of communication), first antechamber, second antechamber, Schlafzimmer, Cabinet, Retirade.

There are records of further work in the ground-floor rooms around the Grottenhof under Karl Albrecht. In 1739 or 1740, Cuvilliés received a commission for "neue Residenzzimmer im sogenannt Stainen Gärttl zunegst der Hofkapelle," which Trautmann believed to be rooms on the west side of the Grottenhof, on the site of the earlier loggia (F. Wolf, 49). In HStA, HR1 108/61/2, there are two requests for payment submitted in 1750 by Hofkistler Johann Michael Schmidt regarding outstanding sums due him for carpentry work in 1740–42 "in die churfrtl. Neuen Zimmer beym sogenannt Stainen Gärttl" (dated November 24) or "in die Zimmer bey der Sacristey" (dated August 8). In 1746–48, the paneling and doors of these rooms were removed and used in the rebuilding of Max III Joseph's new apartment above the Antiquarium; Schmidt's request of August 8, 1750, notes: "Weillen aber dise Zimmer widerumb abgebrochen als nembl. Thüren, Pargeth und Lamperin, dises alles dahin appliciret worden zu Wohnzimmern vor ICD unser allergdisten Herrn." No documentary evidence has been uncovered regarding the nature and purpose of these rooms. On Cuvilliés's plan of around 1760, three rooms are shown here: two rooms designated as "sacristies" and a "chambre" (which is separated from the "sacristies" by a passage). These rooms could well have formed a small apartment. The fact that Schmidt's request for payment of August 8, 1750, is addressed to Dowager Empress Maria Amalie and that, as he notes, the work was done "vor [i.e., für] I Röm Kais Mayt" suggests that this may have been intended as a small private apartment for her.

103. BStB, HsAbt, Cod germ 5456, Preysing, diaries, February 8, 9, 15, March 25, 1739. Several entries in Maria Theresia von Gombert's 1734 diary suggest that the Gelbes Appartement existed by then. On December 20, she wrote that because the elector was not feeling well, he held the conference in bed and then had himself carried upstairs to dine with the electress. In the evening the electress came downstairs to him for supper. This would seem to indicate that Karl Albrecht was then staying in the Gelbes Appartement on the ground floor. Thoma notes that the Gelbes Appartement was erected around 1730 (143) but does not document this conclusion. Braunfels states that, according to a cost estimate of Cuvilliés from March 9, 1754 (HStA, HR1 162/41), this apartment was executed in 1738–42 (*Cuvilliés,* 64).

104. On Max III Joseph's reign, see Spindler, 1034–43.

105. Gunezrhainer spent 8,224 florins; Cuvilliés spent approximately 17,000 florins (Voelcker, 53). Paneling from the rooms on the ground floor next to the Hofkapelle was re-used by Gunezrhainer (see n. 102 above). In the decree of June 13, 1752, ordering the work in the electress's apartment, Cuvilliés was instructed to reuse the existing gilded doors and wall paneling (HStA, HR1 25/89/2, Prod. 19).

106. In 1722–24, the apartments of the electoral prince and princess had been redecorated by Zuccalli and Effner (Hauttmann, *Effner,* 155; see also n. 87 above).

107. This change in the location of the electress's bedroom involved shifting walls.

108. When the location of the electress's bedroom was changed, the octagonal vestibule was enlarged to become a Ritterstube.

109. The subsidiary spaces of the electress's apartment included the former gallery of Henriette Adelaide at the east end of the Residenzgarten, where Verschaffelt's plan of 1799 (fig. 13) seems to place a small apartment of three rooms (antechamber, chamber, cabinet). Unfortunately, on Verschaffelt's drawing the room numbers in the elector's rooms have been inadvertently omitted, so that it is not possible to locate with certainty the rooms listed in the descriptive key.

110. Preysing recorded the fire in his diary on March 5, 1750: "Die grosse Feurbrunst, so nach gestrig. Mitt.nacht in d. Residenz entstanden, und bis gegen ½7 Uhr gedaurt gehabt. Abents ist d. Hof schlaffen gangen nach Nimphenburg" (BStB, HsAbt, Cod germ 5456). On the spread and extent of the fire, see Meitinger, 48 n. 64; and H. Brunner, *Theatre,* 21. A Residenz plan of 1630–58 (see P. Frankl, *MJBK* 10, 1915–18) shows the extent of the damage in poché and describes it in a legend.

111. Preysing noted on July 9, 1751: "In der Früh worde der erste Stein gelegt zum Neubau der Residenz" (BStB, HsAbt, Cod germ 5456).

112. On the building history of the Altes Residenztheater, see H. Brunner, *Theatre;* and *Festschrift zur Eröffnung des Alten Residenztheaters* (Munich, 1958). On the history of opera at the Munich court, see Rudhart.

113. Hojer, "Redoutenhaus."

114. The model was commissioned in 1764 and delivered in 1767 (Braunfels, *Cuvilliés,* 64). Today it is on display in the Ritterstube of the Reiche Zimmer. Cuvilliés's plan and elevation drawings exist only in black-and-white photographs in the possession of the BSV (Museums-Abteilung); the originals are apparently lost. The drawings may have been prepared somewhat earlier than the model, as they show the "schöne Stiege," which was demolished in 1764, still in place; they also show the electress's bedroom along the south or rear side of the Antiquarium tract—where it was presumably located only until around 1761, when it was moved into the enfilade along the Brunnenhof. The elevations and the model differ in certain respects (notably regarding the inclusion of mezzanine stories).

115. The extension of the facade west of the Kaisersaalbau houses a redesigned Schwabingertor on the ground level and the Wehrgang on the upper level. It terminates along the flank of the Theatinerkirche.

116. A good, succinct account of Karl Theodor's succession is found in Bosl (137–38).

117. Charles-Pierre Puille was originally a tapestry and furniture dealer in Paris; he came to Munich with Max IV Joseph and replaced Verschaffelt as director of the Hofbauamt (Hojer, "Residenz um 1800," 692).

118. Adalbert, *Residenz,* 194, 202. Verschaffelt noted in the legend accompanying his 1799 plans of the Residenz that Max IV Joseph intended to occupy the Kaiserzimmer (GHA, Hs 64).

119. Maximilian von Verschaffelt (1754–1818) was active as an architect and sculptor in Mannheim before he came to Munich in the 1790s, replacing Carl Albrecht von Lespilliez as director of the Hofbauamt in 1796. He was dismissed in 1802, after disagreements with the electress, and went to Vienna (biographical sketch in *Klassizismus in Bayern, Schwaben, und Franken: Architekturzeichnungen, 1775–1825,* exhibition catalog [Munich, 1980], 443).

120. Verschaffelt presented his proposal to the elector in the form of a plan drawing of the piano nobile (fig. 14) and elevation drawings of the new facades. Along with these he submitted five floor plans of the Residenz (figs. 12, 13), with an accompanying legend, showing existing conditions and detailing room usage; this material was intended to assist the elector in assigning apartments to family members and lodgings to the household. All the above material is in GHA, Hs 64; Hojer has published the plan and elevation drawings of the new project ("Residenz um 1800").

121. *Carl von Fischer, 1782–1820,* exhibition catalog (Munich, 1983), 70–81. Along the east side of the as yet unformed Max-Joseph-Platz, von Fischer's Königliches Hof- und Nationaltheater would rise in 1811–18. Von Fischer had won a competition in 1802 for its design.

122. In 1814–16, however, the Herkules-Saal was redecorated. The designs, which differ from the execution in certain respects, had been prepared in 1806 by Andreas von Gärtner (Hojer, "Residenz um 1800," 693–94).

123. Oswald Hederer, *Leo von Klenze: Persönlichkeit und Werk,* 2d ed. (Munich, 1981), 41.

124. The lodging of personnel in the opera house is documented in the Residenz furniture inventory of 1769 (HStA, HR1 22/58), in a list of lodgers in the Residenz from 1771 (HStA, FS 776, "Anzaig was von [dem] HofStaat in d Churfrtl alhiesigen Residenz, wie auch in den Chl Neuen OperaHaus und HofGarten logiert und schläft," January 9, 1771), and in Verschaffelt's plans.

125. Hainhofer (1611), 81, 84. On the development of government offices, see Spindler, 545–58, 581–85, 1063–73. On the Alter Hof, see Haeutle, *Residenz,* 2.

126. In 1743, after Karl Albrecht's election as emperor, plans were made to accommodate the Reichskanzlei in the Maxburg, a house in the western part of the city that was built for Wilhelm V in the late sixteenth century and later occupied by adult younger sons and other family members (HStA, HR1 25/89/1, Prod. 150).

In 1733, plans and estimates were drawn up for a small, four-story office building to be located in the Zwinger alongside the enclosed passage leading from the Schwarzer Saal to the Alter Hof (probably on or near the site of the opera house). This structure was to contain a nursery for the gardeners, in the basement; rooms for a Kanzlei and Registratur on the first floor; a Ratsstube on the second floor; and a large library hall on the third floor. Nothing, apparently, ever came of it (HStA, HR1 25/89/1, Prods. 132–41; HStA, Plansammlung 19496–501).

127. Wening, 3, 6.

128. The presence of the Revisionsrat in the Residenz is recorded in 1754 (GHA, Korr Akt 1712/K/II/20, memoranda regarding its removal to a quieter location, December 4, 1754, March 5, 1755) and in 1769 (furniture inventory). The presence of the archives and/or chancellery of the St. Georg Ritterorden is recorded in 1750 (StAM, Ämternachlass Törring 228, "Anzaig der sammentl. in alhiesig. churfrtl. Residenz verhandtenen gehaizten Öfen und Camin," February 17, 1750) and in 1754 (GHA, Korr Akt 1712/K/I/28, "Beschreibung, die in der Residenz bewohnt. und unbewohnten Zimmer betr.," December 24, 1754).

129. The use of this apartment under Max III Joseph is documented in the 1769 furniture inventory and in Cuvilliés's Residenz plan of the early 1760s.

The *départment des affaires étrangeres* was probably a fairly recent organ, resulting from the development of specialized *Fachkompetenzen* within the Geheime Konferenz, the innermost private council established during the late reign of Max Emanuel (see Spindler, 1065).

130. The presence of the Kabinettskasse in the Residenz is recorded in 1754 (GHA, Korr Akt 1712/K/I/28, list of rooms, December 24, 1754).

131. On the Silberkammer, see H. Brunner, *Kunstschätze,* 195–210.

132. Wening notes only one "Frauen-Zimmer-Kuchen." The list of stoves from 1750, however (StAM, Ämternachlass Törring 228), lists three "Herdt" for the ladies—one for the ladies of Dowager Empress Maria Amalie, one for the "kur-fürstliche Damen," and one for the "herzogliche Damen." There was likewise more than one dining room for the ladies. On the dining room, see n. 100 above.

133. Wening, 8. The list of stoves from 1750 gives a total of nineteen kitchens (including the three Herdt for the ladies); among these are kitchens for the Burg-pfleger, Hauspfleger, Leinwandmeisterin, and other officials.

The plans of Cuvilliés and Verschaffelt show a large kitchen on the ground floor under the Weisser Saal, which Verschaffelt calls the "grande cuisine dite de l'empereur." The function of this kitchen is not clear; perhaps it served to provide for highly placed guests or for special banquets held in the Kaisersaal. Wening does not mention it.

134. On the etymology of the word Dirnitz (also Dürnitz, Tirnitz, Türnitz), see Föringer, "Anordnungen," 97–98. It would seem that in the sixteenth century all the male members of the household ate together in the Dirnitz. A Türnitz-Ordnung issued by Wilhelm V in 1589 (published in Föringer, "Anordnungen," 133–38) states that this regulation applies to "allen unsern hofgesindt, grauen, herrn, adl, und allen andern, was standts thuen und wesens sy seyen." In 1607, Maximilian introduced the practice of giving a food allowance to most of the household, and the number of persons who had the right to dine at court was significantly reduced. See chapter 5 (section on dining).

The reference of 1600 is from a building document quoted in Knüttel, 205 n. 7. In the 1769 furniture inventory, this Dirnitz is designated "Turnitz, worin die churf. Edlknaben speisen"; Verschaffelt calls it the "salle à manger des pages."

135. StAM, Hoh Arch A788, "Beschreibung über die ienige Persohnen unnd Diennerschafften, welche in der churfrtl. Residenz logieren," December 1, 1745; HStA, FS 776, list of lodgers in the Residenz, January 9, 1771 (see n. 124 above). The difference between 1745 and 1771 in numbers of personnel housed in the Residenz can be accounted for in two ways: in 1745 the Neuveste was still standing; and in that year there were eight Herrschaften living in the Residenz, whereas in 1771 there were only three. Court personnel also lived in the Maxburg (n. 126 above); according to a 1745 description of that building (StAM, Hoh Arch A788), some sixty to seventy persons had lodgings there. We may also presume that certain stable personnel lived above the stables and that court personnel may well have been housed in buildings owned by the elector elsewhere in Munich.

136. HStA, HR1 25/89/2, Prod. 104.

137. August Freiherr von Müller, *Geschichtliche Entwicklung der königlichen bay-erischen Pagerie von 1514 bis zur Gegenwart* (Munich, 1901), 25–26.

138. Hofkalender 1769; list of lodgers of 1771 (see n. 124 above).

139. Rohr, 71.

140. GHA, Korr Akt 1712/H/39, Instruktion of May 15, 1686. It seems to

have been not unusual for the Obristhofmeister of young Herrschaften to have lodgings at court; there is, for example, a letter of 1744 from the newly appointed Obristhofmeister of Princess Maria Antonia Walburga to Karl Albrecht regarding the allocation of a lodging for him in the Residenz (HStA, MF 10863). On November 13, 1719, Preysing wrote in his diary: "Diese Nacht hat einer vom Nebendienst bei Hof geschlaffen, weil die 2 im Hauptdienst den 14ten früh morgen voraus nach Haag gegangen." (BStB, HsAbt, Cod germ 5456).

141. *Radl-Bett* and *Spann-Bett* are the usual terms for these.

Chapter Three

1. Moser, 2:265–69.

2. "Manche . . . Herren sehen nicht gerne, dass Fremde, ja selbst ihre eigene Diener, welche sie nicht ausdrücklich hierunter favorisieren, ohne Erlaubnis auf die Lust-Häuser hinauskommen. Ordinaire ist der Zutritt auch nicht so frey, als bey Hof in der Residenz, weswegen auch die Cour-Tage und bestimmte Assembleen auf dem Land wegfallen. An grossen Höfen dürfen fremde Gesandte, ohn ausdrückliche Erlaubnis und Benennung, dem Herrn nicht folgen, wann er sich auf das Land retirirt; da ist er mehr ein Particulier, der sich Ruhe machen will, als Regent" (Moser, 2:267–79).

3. Moser, 2:265–69.

4. Hüttl, 27.

5. GHA, Korr Akt 631/5, "Bericht dessen was zu Ankunfft der churfrtl. Prinzessin und deren Bedienung abgeredt, verglichen und von Sr. Churf. Drtl. gnädigst placitirt worden," n.d.

6. HStA, FS 109, "Kurzer Begriff, wie es bey Ankunfft der kaiserlichen und königlichen Maytten. zu Dachau und alhier zu halten," [1653].

7. On Schloss Dachau, see Karl Trautmann, "Der grosse Saal des Schlosses zu Dachau," *Monatsschrift des Historischen Vereins von Oberbayern* 2 (1893): 138–44; Hartig, 198–99; and Elmar Schmid, *Schloss Dachau* (Munich, 1982). Hainhofer left a brief description of Schloss Dachau from his 1611 trip to Munich (131–33).

8. Hainhofer (1611), 119–31; E. Schmid, *Schleissheim*, 24.

9. Mayerhofer, 16.

10. E. Schmid, *Schleissheim*, 39–40.

11. GHA, Korr Akt 631/4, Graf Max Kurz, "Continuation des Diary oder der Verzeichnus, dessen was sich bey hiesigen Churfrtl. Hofstat Denckwürdiges und anders verloffen," January 15, 1651–January 15, 1652.

12. GHA, Korr Akt 638a, Johann Mändl, "Consultatio et Reformatio der übermässigen Ausgaben beim churbayerischen Hof," 1655.

13. Hainhofer (1636), 277–78. The compendium of embassies, 1633–83 (HStA, FS 126½), does, however, contain records of three instances in which audiences were granted at Schleissheim in May and June of 1644.

14. Letter of September 27, 1652, quoted in Merkel, 28.

15. Merkel, 333–96; Straub, 174–244; Bary, passim.

16. Bary, 179–91.

17. Mayerhofer, 24; Bary, 190; E. Schmid, *Schleissheim*, 49; HStA, HR1 227/102/5, "Überschlag was ds zu Schleisshaimb zu erpauen vorhabende neue Pallonhaus ungefehr costen mochte," June 27, 1656. Schleissheim became the Witwen-

sitz of Maria Anna after Maximilian's death (E. Schmid, *Schleissheim,* 40), but seems to have been available to the young electoral couple from an early date.

18. Chapuzeau, 61.

19. The Bucintoro and its fleet are described in Bary, 180–85.

20. Chapuzeau, 135–40. The flotilla continued in use through the eighteenth century.

21. Merkel, 373, 374. The four apartments were presumably intended for the four members of the family at that time—Ferdinand Maria, Henriette Adelaide, Maria Anna Christina, and Max Emanuel (although in August 1663 Henriette Adelaide was pregnant with a third child, Louisa Margarethe Antonia, born September 18, 1663, died November 10, 1665). As built, the apartments of the elector and electress on the piano nobile were composed of only two anterooms, a bedchamber, cabinet, and garderobe. Two additional apartments for Herrschaften could have been located on the third floor, where the layout of rooms on either side of the Saal was virtually identical to that below. The only difficulty would have been that the only access to these rooms was by means of small spiral staircases at the west side of the building. Narrow corridors connected the staircases to the antechambers at the east. On a plan of the ground floor (HStA, Plansammlung 8329) that must predate the beginning of construction in 1664 (as it shows only four pairs of columns in the vestibule, instead of the six that were built; see Hojer, "Residenzen," 159), there is a pair of enclosed staircases projecting from the garden (west) facade. Such staircases could have been intended to link more than just the two lower stories and would have provided a more dignified approach to third-floor "appartements nobles" than the small existing spiral staircases. The walls of the staircases, however, are pochéed in black, whereas those of the house are in pink, so that the staircases may have been a later addition to the drawing. The idea of enclosed, projecting staircases extending from ground floor to third floor is also found on an elevation drawing of the west facade dating from after 1714 (HStA, Plansammlung 8302; see Petzet, "Nymphenburg," 206–7); this suggests the presence of fairly important apartments on the third floor. Clearly, the only way to provide fittingly monumental access to these apartments without encroaching on the apartments of the piano nobile would have been, in fact, to add staircases in front of the building. In the eighteenth century, the third floor was occupied by ladies-in-waiting.

22. Hojer, "Residenzen," 160; E. Schmid, *Nymphenburg,* 10.

23. The original plan of Venaria Reale is preserved in Amadeo di Castellamonte, *La Venaria Reale: Palazzo di piacere . . .* (1672). The name Nymphenburg first appears in building accounts of June 1664 (Bary, 245).

24. Bary, 247; E. Schmid, *Nymphenburg,* 10, 13, 14; Hager, 11.

25. Conte Lantery, quoted in Straub, 246. An example of his self-indulgence: no mourning was laid on for the death of Albrecht Sigmund, Bishop of Freising, on November 4, 1685, as this would have meant an end to the fall hunting; only the following January was a solemn requiem mass said for the deceased prelate, who was also a member of the family (Straub, 270).

26. A detailed account of Max Emanuel's activities in these years, based on the reports, is found in Straub, 246–57.

27. The town of Karlstadt along the canal in front of Nymphenburg—founded by Karl Albrecht, ostensibly to promote industry and trade—never

grew beyond a hamlet (see the discussion later in this chapter). Neither the architectural inadequacies of the Residenz nor the extravagance of several preliminary projects for Schleissheim justify supposing that there was a plan to relocate the seat of government. Hojer's contention that "diese Pläne dokumentieren den Entschluss, die Residenz nach Schleissheim zu verlegen" seems overstated and wishful, in light of the total absence of explicit evidence ("Residenzen," 146).

28. Paulus, 77; *Schloss Lustheim,* 14. Viktoria Berg notes that the last invoice from the frescoists dates from 1687 ("Die Lustheimer Fresken," *Anzeiger des Germanischen Nationalmuseums Nürnberg* [1968], 86–102). Paulus sets the completion date for the building as April 30, 1689 (80). On the imperial visit, see Straub, 292–93.

29. This drawing is in the possession of the BSV (illustrated in Petzet, "Schleissheimer Schlossbauten," 184). Petzet (183–85), and Hojer ("Residenzen," 146) assume that the parterres in the foreground of the drawing are meant to be directly in front of the Altes Schloss. Imhof argues, however, that this garden design already presupposes the new palace (59–60).

30. The electoral apartments were effectively double apartments. Although the 1715 Lustheim furniture inventory (HStA, HR1 209/11) describes only two apartments, the 1731 and 1755 inventories (both HR1 210/16) list two bedchambers on the electress's side. The 1761 inventory (HR1 210/16) describes four apartments—green, red, yellow, and blue—each consisting of antechamber and principal room; the inventories of 1731, 1755, and 1761 mention the Cavaliers-Zimmer.

31. E. Schmid, *Schleissheim,* 61–62. On January 25, 1694, Max Emanuel decreed from Brussels that "die Galerie beim Neugebeu [Lustheim]" was to be finished. The 1755 Lustheim furniture inventory (HStA, HR1 210/16) mentions the "Gallerie"; the 1761 inventory (HR1 210/16) does not. The latter lists much furniture that was removed from Lustheim to Munich in 1755 and 1759; it could have been from the gallery.

32. The latter two views, by Joachim Franz Beich, are illustrated in Imhof, pls. 33, 34.

33. *Ausführliche Relation,* chap. 6. The plan is reproduced by Paulus (pl. 66), who does not cite the location of the original. The architecture of the exterior, as seen in the elevations accompanying the plan, is in general agreement with the Diesel and Beich views. In the Bibliothèque de l'Institut de France in Paris, there are three drawings that show a variant scheme that may represent an earlier design for the gallery (the drawings are reproduced in Petzet, "Schleissheimer Schlossbauten," pls. 1, 2, 3).

34. Good accounts of the evolution of the Schleissheim garden are given in Imhof; and E. Schmid, *Schleissheim,* 123–30.

35. On the canal systems of Schleissheim and Nymphenburg, see Josef Ponten, "Die kurfürstlichen Kanalbauten in der Münchner Landschaft," *Mitteilungen der Geographischen Gesellschaft in München* 21 (1928): 305–39.

36. Mayerhofer, 46–47; E. Schmid, *Schleissheim,* 125.

37. Aerial view in Bibliothèque de l'Institut de France, Paris (illustrated in Petzet, "Schleissheimer Schlossbauten," 196). It and two earlier garden designs (HStA, Plansammlung 8258, 8272; illustrated in Imhof, pls. 10, 14) show sunken parterres lined with wall fountains that were never executed.

38. On Girard at Schleissheim, see Imhof, 104–11. The cascade was erected in 1723–33 to final designs prepared by Effner (E. Schmid, *Schleissheim,* 129).

39. Hauttmann, "Entwürfe," 256.

40. Most of the drawings are in the Plansammlung of the HStA; others are found in the collections of the BSV and the Bibliothèque nationale and Bibliothèque de l'Institut de France in Paris.

41. The studies that have contributed the most to reconstructing the complex planning and building history of Neu-Schleissheim are Hubala; Petzet, "Schleissheimer Schlossbauten"; Ernst Götz, "Beobachtungen am Neuen Schloss Schleissheim zu seiner Planungs- und Baugeschichte unter Zuccalli, 1701–1704," typescript, 1976; Hojer, "Residenzen"; and Riedl.

42. HStA, HR1 227/102/5, decree of January 8, 1700.

43. The aerial view (illustrated in Petzet, "Schleissheimer Schlossbauten," 196) is in the Bibliothèque de l'Institut de France; the letter of April 3, 1700, and accompanying legend are in GHA, Korr Akt 753/42a (R220). The ground-floor plan also exists in another drawing (HStA, Plansammlung 8273); in it the rooms are not numbered, nor does it show the lateral service courts.

The interior layout of the third mezzanine floor corresponds very directly with that of the ground floor. It is therefore difficult to imagine this as a story containing lodgings for ladies and gentlemen. The drawing seems instead to show a piano nobile, and it is possible to identify on this plan many of the rooms of the piano nobile listed in the legend. We should note, however, that in 1735 Schlossverwalter Gillet rearranged one of the mezzanines by dividing up the rooms, which he described as being unnecessarily large, into smaller rooms (see p. 113).

44. GHA, Korr Akt 753/42a (R220), "Punti sopra gli quali si vuole meliore explicatione dal Zuccalli," n.d. [before June 12, 1700].

45. The principal apartments do not have the same number of anterooms as those in the Residenz; see chapter 4 for a discussion of this. It is not possible to identify the princely apartments with certainty on the plan of the third mezzanine floor.

46. GHA, Korr Akt 753/42a (R220), letter of Max Emanuel to Joseph Clemens(?), n.d. [late July or August 1700].

47. GHA, Korr Akt 753/42a (R220). This remark is made specifically in reference to the "grand dessin"; it may refer only to the overall layout, not necessarily to the palace itself.

48. There exists a late project by Zuccalli, clearly postdating the project of 1700, for a three-winged palace without the Altes Schloss; it may have been prepared in response to such criticism by Joseph Clemens. Various drawings were made for this project: a site plan (Plansammlung 8284), a ground-floor plan (8276), plans of the piano nobile (8275, 8277), a perspective view of the courtyard (8254), a garden elevation (8251), and others. Plansammlung 8251, 8254, 8275, and 8276 are illustrated in Hubala.

49. GHA, Korr Akt 753/42a (R220), "Punti sopra gli quali si vuole meliore explicatione dal Zuccalli," n.d. [before June 12, 1700, when Zuccalli wrote that he was preparing responses to the points in the memorandum].

50. This idea apparently came from Max Emanuel, who expressed his intentions regarding the galleries in a letter of late July or August 1700: "The gallery that attaches the new building to the old should be with arches on columns (con

portici sopra colonate), and above this nothing other than a terrace with a balustrade." In a letter of August 7, 1700, Zuccalli pointed out to Max Emanuel that it would be advantageous to plan the galleries in such a way that the side wings, which would ultimately be needed for the accommodation of court offices, could be added at a later time. He therefore recommended keeping the arcades as he had already designed them. Both letters are in GHA, Korr Akt 753/42a (R220).

51. The appearance of the gallery is discussed in chap. 5. Riedl, who draws heavily on Götz's observations of the building fabric during restoration work undertaken in 1958–61 and 1968–72 (see n. 41 above), as well as on careful study of the extant drawings, has argued, very convincingly, that this gallery was not first developed in reaction to the disastrous collapse of part of the central pavilion on July 7, 1702, as Hubala had maintained. An already existing gallery in this location is mentioned in the report of July 29, 1702, that was prepared by the commission of experts appointed to investigate the collapse (HStA, HR1 227/102/5). Furthermore, the two plan drawings of the piano nobile (fig. 26) can be identified as dating prior to the start of construction, as Riedl demonstrates. She does not, however, offer an explanation for the appearance of this gallery to take the place of Hubala's hypothesis that it was an expedient developed in response to structural weakness.

52. GHA, Korr Akt 753/42a (R220).

53. This drawing is in the possession of the BSV, Bauamt (illustrated in Hubala, 181).

54. Imhof, 74.

55. HStA, HR1 227/102/5. See also Götz (n. 41 above), 10.

56. It was reported that in March and April 1704, "die Erste gemachte Stiegen [wurden] abgetragen, ainiche Mäuren durchgeprochen, ain neye Stiegen angelegt" (Riedl, 14).

57. HStA, Plansammlung 8276 (illustrated in Hubala, 163).

58. E. Schmid, *Nymphenburg*, 17.

59. Heigel asserts that the reason often given for the retention of Henriette Adelaide's villa—that Max Emanuel did this out of respect for the memory of his mother—originated with Pierre de Bretagne (*Nymphenburg*, 55).

60. E. Schmid, *Nymphenburg*, 18.

61. Hojer, "Residenzen," 167 n. 78.

62. Hauttmann, *Effner*, 14.

63. Although the name of Effner's teacher is nowhere mentioned in the sources, Boffrand is for various reasons the likeliest candidate (ibid., 26–28). For a brief biographical sketch of Effner, see Samuel J. Klingensmith, "Joseph Effner," *Macmillan Encyclopedia of Architects* (New York, 1983).

64. Hauttmann, *Effner*, 30–36.

65. GHA, Korr Akt 753/52. Plans were sent in August 1714, as witnessed by a letter of August 29 from Generalbaudirektor Baron von Neuhaus to the elector (HStA, FS 147d). This letter mentions reports sent on August 5 and 10. GHA, Korr Akt 753/50, contains two undated reports that describe conditions at the two building sites in the summer of 1714.

66. These two projects are represented in a total of twenty-one drawings in the Cabinet des estampes, Bibliothèque nationale, Paris. They were published in part by Hauttmann in 1911 ("Entwürfe").

67. On the work at Dachau, see Hauttmann, *Effner*, 67–72; and Gerhard

Hanke, "Die Umgestaltung des Dachauer Schlosses durch Joseph Effner," *Amperland* 1 (1965): 5–7. On the work at Lichtenberg, see Hauttmann, *Effner,* 75; and Heym, *Zuccalli,* 84–86.

68. That Schleissheim remained a project to which Max Emanuel attached great expectations is suggested by the choice of the palace as background in the enormous group portrait commemorating the reunion of Max Emanuel, Therese Kunigunde, and their six children in 1715 (Joseph Vivien, 1715–33; see *Kurfürst Max Emanuel,* cat. no. 474). An equestrian portrait of Max Emanuel painted around 1725 (artist unknown)—in which rider and horse are, curiously, placed on a pedestal—also uses Schleissheim (the garden facade and parterre) as background (cat. no. 672).

69. Hauttmann, *Effner,* 38–41.

70. Diesel, 87.

71. Hauttmann states that the original building was the central pavilion (*Effner,* 72–75). The plan of Fürstenried of 1756 (fig. 32), however, identifies it as one of the side pavilions.

72. *Ausführliche Relation,* chap. 11. I have been unable to find a plan of Fürstenried that shows the disposition of rooms. There are, however, furniture inventories from 1717, 1731, and 1759 (all in HStA, HR1 192/2).

73. HStA, FS 1126a, "Détail de la réception de l'Electeur de Treve en Baviere et des fêtes qui luy ont été données pendant son séjour," 1728.

74. Shortly after his accession, Karl Albrecht presented Fürstenried to Maria Amalie as her Witwensitz. In the "Détail de la réception de l'Electeur de Treve" of 1728 (HStA, FS 1126a), Fürstenried is described as belonging to the electress. In 1737, Küchel called it her "Wittibsitz" (546). After Max III Joseph's death, the house became the Witwensitz for Maria Anna Sophia (HStA, HR1 192/4, collection of documents relating to the transfer of Fürstenried to Maria Anna Sophia, 1780–99).

75. This building history of the service blocks is from Hojer, "Residenzen," 167 n. 79; and E. Schmid, *Nymphenburg,* 25–26.

76. The corridors crossing the canals (Wassergänge) were added after 1739 (Hojer, "Residenzen," 159).

77. HStA, FS 147d, contains an estimate of materials and labor for the Passgebäude from January 26, 1723. The game of Pass was invented by Max Emanuel, probably as a diversion from pall-mall. Pass was played by driving small wooden balls around a series of obstacles with a stick or club until the goal was reached. The rules of the game as devised by Max Emanuel were published in full as chapter 16 of the *Ausführliche Relation.* There was also an open course for Pass in the garden at Nymphenburg, inside one of the bosquet compartments flanking the great parterre (see Diesel, fig. 23). On Pass, see *Kurfürst Max Emanuel,* cat. no's. 596, 597.

78. Petzet notes the existence of an estimate dated 1749 for the installation of the kitchens in the former Comedihaus ("Nymphenburg," 209). The BSV, Bauamt, possesses a plan of the Küchenbau entitled "Plan wie in den dermahligen Comodihaus zu Nymphenburg die samentliche Mundt- und Hofkuchln, nebst der Hofmezgt, und ober selbigen die Wohnungen der sammtl. Hofkuchlambtsofficianten, Hof- und Mundtköch &c errichtet werden könten." Hager notes that the resolution to transfer the kitchens was first made under Karl Albrecht but was not carried out until 1749 (89 n. 143).

79. Hager, 19–20. The triangular pediments were removed by von Klenze in the early nineteenth century, as part of a campaign to purge the palaces of their Baroque features. Schleissheim suffered a similar fate.

80. HStA, FS 1126a, "Détail de la réception de l'Electeur de Treve," 1728, (where the room is called "das Appartement-Zimmer oder sogenannter Spiegel-Saal").

81. The Spiegel-Saal and the two apartments of the elector are listed in the 1719 furniture inventory (HStA, HR1 199/11) with a seemingly complete record of their furnishings, implying that the rooms were then furnished. The first mention of the Neues Tafelzimmer occurs in Preysing's diary entry for September 3, 1720 (BStB, HsAbt, Cod germ 5456). Preysing notes that supper was taken that evening in the "neues Tafelzimmer," after which a ball was held in the "Spiegelzimmer."

The term Prinzenbau appears in the *Ausführliche Relation,* chap. 13. Therese Kunigunde was assigned the south apartment in the central pavilion, according to the 1719 furniture inventory (HStA, HR1 199/11), where it is termed "ICD unser gdisten Frauen oder das sogenant rote Apartement." As Therese Kunigunde lived mostly apart from the court, it is probable that she did not require accommodations as extensive as those Max Emanuel furnished for himself in the inner north pavilion. The corresponding apartment along the north side of the Hauptsaal is designated "das sogenandt Griene Apartement, dessen sich vormahls ICD bedient." It could well have served as a guest apartment at this time.

82. This is demonstrated by comparing it with late-eighteenth-century plans of the garden—for example, the 1755 plan owned by the BSV (illustrated in Hager) or Cuvilliés's site plan (fig. 38).

83. On July 16, 1719, Preysing recorded in his diary (BStB, HsAbt, Cod germ 5456) that the Herrschaften took supper at the Pagodenburg and in this way dedicated the building.

84. "ICD haben dieses commode Gebäu selbst anzugeben beliebet" (*Ausführliche Relation,* chap. 15); "C'est SASE de Baviere Maximilien Emanuel de glorieuse memoire qui en a fait le dessein elle même" (HStA, FS 1126a, "Détail de la réception de l'Electeur de Treve," 1728).

85. "Das Getäffel ist auf Arabische und Indianische Art gemahlt, mit allerhand Chinesischen Figuren, und Pagoten, daher es auch den Namen Pagottenburg erhalten" (*Ausführliche Relation,* chap. 15). This source also calls the building the "Indianisches Gebäu."

86. The term "Cammer zu ruhen" is from the *Ausführliche Relation,* chap. 15. I have come across no record of the Herrschaften having slept in the Pagodenburg.

87. HStA, FS 1126a.

88. "[Die] Pagottenburg ist ein Ort vor die hohen Herrschaften, daselbst auszuruhen, wenn Sie auf der Maille-Bahn gespielt haben" (*Ausführliche Relation,* chap. 15). The "Détail de la réception de l'Electeur de Treve" echoes this; the Pagodenburg, it says, is situated "au beau milieu du maille, comme un endroit de repos pour ceux qui se sont fatigués en jouant."

89. *Ausführliche Relation,* chap. 15.

90. BStB, HsAbt, Cod germ 5456.

91. The building was first used in September 1721. Preysing notes that the first supper was held there on September 9; the electoral prince slept there for the first time on September 18 and the elector two days later (ibid.).

92. Hager, 39.

93. E. Schmid, *Nymphenburg,* 60.

94. On the Eremitage, see Hager, 40–43; and E. Schmid, *Nymphenburg,* 64–71.

95. On April 6, 1719, Effner presented a lengthy estimate detailing all work that would be necessary to complete the corps-de-logis (HStA, FS 147d), "Haupt-Uberschlag was über das, von ICD zu bauen gdist resolvierente Corps de Logie bey dem neuen Lust- und Residenz-Gebau zu Schleissheimb . . . an Arbeit- und Material-Uncosten ergehen mechte." Preysing's diaries for 1719 and the early 1720s are full of references to Max Emanuel riding out to Schleissheim to view the progress of the construction (BStB, HsAbt, Cod germ 5456).

This building history of the pavilions is from Hauttmann, *Effner,* 111. Of the galleries connecting the pavilions to the corps-de-logis, the south arm was finished at this time. Only the rear wall of the north arm was erected; it was finished under Ludwig I.

96. The model was produced by Nikolaus Gottfried Stuber. It is kept today at Schleissheim in a room not normally open to the public. See *Kurfürst Max Emanuel,* cat. no. 667.

97. HStA, FS 147d, memorandum from Max Emanuel, "Pour Schleissheimb à faire pendant cette esté de l'année 1724"; HStA, FS 147d, estimate "Yberschlag betr . . . drei Gebäuden für Cavaliers und Frauenzimmer nach der Riss von J. Effner," January 28, 1723.

98. Hauttmann claims that they never progressed beyond the foundations and notes that in his day an underground corridor from the old to the new palace remained under the line of the north gallery (*Effner,* 112, 204 n. 199). The *Ausführliche Relation,* however, in describing Schleissheim, states: "Zuerst kommt man durch grosse Vorhöfe, in deren letztern zu beyden Seiten Gallerien auf Pfeilern stehen" (chap. 6). Gottfried Edler von Rotenstein writes: "Vorne ist ein sehr grosser Hof mit einem eisernen Gatterwerk und 66 Säulen umgeben, auf welchen 38 versilberte Vasen und 28 versilberte kleine Statuen stehen. . . . In diesen Hof kommt man durch vier eiserne Thore von Gitterwerk" (pt. 3:262).

99. On Karl Albrecht's financial policies, see Hartmann, 91–95. On the Cuvilliés petition, see F. Wolf, 79.

100. Plans for the Rondell, which may have been formulated under Max Emanuel, were drawn by Effner.

101. Hauttmann, *Effner,* 169.

102. The observation is by Hauttmann (ibid.).

103. The draft of the patent is published in part by Heigel ("Projekt"). The patent is undated, but is probably from the first several years of Karl Albrecht's reign; a letter of 1728 regarding the requirement that settlers build houses (a provision contained in the patent) is quoted in Hauttmann, *Effner,* 170.

104. "Längst dem Canale von Nymphenburg nach München sollen Gärten und Häuser, jedes von besonderer Bauart, angeleget werden; und weil der itzige Churfürst Nymphenburg sehr liebet, so fürchten einige, dass durch Vergrösserung dieses Ortes, der Stadt München schlechter Vortheil zuwachsen werde." (Keyssler, 61).

105. On the building history of the Amalienburg, see Hager, 44–53. It seems probable that a small garden building already existed on this site (ibid., 45). A

pen-and-ink drawing in the possession of the BSV, dating probably from 1725–28 (on its date, see Hojer, "Residenzen," 169 n. 134), shows a small structure on this site that looks like a menagerie (with small enclosures surrounding it in radial formation).

106. At the time, the *chambre* was not specifically designated a bedroom. Cuvilliés' engraved plan of the Amalienburg in his *École de l'architecture bavaroise* terms it "chambre avec un lit en niche." The Nymphenburg furniture inventories of 1751 and 1769 (both in HStA, HR1 199/11) call it "Gelbes Cabinet" and "Gelbes Zimmer" respectively and note that the room contained a "Rast-Bett." The 1789 "Beschreibung des churfürstlichen Lustschlosses Nymphenburg" (HStA, HR1 200/13) does call this room "Schlafzimmer." The present-day "official" designation is "Ruhezimmer" (Hojer and Schmid, 56).

107. "Die Hunde finden eine grosse Liebhaberinn an ihr, welches man vornehmlich zu Nymphenburg an den übel zugerichteten rothdamastenen Tapeten und Betten abmerken kann. . . . Bey der Tafel stehen eine gute Menge derselben um die Churfürstinn, und auf jeder Seite sitzt einer, die alles wegnehmen, was sie erwischen können" (Keyssler, 50).

108. Hager, 48.

109. Küchel, 544; HStA, HR1 199/11, Nymphenburg furniture inventories, 1755, 1769; HStA, HR1 200/13, "Beschreibung des churfürstlichen Lustschlosses Nymphenburg," 1789. Küchel wrote in 1737 that the mezzanine was intended as lodgings for the Hofdamen (ibid.)

110. E. Schmid, "Schleissheim," 104, 121–22.

111. Kirchgrabner's plans for the staircase (dated 1776) are in BSV, Bauamt.

112. Regarding Schleissheim, the 1779 travelogue of Pater Beda Plank reports only that it is famous "wegen der künstlichsten Malereyen" (Dussler, 352). See also Ulla Krempel, "Max Emanuel als Gemäldesammler," in *Kurfürst Max Emanuel* 1:225.

113. Bianconi, 70.

114. See the memoirs of Stephan Freiherr von Stengel ("Neue Denkwürdigkeiten vom pfalzbayrischen Hofe unter Karl Theodor," ed. Karl Theodor Heigel, *Zeitschrift für allgemeine Geschichte* 4 [1887]: 555–56); he claims much of the responsibility for persuading Karl Theodor to make the electoral picture collections accessible to the public and to remove paintings from Schleissheim, where, he feared, they were perishing from exposure to dampness.

115. Hager, 57–60.

116. In the 1751 furniture inventory (HStA, HR1 199/11), the rooms on the piano nobile of the inner south pavilion are called "ID Unser Gdisten Frauen Neue Zimmer." The 1769 furniture inventory (HStA, HR1 199/11) notes that the bedchamber of the elector's apartment on the ground floor of this pavilion had been completely redone in 1767.

117. HStA, HR1 199/11, Nymphenburg furniture inventory, 1769; Hager, 63.

118. HStA, HR1 200/13, "Beschreibung des churfürstlichen Lustschlosses Nymphenburg," 1789; Hager, 63.

119. In his diaries (BStB, HsAbt, Cod germ 5456), Preysing frequently noted the dates of the beginning and end of the Campagne from 1719 to 1751. Maria Anna Josepha, widowed Margravine of Baden-Baden, also recorded this information in her diary in the 1770s (GHA, Hs 194).

120. StAM, Hofmarken: Ämternachlass Törring, Karton 74, Nr. 115. Preysing gives the following dates for the Campagne during the early reign of Max III Joseph: May 14, 1748; May 12, 1749; May 12–October 3, 1750; and May 14, 1751.

121. BStB, HsAbt, Oefeleana 483, Felix Andreas Oefele, "Journal historique de ce qui s'est passé à la cour de Baviere," 1738–43.

122. In the *Ausführliche Relation,* it is noted that the palace was quite capable of accommodating all necessary personnel: "In allen diesen Pavillons, wie auch über den grossen Ställen sind so viel Apartementer, dass, wie Zahlreich auch die Hofstadt ist, sie doch gar commod daselbst logirt werden kan" (chap. 13).

123. HStA, FS 777, "Liste nach Nymphenburg pro ao. 1770."

124. GHA, Korr Akt 1712/O/VI/16, "Anzeig deren sammentlichen allhiesigen Schloss- und anderen Bedienten, welche zum Theil im Schloss logiren, dann ybrigen ausser dem Schloss sich allhier befuntenten so wohl Haus Inhabern, dann Inwohnern," compiled by Nicolaus Turbert, Schlossverwalter of Nymphenburg, 1766. Four of the ten Rondell pavilions are listed here: Hieberisches Haus (center pavilion, south quadrant), Lespillisches Haus (northernmost pavilion, north quadrant), Kaufmann-Haus, and Hofkistlers Haus (both probably among the four pavilions closest to the mouth of the canal on the east). Only thirty-two of those living in the palace were actively in service; the rest were dependents of former or retired servants.

125. A tabulation of the beds listed in the 1769 furniture inventory (HStA, HR1 199/11) gives a figure of only about 180. This discrepancy may result from the fact that furniture was sometimes moved from palace to palace as the need arose (see HStA, HR1 192/2 and HR1 209/8, for example, which contain much documentation—lists, correspondence, receipts, etc.—from the entire eighteenth century regarding the delivery of furniture from palace to palace) or from the fact that many lower servants slept more than one to a bed or slept on mattresses or strawsacks (which are inventoried but difficult to count). A tabulation of the beds listed in the 1751 furniture inventory (HStA, HR1 199/11) totals 359, so that the palace clearly could accommodate that many persons. In that year, however, there were seven Herrschaften resident at the Munich court (elector, electress, Dowager Empress Maria Amalie, Princesses Maria Anna Josepha and Josepha Antonia, and Duke and Duchess Clemens). In 1769 there were only five, two of whom (the duke and duchess) lived somewhat apart from court and did not always participate in the Campagne.

In 1771, approximately 240 persons, of whom 42 were retired, lodged in the Residenz (HStA, FS 776, "Anzaig was von ID Churfürst und ID Churfürstin dan IH verwittibten Markgräfin von Baaden-Baaden Hofstaat in d. churfrtl. alhiesigen Residenz . . . logiert und schläft," January 9, 1771).

126. The fourteen ladies had twenty-eight servants living in the Residenz. In addition, eight retired servants of ladies lived there. The ladies who moved to Nymphenburg took eighteen servants with them.

127. I have counted beds in rooms specifically designated for kitchen personnel. There may very well have been additional kitchen personnel housed elsewhere in the palace, just as there may have been more persons sleeping in these rooms than is suggested by the number of beds (see n. 125 above).

128. HStA, HR1 199/11, Nymphenburg furniture inventory, 1769.

129. One of the thirteen court officers listed in the 1771 "Liste nach Nymphenburg" (HStA, FS 777) was Baron von Erdt, who was Hof- und Kabinettssekretär. He brought with him a secretary and a protocolist.

130. Preysing's diaries from 1719 and 1720 (BStB, HsAbt, Cod germ 5456) indicate that Hofgärten were held two or three times a week during the summer months—usually on Sunday, Monday, and Thursday—and that very often the Thursday Hofgarten took place at Nymphenburg.

The husbands of ladies invited to stay for supper at Nymphenburg seem to have presented something of a problem. This matter figures among those listed as requiring some thought in an undated memorandum regarding social functions at Nymphenburg (HStA, HR1 34/18, "Unterthännigste Anfrags-Puncta wenn ICD die Sommer Saison in Nymphenpurg zuzubringen gedenken"). Often, the husbands seem to have been invited to stay for supper as well (Pöllnitz, 2:32).

131. J. J. Moser, 11.

132. Pöllnitz, 2:32.

133. BStB, HsAbt, Cod germ 5456, Maximilian Graf von Preysing, diaries, 1717–60. Preysing made his notations, which vary in completeness, in appointment calendars. In 1746, Max III Joseph appointed him Obristhofmeister.

134. Preysing's entries during Max III Joseph's reign are much sparser than previously, so that one is hampered in drawing general conclusions about annual itineraries during this reign. Baron von Widmann, imperial resident in Munich, wrote to Kaunitz on June 8, 1756, that the elector planned to stay at Schleissheim from June 18 to July 19 (letter published in S. Brunner, 1:97).

135. HStA, HR1 227/102/7, invoice from Gillet, January 16, 1736; HStA, HR1 227/102/12, letter from Gillet, October 3, 1735.

136. HStA, HR1 210/15, Schleissheim furniture inventory, 1761. The figure for the Altes Schloss does not include the personnel of the estate farm. Between the apartments on the ground floor and the piano nobile "sind noch andere Zimmer, worinnen die vornehmsten Herren vom Hof, Cavaliers, Ober-Hofmeisterinnen, Hof-Damen, und alle andere Domestiquen logiren, so dass durch die Stiegen, welche an verschiedene Zimmer gehen, die hohen Herrschaften alle diejenige gleich bei der Hand haben, welche die Ehre geniessen, ihnen zu dienen" (*Ausführliche Relation,* chap. 6).

137. The Obriststallmeister, Jägermeister, Vizeobriststallmeister, and Vizejägermeister are listed as having lodgings in the Altes Schloss. The Obristhofmeister, however, had an apartment in the Neues Schloss (lower mezzanine, south wing).

138. J. J. Moser, 10.

Chapter Four

1. Benoist, 29.

2. Farmer, 120–27.

3. Ibid., 365–66.

4. Küchelbecker, 354–55.

5. Ibid., 359–61. The imperial Hofkalender for 1729 (reproduced in Küchelbecker, 222–49) lists forty-eight Fest-Tage and twenty-one gala days.

6. Ibid., 252–53.

7. Straub, 127.

8. It was the Viennese court, where the festival was highly developed, and not the French court, where this sort of pageantry was exceptional, that served in the seventeenth century as a model for the other courts of the Empire in the creation of indigenous festival traditions. Straub, one of whose goals is to delimit and clarify the extent of French cultural influence on the German courts in the seventeenth and eighteenth centuries, notes not only that the tradition of the festival cycle at the French court was less highly developed than elsewhere, but also that the character of festivities there was different (128–29). French lyric opera was preferred to Italian opera and opera in general was less important than tragedy, which was known at almost no other court. Tournaments, moreover, without which a festival was unthinkable in Vienna and at the German courts, were seldom held at the French court.

9. Küchelbecker, 258–59. Each opera was repeated two or three times.

10. During other reigns, carnival at the imperial court may well have been celebrated more lavishly. Henriette Adelaide wrote home to Turin that during carnival in 1663, no one in Vienna seemed to think of anything but how to stage new festivities, despite the threat of Turkish invasion (Straub, 128).

11. Küchelbecker, 263–64.

12. Florinus, 1:137; Moser, 2:486–93. Both writers record that in 1700 a French envoy, the Marquis de Villars, arrived uninvited and unannounced at a Cammer-Fest and was turned away, at which he took great offense.

13. Küchelbecker, 250–51, 354–56.

14. Pöllnitz, 1:214.

15. "Superfluous eating and drinking, gambling, excessive hunting, jousting, and other pastimes and vanities are not desired here. The duke is a good ruler, reads petitions and other state documents himself, even corrects them, and often dictates himself. I hear his extraordinary knowledge and judgment praised by his councillors and by many others" (Hainhofer, 78). A similar characterization is given by the Netherlandish jurist Thomas Fyens, who visited Munich in the 1610s: "They are all frugal, strict, and righteous. All vice has been exiled from this court. Drunken, frivolous, and idle persons are hated and despised by the duke. Everything is directed toward virtue, temperance, and piety" (quoted in Pfister, 97).

16. Coulanges, 11–12; Trautmann, "Aus alten Reisetagebüchern," 482–83.

17. The custom of celebrating family birthdays with theatrical performances existed at the court of Turin (Bary, 297–98).

18. H. Brunner, *Theatre*, 18–19.

19. Quoted in Straub, 244. The report notes that a certain Fräulein von Wartenberg was Max Emanuel's favorite, "und weilen selber [Max Emanuel] zu klein, gestölt er sich bisweillen als wolt er ihr etwas in das Ohr sagen, wan sie aber das Gesicht niederhelt, tuet er sie küssen."

20. Since at least the late sixteenth century, there had been Italian artists and intellectuals in Munich, but it was under Ferdinand Maria that the presence of Italians of standing first became an important factor. This influx of foreigners and the favor they enjoyed with the electress caused suspicion and resentment among the indigenous nobility. The lady-in-waiting who caused the Residenz

fire in 1674 was Italian and feared that popular indignation at the catastrophe would force the elector to banish her (Bary, 317). Initial tensions were eventually smoothed over, and various Italian families who first came to Bavaria in Henriette Adelaide's wake later became established members of the local nobility (ibid., passim).

21. Ibid., 83–93.

22. Straub, 270–71.

23. Pöllnitz, 2:20, 24. Bianconi's assessment of the social character of the European courts in the eighteenth century, while certainly somewhat simplistic, is nonetheless worth noting here: "Der bayrische Hof war seit langem unter den katholischen Höfen Deutschlands eine vorzügliche Schule feiner Galanterie; in seinem Umkreis haben ebenso wie in Versailles und Dresden seit je Höflichkeit, Liebesaffären und infolgedessen Lebenslust geherrscht. . . . Auf Ihrer Reise werden Sie beobacht haben, wie gross der Unterschied der Sitten zwischen den Höfen unseres Bekenntnisses und des protestantischen ist. Sollten Sie daran interessiert sein, der Ursache einer so auffallend merkwürdigen Erscheinung nachzugehen, so wüsste ich keine andere anzuführen als die folgende, wobei ich es Ihnen überlasse, ob Sie meine Erklärung für richtig halten wollen. Nachdem Karl V zum Kaiser gewählt worden war, brachte er spanische Sitte, Art und Gravität nach Deutschland mit und verbreitete sie im übrigen Europa. Die Höfe, die katholisch blieben, erklärten sich fast ausnahmslos für Karl; indem sie ihn nachahmten, führten sie zugleich das spanische Zeremoniell ein. . . . Die Höfe, welche den Glaubenswechsel vollzogen, bildeten beinahe eine Bruderschaft untereinander und verbanden mit den alten nationalen Sitten voll Eifer die leichte und galante Art Franz' I, der als Gegenspieler Karls allzeit ihr Freund und Verbündeter war. Dieser Unterschied hat fast zwei Jahrhunderte lang angehalten. . . . Gegenwärtig beginnen sich die Dinge zu wandeln, und mit dem Andenken an Karl V. verschwindet allmählich die Etikette und die Reserviertheit des burgundischen Hofes" (letter of November 18, 1762, 73–74).

24. Published in S. Brunner, 1:53, 63.

25. GHA, Korr Akt 753/42a/J-R221, letter of February 12, 1721.

26. This description is based on that in Baillie, 185–86.

27. Excellent plans of the king's apartments at Versailles are found in Verlet, 95, 241.

28. Baillie, 190–91. The role of the bedchamber as a room of audience became more important with its move to the center of the palace in 1701. Previously, in the royal apartment in the Louvre, audiences had also been held in the antechamber and in the grand cabinet (ibid., 187). More important envoys were received in an inner room; lesser ones in an outer room—a pattern that is the exact opposite of that at the Bavarian court. When he wished to make an impression, Louis XIV might hold audiences in the Galerie des Glaces or one of its end salons (as at the audiences of the Siamese ambassador in 1686 and the Persian ambassador in 1715; see Farmer, 397, 402). After 1684, the Maundy ceremony was held in the Grande Salle des Gardes (which was adjacent to the queen's guard chamber), not in the guard chamber of the king's apartment. In the Grande Salle des Gardes, *lits de justice* were also held (Baillie, 189).

29. In the second apartment, before Louis XIV moved the bedchamber to the center, the Lever and Coucher were held in the central salon, which was also

called the "salon où le roi s'habille" (Verlet, 246). Presumably, the courtiers simply passed through the bedchamber in order to attend these ceremonies.

The summary of the daily life of Louis XIV given here draws heavily from Farmer (34–42, 154–79), which is based mostly on the memoirs of the Duc de Saint-Simon and on the *État de la France* of 1712.

30. Baillie, 190–91.

31. Farmer, 43–45.

32. The existence of two antechambers in the second apartment at Versailles probably resulted from the need to keep open a path of circulation from the anterooms to the Galerie des Glaces.

33. Dunlop, 133.

34. Quoted in Dunlop, 198.

35. Joseph Clemens, who commissioned designs for his Residenz in Bonn from Robert de Cotte in 1713, carried on an extensive correspondence with the architect in which he often detailed programmatic requirements, as the Frenchman was not familiar with German court usage. In a letter of June 25, 1713, Joseph Clemens wrote, "Pour les appartemens des Princes de moindres consequences il ne faut seulement qu'une Salle des Gardes, une anti-chambre, la chambre du Lict, un Cabinet, une Garderobbe" (Oglevee, 8).

36. Florinus wrote that "Fürstliche Haupt-Zimmer" required the following rooms: Guarde-Kammer, Vorgemach (or two or three), Audienz-Zimmer, Cabinet, Schlaff-Gemach, Guarderobe (2:866).

37. Oglevee, 187.

38. Rohr, 76.

39. Trautmann, "Aus alten Reisetagebüchern," 482–83.

40. Coulanges, 8–11.

41. GHA, Korr Akt 791, "Anmerckungen über das Ceremoniel, so bey künftigen Anwerbung und Trauung Sr Hoheit der Kayserl. Princessin Maria Antonia zubeobachten seyn mechte," 1747. Control at the gates of the Residenz was apparently sometimes rather lax. A decree issued by Max Emanuel on April 10, 1726 (HStA, MF 10892), expresses displeasure at the large numbers of beggars who passed through the Residenz and annoyed people, and it orders that this is to be prevented in the future.

42. GHA, Korr Akt 631/4, Graf Max Kurz, "Continuation des Diary oder der Verzeichnus, dessen was sich bey hiesigen Churfrtl. Hofstat Denckwürdiges und anders verloffen," January 15, 1651–January 15, 1652.

43. Hainhofer (1611), 67–68; Hainhofer (1636), 293.

44. Wening, 4.

45. The ball is described by Hainhofer (1613, 229). Later ceremonial balls are recorded for Karl Albrecht and Maria Amalie in 1722 (*Ausführliche Relation,* chap. 7); for Maria Antonia Walburga and the Electoral Prince of Saxony on June 13, 1747 (GHA, Korr Akt 791); for Max III Joseph and Maria Anna Sophia on July 9, 1747 (HStA, FS 777); for Maria Anna Josepha and the Margrave of Baden-Baden in 1755 (GHA, Korr Akt 796); and for Josepha Antonia and Emperor Joseph II in 1765 (Klueger, 43).

46. GHA, Korr Akt 681, "Diarium was bey denen florent. Heuraths Tractaten und sonst passirt," 1688.

An idea of other public acts that might be held in a guard chamber may be had from a letter written by Joseph Clemens to Robert de Cotte regarding the design of the *salle des gardes* in the Residenz in Bonn. The elector urged the architect to make the room as large as possible: "For since I perform there my principal functions, a great number of people come there and that requires a very spacious and vast place. That is where I receive the homage rendered to me, where I grant fiefs, where I hold the meetings of the estates of my Electorate of Cologne, where on holy Thursday I wash the feet of thirteen poor men, where the Chapter of the order meets, and where, finally, I administer the sacrament of confirmation. All that therefore requires a very extensive room" (letter of December 18, 1714, in Oglevee, 40).

47. StAM, Hoh Arch A867.

48. Rall, *Kuybayern* 341. In this the Bavarian court differed from the imperial court, where Reichsbelehnungen were ceremonial acts. The court of the Margrave of Ansbach was another exception. Although Belehnungen at Ansbach were handled purely as a bureaucratic matter up to approximately 1700, they acquired a ceremonial component in the eighteenth century. The Belehnungsakt differed little from a diplomatic audience and took place in the audience chamber. Because of the fragmented geopolitical structure of regions such as Franconia, many of the margrave's vassals were princes equal to or higher than the margrave in standing; they sent envoys to receive the investiture (Plodeck, 188–94).

Preysing often noted the Maundy ceremonies in his diaries (BStB, HsAbt, Cod germ 5456), but never recorded where they took place. The electress performed a similar ceremony on Maudy Thursday. On that day in 1720 (March 28), Preysing mentioned "die fuesswaschung, die appostln, und auspeisung der 13 Mädln in der Anticamera der Churfürstin." We may infer that the dining of the thirteen girls took place in the electress's antechamber; the washing of the feet may have taken place elsewhere.

49. Moser, 2:287–88.

50. A protocol of a meeting on February 27, 1727, regarding the ceremonial to be observed on the death of Max Emanuel (StAM, Hoh Arch A717), states that setting the body out in the Ritterstube was traditional usage at the imperial court and at the electoral courts. The practice had not been followed at the death of Maximilian and Ferdinand Maria, who died outside the Residenzstadt (Maximilian in Ingolstadt and Ferdinand Maria at Schleissheim); their bodies were transported directly to the church (first to the Georgskapelle and then, on the same day, to the church of their final resting). Henriette Adelaide, however, had been laid out in the Ritterstube, and the ministers recommended that the traditional practice be resumed for Max Emanuel. The body of the elector was displayed, with all his regalia, on a dais of three steps underneath a baldachin. Four altars, where chaplains alternated in saying masses, were set up in the room. Kämmerer and councillors were delegated to maintain a vigil until the church service two days later (Max Emanuel died on February 26 and was laid out in the Ritterstube on February 28; the service was held on the evening of March 2). Virtually the same procedure was observed on the death of Karl Albrecht's five-year-old son, Joseph Ludwig, in 1733; the body was laid out in the elector's Ritterstube (StAM, Hoh Arch A743).

The state acts that took place in the antechamber and audience chamber, rather than the Garde-Saal or Ritterstube, had to do more directly with dynastic affairs and with the elector's relations with fellow sovereigns. In the audience chamber, of course, diplomatic audiences took place. At least in the eighteenth century, marriage pacts and acts of renunciation (to rights of inheritance) were signed ceremonially in the audience chamber. An altar before which the oaths could be taken was set up in the room, and the act was witnessed by several ministers. On December 10, 1722, Preysing recorded, "12 mittags im Audienzzimmer des Churfürsten d. actus renunciarus." The renunciation was taken by the elector, the electoral prince, and the electoral princess, in the presence of two imperial commissaries and five Bavarian officials (including Preysing himself). On the marriage of Maria Antonia Walburga and the Electoral Prince of Saxony in 1747, the "Act der Signation der Heirats-Pact und der Renuntiation" took place on June 12 in the "zweite chf. alte Antecamera" (GHA, Korr Akt 791). On the marriage of Josepha Antonia and Joseph II in 1765, the signing of the marriage pact took place on January 12 in the "churf. 2. Audienz-Saal" (Klueger, 35).

51. Neither Moser, Florinus, nor Rohr mentions the term "Ritterstube." I cannot find the word in any of the standard German dictionaries, of whatever date.

52. GHA, Korr Akt 753/42a (R220), letter of July 4, 1700.

53. HStA, HR1 22/58, Residenz furniture inventory, 1769. By comparison, the inventory lists no furniture in the Herkules-Saal other than one table.

There are occasional records of festivities held in the Herkules-Saal. On February 7, 1690, on the occasion of the visit of the imperial family, a ball was held here in the evening, after the opera (Vehse, 23:217). On February 16, 1719, Preysing noted a ball in the Herkules-Saal (after a tournament earlier in the day) and on February 21, a banquet (in connection with a Bauernhochzeit).

I have found no record of festivities taking place in the electress's guard chamber (the Hartschier- or Lederner Saal).

Although evidence regarding the usage of the Schwarzer Saal is very sparse, this room seems to have been used in the eighteenth century for concerts. Preysing wrote on February 17, 1719, "6 Uhr—Concert de Music im Schwarzen Saal." On September 15, he noted that a rehearsal for an opera was held here (later rehearsals, as well as the performance, took place in the opera house); and on July 2, 1720, "Der Kurprinz . . . machte gegen 6 Uhr eine schöne Music im Schwarzen Saal, wo etliche Damen dabei erschienen." The 1769 inventory lists no furniture in the Schwarzer Saal other than "2 Kästen [probably armoires], worin die Musicalien aufbehalten werden."

54. Florinus, 2:866.

55. Moser wrote that "special rules and limitations" pertained in the matter of entrée to the bedchamber. "Die allgemeinste und sicherste Regel ist, dass der Eingang in dasselbe verstattet wird: Gemahlin, Familie, und Verwandten; Lieblingen und Vertrauten; Obrist-Cämmerer oder seinem Vertreter; CammerHerr oder CammerJunckern vom Dienst; dem oder den Leib- oder Cammer-Pagen; Leib-Medico; dem oder den Cammer-Diener; den geheimen Secretairs; Beichtvater" (2:290–91).

56. Kammerordnung 1589, reprinted in Kern, 2:216. This provision is repeated almost verbatim in the Kammerordnungen of 1597 (Kern, vol. 2), 1628 (HStA, HR1 34/17), and 1654 (HStA, HR1 34/16). The Kammerordnung of 1769 contains a similar provision (par. 7; see app. 5).

The differences between German and French practices in these matters are pointedly revealed in a small misunderstanding between Joseph Clemens and Robert de Cotte. The rebuilding of the Residenz in Bonn was to include construction of a small summer house on the banks of the Rhine, where the elector could receive distinguished visitors arriving by boat and conduct them to the palace by means of a long gallery. In commenting on preliminary plans sent by the architect, Joseph Clemens noted that de Cotte had inadvertently laid out the summer house in such a way that visitors and their suites would have to pass through the elector's bedchamber in order to reach the gallery. This would not do, and he requested the architect to rethink the plans: "There is this difference in our customs, that in France everybody enters and passes through the apartments of the King and of the Princes, and that with us very few enjoy that honor and have that advantage. I must therefore conform, while I am in Germany, to the customs of the country, in order not to shock the nobility, who are very jealous of such entrees, and who contend that this privilege is due only to titled gentry" (letter of August 15, 1714, in Oglevee, 30–31).

57. GHA, Korr Akt 833, "Vormerkungen bey Ankunft Ihro Königl. Hoheit der Erzherzogin Antonia aus Österreich zukunftiger Dauphine von Frankreich, auf den 26., 27., et 28. April 1770."

The Margravine of Baden-Baden recounts the following incident in her diary for November 5, 1773 (GHA, Hs 194): She was alone in her bedchamber with one lady who had come to wait on her. "Pendant qu'elle y fut, Mundel—— [an official] entra par inadvertance pour m'annoncer que le jeun Reis [a Count Reis or Reisen, who was apparently passing through Munich] vouloit me faire la cour. Je me levois et le fis sortir de la chambre à coucher en disant qu'on y entroit point et que je sortois déjà pour lui demander ce qu'il avoit à me dire. Il me fit des excuses sur son inadvertance et je lui dis que Reisen pourroit venir lorsqu'on soneroit à table. Mais contre mon attente il se trouva déjà à la porte. Cependant je rentrois et m'arrêtois encore quelque tems avec la Lodron. Enfin lorsqu'elle fut partie je vis Reisen."

58. Gombert, 94.

59. GHA, Hs 194, January 24, 1774.

60. GHA, Korr Akt 753/42a (R220), letter of July 4, 1700.

61. Letter of June 25, 1713, in Oglevee, 7–8.

62. Florinus, 2:866.

63. Wening describes the "fürstliche Wohnung" in the Rundstubenbau (on the upper floor, one floor above the Georgs-Saal) as comprising the following rooms: Ritterstube (the "Rundstube"), Ante-Cammer, Audienzzimmer, Schlafzimmer, and Retirad-Zimmer (6). The apartment on the upper floor of the Hoher Stock has the same number of anterooms. Both these apartments thus have fewer anterooms than Maximilian's apartment in the Grottenhofbau.

64. BStB, HsAbt, Cod germ 2123, Residenz furniture inventory, 1638.

65. Kammerordnungen 1589 (Kern, vol. 2), and 1597 (Kern, vol. 2), 1628 (HStA, HR1 34/17).

66. The 1654 Kammerordnung (HStA, HR1 34/16) states that the Lever and Coucher took place in the "Audienz-Stube." As private audiences presumably took place in the Zimmer, the latter room is probably meant.

67. HStA, FS 126½, Compendium of embassies, 1633–83.

68. In his discussion of "Fürstliche Haupt-Zimmer," Florinus notes that one sometimes finds an Anti-Cabinet in front of the Cabinet (2:866; see n. 36 above).

69. An estimate from 1633 (HStA, HR1 25/89/1, Prod. 17, March 30) regarding various minor renovations and repairs in the elector's apartment (plan B, 4–10) mentions the erection of a partition wall ("Schidmeirl") in the "Schlaf-Khamer" (plan B, 9). The plan of 1630–58 shows two rooms at the west end of the Kammergalerie (plan B, 8) divided by a wall that has all the appearance of being a later partition wall. On the plan of 1616–30 (plan C), which shows a later state of the elector's apartment than that seen in the plan of 1630–58, there is a small chapel in this location.

70. BStB, HsAbt, Cod germ 2123, Residenz furniture inventory, 1638.

71. Seventeenth-century plans suggest that the changes made to the apartment under Maria Anna may have been more radical than simply the creation of several cabinet-type rooms along the Residenzgarten. The plan of 1616–30 shows a later state of the electress' apartment than the plan of 1630–58; on it, the Grottenzimmer may be seen, but not Henriette Adelaide's Alkovenzimmer. The room that later became the Herzkabinett is occupied by a chapel, which seems to belong to the elector's apartment. The three rooms along the street seen in the plan of 1630–58 have been made into two larger rooms, and the site of Henriette Adelaide's audience chamber (the Goldener Saal) is occupied by a further room somewhat irregular in shape. It is thus possible that the open space that originally existed on this site was filled prior to the 1660s.

72. An estimate from 1687 for stucco work in the Kaiserzimmer lists the rooms as follows: "1. Zimmer, neben ICD unserer gdisten Frauen Saal; 2. Zimmer; 3. Zimmer; Schlafzimmer; Audienzzimmer; AnteCammer; [room] so für die kayl. Ritterstuben oder Tafelzimmer dient" (HStA, HR1 25/89/1, Prod. 118, September 25, 1687). Wening lists the rooms with exactly the same designations, but from the opposite direction (3). This seems to have been an apartment that could be entered from both ends. In two diplomatic protocols of 1726 (HStA, KS 11791, Graf von Schrottenbach from the Archbishop of Salzburg, Graf von Sinzendorf from the emperor), we read that the audience with Clemens August (visiting in Munich at the time) took place in the Kaiserzimmer and that his Obriststallmeister met the envoys in the Lederner Saal. The 1769 furniture inventory describes the Kaiserzimmer ("Alt Kaiserliche Zimmer") as a double apartment, each half with a "Schlafzimmer" and two "antichambres" (HStA, HR1 22/58).

73. Wening describes the Trierzimmer as follows: The north half ("königliche Zimmer"), with entrance from the "Königliche Vorsaal" (Weisser Saal), had an antechamber, audience chamber, bedchamber, and cabinet. In the center of the wing was a "kleines Säalein." The south half ("herzogliche oder Fürsten-Zimmer"), with entrance from the Herkules-Saal, had the same configuration of rooms. This description corresponds to the state seen in the plan of 1616–30. According to Wening, the bedchambers were on the inside, facing the corridor, while the cabinets faced the courtyard. Around 1730, the central Saal was sacrificed to create two small cabinets (Thoma, 59), and a zone of service dégagements was created behind the cabinets and the bedchambers.

74. HStA, HR1 22/58, Residenz furniture inventory, 1769. The possibility of using the Weisser Saal as a Ritterstube must have played a role in the choice of

the north rather than the south half of the Trierzimmer as an apartment for the margravine, despite the greater distance from the state apartments where the public and social life of the court was concentrated. The only other apartment she could have occupied at this time was the Charlottenzimmer. These rooms, however, were perhaps too close to the kitchens.

75. Wening, 5.

76. Ibid.

77. Pallavicino begins his account of the elector's apartment with the antechamber, then moves to the "stanza di SAE," with its "altri superiori & inferiori gabinetti," and to the "contigua galleria," which is followed by the "picciolo gabinetto" (123–35). Pallavicino's description seems to be reflected in the plan of 1616–30 (plan C).

78. Schmid, 186. The terms used below, *Conferenzzimmer* and *Wohnzimmer,* as applied to this apartment, appear in the second half of the eighteenth century.

79. Kammerordnung 1769, par. 3 (see app. 5).

80. Florinus, 2:866.

81. HStA, KS 11824, Compendium of embassies, 1633–1702. On February 21, 1684, Prince Friedrich August von Eisenach was treated in the same manner: a private audience in the Grosses Cabinet, then dinner in the same room (ibid).

82. Florinus comments on the institution of the *cercle,* or *cercle royal,* as he calls it: "Der Cercle Royal ist nur eine Versammlung der Dames, in der Königin- oder Fürstin-Zimmer, da sich dann die höchsten Standes-Personen auf Tabourets um die Prinzessin herum setzen, denen anderen aber ist nur erlaubet dabei zu stehen. Es werden auch Cavaliers eingelassen, die sich aber auch nicht setzen dürfen" (2:136).

83. Schmid, 208.

84. HStA, KS 11817, abstract from protocol on visit of Prince Radzivil, 1776. The nature of the problem of etiquette is not explained in this document.

85. One of the projects with an oval central Saal (HStA, Plansammlung 8270) has bedchambers identified. They are the fourth rooms in sequence from the grouping of central Säle (an oval Saal and two flanking rectangular Säle). If we may assume the rectangular Säle to be Rstterstuben, then these apartments would have the same number of anterooms as the Alexanderzimmer.

86. The plan in fig. 23 shows altogether six rooms on each side along the garden front. The two other projects for a quadrangular palace (HStA, Plansammlung 8272 and 8267) show six and eight rooms respectively. The apartments in the latter project have thus clearly reached the extent of the Alexanderzimmer. If we assume the bedchamber to be the last room before the corner pavilion, as is the case in HStA, Plansammlung 8330, then there would be two antechambers, an audience chamber, and a Grosses Cabinet in front of the bedchamber, and three cabinets in the corner pavilion behind the bedchamber.

87. Effner's estimate of April 1719 (see chap. 3, n. 95) mentions removing the earlier walls in these rooms.

88. Preysing often recorded the order's conferences in his diaries; for example, he noted on April 21, 1730, "OrdensConferenz, darauf die Electio 8 Herren Aspiranten." On the St. Georg Ritterorden, see Hartmann, 85–86; and *Der Königlich-Bayerische Hausritterorden vom Heiligen Georg.* In two diplomatic proto-

cols of 1741, the Grosses Audienzzimmer is also termed Ordens-Capitl-Zimmer and Ordens-Conferenz-Zimmer (HStA, KS 11817, Compendium of embassies, 1739–41, Marquis de Beauvau from King of France, Conte Montijo from King of Spain).

89. Rohr, 79.

90. Around 1740, the emperor's apartment in the Hofburg had the following anterooms: Ritterstube, small or first antechamber, large or second antechamber, and council chamber. Then followed the common private rooms of the emperor and empress (see Raschauer). Audiences took place in either the second antechamber or the Ratsstube. The latter room also served as an ordinary public dining room; the emperor dined in public in the Ritterstube only very occasionally. There was no Saal in front of the Ritterstube, but only a very small Wachtstube.

I do not mean to suggest that it was unusual that the principal apartments in German Residenzschlösser should have more anterooms than the emperor's apartment. We have already noted Joseph Clemens's excessively long apartment in the Bonn Residenz. Even a prince as politically insignificant as the Bishop of Würzburg had more anterooms than the emperor (see Baillie, 197).

91. See chap. 2, nn. 102, 103.

92. The 1769 furniture inventory applies this term only to the rooms along the garden. Moser defines *Parade-Zimmer* as a suite of rooms that "dienen zur Versammlung der Herrschaften an Galatagen und anderen Hoffesten"; he notes that they were seldom lived in, at most by "höhe Gäste" (2:290–91). This latter function was not, of course, assumed by the Reiche Zimmer, as there were sufficient guest accommodations elsewhere in the Residenz.

93. HStA, HR1 22/58.

94. Moser, 2:284.

95. The south apartment in the middle pavilion was occupied by Therese Kunigunde after the return to Bavaria in 1715 (see chap. 3, n. 81). Under Karl Albrecht, it seems to have been occupied by Electoral Prince Max Joseph; in the 1751 furniture inventory (HStA, HR1 199/11), the bedchamber and antechamber of this apartment are designated as "of the Churprinz." Under Karl Theodor, it was occupied by Dowager Electress Maria Anna Sophia, while the north apartment belonged to Duchess Clemens (HStA, HR1 200/13, "Beschreibung des churfürstlichen Lustschlosses Nymphenburg," 1789). Although these apartments consisted of four rooms (two anterooms, bedchamber, and cabinet), the first anterooms formed points of connection between the Hauptsaal and the galleries. They were thus as much parts of the circulation system of the palace as they were components of the apartments.

96. HStA, HR1 199/11.

97. *Ausführliche Relation*, chap. 12.

98. HStA, HR1 199/11, Nymphenburg furniture inventory, 1769. Under Karl Albrecht, this apartment seems to have been occupied by Clemens August, who was a frequent visitor in Munich while he was Elector of Cologne (1723–61). A diplomatic protocol of 1741 calls the bedchamber of this apartment the "Blaues oder churcölln. Schlafzimmer" (HStA, KS 11817, Compendium of embassies, 1739–41, Maréchal de Belle-Isle from King of France). Küchel notes that the Elector of Cologne had the "most beautiful" apartment in the palace—consisting of a "Vorsaal," three "apartements," a cabinet, and a "music zimmer"—and that

the electress had the equivalent apartment on the other side (544). Under Max III Joseph, the "Blaues Appartement" was occupied by Dowager Empress Maria Amalie until her death in 1765. For the remainder of the century, it seems to have been vacant, being referred to usually as the apartment of "die Kaiserin höchstseel. Angedenkens" (HStA, HR1 200/13, "Beschreibung des churfürstlichen Lustschlosses Nymphenburg," 1789).

99. See chap. 6, n. 90.

100. See n. 98 above.

101. Liechtenstein, 108.

102. GHA, Korr Akt 753/42a (R220), letter of July 4, 1700.

103. Schönbrunn, erected in 1696–1700, had a central Saal extending through the entire depth of the building, similar to the Saal in the preliminary projects for Schleissheim. In the plan published in Fischer von Erlach's *Entwurff einer historischen Architektur* (1721), the two principal apartments are shown back-to-back on one side of the palace, so that the Saal would not have been an impediment to private communication (the plan of Schönbrunn was radically revised under Maria Theresia, the first ruler who used the palace extensively). Hans Sedlmayr suggests that this sort of "tiefrechteckiger Mittelsaal" was a plan feature that was very "unmodern" for that time (*Johann Bernhard Fischer von Erlach,* 2d ed. [Vienna, 1976], 97). In late seventeenth- and eighteenth-century French hôtels and chateaux, the central salons along the garden were normally preceded by a vestibule facing the courtyard; in this way, the entire flight of rooms along the garden could be kept free of servants. This coupling of a salon and vestibule (or two large salon-type rooms) at the center of the building seems to have been generally the case in palaces of the period as well. At the Würzburg Residenz, the Kaisersaal functioned as a banquet hall or as an antechamber shared by the two apartments along the garden; the Weisser Saal was the guard chamber (Baillie, 197).

104. HStA, FS 147d.

105. In the furniture inventories of 1755 (HStA, HR1 209/14) and 1761 (HStA, HR1 210/15), the rooms in these locations seem to be designated "Ritterstube" in several instances (in the north apartment on the piano nobile in the 1755 and 1761 inventories; and in the south apartment on the piano nobile in the 1761 inventory).

106. Keyssler, writing in 1729, located the electress's apartment as the north apartment on the piano nobile and continued, "Des Churfürsten Schlafzimmer ist gerade unter der ihr kommen" (59). The 1755 and 1761 furniture inventories indicate these to have been the apartments of Max III Joseph and Maria Anna Sophia as well. Although the allocation of apartments seen in Zuccalli's 1700 project placed the elector and electress symmetrically within the corps-de-logis, with summer apartments on the ground floor and principal apartments above (apartments for the electoral children were located in the side wings), by 1719 this had changed radically. Building documents of 1719–25 (notably various memoranda in HStA, FS 147d) make no mention of an apartment for Therese Kunigunde at Schleissheim; as we know that she lived isolated from the court, this need not much surprise us. The documents mention a principal and a summer apartment ("mon grand appartement d'embas") for Max Emanuel in the south wing and apartments for the electoral prince and princess in the north wing. On Karl Albrecht's accession, he and Maria Amalie seem to have retained

the apartments they had while electoral prince and princess. The upper apartment in the south wing was occupied by Clemens August (the 1755 inventory designates it as the apartment of the Elector of Cologne). When Max III Joseph and Maria Anna Sophia moved into the north apartments on his accession, Dowager Empress Maria Amalie moved to the south apartment on the ground floor. A similar arrangement of the apartments of the major Herrschaften pertained at Nymphenburg (see n. 98 above). At Schleissheim, apartments for minor Herrschaften were found along the court side in the north wing and in the south terminal pavilion.

Chapter Five

1. Rohr, 19, 34–42.
2. StAM, Hoh Arch A707, "Ordnung wornach wir Carl der Sibente . . . künftighin an denen hinnach ausgeworfenen Tägen und Stunden sowohl unsere geh. Conferentien und geh. Raths-Sitze zu halten, als auch sonsten uns von unseren Ministris und Capi . . . über die vorkommende Regierungsgeschäfte alleruntgst referieren zu lassen," Frankfurt am Main, December 16, 1743. A decree of Max Emanuel from 1688 regarding the daily schedule at court contains a similar disclaimer (HStA, MF 10955, decree of October 17, 1688). See chap. 4 regarding Baron von Widmann's complaints about the difficulty of doing business at the Bavarian court. It was not only imperial diplomats who had this problem; Freiherr von Schroff, Palatine resident in Munich, wrote: "Die Divertissements von der Heyrath haben zwar dergestalten ihr ende, dass vor einiger Zeit die ordinaire Conferenzien wiederumb im Gang seyn, welche aber mehrmahlen unterbrochen werden und der Lauf deren Affairen mithin so beschaffen ist, dass die Partien de plaisir und tägliche Excursiones denen Geschäften annoch auf gewisse Arth vordringen" (BStB, HsAbt, Oefeleana 226, report from Schroff to Baron von Wachdendonck, August 16, 17, 1747).
3. Coulanges, 11–12; "Speiss-, Küchen- und Keller-Ordnung," May 22, 1589, in Föringer, "Anordnungen," 115.
4. HStA, MF 10955, decree of October 17, 1688.
5. Maximilian Graf von Preysing's diaries for 1719–23 (BStB, HsAbt, Cod germ 5456) record mass taking place between 11:00 and 12:30. Dinner followed mass almost immediately. The 1743 Ordnung (StAM, Hoh Arch A707, December 16, 1743; see n. 2 above) fixed the dinner hour at one.
6. Preysing occasionally noted in his diaries when there had been heavy drinking at dinner.
7. On March 4, 1726, Preysing wrote to Freiherr von Mörmann, Bavarian resident in Vienna: "Serenissimus hat die Arbeitszeiten genau geregelt: An 3 Tagen der Woche sind Konferenzen mit den 4 Ministern und an einem ist jedesmal voller Staatsrat. Die Stunden hiefür sind von 9–11 Uhr. Die Zeit zwischen 11 und Mittag ist für eine Heil. Messe und Audienzen bestimmt" (Ow, "Beiträge," AM 6:116).
8. Coulanges, 11–12; "Speiss-, Küchen- und Keller-Ordnung," May 22, 1589, in Föringer, "Anordnungen," 115.
9. Coulanges, 11–12.
10. Kammerordnung 1589, reprinted in Kern, 2:215.

11. The 1688 decree (HStA, MF 10955, decree of October 17, 1688) fixes the supper hour at eight; the 1743 decree (StAM, Hoh Arch A707, December 16, 1743), at nine. Preysing's diaries also indicate that the usual supper hour in the eighteenth century was between eight and ten.

12. Christian Wolff, *Gedanken von dem gesellschaftlichen Leben des Menschen* (1740), quoted in Moser, 1:209.

13. HStA, MF 10955, decree of October 17, 1688.

14. Report of Conte Lantery, March 5, 1683, in Straub, 263–64.

15. Stephan Freiherr von Stengel, "Neue Denkwürdigkeiten vom pfalzbayrischen Hofe unter Karl Theodor," ed. Karl Theodor Heigel, *Zeitschrift für allgemeine Geschichte* 4 (1887): 444.

16. Moser, 1:203–5.

17. The Kammerordnungen all contain provisions to the effect that the preferred status of the Kämmerer obliged them, above all other members of the household, to comport themselves with the dignified, courteous manner expected of the courtier. The Kammerordnung of 1589 states: "Nachdem Sy [the Kämmerer] auch fir [vor] ander unser Hofgesündt geehrt, auch mit der praeminenz und vorgang wollen gehalten sein und billich gehalten werden, So gebirth Inen, dass sy auch vor andern mit gueten Tugenden, hoflichhaid und freundlichkheit geziert und erleicht sein, damit nit die unthugend oder böse Qualitates an der Ererbietung, so sy sonst Ires Ambts halben tragen, Sy verhindern und zuruggschlagen und dardurch auch unss und unser Camer wie auch denen, so sich der gebir nach und wol halten, von aines wegen verclienerung ervolge" (in Kern, 2:211). This passage is repeated almost verbatim in the Kammerordnungen of 1597 (Kern, vol. 2), 1628 (HStA, HR1 34/17), and 1654 (HStA, HR1 34/16).

18. Moser, 1:213–14.

19. Föringer, "Hofstat," 239; Pallavicino, 123.

20. *Chur-bayerischer Hofcalender* (Munich, 1738, 1769, 1781).

21. Moser, 1:182.

22. Gualdo Priorato, 42.

23. Westenrieder, 86. The twelve Kämmerer listed in the 1615 "Hofstat" probably represent only "wirklich dienende" Kämmerer, as this list also gives salaries for the entire household. In a description of the court from 1705 (reprinted in Hüttl, 572–74), twenty-two Kämmerer are listed; this clearly represents only Kämmerer in actual service.

24. Moser, 1:213–14.

25. Kammerordnung 1628 (HStA, HR1 34/17). This is repeated verbatim in the 1654 Kammerordnung (HStA, HR1 34/16).

26. Aufwartungs-Ordnung 1739 (see app. 4); Kammerordnung 1769, par. 14 (see app. 5). See also GHA, Korr Akt 1712/H/39, Dienst-Instruktion for Graf von der Wahl as Obristhofmeister of Electress Maria Antonia, May 15, 1686, par. 11; and StAM, Hoh Arch A685, "Havendo Il Sig. Conte Tarino Imperiale dimandato alcuna informazione . . . del modo onde vengono trattati li ministri di suo carattere, ciò é delle teste coronate in questa corte elettorale, . . . ," n.d. (see chap. 6, n. 55). On one occasion during one of his visits to the court of Würzburg in the late eighteenth century, Peter Prosch, the itinerant Tyrolese Hofnarr (court jester), described the courtiers in the antechamber forming lanes as the bishop passed through (71).

27. Moser, 2:483. Preysing and the Margravine of Baden-Baden frequently noted presentations in the antechambers in their diaries.

28. GHA, Korr Akt 791.

29. The ceremonial observed at the wedding of Maria Anna Josepha in 1755 was patterned very closely on that in 1747. Regarding the kissing of the hands after the wedding ceremony in 1755, we read in a memorandum: "Die Dames, und Cavaliers, jene, wie auch die Ministris, so in die Camer tretten därffen, Ihro Mayt in solcher, die Cavaliers aber in durchgehen durch die Anticamera zum Handkuss, und abstattung Ihrer Gratulation gelassen, und in sothannen Neuen Churfürstl. Zimmern wirdet solang verweillet, bis Zeit zur Nacht Taffl ist" (GHA, Korr Akt 796).

30. Straub, 270.

31. Keyssler, 53. Freiherr von Schroff, Palatine resident in Munich, reported home in 1747 that there were almost forty gala days at the Bavarian court. He went on to complain that because of their great number, not to mention all the other festivities, his salary was hardly sufficient to keep up appearances (BStB, HsAbt, Oefeleana 226, report from Schroff to Baron von Wachdendonck, September 2, 1747). By comparison, the imperial Hofkalender for 1729 listed only twenty-one gala days (see chap. 4, n. 5).

32. GHA, Hs 194.

33. Report of Sonnenberg, imperial resident in Munich, to Graf Kaunitz, reprinted in S. Brunner, 1:175.

34. GHA, Korr Akt 1712/K/II/1, "Unterthänigiste Anfrags-Puncten," n.d. [1773 or 1774]. On January 2, 1774, the Margravine of Baden-Baden wrote in her diary, "Nous mimes ce jour pour la lere fois les habits d'appartement que nous seulles, les grandes maitresses et la gouvernante des dames osames porter à la place d'habits de cour les fetes et dimanges" (GHA, Hs 194).

35. Hainhofer (1612), 164.

36. Ibid., 153.

37. Felix Andreas Oefele (tutor to Duke Clemens) reported in his journal in September 1739 that he had to try four times before he was finally successful in presenting his request to the elector on the return from mass—and then it occurred under the most embarrassing circumstances. When he began to speak, he was interrupted by the elector's dogs, who started barking and carrying on, so that the elector was forced to make a sign that someone should quiet them. Oefele had to repeat himself, only to receive the noncommittal princely reply "je verrai" (BStB, HsAbt, Oefeleana 483, "Journal historique de ce qui s'est passé à la cour de Baviere" [1738–43], September 1, 15, 17, 22, 1739).

38. Kammerordnung 1769, par. 10 (see app. 5).

39. Anderson, 285–86.

40. Moser, 2:294–95.

41. Baillie, 190. Baillie notes that Henri III, who had visited the imperial court in Vienna and was impressed with the privacy that Spanish ceremonial afforded the sovereign, tried in 1574 and again in 1584 to introduce ranked entrée to his anterooms, but succeeded only in alienating his nobility (184).

42. An eighteenth-century imperial Aufwartungs-Ordnung, reproduced in Moser, 2:296–97 (Moser does not date it precisely). This Aufwartungs-Ordnung makes it clear that all regnant princes of the empire, regardless of their

status, had entrée to the emperor's Ratsstube. It was only among members of the imperial household and foreign envoys—but not among the emperor's vassals—that distinctions were made between the various places of waiting (four altogether), in much the same way as at the Bavarian court.

43. HStA, FS 109, "Kurzer Begriff, wie es bey Ankunft der k.u.k. Maytten zu Dachau und alhier zu halten," n.d. [1653].

44. Baillie wishes to suggest that whereas rank at the French court was predominantly temporal rather than spatial in nature, the opposite was true at the German courts (194). I prefer to see the spatial nature of rank in Germany as an additional aspect. Temporality is seen in such things as orders of procession and orders of dancing during ceremonial balls.

45. These early Kammerordnungen (1589, 1597, 1628, and 1654) make clear that there were others who had entrée to the antechamber, but do not specify who these persons were, leaving one to suspect that they were probably persons who had been granted this privilege individually.

The right of entrée to the antechamber was often used as a criterion for entrée to various functions. At an Accademie held on April 22, 1752 (during the state visit of the Elector and Electress Palatine), the following persons were requested to attend: "all Minister, Cammerer, und diejenigen, so die Ante Cammer zu betreten erlaubt, auch die adeligen Hof- und Stadtdamen" (StAM, Hoh Arch A806). At the baptism of Maria Anna Josepha on August 7, 1734, the following persons were present: "alle Ministers, Stadt-Damen und Cavaliers, die die Ante-Cammer haben" (StAM, Hoh Arch A746). The 1794 Kammerordnung states that playing cards at the Accademies was permitted only to those who had the Kammer key (Churpfalzbaierische Hof- und Kammerordnung 1794, par. 26; copy in BStB: 2.Bav.960.XXIV.9).

46. Pallavicino, 123.

47. Hainhofer (164), 59–60.

48. HStA, MF 10893, decree of January 16, 1717.

49. "Chur-Cöllnische Hof-Aufwartungs-Instruction," November 7, 1717, published in Leonard Ennen, *Der Spanische Erbfolgekrieg und der Churfürst Joseph Klemens von Köln* (Jena, 1851), 210–19; Moser, bk. 3, chap. 2, passim; bk. 7, chap. 3, passim.

50. Comparison of this Ordnung with the plan of the elector's apartment in the Bonn Residenz makes clear that not all the anterooms were used as places of waiting.

Entrée to the vestibule under the staircase and to the Vorsaal at the top of the staircase was permitted only to persons of very low rank. In the former, for example, the servants and grooms of the electoral officers might wait; in the latter, lackeys of Reichsgrafen passing through Bonn and those of foreign envoys (except when an envoy was having his public audience with the elector, in which case his lackeys might wait in the guard chamber along with the court lackeys). The order of entrée to the last four rooms (guard chamber, Ritterstube, antechamber, and audience chamber) was not dissimilar to that specified in the 1739 Bavarian Aufwartungs-Ordnung.

51. Cologne Aufwartungs-Ordnung 1717, notandum 1. The Bavarian Aufwartungs-Ordnungen contain similar, if less strongly stated, provisions.

52. HStA, MF 10955, decree of October 17, 1688.

53. This Ordnung is transcribed in full in appendix 4.

54. See n. 45 above, regarding other persons having entrée to the antechamber.

55. HStA, HR1 34/17, "Verordnung betr. die churf. Anticamern und Entrée hierzu," 1747.

56. HStA, MF 10955, "Ordnung welche ICD in Bayern . . . bey denen bey Hof vorfallenden Aufwartungen, wie auch sonsten durchgehends mit Besuchung der Anti-Cameren und Ritter-Stuben in Zukunfft gehalten wissen wollen," n.d. [1756].

57. In the 1747 Ordnung, the first antechamber is called "1. Anticamera zu denen sogenanten kays. als nunmehr neuen churf. Wohnzimmern."

58. GHA, Korr Akt 1712/K/I/49, "Ordnung welche ICD in Bayern . . . bey denen bey Hof vorfallenden Aufwartungen, wie auch sonsten durchgehends mit Besuchung der Anti-Kammern und Ritterstuben in Zukunft gehalten wissen wollen," 1766. This Ordnung was published in the 1769 Kammerordnung (see app. 5).

59. Entrée to the antechambers of the private apartment was permitted only to those privileged to enter the second antechamber and audience chamber, according to the 1766 Aufwartungs-Ordnung. The 1756 Ordnung permitted entrée only to those who had been expressly summoned.

60. The memoirs of the Duc de Saint-Simon and the *État de la France* of 1712 are the best primary sources on these ceremonies. Farmer quotes liberally from both in his description of Louis XIV's Lever and Coucher. See also Force, 74–106; Lewis, 45–47; and Elias, 82–87.

61. See chap. 4, n. 66.

62. Rohr, 222–23.

63. This Ordnung is published in full in Kaufmann.

64. Küchelbecker, 358.

65. Preysing, October 12, 1719, May 12, 1720. See also Oefele's note in BStB, HsAbt, Oefeleana 483.

66. HStA, HR1 34/18, "Unterthännigste Anfrags-Puncta wenn ICD die Sommer Saison in Nymphenburg zuzubringen gedenken," n.d.

67. A similar "Entrée au Lever" was published earlier in the reign of Max III Joseph (HStA, FS 772m, "Cammer-Verordnung betr. die Entrée fruhe zum Anlegen SCD," n.d. [before 1756]).

68. Preysing, January 14, 1739.

69. HStA, MF 10955, decree of October 17, 1688.

70. Kammerordnung 1769, par. 7 (see app. 5).

71. Adalbert, "Residenz," 168.

72. Ibid., 194.

73. Quoted in Hüttl, 180. Villars was in Munich in the late 1680s.

74. Bruford, 93.

75. The sixteenth- and seventeenth-century Hofordnungen published in Kern make clear how standard court practices were throughout Germany at the time. See also Buttlar.

76. Plodeck, 116–17.

77. Treusch von Buttlar, 6.

78. Ibid., 6–11, 17–24; Plodeck, 116–28.

79. "Speiss-, Küchen- und Keller-Ordnung," May 22, 1589, in Föringer, "Anordnungen," 114–26.

80. On days when the duke ate privately in his room and the Kämmerer served him, they ate afterwards, receiving the leftovers from the duke's table. The 1589 Speiseordnung contains a special provision that since these leftovers were often neither warm nor adequate, the Kämmerer were to receive certain additional warm dishes (ibid., 116).

This Ordnung also lists the persons who were to receive a morning soup and an evening refreshment. Considerably fewer persons received these meals at court. It was also customary at the German courts that as a matter of special charity, certain persons—usually retired servants who could no longer care for themselves, or other infirm persons—were permitted to receive their meals from the court kitchen. These persons were known as Ausspeiser; the 1589 Ordnung lists them precisely.

81. Kern, 1:xi; Treusch von Buttlar, 6–7.

82. Hofordnung of Herzog Johann Albrecht I von Mecklenburg, 1574 (Kern, 1:212–37); Hofordnung of Herzog Bogislaw XIV von Pommern-Stettin, 1624 (Kern, 1:156–85).

83. HStA, StV 1164, decree of April 14, 1606.

84. Hainhofer (1611), 77.

85. Wening noted eight Dirnitzen (7). Judging from the 1589 Speiseordnung, the kitchen personnel ate in the Küchenstube.

86. Wening noted two rooms with tables for the ladies on the upper floor in their living quarters (4).

87. Wening, 6. Cuvilliés's project for the Residenz from the early 1760s shows a "salle à manger des chevaliers"—in the new corps-de-logis on the site of the Neuveste—that is probably meant to replace the earlier officers' dining room.

88. See chap. 3, n. 118.

89. J. J. Moser, 18. Moser wrote that there were no Marschalls-Tafeln at the imperial or the Bavarian courts (2:512).

90. Lynar, 222.

91. Kammerordnungen 1589, 1597, 1628, 1654. Before the introduction of Kostgeld in 1607, the Kämmerer ate at court; the 1628 and 1654 Ordnungen specify that when the elector was finished dining, they were to go home to eat. When the elector dined in public, the Kämmerer may have dined at court.

92. This is evident from the descriptions of the wedding celebration of Wilhelm V and Renata of Lorraine in 1568 (see chap. 2, n. 10) and from the Kammerordnungen, in which the ceremonial prescribed for dining in private is quite fastidious. The details of Spanish table ceremonial are available in two excellent publications—Ridder and Villa. See also Lünig, 1:336ff.

93. Küchelbecker, 359–62; Moser, 2:507, 512–19.

94. Rohr, 75. See also the Cologne Ordnungen of 1717 (Ennen, 219) and 1726 (published in Hansmann, *Das Treppenhaus,* 128).

95. Hainhofer (1611), 59.

96. Ibid., 65–66.

97. This protocol is transcribed in full in appendix 7.

98. GHA, Korr Akt 796; Klueger, 44–45.

99. StAM, Hoh Arch A867.

100. Moser, 2:499. A memorandum of 1773 or 1774 (see n. 34 above) states that from then on, public dining was to be held only on New Year's and the two festival days of St. George.

101. HStA, FS 126½, Compendium of embassies, 1633–83. This source contains four additional references to visiting princes dining with the elector in the antechamber: a young Pfalzgraf von Neuburg in 1638, the regnant Margrave of Ansbach in 1642, two young Margraves of Baden in 1644, and the old Margrave of Baden in 1645.

102. HStA, FS 109, "Gehorsambstes ProMemoria . . . ," October 13, 1749.

103. Report of Widmann to Kaunitz, May 14, 1756, in S. Brunner, 1:95.

104. See appendix 6.

105. Cologne Hofinstruktionsordnung 1726, par. 12 (Hansmann, *Das Treppenhaus,* 128).

106. Moser, 2:506–7.

107. Preysing rarely noted where meals "à l'ordinaire" or in company were taken. On the few occasions that he did, we may assume that it was an unusual situation. He noted on Sunday, September 10, 1719, "Mittagstafel mit den Damen im Schwarzen Saal"; on February 12, 1719, "Mittagstafel in den Appartements-Zimmern mit den Damen"; and on March 28, 1751 (a gala day), "Mittagstafel mit den Damen pel mel in der Ritterstube."

108. GHA, Korr Akt 1712/K/II/1, "Unterthänigiste Anfrags-Puncten," n.d. [1773 or 1774].

109. J. J. Moser, 11.

110. Ibid., 10.

111. The institution of *pêle-mêle* was probably quite old. The earliest reference to it that I have found, however, is Florinus, 1:135.

112. GHA, Hs 194, December 31, 1773, January 1, 8, 9, 1774.

113. Ibid., January 9, 1774. The introduction of the permanent *pêle-mêle* is also noted in two letters of Sonnenberg to Kaunitz (December 31, 1773, January 11, 1774, in S. Brunner, 1:174–75).

114. Saint-Simon, 254. Entrée to the king's table at Marly was very limited; according to Brocher, it corresponded roughly with the entrée to the carriages of the royal family (40). Normally there was, however, more than one table. Rohr discusses the supper parties of Louis XV (34).

115. Of the forty-one public dinners (öffentliche Tafel) that Preysing recorded in 1719 and 1720, only two were held in the country (February 14, 1719, at Dachau; and August 6, 1720, at Nymphenburg). I have also encountered the following public Tafel at Nymphenburg: July 10, 1733, on Maria Amalie's name day (Preysing); July 26, 1747, on Maria Anna Sophia's name day (see app. 6); and July 26, 1762 (Lynar).

116. E.g., July 17, 1720, October 19, 1720.

117. Moser, 1:274, 2:512–13. See chap. 3, n. 130. In Munich, the elector very often dined at midday with the ladies, which he almost never did in the country.

118. See chap. 3, n. 81. The 1751 furniture inventory (HStA, HStA, HR1 199/ 11) mentions also a "Grosses Nebenzimmer für die Tafelbediente" next to the Tafelzimmer. This would have been the center room along the court side (underneath the Ratszimmer). In the 1769 furniture inventory (HR1 199/11), the Tafelzimmer is called Winter-Speis-Saal.

119. Various descriptions of dinners held in this room survive. On the first day of the Elector of Trier's visit in 1728 (October 11), supper was held at a table for sixty in the main hall, after an Appartement in the Spiegel-Saal (HStA, FS1126a, "Détail de la réception de l'Electeur de Treve en Baviere et des fêtes qui luy ont été données pendant son séjour," 1728). Lynar left an account of a public dinner he witnessed in the main hall in July 1762 (222). Rotenstein described a dinner he witnessed in 1781 in the Kleiner Speisesaal, the center room on the court side of the south pavilion (239–40).

120. The earliest record calling the Viktoriensaal "Speise-Saal" is a building document of December 29, 1723 (HStA, HR1 227/102/6).

121. HStA, HR1 25/89/1, Prods. 123–24, "Anzeig was der Ausmachung und Verfertigung . . . sein möchten," March 31, 1731. There is also reference in this document to a "herunterer Speiss Saal," so that one of the salons at the ends of the ground-floor vestibule may also have been a dining room.

122. Pater Beda Plank, writing in 1779, called this dining room "das ordentliche Tafelzimmer" (Dussler, 349). The room was demolished during construction of the Königsbau.

123. In 1752, at the state visit of the Elector and Electress Palatine, supper was taken one evening in the Vierschimmelsaal after an Accademie in the Kaisersaal (StAM, Hoh Arch A806, protocol of their visit, May 2, 1752).

124. I have found records of only four occasions on which a public Tafel was held in the Herkules-Saal: July 9, 1662, during the visit of Duke Karl of Lorraine (HStA, FS 126½); 1688, during the wedding festivities for Violante Beatrix (GHA, Korr Akt 681); February 21, 1719, at a Bauernhochzeit described by Preysing; and January 10, 1765, during the wedding festivities for Josepha Antonia (Klueger). I have found records of only three instances in which the Schwarzer Saal was used for this purpose: May 28, 1652 (GHA, Korr Akt 631/4, diary of Graf Kurz); July 10, 1662, during the Lorraine visit; and September 10, 1719 (Preysing).

125. The changes made to the Antiquarium around 1600 under Maximilian (the installation of a raised, balustraded platform and a fireplace at the west end of the hall), as well as Hainhofer's reference in 1611 to two large credenzas and a large, beautiful table (71–72), suggest that the room was renovated to serve as a banquet hall. On five occasions in the seventeenth century, there is mention of the Herrschaften dining in the Antiquarium: 1612 (Hainhofer, 168); 1635, during the visit of the Bishop of Würzburg (HStA, FS 126½); 1644, during the visit of Cardinal Rosetti (HStA, FS 126½); June 11, 1651 (GHA, Korr Akt 631/4, diary of Graf Kurz); and 1665 or 1666, during the visit of the three ecclesiastical electors (HStA, FS 126½). I also have found records of two occasions on which ambassadors (from Spain) dined alone in public in the Antiquarium: 1641 (HStA, FS109); and 1651 (GHA, Korr Akt 631/4, diary of Graf Kurz). In the eighteenth century, the Antiquarium seems to have existed as an architectural curiosity. Its treasures were routinely shown to princely visitors, along with the Schatzkammer and the Kunstkammer; but apart from this, it disappears from the records.

126. Wening, 6. Preysing occasionally notes this "Landschafts-Mahlzeit," which took place in March, in his diary (March 20, 1720; March 26, 1734; March 6, 1749 ["Landschaft Mahlzeit. Waren 39 so dabei gespeist"]). He does not, however, note where it took place.

127. On December 8, 1734, Maria Theresia von Gombert recorded in her diary: "Man feierte das Georgi-Ordensfest in der Hofkapelle. . . . Der Kurfürst speiste wie herkömmlich mit den Rittern im Georgen-Saal, die Kurfürstin in ihrem Zimmer" (102).

128. Adalbert, 150. The Ritterstube is known today as the St. Georgs-Rittersaal.

129. HStA, FS 109, "Memorial dessen was bey Ankunfft der drei geistlichen HHH Churfürsten Mainz, Cölln und Trier und deren Tractament alhier in Acht zu nehmen," n.d. [1665 or 1666].

130. HStA, FS 1126a, "Détail de la réception de l'Electeur de Treve," 1728.

131. Straub is the definitive source on festivals at the Munich court. Under Maximilian, festival cycles on dynastic or state occasions were infrequent. In the sixteenth century, lavish festival cycles are recorded in 1530 on the occasion of the visit of Emperor Charles V and in 1568 at the wedding of Wilhelm V and Renata of Lorraine (see chap. 2, n. 10).

132. Straub, 193–98. In 1654, a tournament in the Brunnenhof is recorded (Straub, 193); in 1722, at the wedding festivities of Karl Albrecht and Maria Amalie, there was a tournament in the Küchenhof (*Ausführliche Relation*).

133. The most lavish festivals held in Munich—which were commemorated, as at other courts, in special publications—were those in 1662 at the birth of Max Emanuel (Straub, 217–34); in 1690 at the visit of the imperial family (ibid., 291–93); in 1722 at the wedding of Karl Albrecht and Maria Amalie (*Ausführliche Relation*); in 1727, when the birth of Max III Joseph and the Erbhuldigung of Karl Albrecht were celebrated together (Blondeau and Cavallo); and in 1765 at the marriage of Josepha Antonia to the future Emperor Joseph II (Klueger).

134. Straub, 329.

135. Ibid., 242–43.

136. GHA, Hs 194. The margravine states that this schedule was "comme les autres années."

137. Straub, 260. Preysing frequently noted occasions when the Herrschaften attended carnival functions at the noble houses of Munich.

138. One, sometimes two Bauernhochzeiten were held each carnival season. Preysing occasionally provides short descriptions of them (e.g., February 9, 1723, February 20, 1732). Bauernwirtschaften were traditional at many German courts—including the imperial court, where the first of these may have been celebrated as early as the reign of Emperor Maximilian I, 1493–1519 (Straub, 127). Henriette Adelaide reacted to this old German festivity with distaste at first, but later learned to enjoy it and took great pleasure in designing fanciful costumes for herself and her ladies (see Bary, 99).

139. An excellent description of a Königsmahlfest was given by Conte Lantery on January 11, 1688 (quoted in Straub, 65). According to Straub, the tradition of the Königsmahlfest at the Munich court was probably not as old as the Bauern-hochzeit (237).

140. Saint-Simon, 7.

141. *Mercure galant,* 1682, quoted in Farmer, 365.

142. Quoted in Straub, 271. The institution of the Appartement is mentioned in a Dienst-Instruktion issued by Max Emanuel for Graf von der Wahl as Maria Antonia's Obristhofmeister on May 15, 1686 (GHA, Korr Akt 1712/H/39). This

document and Lantery's description are the earliest records of the Appartement that have come to my attention.

143. We should also note that in 1719 and 1720 (but not in later years), Preysing records a regular social function called the Anticamera, which took place two or three times a week. As with the Appartement, card playing seems to have been the major attraction.

144. Preysing, November 4, November 8, 1719. When guests were lodged in the apartments of the Kaiserhofbau, Appartements were sometimes held there. In 1722, during the wedding festivities of Karl Albrecht and Maria Amalie, an Appartement was held in the Kaiserzimmer on October 22. Afterwards, the company took supper in the Kaisersaal and then proceeded to a ball in the Herkules-Saal ("Entwurff jener Fest . . . Anno 1722"; copy in BStB: Bav.3000.VII.43). In 1728, during the state visit of the Elector of Trier, another Appartement was held in the Kaiserzimmer. Supper was then served directly at the card tables, and a masked ball was held in the Kaisersaal (HStA, FS 1126a, "Détail de la réception de l'Electeur de Treve," 1728).

145. StAM, Ämternachlass Törring 228, "Anzaig der sammentl. in alhiesig. churfrtl. Residenz verhandtenen gehaizten Öfen und Camin," February 17, 1750.

146. The significance of the name Sommerzimmer is unclear. We should note, however, that Schmid/Kalmbach and Wening are the only sources in which the term appears.

147. Preysing, February 20, 1719, February 17, 1721. That this is not a service staircase is suggested by its size and by the fact that there is what is unmistakably a service staircase directly next to it. It is highly improbable that Preysing would have given this name to the Breite Treppe, which led to the Herkules-Saal.

148. Rotenstein, 204.

149. HStA, KS 11817, protocol fragment of 1739–41.

150. StAM, Hoh Arch A806.

151. Kammerordnung 1769, par. 21 (see app. 5).

152. Churpfalzbaierische Hof- und Kammerordnung 1794, par. 25; copy in BStB: 2.Bav.960.XXIV.9.

153. Florinus, 136. Florinus attributes the introduction of the Redoute, or Accademie, in Germany to Ernst August, Elector of Hanover (reigned 1679–98)—who, he claims, spent much time in Venice. Max Emanuel and Karl Albrecht also had firsthand knowledge of the Venetian carnival (from 1687 and 1715–16, respectively). Ferdinand Maria and Henriette Adelaide made a trip to Venice in the spring of 1667.

154. The earliest record of Accademies at court is in Preysing's diary for 1720.

155. S. Brunner, 1:62.

156. HStA, FS 1126a, "Détail de la réception de l'Electeur de Treve," 1728.

157. Churpfalzbaierische Hof- und Kammerordnung 1794, par. 26; copy in BStB: 2.Bav.960.XXIV.9.

158. Hertling, 244.

159. Straub, 285.

160. On the Redoutenhaus, see Straub, 298; and Hojer, "Redoutenhaus." In 1818–19, this building was transformed into the first Bavarian parliament (Landtagsgebäude); the large Redoutensaal was clearly well suited to accommodate legislative sessions.

161. Only somewhat later, in the mid-1720s, did Preysing begin to record Accademies held in the Residenz.

162. Letter of December 14, 1774, in Anderson, 250. Lynar also left a description of the Redoutensaal from 1762 (223).

163. See chap. 2, n. 120.

164. See chap. 2, n. 122. See also Hübner, pt. 1, vol. 1:160.

Chapter Six

1. Moser, 2:550.

2. An anonymous manuscript in the BStB entitled "Unterricht und zusammengetragene Verfassung vor jene, welche sich seiner Zeit zu Gesandtschaften tauglich machen wollen," written in 1773, indicates the sanctity of diplomatic ceremonial: "Deswegen und obschon ein Fürst an seinem Hofe die Ceremonien abschaffen, oder so gering machen kann als er will, so müsste er doch in Ansehung auswärtiger Gesandten nicht so diffizil seyn. An den meisten Höfen hat man ein regulirtes Ceremoniell, und pflegt man sorgfältig dabei zu verharren" (BStB, HsAbt, Cod germ 3816, par. 17; the entire work is reprinted in S. Brunner).

3. An excellent short introduction to the history of European diplomacy, which was of great use in preparing the present study, is Gerbore.

4. Byzantine ceremonial was codified by Emperor Constantine VII Porphyrogenitus (reigned 913–59) in his *Book of Ceremonies,* the first extant treatise on diplomatic ceremonial. Modern editions of it are in *Corpus scriptorum historiae byzantinae,* vols. 9–10 (Bonn, 1829), and A. Vogt, ed., *Le livre des cérémonies* (Paris, 1935), bk. 1.

5. Gerbore, 19–21.

6. Krauske; Schaube; Pieper.

7. Gerbore, 13, 14; Ernst. It is noteworthy that the emergence of permanent embassies attracted little notice among contemporaries.

8. For a discussion of the development of the Bavarian diplomatic service in the period 1508–1726, see Riezler, 6:94–99, 8:456–60.

9. Gerbore, 68–69.

10. Wicquefort, 2:113.

11. Quoted in Gerbore, 190.

12. Stieve, 261.

13. See, for example, Stieve, 146, 190–93, 234.

14. The ceremonial mission was fulfilled within the framework of the reception or audience.

15. The variety in ceremonial usage from court to court obviated all but the most general discussion of the diplomatic reception in the theoretical literature. See Moser, 2:550–51, where the reader desiring further enlightenment on the subject is referred to Lünig, an enormous compendium of Hofordnungen and protocols of specific ceremonial acts at various courts.

16. Moser, 1:27–41; Rohr, 16–18; Florinus, 1:45.

17. Moser, 1:27.

18. Rohr, 17–18.

19. Moser, 1:32; Rohr, 17.

20. Moser, 1:32. One indignity they suffered was that Louis XIV refused to

recognize their envoys as ambassadors, while at the same time he received ambassadors from the Italian princes (Wicquefort, 1:40).

21. Moser, 1:33–35. Fürstenvereine and Reichsversammlungen were various assemblies of princes and other rulers in the empire.

22. HStA, KS 11852, letter from the Elector of Brandenburg to the Elector of Bavaria, August 29, 1671.

23. With the acceptance by the participating states at the Congress of Vienna of the general "Règlement sur le rang entre les agents diplomatiques" (signed March 19, 1815), European diplomatic ceremonial ceased to be the source of controversy that it had been in the previous period (Gerbore, 95).

24. Plodeck, in her study of ceremonial at the court of Ansbach, was able to establish that at least there, and probably at many other Fürstenhöfe, the *Protocollum Particulare* was followed fairly closely in subsequent decades (138–40).

25. HStA, FS 109, "Verzeichnus etlicher puncten, so auff ankonfft allerlei Abgesandten, aus unsers gdsten Fürsten und Herrns bevelch zuebenachschlagen sein," n.d.

26. HStA, FS 109, "Unnderricht wie unnser genedigister Fürst und Herr Herzog Wilhelm in Bayrn es hinfüran mit den Gesandten zuhallten gedacht," 1581.

27. This idea was a commonplace in political theory from the fifteenth century on; see Gerbore, 87.

28. I have chosen to use *envoy*—a word more neutral in its associations than *legate* or *ambassador*—in a generic sense, although, technically speaking, it denotes only diplomats of the second rank.

29. Callières, 63. The distinction between extraordinary (ausserordentlich) and ordinary (ordentlich) ambassadors was often made in the theoretical literature. An extraordinary ambassador was sent on a specific mission, without intent to reside at the foreign court to which he was accredited. Once the mission was accomplished, he returned home (see, for example, Stieve, 248–51). Extraordinary ambassadors were often received with greater ceremony than ordinary ambassadors and in most cases were considered to have precedence over them (Stieve, 249; Callières, 63–64). It could, however, be taken as an insult to send only occasional extraordinary ambassadors instead of an ordinary ambassador. To demonstrate this, Stieve notes that the Duc d'Estrée remained in Rome for ten years as extraordinary ambassador, because the pope sent no nuncio to Paris (251). Neither Stieve nor Callières extends the extraordinary/ordinary distinction to envoys; Rohr, on the other hand, does (378).

30. Callières, 67–68. He notes, however, that at the papal court envoys and residents were accorded equal honors. See also Stieve, 379.

31. Wicquefort, 1:57.

32. Callières, 68.

33. Gerbore, 94. Among the treatises on ceremony addressed to a general readership, Stieve provides perhaps the most thorough discussion of diplomatic usage. There were two classes of ranking envoys: (1) those with Character, called "ambassadeurs, Botschafter, Gesandte, or legati" (the papal equivalent was the nuncio); and (2) those without Character, called "envoyés Abgesandte, Ablegati, or inviati." Residents and agents made up a third class of diplomats; they had no rank. A plenipotentiary, or Bevollmächtigter (a title that turns up occasionally in the records), was a diplomat to whom no fixed rank was assigned by his princi-

pal; use of this title was a way of avoiding disputes over precedence (Stieve, 190–93, 256, 264). The terms used in the Bavarian diplomatic records (see app. 8) do not agree completely with Stieve's system. The title *Abgeordneter* was in common use from at least the 1670s and clearly designated an envoy of lower class. During Maximilian I's reign, the term *Abgesandter* referred to envoys of the first class. Later, the term became less frequent and seems to have been replaced by *Gesandter* (although the two terms appear side by side in the eighteenth century; what the difference might have been is not entirely clear).

34. HStA, KS 11842, letter from the Elector of Brandenburg to the Elector of Bavaria, January 11, 1666; reply, February 2, 1666.

35. These protocols are found mostly in HStA, FS 109; and HStA, KS 11760–ca. 11850.

36. HStA, KS 11791, "Information wie es mit dem anhero geschickten kayl. formal-Gesandten . . . Grafen von Nostiz . . . gehalten worden," [1726].

37. The following two copies of the compendium have been used in the present study: HStA, FS 126½, "Beschreibung derenjenigen Gesandt-Schafften welchige sich bey dem churfürstl. bayerischen Hoff haben einbefundten . . . " (covering the years 1633–83); and HStA, KS 11824, "Kurze doch Begrundte Beschreibung deren hochen Potentaten . . . wie auch andere Gesandschafften, so von allen hochen Ohrten, an ds durchleuchtigisten Churhaus Bayern seint abgeschicht . . . " (covering the years 1633–1702). There are other copies in the following places: StAM, Hofmarken: Ämternachlass Törring, Karton 61 (1633–1701); and HStA, FS 115 (1633–1733). There is also a fragment of a later composition, covering the years 1739–41, in HStA, KS 11817.

38. StAM, Hoh Arch A685, "Havendo Il Sig. Conte Tarino Imperiale dimandato alcuna informazione del Ceremoniale di SAE di Baviera e del modo onde vengono trattati li ministri di suo carattere, ciò é delle teste coronate in questa corte elettorale, percio in sequenti punti gli serviranno d'avviso," n.d. The diplomat's name, as ascertained from Bittner, was Vittorio Conte Tarini Imperiale di Cossambrato. As the Duke of Savoy achieved the royal dignity in 1713 with the acquisition of Sicily, it is most plausible to date the memorandum shortly after Max Emanuel's return to Bavaria in 1715. Dating it much later than that has been ruled out, as there is no mention in the memorandum of Nymphenburg as a regular country residence of the Bavarian court.

39. HStA, KS 11817, "Nota zur Ankunft eines kaiserlichen, königlichen oder churfürstlichen Gesandtens 2ten Ranges an den churf. pfalzbayer. Hofe zu München," n.d. The memorandum was issued under Karl Theodor, who reigned as both Elector of Bavaria and Elector Palatine from 1777 until his death in 1799. As the memorandum notes procedures to be followed at audiences with Duchess Clemens, who died in 1790, the latter date is a terminus ad quem in dating the document.

40. Stieve, 220. What these protocols do not tell us, except occasionally in the case of ceremonial embassies, is the purpose of the mission. It is thus impossible, without laborious additional research, to judge the extent to which political considerations might have affected the conduct of the reception.

41. Suites varied according to the envoy's rank and importance. They almost always included one or several personal servants, as well as liveried footmen or lackeys. Most envoys were accompanied by a legation's secretary and quite often, especially in the case of ceremonial embassies, by at least one gentleman.

42. It was exclusively the duty of the Obristkämmerer to announce the arrival of envoys to the elector and to arrange audiences. See BStB, HsAbt, Cod germ 1962, "Instruction eines Obristen Cammerers de ao 1654"; and BStB, HsAbt, Cod germ 1962, "Obristhofmeisters Instruction 1702."

43. BStB, HsAbt, Cod germ 1962, "Obristhofmeisters Instruction 1702." More elevated envoys were often waited upon by a Kämmerer, less elevated ones by a secretary.

44. The Abholung in a six-horse carriage was standard for envoys of at least the second rank sent by sovereign princes, including virtually all Reichsfürsten. Envoys from nonpotentates, such as imperial cities or cathedral chapters, were picked up in two-horse carriages, with only one lackey in attendance, and were required to descend outside the Residenz.

45. Hojer goes so far as to claim that a proliferation of courts (Vielhöfigkeit) was itself a form of political representation, an assertion that he does not document other than to cite Matteo Alberti's project for a Palatine residence ("Residenzen," 146).

46. Moser, 2:275.

47. As an example of such a regulation, Moser prints a 1695 imperial regulation regarding the right to drive into the Hofburg (2:280–81).

48. GHA, Korr Akt 1712/J/40, "Lista der hohen Minister und hohen Officier welche befugt sind, in die chl. Residenz hineinzufahren, iedoch sich unter wehrenter Hochamt und Predigt enthalten, wie nit weniger die Laque sowohl in hinein als herausfahren auf die Gutschen niemahlen aufzustehen sich understehen sollen," August 10, 1727. Various other eighteenth-century regulations regarding the right to drive into the Munich Residenz also survive in the Bavarian state archives.

49. "Ordnung, so mit der Einfahrt in die Churfürstliche Residenz zu beobachten," January 5, 1748 (copies in StAM, Hoh Arch A806 and in HStA, MF 10893).

50. Kammerordnung 1769 (see app. 5). A regulation regarding driving into the Residenz published in an Aufwartungs-Ordnung of 1766 (GHA, Korr Akt 1712/K/I/49) does not permit the Kämmerer to drive in.

51. Podstasky to Kaunitz, April 6, April 27, 1770, in S. Brunner, 1:165–66.

According to Wening, the carriages of courtiers and visitors were parked in the Brunnenhof (7), although one wonders whether this was still true in the second half of the eighteenth century, when the private rooms of the elector and electress faced onto this courtyard. The Kaiserhof normally came into use only on ceremonial occasions, particularly at formal entries of visiting personages who were to be lodged in the Kaiser- or Trierzimmer. On these occasions, the portal leading into the Kaiserhof was thrown open for the procession, although we sometimes read that—apparently for the sake of pomp and circumstance—a procession entered via the Kapellenhof and proceeded through all the courtyards before coming to a stop in the Kaiserhof in front of the "Vier Schäften." This was the case at the entry of Henriette Adelaide in 1652 (GHA, Korr Akt 631/5, "Bericht dessen was zu Ankunfft der churfrtl. Prinzessin und deren Bedienung abgeredt, verglichen und von Sr. Churf. Drtl. gnädigst placitirt worden," n.d.).

52. GHA, Korr Akt 791, "Anmerckungen über das Ceremoniel, so bey künftigen Anwerbung und Trauung Sr Hoheit der Kayserl. Princessin Maria Antonia zubeobachten seyn mechte," 1747. The name of the ambassador is not mentioned

in the memoranda. One of the points of agreement between the two courts was that in order to spare expense, the ambassador would not make a formal entry into Munich.

53. It is not clear how far the commissary accompanied the envoy. In some cases, at least, he went as far as the audience chamber. It is recorded that in 1726, at the audience of the imperial ambassador, Graf von Sinzendorf, the commissary pulled back his chair in the audience chamber—in this case, the antechamber of the apartment in the Trierzimmer facing the Herkules-Saal, where the elector was staying at the time (HStA, KS 11791).

54. GHA, Korr Akt 791.

55. StAM, Hoh Arch A685, par. 6. There is virtually no information on how courtiers were deployed in the anterooms during receptions; the subject is not addressed in the protocols. There is, however, no reason to believe that the information in the above memorandum does not reflect standard practice.

56. The documentation from the 1660s on the greeting of envoys varies in completeness. In the compendium of embassies, there is virtually no information on this aspect of the diplomatic reception, and information from the reign of Maximilian I is relatively sparse.

57. In at least one instance, in 1640, Maximilian went out to meet an imperial envoy at the head of the staircase (HStA, FS 126½). There is no indication why this particular envoy was accorded this singular mark of distinction.

58. In these cases, the descriptions in the compendium of embassies contain a statement such as the following: "[Der Kurfürst] ist [dem Abgesandten] nit entgegengangen, sondern hat ihn in dem Audienzzimmer gewartet."

59. HStA, KS 11791; HStA, FS 126½.

60. HStA, KS 11824.

61. HStA, FS 126½. The memorandum for Conte Tarini (StAM, Hoh Arch A685) specifies the following regarding the greeting of envoys of his rank in the anterooms: the commissary conducts the envoy "sin'alla porta della seconda anticamera [the first antechamber is meant], ove il Sig Cameriere maggiore lo riceve, e l'accompagna in mezzo d'altri gentiluomini di Camera, che lo stanno aspettando, sin'alla porta della Camera dell'Udienza nella quale SAE l'aspetta."

62. HStA, KS 11817. As I have found no protocols for individual receptions from Karl Theodor's reign, I am not able to determine whether the theoretical reception outlined in the memorandum reflects current practice or standardizes the diverse three-part receptions held in the previous reign.

63. GHA, Korr Akt 791.

64. GHA, Korr Akt 796, "Anmerckung über das Ceremoniel, so bey konftiger anwerb- und Trauung Sr Hochheit der Kayserl. Princessin Maria Josepha, khönnte in beobachtung khommen," 1755.

65. Moser wrote the following regarding private audiences: "Die Privat-Audienzen geschehen entweder ganz ohne Ceremoniel, mit blosser Anmeld-Einführ- und Entlassung dessen, so Audienz bekommt, oder mit einer gewissen ihm angemessenen Art des Ceremoniels, so aber nicht den ganzen Hof, sondern nur ein- und andere hohe oder in der Aufwartung ohnehin stehende Hof-Bediente bemühet" (2:551).

66. HStA, KS 11810. Leonroth's name often turns up as commissary in subsequent diplomatic protocols.

67. Letter from Podstasky to Kaunitz, September 24, 1765, in S. Brunner, 1:149.

68. The *Protocollum Particulare* of 1700 specified that "[es] stehet zu eines jeden Regenten Belieben, stehend oder sitzend den Besuch anzuhören" (quoted in Plodeck, 149; see also Stieve, 224).

69. Callières, 67.

70. Moser, 2:557.

71. StAM, Hoh Arch A685.

72. Stieve, 224–25. In some cases, the entire audience was conducted without hats.

73. GHA, Korr Akt 791.

74. Moser, 2:558.

75. Quoted in Plodeck, 151. At audiences of imperial ambassadors, these distinctions were sometimes eliminated. At the audience of Graf von Sinzendorf in 1726, for example, the ambassador and the elector sat on identical fauteuils under the baldachin, and the elector allowed the ambassador the right hand (HStA, KS 11791).

76. Quoted in Plodeck, 150.

77. HStA, KS 11794, "Pièce communiquée par M. le Maréchal de Belle-Isle," May 1, 1741.

78. J. Schmid, 186. As the precursor of the Grosses Cabinet of the Alexanderzimmer, Maximilian's Zimmer (plan B, 7) was very likely used for private audiences.

79. Wening, 4.

80. HStA, KS 11824. Prince Eugene had come on an unspecified, although apparently official, mission—not from the emperor, but from another, unnamed member of the imperial family. He was also a comrade-in-arms of Max Emanuel in the Turkish campaigns of the 1680s.

81. Küchel, 545; Rotenstein, 205–6. The 1769 furniture inventory (HStA, HR1 22/58) lists baldachins, with fauteuils or Audienz-Sessel. The furnishings of the antechamber included two fauteuils; one stood under the baldachin and the other, which had a higher back than the first, may have stood elsewhere in the room. The only other seating in these three rooms were tabourets and benches. Baldachins were often hung in antechambers as symbols of the presence of the prince and cannot necessarily be taken as an indication that audiences were held in these rooms. The 1638 furniture inventory (BStB, HsAbt, Cod germ 2123) lists a baldachin in the elector's antechamber.

82. BStB, HsAbt, Cod germ 5456, Maximilian Graf von Preysing, diary, January 15, 1739; HStA, KS 11817.

83. HStA, KS 11817. According to the 1769 Residenz furniture inventory (HStA, HR1 22/58), the Grosses Cabinet contained no baldachin. The central feature of the room was instead a conference table, with seating consisting of a fauteuil, a canapé, four benches, and four tabourets. In three instances—in 1740, 1752, and 1756 (see app. 8)—protocols list audiences as having taken place in the "Grosses Cabinet, wo der reiche Baldachin ist." It seems more likely, however, that these audiences, which were unmistakably public, actually took place in the Grosses Audienzzimmer, where there is evidence for the existence of a baldachin. In 1750, the audience of Freiherr von Schroff, then Bevollmächtigter from the

Elector Palatine, took place "in dem dritten Zimmer unter dem Reichen Pal-takün" (HStA, FS 109).

84. Audiences with family members who resided in the Maxburg (see chap. 2, n. 126) were often held on subsequent days.

The memorandum for Conte Tarini stated: "Se l'inviato desidera d'aver udienza appresso la Ser. Sig'la Elettrice ne ricerca il Suo Maggiordomo maggiore, che gliela procura, e si suole condurlo a questa immediatamente dopo l'udienza del Ser Sig Elettore" (StAM, Hoh Arch A685, par. 13).

The widowed Margravine of Baden-Baden, ever sensitive about her position as a poor relation at her brother's court, wrote in her diary on June 19, 1774, that she had deliberately delayed her return from Nymphenburg to Munich that day, because the English envoy Eliot had not requested an audience with her and she did not wish to be present at court while he was with the elector. Several days later, Eliot was seated next to her at the supper table. "He excused himself for not having requested an audience and placed the blame on his commissary, who had neglected to remind him of it. I replied that I was quite convinced that this oversight did not result from lack of attention on his part" (GHA, Hs 194, June 19, 24, 1774).

85. GHA, Korr Akt 791.

Public audiences did not as a rule take place in the country palaces. The memo-randum for Conte Tarini makes this clear: "When, at the arrival of an envoy, the elector is in residence outside his capital, at Schleissheim or Dachau, and finds it inconvenient to betake himself to Munich, it is customary to have the envoy driven out to the country seat and there to grant him the usual audience" (StAM, Hoh Arch A685). The protocols, in fact, often mention the Herrschaften return-ing to Munich to grant audiences to envoys. Audiences were nonetheless held not infrequently in the country (very often, for example, an envoy had his departure audience at Nymphenburg or Schleissheim), but with considerably less cere-mony than in the Residenz. Usually, no courtiers were expressly appointed to wait, and only the officers on duty and those who happened to have come out from the city were on hand in the anterooms.

86. The seventeenth-century protocols reveal that some envoys were taken from the inn to their new lodgings before the audience.

87. Hainhofer wrote, "Inn der neuen Vesten losieren Ihre Frstl. Dhlt. keine gesandte, sondern allein geborne oder gemachte [i.e. ecclesiastical] Fürstliche Persohnen, Item Keyserl. und Königliche gesandten" (1611, 77).

88. Klueger, 12–13.

89. HStA, FS 126½. It is reported that in 1641, the Spanish ambassador, Don Francisco di Melo, who was lodged in the Mittlere Rundstube, dined in public not only in his Tafelstube, but also once in the Antiquarium (HStA, FS 109).

90. HStA, FS 126½.

In the country palaces, there were no guest apartments set aside for the accom-modation of envoys. In 1726, the imperial ambassador, Graf von Sinzendorf, spent several days with the court at Nymphenburg and had to be lodged in Duke Johann Theodor's old apartment in the inner south pavilion (HStA, KS 11791). The Maréchal de Belle-Isle, who had demanded the privilege of lodging at court during his embassy in 1741, was put up in Duchess Ferdinand's apartment at Nymphenburg (on the third floor of the inner south pavilion). Belle-Isle's brother received the bedroom and cabinet of Duke Ferdinand's apartment, while one of his gentlemen slept in the antechamber (HStA, KS 11817; HStA, KS 11794, "Liste sur le logement assigné à l'ambassadeur de France et à sa suite, partie à Nymphenbourg, et partie en ville," 1741).

91. An earlier Gesandtenhaus, demolished in 1602, had stood on the site of the Residenz. Busch assumes that it stood on the site of the later Triertrakt (403). Knüttel disputes this, maintaining on the basis of archival evidence that it stood in the southern zone of the Residenz, near the monastery that adjoined the Residenz on the south (210 n. 81). Because of lack of space, envoys' suites often had to be accommodated elsewhere in the city.

92. Trautmann states that the site was given to Piosasque de Non by Max Emanuel (110–11). This is impossible, however, as Max Emanuel died on February 26, 1726. The building dates of the Piosasque-Palais, the facade of which remained virtually intact until World War II, are not known; presumably, it was erected quite soon after the acquisition of the site (Braunfels, *Cuvilliés*, 83).

93. GHA, Korr Akt 1712/J/1, decree of Karl Albrecht, November 24, 1727. The decree gives as reason the fact that "bei anderen Höfen die frembde Gesandten, Envoyés, und dergleichen Personen nit mehr von Hoff aus tractiert: oder wie zum thaill bishero an disem Hof geschehen, absonderlich logiert: und ausgespeiset worden." It was reiterated in a decree of July 12, 1741 (also Korr Akt 1712/J/1). There were also other houses in Munich owned by the elector in which envoys were occasionally lodged—for example, a house on the Rindermarkt, in which the Marquis de Maillebois, French envoyé extraordinaire, was lodged in 1726 (HStA, KS 11794).

94. J. J. Moser, 18.

95. There is never any explanation given in the protocols for lodging envoys in private houses and not in the Gesandtenhaus. On certain occasions, however—such as in June and July of 1679, when large numbers of envoys were present in Munich after Ferdinand Maria's death—guest apartments were clearly at a premium.

96. BStB, HsAbt, Cod germ 1962, "Obristhofmeisters Instruction 1702"; BStB, HsAbt, Cod germ 1964, "Hofmarschalckhs Instruction 1657"; HStA, FS 109, Gesandtschafts-Protokoll vom kurmainzischen Gesandten Baron von Kesselstadt, 1740.

97. Hainhofer, 77; HStA, FS 109.

98. StAM, Hoh Arch A665, decree of Max Emanuel, June 27, 1682. An Obristhofmeisters-Instruktion of 1702 (BStB, HsAbt, Cod germ 1962) contains the explicit provision that the Obristhofmeister is responsible for seeing that unauthorized persons do not attach themselves to the envoy's table.

99. The 1739 and 1744 Aufwartungs-Ordnungen (HStA, HR1 34/17) assign *charakterisierte* Gesandten to the second antechamber. The Ordnungen of 1756 and 1766 (HStA, MF 10955) place unaccredited Ministers and residents in the first antechamber and accredited Gesandte and Ministers in the audience chamber.

100. BStB, HsAbt, Cod germ 1983.

101. HStA, KS 11817.

102. HStA, KS 11773.

Bibliography

Archives Consulted

Munich, Bayerisches Hauptstaatsarchiv (HStA).
  Holdings:
    Finanzministerium (MF)
    Fürstensachen (FS)
    Hofamtsregistratur 1 (HR1)
    Karstensammlung
    Kasten schwarz (KS)
    Plansammlung
    Staatsverwaltung (StV)
Munich, Geheimes Hausarchiv (GHA), Abteilung III des HStA.
  Holdings:
    Handschriften (Hs)
    Hof-Haushaltakten 1712 (Korr Akt 1712)
    Korrespondenzakten (Korr Akt)
Munich, Staatsarchiv München (StAM).
  Holdings:
    Familienarchiv Törring-Jettenbach
    Hofmarken: Ämternachlass Törring
    Hohenaschauer Archiv (Hoh Arch)
Munich, Bayerische Staatsbibliothek (BStB), Handschriften-Abteilung (HsAbt).
  Holdings:
    Cod germ
    Oefeleana
Munich, Bayerische Verwaltung der staatlichen Schlösser, Gärten und Seen (BSV), Bauamt.
  Holdings:
    Plansammlung

General Works

Adalbert Prinz von Bayern. *Als die Residenz noch Residenz war.* Munich, 1967.
———. *Nymphenburg und seine Bewohner.* Munich, 1950.
Anderson, Emily, ed. and trans. *The Letters of Mozart and His Family.* 2d ed. London and New York, 1966.
Aufleger, Otto, and Schmitz, Wolfgang Maria. *Die Kgl. Residenz in München: Historische Beschreibung und Führer.* 1897. 2d ed.: Munich, 1908.
Ausführliche Relation von denen herrlichen Festivitäten . . . wegen der hohen Vermählung des Chur-Printzen zu Bayrn Caroli Alberti mit Ertz-Herzogin Maria Amalia. Augsburg, 1723. German edition of Bretagne.
Bachmann, Erich. "Neuveste und Maximilianische Residenz." *Bayerland* 62 (1960): 121–26.
Baillie, Hugh Murray. "Etiquette and the Planning of the State Apartments in Baroque Palaces." *Archaeologia* 101 (1967): 169–99.
Bary, Roswitha von. *Henriette Adelaide von Savoyen, Kurfürstin von Bayern.* Munich, 1980.
Beauvau, Marquis Henri de. *Mémoires.* N.p., 1688.
Benoist, Luc. *Versailles et la monarchie.* Paris, 1947.
Bianconi, Gian Lodovico. *Briefe über die vornehmsten Merkwürdigkeiten der churbayerischen Residenzstatt München und der umliegenden Lustgegenden.* 1771. New ed.: Mainz, 1964.
Bittner, Ludwig. *Repertorium der diplomatischen Vertreter aller Länder seit dem Westphälischen Frieden.* Oldenburg i.O/Berlin, 1936ff.
Blondeau, Philipp, and Cavallo, J. A. *Vollständiger Bericht von allen sehenswürdigsten Freudenfesten . . . anno 1727.* Munich, 1727.
Bosl, Karl. *Bayerische Geschichte.* Munich, 1980.
Böttger, Georg. *Die Innenräume der königlichen alten Residenz in München.* Munich, 1893–95.
Braunfels, Wolfgang. *François de Cuvilliés: Ein Beitrag zur Geschichte der künstlerischen Beziehungen zwischen Deutschland und Frankreich im 18. Jahrhundert.* Würzburg, 1938.
———. *Die Kunst im Heiligen Römischen Reich Deutscher Nation.* 3 vols. Munich, 1979–81.
Bretagne, Pierre de. *Réjouissances et fêtes magnifiques, qui se sont faites en Bavière l'an 1722 au mariage de S.A.S. monseigneur le prince electoral . . . et une description abregée des palais de S.A.S.E.* Munich, 1723.
Brocher, Henri. *Le rang et l'étiquette sous l'ancien régime.* Paris, 1934.
Bruford, W. H. *Germany in the Eighteenth Century: The Social Background of the Literary Revival.* 1935. Cambridge, 1971.
Brunner, Herbert. *Die Kunstschätze der Münchner Residenz.* Munich, 1977.
———. *The Old Residence Theatre in Munich.* Munich, 1960.
———. "Die Residenz im 18. Jahrhundert." *Bayerland* 62 (1960): 127–34.
———, and Hojer, Gerhard. *Residenz München.* Munich, 1982.
Brunner, Sebastian. *Der Humor in der Diplomatie . . . des 18. Jahrhunderts.* 2 vols. Vienna, 1872.
Busch, Karl. "Das Erbprinzenhaus der Münchener Residenz." *Zeitschrift für Kunstgeschichte* 2 (1933): 399–404.

Callières, François de. *The Art of Negotiating with Sovereign Princes*. London, 1716.

Chapuzeau, S. *Relation de l'estat présent de la maison electorale et de la cour de Bavière*. Paris, 1673.

Chur-bayrischer Hofcalender. Munich, 1727–1802.

Claretta, Gaudenzio. *Adelaide di Savoia, Duchessa di Baviera e i suoi tempi*. Turin, 1877.

Coulanges, M. de. "Extrait d'un manuscrit de M. de Coulanges, intitulé: Relation de mon voyage d'Allemagne et d'Italie cz [*sic*] années 1657 et 1658." In *Mémoires de M. de Coulanges*. Paris, 1820.

Cuvilliés, François de. *École de l'architecture bavaroise*. N.p., n.d.

Diemer, Peter. "Materialien zu Entstehung und Ausbau der Kammergalerie Maximilians I. von Bayern." In Hubert Glaser, ed., *Quellen und Studien zur Kunstpolitik der Wittelsbacher vom 16. bis zum 17. Jahrhundert*, 129–174. Munich, 1980.

Diesel, Matthias. *Kurbayerische Schlösser nach einer Vedutenfolge um 1720*. ed. Peter Volk. Dortmund, 1981. New edition of Diesel's *Erlustierender Augen-Weyde zweyte Fortsetzung*. Augsburg, n.d.

Doeberl, Michael. *Bayern und Frankreich, vornehmlich unter Kurfürst Ferdinand Maria,* Munich, 1900.

Dunlop, Ian. *Versailles*. London, 1956.

Dussler, Hildebrand, ed. "Zwei österreichische Benediktiner besichtigen i. J. 1779 Altbayern, insbesondere München." *OA* 97 (1973): 345–358.

Ehalt, Hubert. *Ausdrucksformen absolutistischer Herrschaft: Der Wiener Hof im 17, und 18. Jahrhundert*. Munich, 1980.

Elias, Norbert. *The Court Society*. Translated by Edmund Jephcott. New York, 1983.

Ernst, Fritz. "Über Gesandtschafteswesen und Diplomatie an der Wende vom Mittelalter zur Neuzeit." *Archiv für Kulturgeschichte* 33 (1951): 64–95.

Ertel, Anton Wilhelm. *Kur-Bayerischer Atlas: Ansichten und Beschreibungen altbayerischer Städte aus dem Jahre 1687*. Edited by H. Bleibrunner. Passau, 1968.

Farmer, James. *Versailles and the Court under Louis XIV*. New York, 1904.

Fauchier-Magnan, Adrien. *Les petites cours d'Allemagne au XVIII siècle*. Paris, 1963.

Fischer von Erlach, Johann Bernhard. *Entwurff einer historischen Architektur*. Vienna, 1721.

Florinus, Franciscus Philippus. *Oeconomus prudens et legalis continuatis, oder Grosser Herren Stands und adelicher Haus-Vatter*. 2 vols. Nürnberg, 1719.

Force, Duc de la. *Louis XIV et sa cour*. Paris, 1956.

Föringer, Eustos, ed. "Anordnungen über den Hofhalt in München während des 16. Jahrhunderts." *OA* 9 (1848): 97–138.

———. "Hofstat oder Beschreibung aller unnd Jeder der Frstl. Drtl. Unnsers genedigisten Herrn Herzog Maximilian in Bayrn etc. hoher unnd annderer Offizier, unnd Diener etc. . . . anno 1615." *OA* 31 (1871): 238–63.

Gerbore, Pietro. *Formen und Stile der Diplomatie*. Reinbek bei Hamburg, 1964.

Gombert, Maria Theresia von. "Was sich im Jahre 1734 ereignete: Tagebuch des Fräuleins Maria Theresia von Gombert." Translation of Gombert's manuscript diary from French by F. X. Zettler. *AM* 5 (1905): 89–104.

Gualdo Priorato, Conte Galeazzo. *Relatione della corte e stati del Serenissimo Ferdinando Maria Elettore di Baviera.* Leyden, 1668.

Haeutle, Christian. *Genealogie des erlauchten Stammhauses Wittelsbach.* Munich, 1870.

———. *Geschichte der Residenz in München.* Leipzig, 1883.

Hager, Luisa. *Nymphenburg: Schloss, Park, und Burgen.* Munich, 1955.

———, and Hojer, Gerhard. *Schleissheim: Neues Schloss und Garten.* 4th ed. Munich, 1976.

Hainhofer, Philipp. Accounts of his trips to Munich and other cities in Germany, 1611, 1612, 1613, 1614, 1636. Edited by Christian Haeutle. *Zeitschrift des Historischen Vereins für Schwaben und Neuburg* 8 (1881).

Hansmann, Wilfried. *Baukunst des Barock: Form, Funktion, Sinngehalt.* Cologne, 1978.

———. *Das Treppenhaus und das Grosse Neue Appartement des Brühler Schlosses.* Düsseldorf, 1972.

Hartig, Otto. "Die Kunsttätigkeit in München unter Wilhelm IV. und Albrecht V., 1520–1579." *MJBK* 10 (1933): 147–225.

Hartmann, Peter Claus. *Karl Albrecht-Karl VII.: Glücklicher Kurfürst, unglücklicher Kaiser.* Regensburg, 1985.

Hauttmann, Max. "Die Entwürfe Robert de Cottes für Schloss Schleissheim." *MJBK* 6 (1911): 256–76.

———. *Der kurbayerische Hofbaumeister Joseph Effner.* Strasbourg, 1913.

Heigel, Karl Theodor. *Nymphenburg: Eine geschichtliche Studie.* Bamberg, 1891.

———. "Das Projekt der Gründung einer Stadt 'Karlstadt' zwischen München und Nymphenburg." *JMG* 2 (1888): 335–40.

Hertling, Karl Freiherr von, ed. "Ein Besuch in München 1785: Nach dem Tagebuch des Ministers Johann Friedrich von Hertling." *Bayerland* 24 (1913): 244.

Heym, Sabine. *Henrico Zuccalli, der kurbayerische Hofbaumeister.* Munich and Zurich, 1984.

———. "Schloss Lustheim, Jagd- und Festbau des Kurfürsten Max II. Emanuel von Bayern." *OA* 109 (1984): 7–125.

Hojer, Gerhard. "Die Münchner Residenz um 1800: Projekte für Kurfürst Max IV. Joseph." *Weltkunst* 50 (1980): 690–94.

———. "Die Münchner Residenzen des Kurfürsten Max Emanuel: Stadtresidenz München, Lustheim, Schleissheim, Nymphenburg." In *Kurfürst Max Emanuel* 1: 142–70.

———. "Vom Redoutenhaus zum Ständesaal: Das erste bayerische Parlamentsgebäude in München." *Weltkunst* 50 (1980): 1014–16.

———, and Schmid, Elmar. *Nymphenburg: Schloss, Park, und Burgen.* Munich, 1983.

Hubala, Erich. "Henrico Zuccallis Schlossbau in Schleissheim: Planung und Baugeschichte, 1700–1704." *MJBK* 17 (1966): 161–200.

Hübner, Lorenz. *Beschreibung der kurbaierischen Haupt- und Residenzstadt München und ihrer Umgebung.* 2 vols. Munich, 1803–5.

Hüttl, Ludwig. *Max Emanuel, der Blaue Kurfürst, 1679–1726. Eine politische Biographie.* Munich, 1976.

Imhof, Gabriele. *Der Schleissheimer Schlossgarten des Kurfürsten Max Emanuel von Bayern.* Munich, 1979.

Kalmbach, Christoph. *Triumphierendes Wunder-Gebäu der churfürstlichen Residenz zu München*. Munich, 1719. Updated edition of J. Schmid.

Kaufmann, Paul, ed. "Die 'Cammer-Ordnung' des Kurfürsten Joseph Klemens vom 24. Dezember 1698." *Bonner Geschichtsblätter* 1 (1937): 200–224.

Kern, Arthur, ed. *Deutsche Hofordnungen des 16. und 17. Jahrhunderts*. 2 vols. Berlin, 1905–7.

Keyssler, Johann Georg. *Neueste Reisen durch Deutschland . . . 1740*. 2d ed.: Hanover, 1751.

Klueger, Mathias. *Wahrhafte Beschreibung aller derjenigen Ereignissen, Begebenheiten und Festinen, welche . . . zu höchsten Ehren . . . Josepha Antonia . . . als erwählt und verlobten römischen Königs-Braut sowohl vor, als nach der allerhöchsten Vermählungs-Festivitäten in allhiesiger Haupt- und Residenz-Stadt München auf das feierlichste angestellet und begangen worden*. 1765. New ed.: Munich, 1816.

Knüttel, Brigitte. "Zur Geschichte der Münchner Residenz, 1600–1616 (I)." *MJBK* 18 (1967): 187–210.

Der Königlich-Bayerische Hausritterorden vom Heiligen Georg, 1729–1979. Exhibition catalog. Munich, 1979.

Kraus, Andreas. "Das Haus Wittelsbach und Europa: Ergebnisse und Ausblick." *ZBLG* 44 (1981): 425–52.

Krauske, Otto. *Die Entwicklung der ständigen Diplomatie vom 15. Jahrhundert bis zu den Beschlüssen von 1815 und 1818*. Leipzig, 1885.

Kruedener, Jürgen Freiherr von. *Die Rolle des Hofes im Absolutismus*. Stuttgart, 1973.

Küchel, Johann Jakob. "Ein Reisebericht über München und seine Umgebung aus dem Jahre 1737." Edited by Johannes Mayerhofer. *JMG* 3 (1889): 541–47.

Küchelbecker, Johann. *Allerneueste Nachricht vom Römisch-Kayserl. Hofe*. Hanover, 1730.

Kurfürst Max Emanuel: Bayern und Europa um 1700. Vol. 1, *Zur Geschichte und Kunstgeschichte der Max-Emanuel-Zeit*. Edited by Hubert Glaser. Vol. 2, catalog of exhibition at Schleissheim, 1976. Munich, 1976.

Lafue, Pierre. *La vie quotidienne des cours allemandes au XVIIIème siècle*. Paris, 1963.

Lewis, W. H. *The Splendid Century*. Garden City, N.Y., 1957.

Liechtenstein, Karl Eusebius von. *Werk von der Architektur*. N.d. Manuscript text published by Viktor Fleischer. Vienna and Leipzig, 1910.

Löhneys, Georg Engelhardt von. *Hof-, Staats- und Regier-Kunst*. Frankfurt, 1679.

Lünig, Johann Christian. *Theatrum ceremoniale historicopoliticum, oder Historisch- und Politischer Schau-Platz aller Ceremonien*. 2 vols. Leipzig, 1719–20.

Lynar, Graf Friedrich Ulrich. Account of his trip to the Bavarian court in 1762. In Georg Jacob Wolf, ed., *Das kurfürstliche München, 1620–1800*, 222–25. Munich, 1930.

Malortie, Carl Ernst von. *Der Hof-Marschall: Handbuch zur Einrichtung und Führung eines Hofhalts*. 2d ed.: Hanover, 1846.

Mayerhofer, Johannes. *Schleissheim: Eine geschichtliche Federzeichnung aus der bayerischen Hochebene*. Bamberg, 1890.

Meitinger, Otto. "Die baugeschichtliche Entwicklung der Neuveste. Ein Beitrag zur Geschichte der Münchner Residenz." *OA* 92 (1970): 3–295.

Merkel, Carlo. *Adelaide di Savoia, Elettrice di Baviera*. Turin, 1892.

Moser, Friedrich Carl von. *Teutsches Hof-Recht.* 2 vols. Frankfurt and Leipzig, 1754–55.

Moser, Johann Jakob. *Geschichte und Thaten des Kaysers Carls VII.* Frankfurt and Leipzig, 1745.

Oertel, Friedrich. *Schloss Nymphenburg.* Munich, 1899.

Oglevee, John Finley, ed. *Letters of the Archbishop-Elector Joseph Clemens of Cologne to Robert de Cotte, 1712–1720.* Bowling Green, Ohio, 1956.

Ow, Anton Freiherr von. "Beiträge zur Geschichte Max Emanuels aus den Mörmann'schen Papieren mitgeteilt." *AM* 3 (1901–2): 86–105, 141–52, 161–79; 4 (1903–4): 101–14, 127–42, 165–72; 5 (1905): 25–36, 129–36, 175–76; 6 (1906): 113–24; 7 (1907): 143–53; 8 (1908): 134–37.

———. "Die Familie Mörmann im Dienste des bayerischen Fürstenhauses." *AM* 3 (1901–2): 15–23.

Pallavicino, Marchese Ranuccio Sforza. *I trionfi dell'architettura nella sontuosa Residenza di Monaco.* Munich, 1667. Also see J. Schmid and Kalmbach.

Paulus, Richard. *Der Baumeister Henrico Zuccalli am kurbayerischen Hofe zu München.* Strasbourg, 1912.

Petzet, Michael. "Entwürfe für Schloss Nymphenburg." *ZBLG* 35 (1972): 202–12.

———. "Unbekannte Entwürfe Zuccallis für die Schleissheimer Schlossbauten." *MJBK* 22 (1971): 179–204.

Pfister, Kurt. *Kurfürst Maximilian von Bayern und sein Jahrhundert.* Munich, 1948.

Pieper, A. *Zur Entstehungsgeschichte der ständigen Nuntiaturen.* Freiburg, 1894.

Pistorini, Baldassare. "Descrittione compendiosa del palagio sede de Serenissime di Baviera." Ms. BStB, HsAbt, Cod ital 409. 1644.

Plodeck, Karin "Hofstruktur und Hofzeremoniell in Brandenburg-Ansbach vom 16. bis zum 18. Jahrhundert: Zur Rolle des Herrschaftskultes im absolutistischen Gesellschafts- und Herrschaftssystem." *Jahrbuch des Historischen Vereins für Mittelfranken* 86 (1971/72): 1–260.

Pöllnitz, Karl Ludwig Freiherr von. *Mémoires.* 4 vols. 2d ed.: Amsterdam and London, 1735.

Prosch, Peter. *Leben und Ereignisse des Peter Prosch, eines Tyrolers von Ried im Zillerthal; oder das wunderbare Schicksal.* 1789. New ed.: *Peter Prosch, König der Spassmacher: Die Erinnerungen des berühmtesten Hofnarren seiner Zeit.* Edited by Walter Hansen. Pfaffenhofen, 1984.

Rall, Hans. *Kurbayern in der letzten Epoche der alten Reichsverfassung, 1745–1801.* Munich, 1952.

———. *Wittelsbacher Lebensbilder von Kaiser Ludwig bis zur Gegenwart: Führer durch die Münchner Fürstengrüfte.* Munich, 1979.

———, and Hojer, Gerhard. *Kurfürst Max Emanuel, der 'Blaue König.'* Munich, 1979.

Raschauer, Oskar. "Die kaiserlichen Wohn- und Zeremonialräume in der Wiener Hofburg zur Zeit der Kaiserin Maria Theresia." *Anzeiger der phil.-hist. Klasse der Österreichischen Akademie der Wissenschaften* 20 (1958): 283–91.

Ridder, Alfred de, ed. "Les règlements de la cour de Charles-Quint." *Messager des sciences historiques, ou Archives des arts et de la bibliographie de Belgique* 1893:392–418; 1894:36–52, 180–201, 280–91.

Riedl, Dorith. *Henrico Zuccalli. Planung und Bau des Neuen Schlosses Schleissheim.* Munich, 1977.

Riezler, Sigmund. *Geschichte Baierns.* 8 vols. Gotha, 1878–1914.

Rohr, Julius Bernhard von. *Einleitung zur Ceremoniel-Wissenschaft der grossen Herren.* Berlin, 1729.

Rotenstein, Gottfried Edler von. "Reise nach Bayern im Jahre 1781." In Johann Bernoulli, ed., *Archiv zur neuern Geschichte, Geographie, Natur- und Menschenkenntnis.* Parts 2 and 3. Leipzig, 1786.

Rudhart, Fr. M. *Geschichte der Oper am Hofe zu München.* Freising, 1865.

Saint-Simon, Louis Duc de. *Versailles, the Court and Louis XIV.* Memoirs. Edited and translated by Lucy Norton. New York, 1966.

Schattenhofer, Michael. "München als kurfürstliche Residenzstadt." *ZBLG* 30 (1967): 1203–31.

Schaube, Adolf. "Zur Entstehungsgeschichte der ständigen Gesandtschaften." *Mitteilungen des Instituts für österreichische Geschichtsforschung* 10 (1889): 501–52.

Schloss Lustheim: Meissener Porzellan-Sammlung Stiftung Ernst Schneider. 6th ed.: Munich, 1981.

Schmelzle, Hans. *Der Staatshaushalt des Herzogtums Bayern im 18. Jahrhundert mit Berücksichtigung der wirtschaftlichen, politischen, und sozialen Verhältnisse des Landes.* Stuttgart, 1900.

Schmid, Elmar. *Nymphenburg: Schloss und Garten, Pagodenburg, Badenburg, Magdalenenklause, Amalienburg.* Munich, 1979.

———. *Schloss Schleissheim: Die barocke Residenz mit Altem Schloss und Schloss Lustheim.* Munich, 1980.

Schmid, Joanne. *Triumphierendes Wunder-Gebäu der churfürstlichen Residentz zu München.* Munich, 1685. Updated German edition of Pallavicino. Also see Kalmbach.

Seckendorff, Veit Ludwig von. *Teutscher Fürstenstaat.* Frankfurt, 1656.

Seelig, Lorenz. "Die Ahnengalerie der Münchner Residenz. Untersuchungen zur malerischen Ausstattung." In Hubert Glaser, ed., *Quellen und Studien zur Kunstpolitik der Wittelsbacher vom 16. bis zum 17. Jahrhundert,* 253–327. Munich, 1980.

Spindler, Max, ed. *Handbuch der bayerischen Geschichte.* Vol. 2, *Das alte Bayern: Der Territorialstaat vom Ausgang des 12. Jahrhunderts bis zum Ausgang des 18. Jahrhunderts.* Munich, 1966.

Stierhof, Horst. "Die Münchener Residenz." *Bayerland* 82/4 (1980): 2–30.

Stieve, Gottfried. *Europäisches Hof-Ceremoniel.* Leipzig, 1715.

Straub, Eberhard. *Repraesentatio maiestatis oder churbayerische Freudenfeste: Die höfischen Feste in der Münchner Residenz vom 16. bis zum 18. Jahrhunderts.* Munich, 1969.

Strich, Michael. "Der junge Max (II) Emanuel von Bayern und sein Hof." *AM* 13 (1915/16): 43–73.

———. *Das Kurhaus Bayern im Zeitalter Ludwigs XIV und die europäischen Mächte.* 2 vols. Munich, 1933.

Thoma, Hans, and Kreisel, Heinrich. *Residenz München. Amtlicher Führer.* Munich, 1937.

Trautmann, Karl, ed. "Aus alten Reisetagebüchern: Zwei unbekannte Beschreibungen Münchens aus den Jahren 1661 und 1782." *JMG* 2 (1888).

―――. "Der kurfürstliche Hofbaumeister Franz Cuvilliés der Ältere und sein Schaffen in Altbayern." *Monatsschrift des Historischen Vereins für Oberbayern* 4 (1895): 86–136.

―――, and Aufleger, Otto. *Die Reichen Zimmer der königlichen Residenz in München.* Munich, 1893.

Treusch von Buttlar, Kurt. "Das tägliche Leben an den deutschen Fürstenhöfen des 16. Jahrhunderts." *Zeitschrift für Kulturgeschichte* 4 (1897): 1–41.

Vehse, Eduard. *Geschichte der deutschen Höfe seit der Reformation.* Vols. 23–27, *Bayern, Württemberg, Baden, Hessen.* Hamburg, 1851–59.

Verlet, Pierre. *Versailles.* Paris, 1961.

Villa, Antonio Rodriguez. *Etiquetas de la Casa de Austria.* Madrid, 1913.

Voelcker, Helene. *Die Baumeister Gunezrhainer.* Munich, 1923.

Voigt, Johannes. *Deutsches Hofleben im Zeitalter der Reformation.* Dresden, n.d.

Wagner-Rieger, Renate. "Gedanken zum fürstlichen Schlossbau des Absolutismus." In *Fürst, Bürger, Mensch: Untersuchungen zu politischen und sozial-kulturellen Wandlungsprozessen im vorrevolutionären Europa,* 42–70. Munich, 1975.

Wening, Michael. *Historico-Topographica Descriptio, dass ist: Beschreibung des Churfürsten- und Herzogthumbs Ober- und Nider-Bayrn.* 1701–26. Reprint ed.: Munich, 1975ff.

Westenrieder, Lorenz. *Beschreibung der Haupt- und Residenzstadt München.* 1782. Reprint ed.: Munich, 1984.

Wicquefort, Abraham de. *L'Ambassadeur et ses fonctions.* 2 vols. The Hague, 1682.

Wolf, Friedrich. "François de Cuvilliés (1695–1768), der Architekt und Dekorschöpfer." *OA* 89 (1967): 1–128.

Wolf, Georg Jacob, ed. *Das kurfürstliche München, 1620–1800.* Munich, 1930.

Index

Page numbers in bold refer to illustrations. Plurals or pluralizing suffixes of German nouns appear in parentheses.

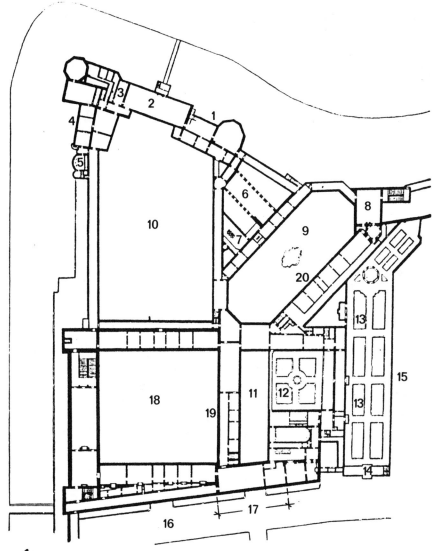

N◁

Plan A. Munich, Residenz, plan of piano nobile ca. 1630–58 as redrawn by Paul Frankl, showing Neuveste and later construction. (Prestel Verlag, Munich)

1. Rundstubenbau
2. Georgs-Saal
3. Georgskapelle
4. Hoher Stock
5. Katherinenkapelle
6. Ballhaus
7. Kitchen
8. Schwarzer Saal
9. Brunnenhof
10. Küchenhof
11. Kapellenhof
12. Grottenhof
13. Residenzgarten
14. Former Witwenbau
15. Site of Franziskanerkloster
16. Schwabingergasse; now Residenzstrasse
17. Approximate extent of former Erbprinzenbau
18. Kaiserhof
19. Hofdamenstock
20. Antiquariumsbau

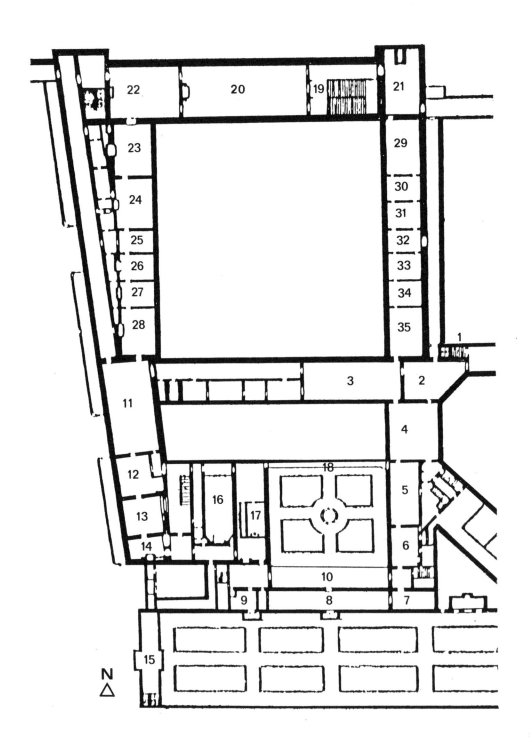

Plan B. Munich, Residenz, detail of plan A, showing electoral apartments and Kaiserbau.

1. Breite Treppe
2. Vorsaal
3. Herkules-Saal

Elector's apartment under Maximilian.

4. Ritterstube
5. Antechamber
6. Audience chamber
7. Zimmer
8. Kammergalerie
9. Bedchamber
10. Altana or terrace

Electress's apartment.

11. Tafelstube
12. Anteroom
13. Anteroom
14. Bedchamber
15. Gallery

16. Hofkapelle
17. Schöne Kapelle or Reiche Kapelle
18. Gläsernes Gängl
19. Kaisertreppe
20. Kaisersaal
21. Halle beim schwarzen Hund; after 1805, Weisser Saal

Kaiserzimmer.

22. Ritterstube or Tafelstube; Zimmer der Planeten; in the 18th c., Vierschimmelsaal
23. Antechamber; Zimmer der Elemente
24. Audience chamber; Zimmer der Welt
25. Bedchamber; Zimmer der Jahreszeiten
26. Fifth room; Zimmer der Ewigkeit
27. Sixth room; Zimmer der Religion
28. Seventh room; Zimmer der Kirche

Trierzimmer.

29. Antechamber
30. Audience chamber
31. Bedchamber
32. Saal
33. Bedchamber
34. Audience chamber
35. Antechamber

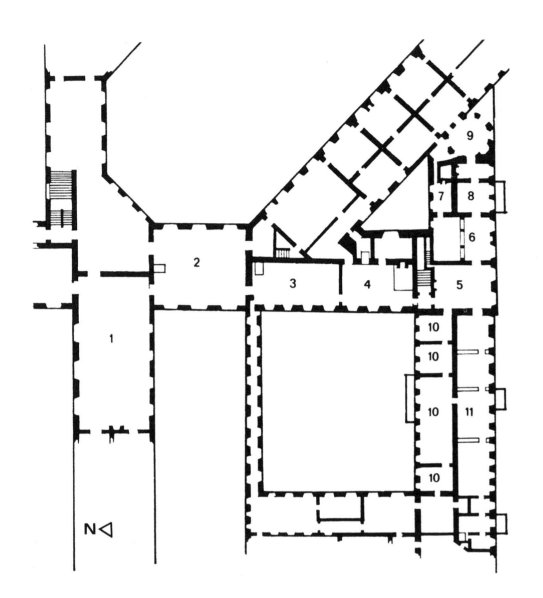

Plan C. Munich, Residenz, detail of piano nobile ca. 1610–30, showing the Alexanderzimmer (redrawn from a plan published in the exhibition catalogue *Kurfürst Max Emanuel,* Munich, 1976).

 1. Herkules-Saal
 2. Ritterstube
 3. Antechamber
 4. Audience chamber
 5. Inneres Audienzzimmer or Grosses Cabinet
 6. Bedchamber or Alkovenzimmer
 7. Geheimes Cabinet
 8. Ankleidezimmer
 9. Höllandisches Cabinet; later, Cäcilienkapelle
10. Sommerzimmer
11. Gallery

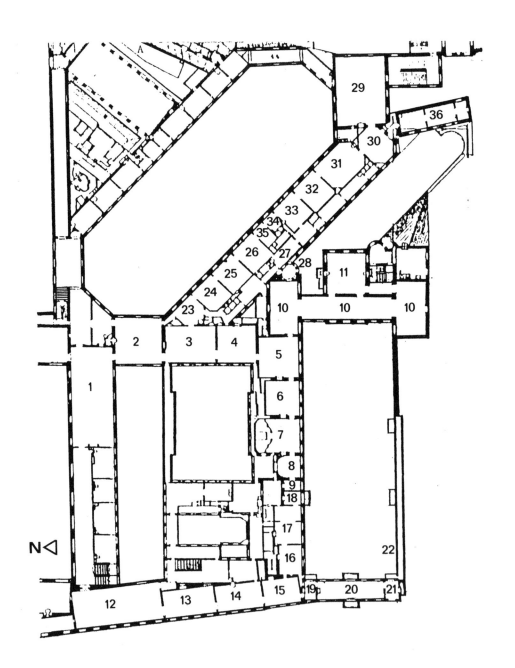

Plan D. Munich, Residenz, detail of piano nobile in 1799, showing the Reiche Zimmer, Henriette Adelaide's apartment, and the Kurfürstenzimmer (redrawn from Verschaffelt's plan [fig. 13]).

1. Herkules-Saal
2. Ritterstube

Reiche Zimmer.
3. Antechamber
4. Second antechamber or first audience chamber
5. Grosses Audienzzimmer
6. Grosses Cabinet or Konferenzzimmer
7. Bedchamber
8. Spiegelkabinett
9. Cabinet der Miniatur-Gemälden
10. Grüne Galerie
11. Speise-Saal; before 1764, staircase

Electress's apartment.
12. Hartschiersaal or Lederner Saal
13. Ritterstube
14. Antechamber
15. Audience chamber or Goldener Saal
16. Grosses Cabinet or Grottenzimmer
17. Bedchamber or Alkovenzimmer
18. Herzkabinett
19. Liebeskabinett
20. Gallery
21. Rosen- und Lilienzimmer
22. Library

Kurfürstenzimmer (elector's apartment).
23. Kleine Ritterstube
24. Antechamber
25. Audienz- und Konferenzzimmer
26. Bedchamber
27. Cabinet
28. Cäcilienkapelle

29. Schwarzer Saal

Kurfürstenzimmer (electress's apartment).
30. Ritterstube
31. Antechamber
32. Audience chamber
33. Bedchamber
34. Cabinet
35. Cabinet
36. Former gallery of Henriette Adelaide

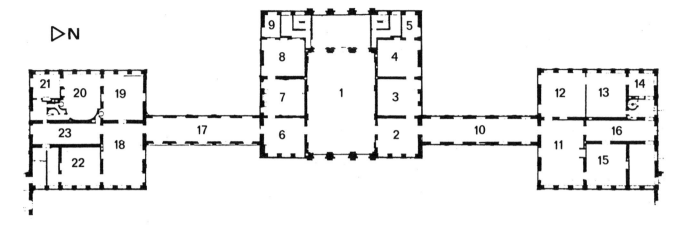

Plan E. Nymphenburg, Schloss, piano nobile (redrawn from a plan of ca. 1785, BSV, Bauamt, neg. 20.851).

1. Hauptsaal

North apartment or Grünes Appartement.
2. Kleiner Saal or Ritterstube
3. Antechamber
4. Bedchamber
5. Cabinet

South Apartment or Rotes Appartement:
6. Kleiner Saal or Ritterstube
7. Antechamber
8. Bedchamber
9. Cabinet

10. North gallery

Principal apartment of the inner north pavilion (Max Emanuel's "Neue Sommer-Zimmer"; under Karl Albrecht, apartment of the Elector of Cologne; under Max III Joseph, apartment of Dowager Empress Maria Amalie).
11. Saal
12. Antechamber
13. Bedchamber
14. Cabinet
15. Ratszimmer; also called Grosses Cabinet der Malereien
16. Kleine Galerie

17. South gallery

Principal apartment of the inner south pavilion (under Karl Albrecht and Max III Joseph, electress's apartment).
18. Saal
19. Antechamber
20. Bedchamber
21. Cabinet
22. Grosses Cabinet
23. Kleine Galerie

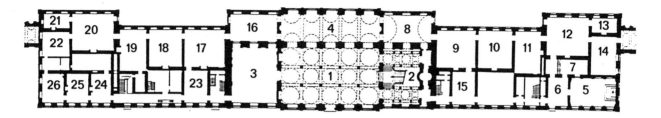

N◁

Plan F. Scheissheim, Schloss, plan of ground floor in 1970.

1. Vestibule
2. Haupttreppe
3. Garde-Saal; after 1774, Neue Speise-Saal
4. Sala Terrena
5. Grosse Kapelle or Maximilianskapelle
6. Vestibule
7. Lower sacristy

South apartment (Max Emanuel's summer apartment; under Max III Joseph, apartment of Dowager Empress Maria Amalie).
8. Anteroom
9. Antechamber
10. Audience chamber
11. Bedchamber
12. Grosses Cabinet

13. Cabinet
14. Oratory
15. Waiting room

North apartment (under Karl Albrecht and Max III Joseph, elector's apartment).
16. Anteroom; on Altmannshofner's plan of 1812, Hartschier-Stube; today, Musik- oder Billiardsaal
17. Antechamber
18. Audience chamber
19. Bedchamber
20. Grosses Cabinet or Konferenzzimmer
21. Stukkatur-Cabinet
22. Drechsel-Cabinet
23. Waiting room; on Altmannshofner's plan of 1812, Billiarde-Zimmer

Small north apartment.
24. Antechamber
25. Bedchamber
26. Cabinet

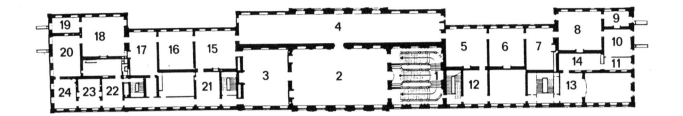

Plan F. Scheissheim, Schloss, plan of piano nobile in 1970.

1. Haupttreppe
2. Weisser Saal
3. Viktoriensaal or Speise-Saal
4. Gallery

South apartment (Max Emanuel's apartment; later, apartment of the Elector of Cologne).

5. Antechamber
6. Audience chamber
7. Bedchamber
8. Grosses Cabinet
9. Rotes Cabinet
10. Cabinet der flamändischen Malereien or Niederländisches Tafel-Cabinet
11. Oratory
12. Waiting room for liveried servants

13. Chapel balcony
14. Upper sacristy

North apartment (under Karl Albrecht and Max III Joseph, electress's apartment).

15. Antechamber
16. Audience chamber
17. Bedchamber
18. Grosses Cabinet
19. Kammerkapelle
20. Cabinet
21. Waiting room

Small north apartment.
22. Antechamber
23. Bedchamber
24. Cabinet